BUY NOW

Distribution Matters Series

Edited by Joshua Braun and Ramon Lobato

The Distribution Matters series publishes original scholarship on the social impact of media distribution networks. Drawing widely from the fields of communication history, cultural studies, and media industry studies, books in this series ask questions about how and why distribution matters to civic life and popular culture.

Emily West, *Buy Now: How Amazon Branded Convenience and Normalized Monopoly*

BUY NOW

HOW AMAZON BRANDED CONVENIENCE AND NORMALIZED MONOPOLY

EMILY WEST

THE MIT PRESS   CAMBRIDGE, MASSACHUSETTS   LONDON, ENGLAND

The MIT Press would like to thank the anonymous peer reviewers who provided comments on drafts of this book. The generous work of academic experts is essential for establishing the authority and quality of our publications. We acknowledge with gratitude the contributions of these otherwise uncredited readers.

This book was set in Stone Serif and Avenir by Westchester Publishing Services. Printed and bound in the United States of America.

Library of Congress Cataloging-in-Publication Data

Names: West, Emily, author.
Title: Buy now : how Amazon branded convenience and normalized monopoly / Emily West.
Description: Cambridge : The MIT Press, [2022] | Series: Distribution matters | Includes bibliographical references and index.
Identifiers: LCCN 2021014621 | ISBN 9780262543309 (paperback)
Subjects: LCSH: Amazon.com (Firm) | Electronic commerce. | Retail trade.
Classification: LCC HF5548.32 .W466 2022 | DDC 381/.14206573—dc23
LC record available at https://lccn.loc.gov/2021014621

10 9 8 7 6 5 4 3 2 1

In memory of my grandfather, Selwyn John, who loved to go to the shops.

CONTENTS

FIGURE LIST

ACKNOWLEDGMENTS

I would like to acknowledge and thank the many people and institutions who encouraged and supported me in this project. The seeds of this book are in an International Communication Association pre-conference in 2017 called Distribution Matters, organized by Joshua Braun, Ramon Lobato, and Amanda Lotz. This inspiring one-day event encouraged me to pursue this project, which ended up in the MIT Press book series Distribution Matters coedited by Josh Braun and Ramon Lobato. It's not an exaggeration to say that there would be no Amazon book, at least not by me, without their expertise, professionalism, and care. Thank you to Gita Devi Manaktala and Justin Kehoe at the MIT Press who between them have shepherded this book to the finish line, with the right balance of patience and deadline setting during the challenges of 2020–2021, and the anonymous reviewers for their expert feedback on the manuscript.

Conferences and workshops have been a key way for me to stay focused on this project, be inspired and informed by other scholars' work, and get much needed encouragement and energy from others' responses. In particular I'd like to thank danah boyd for her invitation to the Environmental Impacts of Data-Driven Technologies Workshop at Data & Society, Candace Roberts and Myles Ethan Lascity who organized the Consumer Identities & Social Change Symposium at St. John's University, and Richard R. John for welcoming me to a roundtable on communications and globalization at the World Economic History Forum.

Two of this book's chapters draw from previous publications, and I extend thanks to those who gave permission to partially reprint that material here. Chapter 3 appears in part in a volume coedited by Daniel Herbert and Derek Johnson, *Point of Sale: Analyzing Media Retail* (2019), published by Rutgers University Press. Chapter 4 builds on an earlier piece published in 2019 in a special issue of *Surveillance & Society* focused on platform surveillance, coedited by David Murakami Wood and Torin Monahan.

My academic home in the Department of Communication at the University of Massachusetts Amherst, housing my tremendous colleagues and engaged graduate students, has been an ideal environment for pursuing this work. I'm grateful to current and former chairs Erica Scharrer, Sut Jhally, and Mari Castañeda for helping protect my research time at crucial moments.

Outside of formal institutional support I'm very fortunate to have a deep bench of mentors/colleagues/friends who have encouraged and advised me at key moments, including Lynn Comella, Laura Grindstaff, Lisa Henderson, Carolyn Marvin, Matt McAllister, Amy Schalet, Katherine Sender, Claire Wardle, and Louise Woodstock. Special thanks go to Ryan Olbrysh for his assistance with the book cover. Through a virtual writing accountability group generously organized by Josh Braun, I've also received advice and weekly encouragement from wonderful colleagues in digital media and technology studies.

Thank you to my family in Canada for supporting me and showing great patience in what no doubt has seemed an extremely slow process from idea to book. Special thanks to my father, Richard P. West, who has far surpassed me in book publishing during this period as well as educated me about the world of self-publishing on Amazon. Thank you to our wonderful Valley friends for promoting joy and balance amidst work and responsibilities, especially during the pandemic times. And to my husband, Kevin, and children, Gryffith and Ivar, thank you for your unconditional love, enthusiastic encouragement, practical support, and letting me monopolize the "office/music room" in order to finish this book.

INTRODUCTION: BUY NOW—THE BRANDING OF CONVENIENCE

In August 2015, I found myself transfixed by a *New York Times* article that appeared on my smartphone: "Inside Amazon: Wrestling Big Ideas in a Bruising Workplace."[1] Detailing the harsh workplace conditions at Amazon headquarters in Seattle that housed programmers and other white-collar employees, as well as reviewing existing reports of abuses in Amazon's warehouses, the article revealed disturbing allegations about the human costs being extracted in order to provide a fast, seamless, inexpensive, and convenient consumer experience. As a longtime Amazon customer (since 2000, my online account informed me), I was suddenly and painfully aware of my own complicity in supporting these workplace practices through my purchases, and perhaps, even by my behavioral responses to Amazon over the years. How many times had I discussed a product with a friend, and punctuated the conversation with "you can get it on Amazon." "It's probably on Amazon." "Check Amazon." Baby gear, jewelry display stands, left-handed spatulas, replacements for lost AC adaptors, and oh yes, books, can all be found on Amazon, ordered within seconds, and received often within a day or two.

My first encounters with the company were in my final year of my university studies, searching for books on what was at the time the new Amazon.com website. I wasn't yet able to purchase them, at least not for a reasonable shipping fee, because I lived in Canada, and Amazon .ca had not yet been established. Even then, I found the way Amazon (as it now prefers to be called, and as most people refer to it) functioned as a digital library useful for discovering or learning more about resources for school projects, some of which I could then track down from other bookstores or libraries. An avid reader from a young age, the online bookstore was my favorite corner of the young internet, which I mostly accessed via a painfully slow dial-up connection. As I thought about what kind of work to pursue after graduation, I looked into employment with Amazon—combining my love of books with involvement in the emerging digital economy seemed like a dream job—but my citizenship would be an obstacle. A few years later, having moved to the United States for graduate school, I finally summoned the courage to put my credit card information online in order to start buying books from Amazon. About ten years later I was in Seattle, attending a workshop for expectant parents, and a fellow parent who was an Amazon employee told everyone about a new "Amazon Mom" program—free two-day shipping in exchange for sharing the date of your impending birth with the company. I signed up. Baby gear from Amazon started to arrive. I even registered for the baby shower on Amazon. That was the gateway for using Amazon not just for books anymore, but all manner of household items, some of which I purchased using the "Subscribe & Save" feature. I eventually became a Prime customer in order to access the Prime Video content as well as the free two-day shipping no matter the size of my order. When I finally gave some conscious thought to my relationship with the ecommerce giant, prompted by the investigative reporting by Jodi Kantor and David Streitfeld, I realized that incrementally Amazon had become a regular habit for me; I had certainly spent thousands of dollars at the retailer over the years. Like other Amazon customers, including many who commented on the *New York Times* article, I stopped buying from the company. Then Christmas came.

The story of my own entanglement with Amazon is far from unique. In twenty-five years, Amazon has transformed from an ecommerce upstart, puzzling through how to overcome Americans' hesitation to buy things online, to a brand that many people in the United States and beyond interact with on a daily basis. From streaming Amazon Prime Video via a Fire TV stick, to reading books on an Amazon Kindle, to interacting with Alexa on an Amazon Echo, to receiving smartphone updates about the progress of the latest Amazon order, Amazon and its sub-brands have inserted themselves into our daily lives. This doesn't even consider Amazon's role in providing key digital infrastructure to ecommerce, streaming media, and businesses of all kinds via its cloud computing arm Amazon Web Services. Amazon's growth and expansion into new businesses have been so steady that its market dominance and ubiquity have somewhat snuck up on our collective consciousness, just as my own dependence on Amazon snuck up on me. It's almost hard to remember a time pre-Amazon, despite the fact that the company was formed in 1994, not long after the internet became open to commercial activity, famously run at first out of Jeff Bezos's garage in Bellevue, Washington, and launched in 1995.

Buy Now is about our relationship with Amazon—how this brand grew so quickly by obsessing over our consumer experience, and attained a level of ubiquity in our lives while hiding in plain sight. By offering in-depth accounts of Amazon's major consumer-facing services including its focus on fast and seamless ecommerce delivery, streaming media, book retailing, and AI voice-enabled smart speakers, this book offers a cultural study of bigness in today's economy. I present Amazon's market dominance and our increasing dependence on its convenient services in relation to the resulting costs—on product sellers, market diversity, labor, and the environment, and on our own power as consumers. In this book I explain how Amazon's branding practices and the nature of its services cultivate personalized, intimate relationships with consumers that normalize its outsized influence on ourselves and our communities.

Especially for Americans, Amazon has become ubiquitous—a mundane part of our symbolic and material environment, in addition to being an often unseen source of infrastructure for our digital worlds. Journalist Franklin Foer argues, "We've never seen a company that's become so integrated into existence. At a certain point, it becomes unavoidable."[2] Amazon's very ubiquity and everydayness can cause it to fade into the background, too often evading consideration of what its rise has meant for how we access media, learn about and acquire consumer goods, read books, listen to music, and access information online—all this, despite the fact that Amazon is undeniably big. It's one of the most market-capitalized companies in the world, founded by the richest person in the world, the biggest online retailer (by far) in America, the biggest seller of cloud computing services in the world, the biggest seller of books and ebooks in the

United States, and the biggest seller of smart speakers. Amazon is very big in multiple respects, but prefers that we don't notice.

Political economist of communication Vincent Mosco warns against the tendency to allow digital communication, and the companies that facilitate it, to become invisible in their ubiquity. Just as the material objects that make digital communication possible—the cables, wires, and large devices such as desktop computers—disappear from everyday view, so does digital become more embedded in everyday life, and in so doing, grow more powerful. Mosco draws an analogy with the early days of electricity, which similarly became more infrastructural just as its network of wires started to disappear behind walls: "We once viewed electricity outside ourselves, embodied in very material technologies obviously external to people who used them." Similarly, he writes, while "not quite ubiquitous, computers are nevertheless increasingly embedded in so many devices and bodies, including our own, that they appear to be everywhere, yet nowhere in particular."[3] This trend has been identified as a move toward "ubiquitous computing," most fully realized by the Internet of Things (IoT).[4]

Just as the technologies of digital communication become ubiquitous and fade into the woodwork, so do the tech brands—Google, Facebook, Apple, and Amazon—that bring them to us. These platform giants blend into our homes and lives when we access them through ever-smaller devices, or merely through voice, as people now do with speakers such as the Amazon Echo, Google Home, or Apple HomePod that are designed to blend into home décor. And the giant most likely to be in the living room is Amazon, with its leading digital voice assistant, major investments in Internet of Things technologies, and natural advantage as the dominant ecommerce site selling objects for the home.

I approach the normalization, even the banality of Amazon's ubiquity not as something to take for granted, but as an industrial and cultural accomplishment that requires explanation, theorization, and critique. This book is an effort to make this ubiquity—which tends toward invisibility very much by design—visible, thereby making it more available to challenge and critique. It offers a cultural study of corporate bigness and ubiquity, and an investigation of how the rise of such a large company laser-focused on serving the consumer with convenience is shifting what it means to be a consumer, and beyond that, the self.

Why focus on Amazon? Other tech giants like Facebook and Google have achieved similar levels of everyday usage for millions, if not billions, of people worldwide. Facebook, Google, and Netflix have enjoyed rapid ascent to ubiquity and achieved unprecedented power in our information environment.[5] Facebook has risen from a dorm room dream to a massive economic and cultural force quicker than Amazon. And Google has perhaps an even greater claim on everyday ubiquity, as it undergoes "genericide"—when a specific brand name starts to be used in the language as a generic term for something, in this case to "google" as the widely used term for "doing an internet search." However, Amazon thus far has eluded the extensive scholarly critique these other companies have received. The auction-based ecommerce site eBay likewise has inspired in-depth scholarly treatment, notably in Michele White's *Buy It Now*, named after that all-important button on that site.[6] In comparison, scholarly consideration of Amazon as a key player in the digital economy and, by extension, our culture may have lagged because Amazon's primary association with something as prosaic as retail—and even more quaint, its origins in bookselling—arguably insulate it from being taken as seriously as it should be.

However, popular and press investigation of Amazon has burst on the scene in recent years, with the Kantor and Streitfeld article heralding a turn to greater journalistic scrutiny, Jason Del Ray's *Vox* Land of the Giants podcast (2019) digging in depth into different parts of Amazon's business model, and James Jacoby's *Frontline* episode "Amazon Empire" (2020) consolidating many of the critiques of the tech giant among journalists and activists. With the arrival of the COVID-19 pandemic in 2020, Amazon's infrastructural pervasiveness has achieved greater social recognition. Seemingly overnight, people all over the world discovered that the people who worked in retail distribution systems were "essential," although their level of pay and rights in the workplace might suggest otherwise. Online shopping was no longer just a convenience but in fact a necessity for some people, while for most, getting things delivered made sheltering in place more feasible and tolerable. Markets formerly resistant to Amazon's charms, notably American seniors who had yet to adopt online shopping habits, and Italians, for whom going to shops had been an important part of the culture, and cash their preferred form of payment, were suddenly won over.[7] Amazon's streaming media services similarly played a greater role in people's lives, as libraries, bookstores, and movie theaters closed, and new programming on television dried up. As warehouse workers in particular were required to continue going to work, under the greatest pressure ever to fulfill customer orders, Amazon's role as one of the country's largest employers and the way that it consistently seemed to prioritize the delight and satisfaction of its customers over the well-being of its workers came to sustained national attention in the United States. As Amazon made a public stand in June 2020 in support of the Black Lives Matter protests taking place all over the United States and beyond, it also announced a one-year moratorium on selling its controversial facial recognition technology (called Rekognition) to law enforcement, thereby making a rare connection between the values of its consumer-facing activities and its business-to-business activities.

As Amazon has developed into much more than an online book retailer, the lack of clarity and even knowledge of what kind of company Amazon is has also helped it fall under the radar. Ontological uncertainty about the very nature of Amazon and its business isn't limited to observers or average consumers—it's a theme that emerges in commentary about Amazon from its very core, including founder and longtime CEO Jeff Bezos, who has grappled with what Amazon actually is since its earliest days. As Bezos tried to explain what kind of company Amazon was in 1999, he said that it wasn't a business that sold things so much as a business focused on "helping people make purchase decisions. . . . The closest thing that I can come to is that we're not trying to be a book company or trying to be a music company—we're trying to be a customer company."[8]

As implied by this comment, Amazon's business activities and core competencies are a rapidly moving target. However, the idea that Amazon is a platform business, a particular expression of digital capitalism, offers some explanation for how and why one company can move so rapidly into new business areas, and not just grow into them, but soon dominate them. This book is about a company called Amazon and how it persuades consumers to welcome it into almost every corner of their lives. On another level, it's about what it looks like and feels like to be a consumer in platform capitalism.

DISTRIBUTION MATTERS

For many years, it was tempting to overlook Amazon as a tech giant because of its association with retail rather than media, information, or computing. Similarly, for too long the economic and cultural importance of digital distribution companies like Facebook, Google, and YouTube (a subsidiary of Google that in turn resides within Alphabet) were underestimated. After all, these companies didn't produce their own content, and wasn't it really the messages that mattered? In recent years that misapprehension has been corrected, with scholars, activists, and eventually, politicians raising the alarm bells about how new regimes of digital distribution have disrupted long-standing economic and cultural norms in news, politics, and entertainment.

While it's clear that disrupting the distribution of news is of prime importance for politics and the public sphere, it may have been less obvious why we should care about online shopping. However, retail is a key stage in the distribution of cultural and informational goods, including books, which was Amazon's first product category, but also music, movies, and television. While production and consumption have typically received the bulk of attention in media studies scholarship, the ways that digital has upended dominant paradigms of media distribution has inspired renewed interest in media distribution among critics and scholars.[9] Related to this development, recent scholarship draws attention to the cultural significance of retail as a key aspect of media distribution, not coincidentally as our retail environment—especially in terms of brick-and-mortar enterprises—is being transformed precisely because of the explosion in ecommerce led by Amazon.[10]

Shopping has long been trivialized due to its association with feminine domesticity, consumption rather than production, and the pursuit of meaningless, fleeting pleasure. Although shopping and retail might conjure the realm of the frivolous and extraneous, in fact the vast majority of shopping we do involves the routine provisioning that keeps households and lives running.[11] Amazon has steadily moved into these household categories of consumption, including groceries, as with its 2017 acquisition of the Whole Foods grocery chain.

As a scholar of consumer culture, my interest in Amazon is because of, not despite, its association with retail and shopping. Consumer identities are socially and politically consequential; the ways that ecommerce and digital technologies reshape consumer identities matter. Rightly or wrongly, the things that we buy are important resources in how we construct and communicate identities and make everyday culture. Retail spaces have long been prominent, if not the dominant, public spaces where people encounter each other, either directly, or through the products that other people are buying. Retail has also shaped our communities, via both infrastructure and employment.

The social and cultural value of retail spaces and employment became more noticeable as they were taken away with widespread lockdowns in 2020. Online shopping became not just an option but a seeming necessity, at the same time that the conditions and dangers of the warehouse and delivery jobs became much more of a consideration as consumers navigated decisions about what to buy, from whom, and with what modalities. As Paul N. Edwards explains, infrastructure is what remains invisible to most people until it stops working, and that was certainly the case during the pandemic shut downs, with longer shipping times and lack of availability for certain products drawing consumer attention to the supply chains and labor enabling the distribution of so many goods.[12]

In recent years, the sheer speed with which Amazon has entered and then succeeded in, or even come to dominate new businesses has not escaped the attention of business analysts, legal scholars, and legislators. Amazon's business expansions have attracted substantial press attention and awareness among the public, including the aforementioned purchase of Whole Foods Market in 2017, Amazon's launch of its own streaming channel and production company that competes with Netflix, its invitation to North American cities to compete to be the second Amazon headquarters, its testing of drone deliveries, its consumer electronics including the Kindle, Fire TVs and Fire Tablets, Echo smart speakers, and Alexa, the AI digital assistant.

Other business expansions may be less well known among the general public, but are no less noteworthy in terms of understanding Amazon's market dominance: Amazon Marketplace and Fulfillment by Amazon—services for third-party sellers; the development of Amazon Web Services, a company that provides cloud-based data storage and software services to millions of companies, including big players in digital media like

Netflix and Comcast and government agencies like the Central Intelligence Agency; its purchase of Kiva, a robotics firm, and its subsequent rollout of robotic technologies in its fulfillment centers; growth in its logistics, shipping, and delivery services; and Amazon Mechanical Turk, a crowdsourcing platform on which people do digital piecework.[13]

In addition to these discrete businesses, the data analytics side of Amazon—the ways it collects data about customers and transactions that are then fed into "models, analytics, and algorithms" for both its own purposes and to sell information products to third parties—is key to the company's success and ability to grow into new businesses, but is far from transparent to the average consumer.[14] In sum, while Amazon began as simply an online retailer, and remains that in many of our minds, in fact it is a type of business that is coming to define the digital economy—a platform.

PLATFORMS IN THE DIGITAL ECONOMY

Essential to the digital economy, platforms are often defined, including by theorist of platform capitalism Nick Srnicek, as digital intermediaries.[15] The term "platform" evokes a foundation—some kind of digital space or software capability—that allows different stakeholders (consumers and sellers, users and advertisers, companies and gig workers) to interact. Amazon is a platform company in this sense. More than half of the goods the company sells are through the Amazon Marketplace and Fulfillment by Amazon (FBA) programs, the former where sellers use the site to sell their goods but take care of the delivery themselves, and the latter where sellers also pay Amazon to warehouse their goods and arrange their delivery. Amazon is also a retailer in its own right, meaning it stocks product and increasingly produces items, such as personal electronics, fashion, and beauty products, under its own labels. This distinguishes it from ecommerce sites that are pure platform, such as eBay, Etsy, and Chinese ecommerce giant Alibaba.

Allowing other sellers—often selling at cheaper price points—to use its retail platform to reach consumers might seem counterintuitive. However, the more product choices that are on Amazon, the more consumers will visit it, which creates network effects. Network effects refer to a success-breeds-success dynamic that has been particularly pronounced for the GAFAM (Google, Apple, Facebook, Amazon, and Microsoft) tech giants: the scale of the company is part of the value proposition for users. As more products are available on Amazon, more consumers use the site to shop, and as more consumers use the site, more sellers want to sell there. Thanks to network effects, platform companies that arrive first or achieve early momentum have a tendency toward tremendous market dominance, sometimes approaching or achieving monopoly status.[16]

Amazon reportedly understood from its earliest days the value of being the middle man. Business journalist Brad Stone locates Amazon's first efforts to "become a platform and augment the e-commerce efforts of other retailers" to 1997 when it launched its first effort at an eBay-like service with Amazon Auctions.[17] In 1998, one of the newly public Amazon's first acquisitions was an online shopping comparison company called Junglee from which it developed its own shopping comparison site, Amazon's "Shop the Web." Even though the service would allow shoppers to see if a product was being sold cheaper somewhere other than Amazon, Amazon still received a commission on delivering that customer through the service, and built the brand equity of being a trusted destination for online shopping. These early attempts at being an ecommerce platform morphed into today's Amazon Marketplace and Fulfillment by Amazon services, through which Amazon collects a cut of every transaction that occurs thanks to bringing buyers and sellers together, a revenue stream yielding higher margins than selling its own products, and growing all the time as Amazon extracts higher commissions from and charges ever more fees to its sellers.[18] As one of Amazon's first chroniclers, Robert Spector, put it, "Amazon.com made it obvious that it intended to be *the* commerce portal of the World Wide Web."[19]

The term "platform" is also understood in the digital economy as hardware, software, or a service upon which other companies can build their own products and services, typically via APIs, or application programming interfaces. As Nick Montfort and Ian Bogost define platforms, they are "the underlying computer systems" that "enable, constrain, shape, and support the creative work that is done on them."[20] Developers can build games for people to play on Facebook, third parties can integrate Google Maps into their own websites and services, and companies can create Alexa "skills" so consumers can access their services via voice. Amazon runs multiple platforms upon which third parties can develop their own products and services, including its retail site, Alexa, the Amazon App Store, and Kindle Direct Publishing.

In turning Amazon into a platform company, Bezos was reportedly influenced by internet thought leader Tim O'Reilly, who met with the CEO in 2002 to convince him of the wisdom of platformizing the Amazon site by providing APIs to sales data that other companies, such as book publishers, could use to track trends.[21] Opening up the Amazon site to developers in addition to consumers and sellers started Amazon on the path toward conceptualizing their internal computer storage and software capacities as services for third parties, culminating in what is today Amazon Web Services, the first-to-market cloud computing service at its official launch in 2006 and continued leader, estimated to control 32 percent of the global market in 2020.[22] AWS, as it is commonly known, is one of Amazon's primary platform businesses, and its most profitable to boot. In fact, Amazon's cloud computing arm is largely responsible for the company's overall profitability—accounting for more than half of its profit in the fourth quarter of 2020, for example—allowing the company to subsidize other parts of its business that are losing money or still growing.[23]

The customers for Amazon Web Services are businesses and organizations. Since AWS is not consumer-facing, it does not get in-depth treatment in this book despite how significant it is to both Amazon and the business community. Just as the average computer user has gradually moved their data storage and software from their hard drives to the cloud, so have businesses. AWS's cloud computing services allow businesses to, essentially, rent data storage, computing power, database infrastructure, software services, and data analytics from Amazon on an as-needed basis. This arrangement gives businesses the flexibility to grow or shrink their usage as needed, and avoid the outlay of overhead and fixed costs on IT infrastructure and staff. While Amazon offers dozens of its own AWS services, it also allows other companies to produce their own services that sit "on top of" AWS, known as "AWS Partners," as well as "Independent Software Vendors" who have adapted their software to work with AWS.[24] In this formulation, it's the programmability of the service, and therefore the ability of the user to customize it for their own uses that make it a platform.[25]

AWS is used by government agencies, large companies, and more than a million small and medium-sized businesses and startups. It's the platform of platforms, in the sense that it provides the cloud-based computing infrastructure for Amazon's own services, as well as for numerous other platform businesses, including Lyft, Expedia, Slack, and Zoom, as well as more conventional companies like McDonald's and General Electric. Its importance to Amazon became clearer than ever when its CEO Andy Jassy was named Jeff Bezos's successor when Bezos stepped down as CEO of the whole company in 2021. Similar to so many infrastructures, but especially digital ones, Amazon's cloud services are an aspect of its ubiquity far beyond the average consumer's ken.

A third insight about platforms in the digital economy is that their primary business, even with appearances to the contrary, is extracting and processing data.[26] Market dominance has always meant the ability to shape market conditions in order to defeat competitors, through the benefits of economies of scale, or keeping prices artificially low. However, in the digital economy the ability to collect data about all your users and use that data not only to make your own business activities more competitive, but also to sell either the data itself, or products and services informed by that data, to third parties is a tremendously powerful and self-perpetuating advantage. Amazon collects huge amounts of data about consumer behavior that it can use to create predictive models and algorithms that make its products and services ever more irresistible to consumers. As I'll discuss in this book, the breadth and detail in the data that Amazon collects from consumers has been key to much of its growth and success, while the drive to collect an ever-greater variety and amount of data about us informs the design of many of Amazon's products and services.

In sum, Amazon is a platform in all three senses of the term: it's an intermediary, its platform businesses provide digital infrastructures upon which third parties build products and services, and its business is profoundly shaped by the data commodities resulting from its intermediary position. There is a politics to the term "platform," as Tarleton Gillespie has argued, particularly in how it obscures the extractive, structuring, and enclosing nature of many platforms in favor of the image of a neutral and open foundation.[27] Platform companies like to present themselves as "merely the platform" that facilitates others' innovations and accomplishments. Today, platform companies like Amazon are among the most valuable (as measured by market capitalization) in the world, and are the brands that people spend the most time with, and report the greatest appreciation for.

BRANDS IN PLATFORM CAPITALISM

There is no small slippage in how the term "platform" is used.[28] In addition to definitions focused on the technical qualities of digital platforms, brands themselves have been conceptualized as platforms,[29] a "figurative" usage according to Gillespie's typology for the term.[30] In this book, I approach Amazon primarily as a brand, and use the case of Amazon to examine how brands are changing with the rapid growth of digital technologies and the rise of platforms. While focusing on distribution infrastructures exposes the structural foundations of Amazon's market dominance, looking at platforms through the lens of branding draws our attention to the cultural and symbolic determinants of its ubiquity. The way a platform brand like Amazon has normalized its own ubiquity should be viewed as an accomplishment borne of branding, public relations, and relationship marketing.

Why foreground Amazon as a brand, rather than how it is organized technically, from a business perspective, or how it functions within current law and regulation? While I will consider all these aspects of Amazon throughout this book, I privilege branding for a few reasons. First of all, centering the brand trains our focus on the *relation* between the company and the public, and the ways in which that relation is made *meaningful*. A brand is the symbolic aspect of a business that consumers interact with and relate to; it is the "face" of the company, be that in literal terms—such as with the Quaker of Quaker Oats, or more figuratively—as the identity with which consumers cultivate a parasocial relationship. As Sarah Banet-Weiser puts it, a brand is "typically understood as the cultural and emotional domain of a product, or the cultural expression of a company or corporation."[31] Approaching Amazon as a brand draws our attention to consumer experience, affect, and meaning. It is only through consumer use, motivations, and meanings that companies flourish. As brand theorist Adam Arvidsson argues, brands depend on the immaterial labor of consumers and users who complete and perpetuate brand meanings through their consumption and communication.[32]

Ubiquity is a goal for all brands. As Arvidsson puts it,

For the big brands, with a lot of resources at their disposal, the ideal is ubiquity: To make the brand part of the biopolitical environment of life itself, no different from water and electricity, and to thus make life in all its walks contribute to its continuous and dynamic reproduction. As Ira Herbert, former marketing director for the Coca-Cola Company, described this strategy: "the ideal outcome . . . is for consumers to see Coca Cola as woven into their local context, an integral part of their everyday world."[33]

But for most brands, especially those linked to particular products, like Coca-Cola, ubiquity will remain aspiration rather than reality. In contrast, digital platform brands like Amazon can achieve ubiquity in people's lives to an unprecedented extent.

It's well established that the consumer product and services brands that dominated brand value and brand affection metrics in the 1990s—brands like Coke, Nike, and McDonald's—succeeded in large part because they sold not just stuff that people liked, but lifestyles. To be somewhat reductive, Coke sells Americanness, Nike sells athleticism, and McDonald's sells family. The strength of these brands is that they can inspire consumers with ideas, emotions, and aspirational lifestyles rather than merely touting their product features. There's always something slightly new to say in advertising and promotional materials about the brand's meaning, which gives these brands new materials for their marketing campaigns, and consumers new reasons to pay attention. The drawback is that no brand image or lifestyle can encompass absolutely everyone. Coke's emphasis on classic American fun opens the door for Pepsi to claim youth and irreverence. Nike's brand story about striving through sports allows a brand like Adidas to distinguish itself by offering street-ready athletic fashion. McDonald's family-friendly vibe makes space for Burger King to siphon off irreverent young men, the most loyal customers for fast food.

Counter to what seemed like the zenith of brand culture in the late twentieth century, when every brand had its tribe and the consumer market could be sliced and diced finer and finer, tech brands that benefit from network effects follow different brand logics. Distribution brands like Amazon, eBay, Facebook, and Google don't set out to have a market segment; they aim to capture everyone. Amazon in particular wants to be the "everything" brand for "everyone." To do so, it avoids telling a brand story specific enough to bring to mind a certain kind of consumer. Anna Weiner argues in the *New Yorker* that even compared to other tech giants, who "promote idealistic, utopian, or progressive narratives about community or connection," Amazon "strives, almost always, to present itself as a kind of infrastructure."[34] By *not* cultivating an elaborated brand image (other than the instantly recognizable logos) or offering itself as a lifestyle brand, Amazon avoids the semiotic specificity that would open up space for other brands to plant a flag on unclaimed semiotic, and therefore, demographic territory. The understated touch that Amazon uses in its branding and advertising is not an accident, as it seeks to be an innocuous, mutable brand that achieves maximum familiarity with minimum identity. Amazon is a fragmented, relational brand. Its meaning need not be as coherent, stable, or representational as brands traditionally have been. Customizing experiences for individuals is what allows brands like Amazon, Facebook, and Google to be brands of ubiquity, rather than the traditional brands of distinction. Using another conceptualization, many of these tech giants are "service brands," emphasizing a service or overall experience that they provide rather than a specific product or image.[35] For Amazon, that service is defined by the convenience and ease of the consumer.

Platform brands that provide services, like Amazon, are ideally suited to marketing and relationship building with consumers in the digital age. Today, product brand marketers are trying to emulate the success of the Amazons of the world by shifting from traditional marketing logics, wherein you create an eye-catching, memorable, emotional campaign and promote it largely through television spot advertising, to digital-era marketing logic, wherein you approach people not as potential buyers, but as users.[36] In this logic, rather than focusing on the brand's image or story, you focus on an experience or benefit you can provide your user, also known as relationship marketing.[37] You don't necessarily invest all your marketing dollars up front to get that initial purchase; you also focus on optimizing the service experience during and after the purchase. Based on their survey research with 5,000 consumers, business researchers Mark Bonchek and Vivek Bapat summarize the distinction: a traditional brand is "a brand that people look up to" whereas a newcomer brand like Amazon is a brand that "makes my life easier."[38] While the Cokes and Nikes of the world have long focused on positioning the brand in people's minds, tech brands typically focus on positioning their brand in people's lives. Bonchek and Bapat found measurable benefits for "usage brands" over "purchase brands": "Survey respondents show more loyalty to usage brands. They had stronger advocacy in the form of spontaneous recommendations to others. And they showed a higher preference for usage brands over competitors, not just in making the purchase but in a willingness to pay a premium in price."[39]

In *Advertising Age*, Garfield and Levy report on "brand sustainability" being predicted both by frequency of transaction and level of consumer trust. Brands like Amazon, which ranks high on both measures, "typically spend little on advertising—because they don't need it."[40] In its most established markets Amazon has hardly been known for traditional forms of advertising such as TV spots, billboards, print ads, or direct mail. In its first year, the company did minimal paid advertising, relying instead on word-of-mouth and other forms of buzz online.[41] Preferring to drive traffic to sites via "associates," or other websites that would link specific book titles to the Amazon site in exchange for a small cut of any resulting purchase, the company spent only 10 percent of its sales revenue on advertising and marketing, compared to the 119 percent of typical internet startups in the 1990s.[42] In 2001, when Amazon was struggling to weather the dot.com bust, Bezos started to question the company's return on investment on the expensive forms of traditional advertising it had begun such as TV advertising, and ended up radically rethinking advertising and marketing.[43] Bezos decided to reroute those advertising dollars into improving the experience of individual consumers, via lower prices and fast, free shipping, betting that word of mouth and customer loyalty would be the payoff. He said, "In the old world, you devoted 30 percent of your time to building a great service and 70 percent of your time to shouting about it. In the new world, that inverts."[44] The shift in strategy was successful, making Amazon one of the fastest-growing ecommerce companies of the twenty-first century.

Starting in 2004, Amazon did start to increase its ad spend year over year, with particularly large increases in the late 2010s. With a 34 percent increase in spending from 2018, Amazon became the world's largest advertiser in

2019, vaulting from the number 5 to the number 1 spot.[45] As Amazon has launched new products (Echo smart speakers, Fire TV, Amazon fashion) and services (Prime Video, Alexa, Amazon Music), as well as launched a new retail "holiday"—Prime Day, a massive sale usually in the summer meant to boost sales during a traditionally slow season, the company has had reason to address consumers directly about something other than their specific purchases. A significant portion, close to 40 percent, of the massive 2019 ad spend was focused on markets outside the United States, as Amazon continues to invest in its international markets.[46]

Today many companies are trying to figure out how to switch their product brands from "purchase" to "usage," which is not always an easy fit. Create an app with household cleaning tips for your cleaning products? Create an online game that consumers can play with QR codes on the products that they buy? Creative ideas, but realistically the rate of adoption and usage of these features will be modest, if they take off at all. In contrast, a brand like Amazon that provides multiple consumer-facing services has a built-in reason to be useful to the consumer throughout their day. Over the last twenty-five years a loyal Amazon customer may have gone from interacting with the brand a few times a year to buy hard-to-find books, to several times a day, especially if they use Amazon's mobile app or interact with Alexa via an Echo device. If using the streaming services, they spend extended periods connected to Amazon. It's hard to imagine that kind of exponential increase of consumer touches with a brand that produces physical products, or even specific services like hotel accommodations, although these brands are certainly trying.

The explosion in smartphone and tablet use is a significant factor in increasing the frequency of interactions between consumers and brands. Apps and push alerts for mobile, smart speakers, AI-enabled digital assistants, and smart things are all tools of the ubiquitous, convenient brand. As Amazon can be reached through more devices, and as it provides more products and services, it gets closer to its goal of being always with us.

AMAZON, THE AFFECTIVE BRAND

One day I made an impulsive purchase on Amazon. I bought animal-print kitten heels that I was convinced I would rock at extremely hypothetical parties and in particularly confident teaching moments. I bought them on Amazon from a third-party seller, and they took quite a while to arrive, unlike products that I buy with some regularity using my Prime membership. When they came, they were too big, very stiff, and not as cute as I had imagined them to be. I figured out how to make a return and put them in the mail within the week, thinking no more about it until about six weeks later I received an email from Amazon pointing out that I had indicated a return on the site but had not yet received my refund. I realized that this was the case, confirmed it with Amazon as instructed, and within a couple of days the refund arrived. I'm well aware that the prompt was almost certainly automated, likely flagged by an algorithm on the lookout for slow refunds of returned merchandise. But I can honestly, and with some embarrassment, report that I felt very "cared for" and "seen" by Amazon in that interaction. The company identified a problem I didn't even know I had, and went out of its way to solve it for me. Amazon's number one principle has always been "customer obsession," and this was a clear example of that orientation.

Amazon is not typically conceptualized as an emotional or affective brand, but I argue that Amazon is highly affective, albeit in a subtle way. People may not get Amazon tattoos, like they do for beloved brands like Nike or Harley Davidson, and you are unlikely to see people wearing Amazon-branded gear (because Amazon doesn't make it), but the attachment is nonetheless there. The evidence is in the repeated purchases, the depth of trust, the consumer loyalty, and the brand affection.

Amazon is an affective brand whose techniques for producing strong relationships with consumers exemplify broader trends in branding and marketing in the digital age, characterized by a shift in emphasis from traditional forms of advertising aimed to the masses, or even to niches, to highly individualized relationship marketing, made possible by the affordances of interactive, digital communications. Recent years have seen increasing interest among scholars in theorizing the affective aspects of capitalism.[47] Affect captures the idea of intensity or feeling that moves us to act or affects our body in some way, even if we don't have the language to explain the experience, or possibly, even if we are not conscious of it. Affect is a useful lens for considering how a social relationship, even a sense of intimacy, develops between consumers and brands. The analysis of affect brings our attention to brand attachments, trust, and the energy that puts people and things into motion, be it through purchasing, online forms of expression, or seeking out other consumers.[48]

Amazon is a brand with little explicit emotional content but a powerful affective presence. Many successful brands have used emotional appeals— Nike's "Just Do It," Hallmark's "They'll Never Forget You Remembered," Disney's "The Happiest Place on Earth," and L'Oréal's "Because I'm Worth It." Amazon, rather than telling an affective *story* per se, builds an affective relationship with its customers through *interaction*. And a key part of that interaction is reliable access to and efficient delivery of goods, making the affective relation tangible and touchable on a regular basis through goods and the boxes they come in.

Critical scholar Sara Ahmed looks to Marx's conceptualization of circulation as a metaphor to understand the accumulation of social affects. She argues that we misrecognize emotions as "belonging" or "attaching" to objects or persons (in her analysis, the case of "hate" toward groups seen as "other"), when our sense of this is only produced through an "affective economy" created by the *circulation* of affect, across discursive moments through time. Just as the circulation of money-capital-money leads to the accumulation of value, so does the circulation of discourse create affective accumulation.[49] While capital "gains its power through circulation,"[50] affect also accumulates its power through circulation. What does it mean to focus on the accumulation of affect through circulation? In the worlds of branding and marketing, it means looking at interactions with a brand over time, how a brand seeks to be "with us" on our phones or other devices, the "touches" between consumer and brand, and how a brand communicates responsiveness by acknowledging and even anticipating consumer needs and desires. As Andrew McStay has argued, it's an *ecological* rather than *representational* approach to analyzing, and producing, advertising.[51]

Representationally Amazon might seem simple. In 2000 the company launched its current logo with its brand name "Amazon" in its distinctive typeface (see figure 0.1). The orange arrow points from the "a" to the "z" of "amazon," signaling the company's transition from solely an online bookstore where you might purchase titles starting from "a" to "z," to where all products from "a" to "z" can be found.[52] The arrow is also a dynamic element that emphasizes Amazon as a brand that *delivers*, from its warehouses to customers' doorsteps. And the orange arrow resembles a smile, an iconic nod to the affective relationship Amazon seeks to cultivate with its customers.

Industry research shows that consumers are indeed very attached to the brand. Amazon is consistently at or near the top of lists of Americans' most-loved brands. Amazon topped the 2017 Love List Brand Affinity Index produced by Condé Nast with Goldman Sachs, based on a survey with millennials and "gen z."[53] It was number 1 on Morning Consult's 2019 list of America's Most Loved Brands.[54] The Harris Poll's 2018 reputation rankings for brands found Amazon.com in the number 1 spot—meaning it is both visible and has a positive reputation—and at or near the top of most of the components of reputation they measure, including Emotional Appeal, for which Amazon was also in the number 1 spot, ahead of brands like Chick-fil-A and Nike.[55]

Trust is one of the most powerful feelings people can have about a brand, particularly a digital brand like Amazon where people may never interact with a human representative of the company. Organizations identify America's "most trusted brands" using different methodologies, but Amazon comes out on top on many of these lists, such as one put out by The Values Institute, which found Amazon to be the country's most trusted brand in 2017 based on a survey measuring attitudes to brands on the following factors: Consistency, Competence, Candor, Concern, and Connection.[56] Amazon also came in at number 10 on Forbes' top 100 most trustworthy brands, and Interbrand found Amazon to be the fourth most trusted brand in 2018.[57] Somewhat shockingly, the Baker Center at Georgetown University, in their 2018 poll on American Institutional Confidence, found Amazon to be the number 2 institution in which

0.1 Amazon's logo since 2000. *Source:* "Images and Videos: Logos," *Amazon Press Center*, n.d., https://press.aboutamazon.com/images-videos, accessed May 23, 2021.

Americans have the greatest confidence, second only to the military, and ahead of all other levels of government, colleges and universities, non-profits, and even major companies in general.[58] For Democrats, Amazon was number 1.

Like all brands, Amazon is very attentive to how people perceive it and feel about it—the heart of its brand value. In 2011, in the wake of a scandal about a price comparison app that Amazon had launched that seemingly encouraged consumers to "spy" on other retailers and report on their prices, Jeff Bezos wrote a memo to his senior executives that came to be known as the "Amazon.love memo."[59] Drawing from his own observations of what led some companies, like Apple, Nike, and Disney to be beloved, while equally successful companies like Walmart, Microsoft, and Goldman Sachs were disliked or feared, Bezos generated a list of what consumers found to be "cool" or "not cool," reproduced in part here:

Rudeness is not cool.
Defeating tiny guys is not cool.
Close-following is not cool.
Young is cool.
Risk taking is cool.
Winning is cool.[60]

Although Amazon tries to control how people see the brand, and especially how the press covers it, through their public-facing communications, the company's most powerful tool for getting people to "love" it is the nature of each and every interaction it has with its customers. While Amazon is a brand for which explicit promotional content is not generally emotional (the reading of the logo's arrow as a smile notwithstanding), it creates strong affective connections, even intimacy, with consumers through ongoing "touches," be these virtual or physical. Getting what you want on your doorstep in a short amount of time, in the plain brown box with the recognizable tape and the Amazon logo—these are all elements designed to produce an affective response. Perhaps the response is relief, or gratitude, or joy, or satisfaction, or the comfort in a predictable relationship. The response may not have a name, or be the same every time, but the repeated touches over time accumulate into an affective relation. Given the company's focus on "customer obsession," our feelings have most likely been carefully calibrated to maximize trust and loyalty and minimize reflection and scrutiny. The way we relate to Amazon is crucial to the question of whether and how we will use our agency as consumers and responsibility as citizens to grapple with the impact of Amazon's market dominance on our society and our planet.

SCOPE OF THE BOOK AND ORGANIZATION

Given my focus on Amazon as a brand, *Buy Now* focuses squarely on Amazon's consumer-facing products, services, and marketing. As such I draw on Amazon's website; the programs, products, and services it offers its consumers; its advertising and marketing materials; its press releases and public relations efforts; news coverage of the company and other evidence of its public image; trade press and industry reporting about its strategies and place in the market; industry reports on consumer use and response; and fieldwork in Amazon's consumer spaces, including brick-and-mortar store concepts and fulfillment center tours for the public. These investigations primarily look at the US context, where Amazon was founded and where it enjoys its greatest market dominance, but also considers Amazon's activities beyond US borders, particularly in chapter 7, which focuses on Amazon's global ambitions. I consider the "behind-the-scenes" of Amazon's operations to the extent that what we know from reporting about Amazon's infrastructures, labor conditions, and business practices conflicts with the image and relationship it presents to customers. Amazon is very active in business-to-business services including Amazon Web Services, Amazon Marketplace, and Fulfillment by Amazon—while I consider these for their role in Amazon's overall business strategy, they are not my primary focus. This book does not offer original reporting from Amazon employees, current or former (most of whom are subject to nondisclosure agreements), or proprietary documents and spaces.

This project seeks to contribute to interdisciplinary conversations about the relationships among the spheres of technology, culture, and the economy. I am careful not to err on the side of saying that the digital economy is a source of *sui generis* disruption that is remaking our culture from the ground up. Rather, I aim to show how Amazon, as one of the current behemoths of the digital economy, is building on existing trends in the commodification of data and culture, as well as driving disruptive change in some areas. Similarly, although founder and executive chairman of Amazon Jeff Bezos will get his due, I don't focus exclusively on him as a business genius as a number of other books have done, preferring instead to see him as particularly attuned to shifts in technology, economy, and culture, and the resulting opportunities therein.

The book is organized in three parts that reflect my explanations for how Amazon has achieved ubiquity and market dominance with relatively few obstacles and proportionately little pushback on the part of consumers or governments. The reasons for this rapid rise of Amazon's platform ubiquity are structural, cultural, and semiotic, and the three parts on Distribution, Culture, and Image map onto these. Part 1, "Distribution," focuses on Amazon's core function of circulating information and goods. Chapter 1 establishes historical context for distribution brands, looking back to Sears as a precursor distribution brand, and across the marketplace today to Amazon's distribution partners and competitors USPS, UPS, and Walmart. Distinguishing disruption from continuity in the digital economy is central to this chapter, as I apply Marxist analyses of the circulation of capital to Amazon's business model, and highlight what has shifted with the turn to digital capitalism and, relatedly, platform capitalism. This chapter also considers how all distribution brands, to some extent, are affective brands built on service rather than image-based marketing, and how Amazon has been able to use the affordances of digital communication technologies to achieve that to the nth degree.

In chapter 2 I highlight how Amazon achieves affective connections with consumers less through symbolic means than material and interactive ones, beginning with the materiality of the branded brown box. While a key part of Amazon's business model is to speed up the circulation of capital, by reducing friction in purchasing and time from click to ship to delivery, the company generally discourages consumers from knowing about or reflecting on the labor and infrastructure required to deliver their goods in unprecedented short delivery windows. From a Marxist perspective, I characterize this consumer relation with Amazon's delivery capabilities as "distribution fetishism." As Amazon starts to respond to public pressure to be more transparent about its warehouse conditions and environmental impacts, I consider the optics of Amazon's public fulfillment center tours and public relations efforts around climate and waste, and conclude that rematerializing our understanding of digital distribution means more than rendering it visually "transparent."

Part 2, "Culture," focuses on Amazon's media and communication services, including book retailing, media streaming, and smart speakers. Amazon doesn't just purvey books, movies, and information; it uses these products and services to forge personalized relations with its customers. It uses our interest in cultural products to hook us into its Prime "ecosystem." Amazon is converting its early focus on retail sales into the provision of cultural "services" so it can collect ever more data about us, with which it can offer us the service of personalized convenience. Beginning with chapter 3, I consider Amazon's origin and evolution as a bookseller, with an eye to what platformization has meant for the books business, bookstores, and readers. Like the big box retailers that came before it, Amazon has used the tools of the digital economy to intensify the commodification of books, inspiring anxiety from authors, publishers, booksellers, and readers about the commercialization of this revered form of culture. Being more than just a large company—a platform—has afforded Amazon the ability to vertically integrate its business in books to an unprecedented extent, and therefore achieve a position of market dominance and control in publishing and marketing books. This chapter considers Amazon's development of the Kindle and the associated explosion in ebooks, as well as the world of brick-and-mortar retail, which Amazon moved into for the first time with the introduction of its Amazon Books retail locations in the United States. Focusing on these stores, I examine how Amazon uses the techniques of online retail to personalize even physical retail spaces for its customers, which serves to strengthen the relationship between consumer and brand while dividing and discriminating among consumers as a bloc.

In chapter 4 I turn my attention to one of Amazon's most successful electronics products, the Echo smart speaker, and its associated AI (artificial intelligence)–enabled digital assistant, Alexa. This chapter continues my focus on Amazon's media-related products and services, while turning to an issue relevant not just to Amazon but also to other tech brands—the commodification of personal data in platform capitalism. I argue that rather than obscuring its surveillance capacities, Amazon generally sells surveillance as a service, and uses it to build intimacy with the consumer, borne of domestic familiarity and responsiveness to the self. While personalized service has been a longstanding aspect of Amazon's business strategy and brand promise, with Alexa we see an intensified version of personalized service that positions the consumer no longer as a choosing subject, the typical subjectivity of consumer culture, but as a served self, transferring agency and decision power from consumer to brand. I posit that the subjectivity of the served self is one of the costs of convenience that conspires to limit critical reflection and resistance from consumers to Amazon's intrusiveness and market dominance.

In chapter 5 I turn to Amazon's streaming services and examine how ecommerce commodifies culture in new ways. I consider the implications of a service brand like Amazon—known primarily in many markets for good deals and quick delivery on everything from diapers to electronics to groceries—also becoming a media brand. I argue that in many of its promotions for its media holdings, Amazon doesn't just commodify media, but commoditizes it, through its emphasis on Prime Video as a value proposition for the consumer. In fact, Amazon promotes Prime Video in two ways—as a commoditized value proposition, and as an irreplaceable destination for exclusive content. By extending its ubiquity and emphasis on convenience to the world of media, Amazon presents media content as just another service that it can provide, and uses entertainment to recruit Prime members and keep them firmly in the fold.

Part 3, "Image," steps back from specific services in order to examine the rhetorical and promotional strategies that Amazon uses to influence how people conceptualize and feel about it, considering both consumers and regulators as key constituencies. In chapter 6 I highlight the techniques Amazon uses to normalize its market dominance and the ubiquity of its platforms. In addition to reviewing the legal and regulatory conditions that have allowed platforms like Amazon to achieve their market dominance relatively uncontested (until recently), especially in the United States, I draw attention to the way Amazon has crafted itself as a brand of ubiquity through the use of naturalistic metaphors, such as "ecosystem," "cloud," and the brand name itself. Branding techniques that frame Amazon's ubiquity as natural produce a taken-for-granted invisibility that is politically useful as concerns over its conflicts of interest as a platform business, the consequences of market concentration, its outsized power in labor markets, and the environmental impacts of the digital economy put Amazon into an unwelcome spotlight.

I continue stepping out to see the bigger picture in chapter 7, in which I examine Amazon's global activities through the lens of "platform imperialism."[61] I recount Amazon's efforts to spread across the globe, and how different countries have responded to these moves. Considering both Amazon's successes, like India, and its failures, as in China, the chapter notes that Amazon's goal of achieving global ubiquity is far from complete, and that it presents itself differently to foreign markets than at home, in part because it comes already marked by its Americanness. Amazon's efforts at localizing its image and services have met with mixed success, but its business advantages as a platform company with very deep pockets that make it possible to subsidize the investments required to grow in new markets make it a formidable competitor.

In the concluding chapter I acknowledge one of the greatest sources of pushback against Amazon's ubiquity and market power—its workers. I recount not just what efforts Amazon workers have made and with what success, but also why it is among workers rather than consumers or competitors that we see the most visible and effective activism. In this concluding chapter I ask: What do consumer politics and subjectivities look like in the age of ubiquitous platform brands like Amazon? What are the possibilities and obstacles for resistance and change in the context of platform capitalism? This investigation considers how Amazon's brand logic fragments consumers as a political bloc, and forges brand intimacies via surveillance and personalization that undermine the subjectivity of consumer-as-citizen. While distribution fetishism, cultivation of the served self, and naturalistic metaphors all work to normalize Amazon as a brand of convenience and therefore its ubiquity in our lives and our societies, I point to ways of thinking and acting that people could adopt to reclaim some of their consumer power and rights as citizens relative to the power of platforms.

I

DISTRIBUTION

1

A NEW KIND OF DISTRIBUTION BRAND

Amazon is one of the most loved, trusted brands in America. It creates affective relationships with its customers by connecting them regularly and reliably to products, services, and entertainment. Even though it creates some of those products itself it is, primarily, a brand of distribution. Amazon is far from the first distribution brand to win consumers' affections. Like other distribution brands, it has reshaped commerce, consumer experience, and even perceptions of space and time through innovations in distribution. From the Sears catalogue as a tool for broadening the reach of not just consumer goods but also consumer desires, to Walmart's mastery of logistics, to the United States Postal Service's historic role as the primary distributor of printed material and packages, to UPS as a privately held but ubiquitous delivery brand, the historic importance of distribution brands to both the economics and culture of the United States cannot be underestimated.

In this chapter I consider each of these companies as either partners or competitors of Amazon or, in some cases, both. Through these comparisons I aim to provide enough historical grounding to establish that Amazon is not, in fact, a disruptor company the likes of which has never been seen before, as it is sometimes characterized. Rather, there are significant continuities between Amazon's activities and strategies and those of its precursors that arise from the constraints, incentives, and logics of capital, and the particular place that brands of distribution inhabit in the economy. Like distribution brands before it, Amazon has gained consumers' trust and affection through its ubiquity and focus on service, coming to seem more like a utility than a private company. We'll see that Amazon's ubiquity is similar to its fellow distribution brands, in part because they thrive on network effects and the efficiencies that come with economies of scale. But we'll also see that the logics of *digital* capitalism have launched Amazon into a sphere of market dominance and expansion into horizontal and vertical integrations that are unprecedented relative to its fellow distribution brands.

We can look to Karl Marx's discussion of circulation in the second volume of *Capital* for tools to theorize distribution. In this framework, capital must change form in order to accumulate value, and the faster these conversions happen, the more rapid the process of capital accumulation. In other words, the quicker raw materials are transformed into commodities with exchange value, the less time they spend in inventory, and the quicker and cheaper they get to customers who pay for them (i.e., distribution), the more money you make.[1]

Amazon is an ideal case for considering how the rise of digital communication technologies, computing, and the internet—which have constituted the era of "digital capitalism"—have sped up and transformed the circuit of capital to enhance capital accumulation.[2] The picture that emerges from the brief history offered here is the power that *any* distribution brand that is large enough has in the economy. But that power is particularly pronounced in digital capitalism, where new tools can produce heretofore unimagined speedups, and advantages in distribution can be parlayed into dominance in other business areas in ways that may be truly unprecedented.

Distribution comes in two main flavors—transportation and communication. The idea that these are separate activities is a relatively recent one, dating to the invention of the telegraph, according to James Carey, who memorably pointed out that the word "communication" was used interchangeably with "transportation" before this mode of instantaneous electronic communication conquered space.[3] But even before the telegraph, the railroad struck observers as both a tool to "annihilate space and time" and the engine, so to speak, accelerating industrial capitalism.[4]

Retail and media distribution brands are built on top of these fundamental modes of distribution. What the stories of these companies make clear is that there are multiple types of distribution that need to be in place for a distribution brand to thrive. Retail brands, in particular, require networked communication, transportation of goods, and ways for money and credit to circulate. As Richard K. Popp puts it, these networks of distribution come together to form "a kind of infrastructural ensemble" that supports the various forms of circulation in retailing.[5] As I introduce two main kinds of distribution brands—retail brands and delivery brands—I'll connect these consumer-facing organizations to the transportation and communication networks they depend upon. With Amazon, we'll see that part of its "platformization" has been to slowly but steadily move the purview of its business into these very distribution infrastructures.

COMPETITORS: SEARS AND WALMART, UBIQUITOUS RETAIL BRANDS

More than one hundred years before Jeff Bezos started Amazon.com out of his garage, another entrepreneur named Richard Sears started his retail empire in 1886 from his position as a station agent for the Minneapolis and St. Louis railroad in Minnesota, getting into the mail-order business in watches. Sears acquired a partner with expertise in watches, relocated to Chicago, the railroad hub for the Midwest, and then expanded into more products.[6] The business that started out as the R.W. Sears Watch Company eventually became the dominant force in American retailing, combining the catalogue on which it had built its relationship with rural consumers with brick-and-mortar stores that reached urban and suburban consumers acquiring automobiles. The Sears, Roebuck mail-order business depended on the late nineteenth-century rapid expansion of both the railroad networks and the postal service into rural communities, just as Amazon would depend on a variety of distribution infrastructures in the late twentieth century, including the royalty-free, open-access technical standards of the World Wide Web.[7]

The parallels between the United States' first nationally dominant retail brand Sears, as it came to be known, and Amazon are striking. Both founders originally worked in close proximity to a distribution network that would be key to their business, Sears being a station agent for the railroad, and Bezos working for a hedge fund that was using the new affordances of high-speed computing and the internet to transform that business. Each started with a single product and expanded to eventually become "everything stores"[8]—in Sears's case, facilitated by the size and variety of its catalogues, and in Amazon's, by the limitless nature of online shelf space. Both began as a mail-order retail business of sorts and *then* moved into brick-and-mortar retailing. Both companies were decried by local, independent store owners, particularly in rural areas and small towns in the case of Sears, as existential threats to their businesses—and by extension—a whole way of life.[9] Both retailers had to find ways to establish trust with consumers via the mail, in Sears's case, and the internet, in Amazon's. Richard Sears built up his company's reputation initially by sending watches just for payment of a deposit, as well as with the famous "Satisfaction Guaranteed or Your Money Back" brand promise.[10] For its part, Amazon initially gave consumers the choice of phoning in their credit card or providing it on a web-based form, and emphasized consumers' data security from early on, facilitated by the encryption technologies that reassured users that websites were secure.[11]

For a good chunk of its history, Sears had the quality of retail ubiquity that Amazon clearly aspires to, being the "everything store" for "everyone," and thereby fading into the background. As the store's biographer Gordon L. Weil put it, "Many customers look upon the company more as a public utility than as a profit-making corporation. It has been around for a long time, so people do not consider it an impersonal outfit. They do not hesitate to ask it to help them out with their personal problems. They look upon it as a friendly neighbor."[12] Amazon's reputation as an almost infrastructural feature of the retail and distribution landscape, especially in the United States, has attained a similar level of trusted ubiquity.

Starting out with a focus on the rural customer, in the early days Sears understood its customers to be the growing number of working people who sought the best possible quality for the lowest prices. However, in the postwar period, as urbanization increased and Americans became more affluent, Sears gradually morphed into a store for the middle class.[13] Weil points out that while Sears may have imagined the middle class to be "just about everyone," in fact by later in the twentieth century that image and the associated price points were losing the large segment of the lower middle-class being vigorously courted by discount retailers like Kmart and Walmart, while on the upper end, the store was disdained by upwardly mobile consumers for whom Sears was hopelessly unfashionable.[14] Therefore, while Sears may have still been the "everything store" it was no longer for "everyone," posing a challenge for its competitiveness and potential for growth. While Amazon skews toward better-off consumers than retail competitors such as Walmart, it otherwise avoids a specific brand identity in relation to social class, at least in relation to its core consumer-facing brands that include Amazon, Prime, and Fire electronics.

A less well-known chapter in Sears's history that also parallels Amazon's is its investment in internet services as one of the co-owners of Prodigy, an early portal along the lines of AOL, in the 1980s and 1990s. Sears envisioned the strategies of selling users' eyeballs to advertisers and launching an online shopping network, both ideas that turned out to be ahead of their time by a few years.[15] The Prodigy portal, despite having a business model that anticipated many of the ways the internet would be used, disappeared by the late 1990s, losing ground quickly to users' enthusiasm for the open web.[16] Just as Sears moved into distribution businesses that paralleled and supported its core retail business, so has Amazon moved into cloud computing, logistics, and media distribution, but much more successfully.

The company that owns both Sears and Kmart barely survived a Chapter 11 bankruptcy that initially allowed it to keep 400 stores open;[17] as of 2020 industry observers were in "death watch" mode.[18] After shaping the contours and traffic patterns of so many communities with the locations of its stores, Sears's decline was a harbinger of the "retail apocalypse" routinely discussed in the media.

Amazon's greatest competitor today is the world's leading retail distribution brand as measured by sales—Walmart.[19] Walmart is also the leading retailer in the United States, with close to $400 billion in sales in 2019.[20] Amazon comes a distant second with $193 billion in US sales, a figure that includes not only its ecommerce business but also sales at new brick-and-mortar store concepts like Amazon Books as well as its Whole Foods Market acquisition.[21] When it comes to ecommerce, though, the retailers swap places in the rankings, with Amazon controlling between 37 and 52 percent of US ecommerce in the late 2010s according to different estimates (with the modal estimate in the high 40 percent range), and Walmart only 4.6 percent (after eBay with 6.1 percent).[22] Amazon's dominance of close to half of online sales in the United States still only comprises 5.1 percent of all retail sales,[23] but Walmart's focus on ecommerce and its determination to try and catch up to Amazon in ecommerce is apparent.

In addition to being market leaders and close competitors, Walmart and Amazon have both sought to serve consumers by being competitive on price, and each in their own way, like Sears before them, being "everything stores." Walmart is well known for putting the "discount" in discount retailing. It has also pushed the envelope in terms of the size of its stores and scope of product categories. For example, Walmart expanded the boundaries of the discount retailer category by introducing groceries in 1988, becoming the country's leading grocer by 2010.[24]

Similarly, Amazon is well known for being competitive on price, be it setting low prices on its own product lines, incentivizing lower price points from third-party sellers through the design of search algorithms, disciplining sellers whose products ever appear elsewhere for a lower price, or offering its own discounts on third-party products by reducing its cut of sales.[25] All of this is despite the fact that antitrust law forbids Amazon from interfering with third-party sellers' pricing, a practice the company told the Federal Trade Commission it would stop doing in 2019.[26] Amazon, of course, has long had the reputation of having a massive product selection because since 1999 it has not just sold items that it actually stocks, but also turned its retail site into a platform for third parties to sell their goods.

Both Walmart and Amazon have their own "circuits" that are reminiscent of Marx's circuit of capital, Amazon having developed its "flywheel of growth" model inspired by Walmart founder Sam Walton's "productivity loop" (see figure 1.1).

Industry observer Brad Stone translates Amazon's "flywheel of growth" in the following way: "Lower prices led to more customer visits. More customers increased the volume of sales and attracted more commission-paying third-party sellers to the site. That allowed Amazon to get more out of fixed costs like the fulfillment centers and the servers needed to

Walmart's Productivity Loop

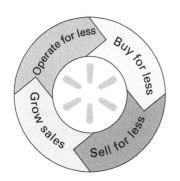

Amazon's Flywheel of Growth

1.1 Walmart's productivity loop and Amazon's flywheel of growth. *Sources:* Paul, "The Productivity Loop (Walmart's Feedback Loop)," July 30, 2012, *Understanding Amazon* (blog), http://understandingamazon.blogspot.com/2012/07/the-productivity-loop-wal marts-feedback.html; and Franz Jordan, "Applying the Amazon Flywheel to Your Online Business," last updated February 14, 2020, https://sellics.com/blog-applying-amazon-fly wheel-to-your-online-business/.

run the website. This greater efficiency then enabled it to lower prices further."[27] While other retailers might have raised those prices to satisfy shareholders, Amazon has long been able to keep prices down and business investment way up, with the promise that profits would be forthcoming, eventually. Through a combination of Jeff Bezos's persuasive zeal, and investors' belief that an internet-based company had potential for growth that traditional retailers didn't, Amazon was largely successful on the stock market (minus a few notable bumps) from when it went public in 1997 to 2003, when it posted its first-ever annual profits. The company's profits remained relatively modest, and even dipped below profitability in 2012 and 2014, until 2015 when it became consistently profitable. Nevertheless, Amazon became one of the most highly market-capitalized companies in the world on the strength of growth that is fueled, in no small part, by keeping both product and shipping prices low for longer than its competitors can often bear.

The last few decades have seen a shift away from the presumed dominance of the manufacturing sector in a Fordist economy, characterized by the rise of mass production by large corporations in much of the twentieth century, and toward what historian Nelson Lichtenstein argues is akin to eighteenth century-style merchant capitalism.[28] This is a shift in market power from companies that *produce* goods to those that *distribute and retail* them. Large retailers, like Sears, have long been in the driver's seat vis-à-vis their suppliers. By the 1970s, Sears was partial owner of the firms that produced 30 percent of the goods that it sold.[29] Richard Sears himself reportedly discovered that "the company was such a large purchaser of other people's products that it could demand that the goods be made to its specifications."[30] In a 1938 *Fortune* report that sounds like it could have been written about Walmart or Amazon today, we learn that "the antimonopolists contend that by bringing this massive buying power to bear against small manufacturers and threatening to whisk it away once they have been ensnared, Sears can force them to submit to prices on which a living profit is impossible."[31] The company's influence extended to telling manufacturers where they should locate, in order to minimize transportation costs for both raw materials and delivery to the nearest Sears distribution center.[32] The company developed its own research lab to test products and develop innovations to existing products, which it then asked manufacturers to produce, known as "specification buying."[33]

The history of Sears demonstrates that any retailer that is large enough shifts the center of gravity from manufacturers to distributors, when it comes to who is calling the shots on product development and pricing. It continues to be the case that as retailers get big they start to blur the boundaries between production and distribution, whether through actual ownership and acquisition of manufacturing companies or the extent of influence over their activities. Walmart exemplifies the shift from a "push" to a "pull" economy, where it's no longer manufacturers pushing the products they are making onto retailers who must find a way to move them, but retailers who have a monopoly on market information and the monopsony power to list terms to manufacturers.[34] Walmart demands of its suppliers "just-in-time" delivery of specific goods, the mass production of customized products, particular packaging and labeling specifications, and makes specific suggestions on how to cut manufacturing costs.[35] Lichtenstein argues that while Walmart technically is not a manufacturer, its power over its suppliers means that it should be regarded as de facto in the manufacturing business.[36]

In addition, strong retail brands like Sears, Walmart, or Amazon can erode the value of product brands. Retailers generally carry particular product brands to bring consumers into their stores. But Sears's own brand name was so strong that, until the 1970s, it emphasized its own brand names, even though the products were usually manufactured especially for the chain by well-known companies, such as Sears's brand home appliances that were made by Whirlpool.[37] Sears reasoned that its hard-earned consumer trust in Sears's value and quality outpaced the attraction of most specific product brands.[38] Amazon has also leveraged the trust that consumers have in its brand to launch sub-brands for various product categories, such as Kindle, Amazon Basics, the Fire line of personal electronics, the Echo suite of smart speaker devices, and clothing brands such as Amazon Essentials. Amazon's brand identity is service itself. It may have begun by selling books, but it has extended its brand farther than business professors and consultants thought could ever be possible—beyond consumer items into cloud computing services, shipping and logistics, and media production. Amazon's brand can stretch like taffy because its focus is not the things it sells so much as the service relationship it cultivates with customers. As a result, as noted previously, Amazon is one of the most trusted brands in America.

Today most product brands feel that they have to sell on Amazon or at Walmart, as opposed to the pressure being the other way around. Both retailers emphasize low prices, which encourages consumers to shop on price rather than brand name; if consumers have enough trust with the retail brand, they are less likely to require a trusted product brand name to make a purchase. Amazon's platform characteristics and relationship with consumers position it particularly well to erode the value of well-known product brands. The ability to sort product searches by price, the availability of customer reviews, and advantageous placement in searches (at a cost) can all level the playing field across brands.

Since 2015, products that perform well on price, customer reviews, return rate, and availability to ship immediately via Prime have the chance to be highlighted as "Amazon's Choice" (although the exact formula and decision process remains a mystery, even to companies whose products are chosen).[39] In addition, since 2012, companies can pay to be a sponsored search result. Sponsored search results have steadily risen over recent years, or at least, more of them are appearing near the top of searches.[40] Even a well-known name like the luggage brand Samsonite finds it has to pay Amazon to appear in searches for its own brand name.[41] At the same time, it's competing against Amazon's own branded products that, according to both consumer observation and investigative reporting, are increasingly advantaged by Amazon's search algorithm.[42]

New York Times technology columnist Farhad Manjoo explored the power of Amazon's retail platform to shake up the hierarchy of product brands by drawing attention to a consumer technology brand like Wyze, which makes smart home devices like motion-sensitive cameras, and has massively undercut better-known brands on price in order to establish itself in the market through high-volume, low-margin sales.[43] As more online product searches begin on Amazon (close to half, according to a number of industry estimates), the way products appear in search becomes more significant.[44] Although in theory Amazon's digital shelf space is limitless, in practice the first few results—especially those on the first page of the smartphone screen—are tremendously important. According to industry research, more than two-thirds of product clicks happen on the first page of Amazon's search results, with half of those focused on the first two rows of products that appear.[45] If a new or unfamiliar brand can pay for or earn strong placement in search, the trust that consumers have with Amazon, particularly guarantees around returns and delivery times, as well as its reputation as a source of product information, can rub off on them. *New York Times* tech columnist Shira Ovide notes this happening regularly with various fashion trends such as the "Amazon coat" in 2019, which was actually from an obscure brand but was available for purchase on Amazon's retail site.[46] As much as Amazon can recede into the background due to its ubiquity, the depth of the relationship that consumers have with it increasingly makes it the dominant brand, at least in terms of powerful affects like trust, relative to product brands that appear on its site.

One powerful brand that dipped its toe into Amazon's orbit, only to retreat again after two years, is Nike. Reportedly motivated to start wholesaling to Amazon in order to qualify for a "brand registry" program through which Amazon cracks down on counterfeit products, Nike changed its mind after finding that Amazon's efforts did not make much of a dent in the fake Nikes flooding the site. Nike has now shrunk the outlets that can sell its products to only those that can offer it "distinctiveness" in terms of space and signage, signaling Nike's specialness relative to other athletic brands. On Amazon's site, Nike products appeared cheek by jowl with competing and lesser brands, including "unauthorized sellers" of Nikes offering them at lower prices, with no distinction in size or appearance of the product listing, and favorable search results only coming at a price. These issues are why many luxury brands decline to sell on Amazon, recognizing that any increase in sales may be accompanied by an erosion in their brand equity.[47] Nike had confidence in the power of its brand to leave Amazon, but as one industry analyst put it, "I don't think as many brands can be as selective as Nike."[48]

While Walmart and Amazon have come to occupy a powerful position vis-à-vis product brands and manufacturers, their dominance has also afforded them considerable political power, not just over the decisions made by those in elected office, but also in terms of how their own activities take on the qualities of governance in communities and markets. Since the late nineteenth century, the US government has sought to limit the market dominance of any single company in order to preserve the competition thought to be necessary for innovation and consumer welfare. However, corporations whose main activity is the distribution of goods, people, or information have sometimes been able to argue that monopoly, or something close to it, is in fact "natural" for any business that requires a comprehensive network. Certainly, that's an impression that Amazon would like to cultivate—that its market dominance in any given area is merely a result of the efficiencies that accrue with greater size and reach, and a just reward for a job well done.[49] The history of distribution companies that claimed or seemed to enjoy "natural monopolies" reminds us, though, that a concentration of market power almost inevitably means a significant amount of power over politics and governance as well.[50] As Lichtenstein argues about Walmart:

No company of Wal-mart's size and influence is a "private enterprise." By its very existence and competitive success, it rezones our cities, determines the real minimum wage, channels capital throughout the world, and conducts a kind of international diplomacy with a score of nations. In an era of weak unions and waning governmental regulation, Wal-mart management may well have more power than any other entity to "legislate" key components of American social and industrial policy.[51]

Beyond the power of large retailers over manufacturing, the outsized political power of Amazon and Walmart can be attributed to the number of people they employ, or promise to employ if communities lay out the welcome mat. As of this writing, Walmart and Amazon are the two largest private employers in the United States. Worldwide, Walmart employs 2.2 million people and Amazon 1.3 million, with Amazon's hiring exploding during the 2020–2021 COVID-19 pandemic as it seeks to keep up with the greater demand for online shopping.[52] When jobs at this scale are on the line, especially for companies like Walmart and Amazon that have some discretion as to where they locate their stores and distribution infrastructures, then the distribution brands hold all the cards.

PARTNERS: THE UNITED STATES POSTAL SERVICE AND UPS, DELIVERY BRANDS

The famed Philadelphia-based department store Wanamaker's at one time used the slogan "Everything from Everywhere to Everybody!," but its founder John Wanamaker arguably turned that promise into a reality more through his service as US Postmaster General from 1889 to 1893 than through the store itself.[53] Certainly, Sears's approximation of that brand promise would not have been possible without existing infrastructures of distribution, including the railroads where Richard Sears first developed his mail-order scheme, but also the Post Office Department of the United States' federal government, as the United States Postal Service (USPS) was then known.

The social and political significance of the Post Office far exceeds the role it played in facilitating mail-order shopping. Historians have argued that the Post Office's mission to deliver mail to every part of the United States was what allowed the nation to "commune"—to be a community—in a fundamental sense.[54] The history of the USPS illustrates that affordable, efficient, content-neutral structures of information distribution are not just community making, but nation making, as well as commerce making.

Beyond the circulation of news and personal correspondence, the Post Office has long been crucial to the market economy. In the late nineteenth century, when consumer capitalism was exploding, the low-cost second-class category of mail, intended for newspapers and periodicals, also applied to some commercial materials, not to mention the advertising that increasingly appeared in the pages of those publications.[55] Because the mail-order catalogue was deemed "educational material" and therefore eligible for the favorable second-class postage rate, Sears concluded early on that the Post Office was in fact subsidizing the circulation of his catalogues.[56] But the real boon to Sears's business, which in the early days was focused mostly on rural consumers, was rural free delivery (RFD), which meant that starting in 1902 mail would be delivered to all homes regardless of their proximity to towns. The popularity of RFD paved the way for parcel post in 1913, which meant that for the first time these rural addresses could get packages of more than four pounds also delivered right to their homes, shipped via the Post Office for a reasonable rate.[57] Wanamaker had passionately advocated for both rural free delivery and parcel post, although they weren't ultimately adopted until after his tenure at the Post Office. But his experience in retailing made him aware of not just the value to consumers of being able to order goods delivered straight to their homes in a way that avoided the exorbitant fees charged by the private express companies of the time, but also the value to businesses of being able to deliver marketing communications to the mailboxes of the nation's consumers.[58] As USPS historian Winifred Gallagher puts it, "Simply by delivering a newspaper to every home, it would draw new customers into the national market and benefit businesses from publishers to the fledgling mail-order merchants and advertising agencies."[59] According to communication historian Richard B. Kielbowicz, "Parcel post formed the capstone in a postal communication and transportation system that already promoted marketing on a national scale."[60]

The significance of this shift was not lost on the stakeholders of the day. As Kielbowicz documents, the extended debate about parcel post revealed "all the hopes and anxieties associated with the expansion of mass society at the turn of the century" that the seemingly simple act of delivering packages to homes unleashed: "Opponents of parcel post foresaw a decline of small towns, a centralization of production and distribution, a disruption of the 'natural' relations among labor, retailers, and consumers, and the aggrandizement of urban culture. At the other extreme, proponents claimed that parcel post would increase consumer choice, reduce the cost of living, and bridge the widening chasm between urban and rural life."[61] Rural free delivery and parcel post were key inflection points in the improvements to the nation's communications and distribution networks that paved the way for truly national retailing and branding. Another would be the introduction of 1-800 numbers in 1967, which quickly made "mail-order" retailing actually "shopping by phone" most of the time, introducing a meaningful efficiency into the moment of exchange.[62]

Embedded in the debates about rural free delivery and parcel post from a century ago are concerns that continue today, as people try to make sense of how ecommerce has disrupted shopping routines previously organized around main streets and malls. At the time, opponents raised concerns about the government's role in promoting national parcel delivery, thereby competing with private companies that had deemed such services insufficiently profitable.[63] Deep cultural ambivalence about the government providing services that could conceivably be privatized continues to shape the fortunes and misfortunes of the United States Postal Service. Today USPS must be self-supporting (i.e., it is not funded with any tax dollars) at the same time that it is operating in the red, largely due to a burdensome requirement to pay retiree health benefits into an account in advance, a requirement unique among all government agencies. At the same time that the United States Postal Service is tasked with acting as if it were a private business (minus the tax burden, not that many large businesses—including Amazon—are paying much tax these days anyway), it is legally prevented from expanding into new business areas, as a real private entity would no doubt be doing, while required to operate according to its public-service mission—providing mail and package delivery to every corner of the nation.

Although the exact numbers are a fairly well-kept secret, it's widely thought that the USPS delivers the greatest proportion of Amazon packages out of all the delivery services the company works with—54 percent in 2018 according to one estimate.[64] While Donald Trump declared loudly and often during his presidency that Amazon is ripping off the USPS and getting too good a deal on its rates, going so far as to threaten to withhold a crucial line of credit and install a new postmaster general tasked with raising package delivery rates,[65] it's generally thought that package delivery has become core to USPS's business model and helped it sustain its shrinking mail delivery operations.[66] Even if Amazon is a ruthless negotiator (as is widely assumed), the Post Office is required by law to make money on its corporate accounts. Whether the profit margins are sufficient is a topic of debate among analysts, since the fine print is secret.[67]

It's worth pausing to consider the importance of public distribution infrastructures, like USPS, for a business such as Amazon's. Whether it's the United States Postal Service, the research and development of internet and telecommunications infrastructure, or even the roads, Amazon is a distribution brand that sits atop transportation and communication networks that had already made fairly instantaneous home shopping a reality. As Amazon significantly ramps up the amount of goods that it delivers (delivering 66 percent of its own packages by the middle of 2020),[68] and increases its distribution footprint accordingly, the support from public infrastructures only becomes greater.

Widely thought to be the largest carrier of Amazon packages after USPS and Amazon itself is UPS, a company that shares a great deal of brand DNA with its biggest client, including its identity as a service brand. The origin of the United Parcel Service is founder Jim Casey's childhood employment in on-foot delivery for a department store, a teahouse, and a telegraph company (a reminder that the telegraph only partially severed communication from transportation).[69] Forming a new delivery company in Seattle, Casey and his business partners first focused on delivering packages for department stores.[70]

After starting out on motorcycles, by 1913 the then "Merchants Parcel Delivery" company acquired a Model T Ford that they adapted for deliveries. Three years later they had a fleet of delivery vehicles they initially planned to paint bright yellow, until one of the company's partners argued instead for a color that would blend into the background, to avoid competing with the brands of the department stores that were their clients. This is the origin of the UPS brown that defines this brand, originally "Pullman brown"—the color of Pullman train coaches, which conveyed sober, established respectability at the time.[71]

Since then, UPS has embraced the understated ubiquity and ability to blend into the background represented by its chosen brown. The company's biographer in *Big Brown: The Untold Story of UPS* certainly sees it that way, writing, "Yet, despite the P.R. . . . despite UPS's much increased advertising budget, despite the company's presence on the NASCAR circuit, despite the 19 million hits on www.ups.com daily, UPS still isn't flashy. Big Brown, though ubiquitous, still *feels* 'under the radar.'"[72] Common across distribution brands is a focus on service, and this is particularly true of UPS's brand story. The same business partner who insisted on brown for the delivery vehicles also insisted, when the company was undergoing a name change as it expanded into California, that it should be called "United Parcel Service" rather than "United Parcel Company."[73]

The idea that the company has "nothing to sell except service" was reportedly a focus for founder and CEO Casey as well, who is remembered for saying: "Our real, primary objective is to serve—to render perfect service to our stores and their customers."[74] Amazon's own understanding of itself as fundamentally a service brand will become more than clear throughout this book, but an early hint came from Jeff Bezos in 1999: "When we first started Amazon.com, we had very conscious discussions where we talked about the fact that we were not a bookstore, but we were a book service. I do think that is a better way to think about it. Thinking of yourself as a store is limiting. Services can be anything."[75]

Although UPS reported in 2018 that no single client comprises more than 10 percent of its business, it's also the case that Amazon's steady movement into the delivery and logistics business is cause for concern for the delivery giant,[76] and widely attributed to be behind FedEx's 2019 decision to no longer deliver for Amazon.[77] As a platform business, Amazon frequently blurs the lines between business partner and competitor, whether with delivery partners like FedEx and UPS, or the companies that sell products on its site. As Amazon moves into more business areas, this will only happen more often.

DIGITAL CAPITALISM AND DISTRIBUTION

Beyond the retail fundamentals of offering a large selection at low prices, both Walmart and Amazon exemplify how digital communication and computing technologies have been deployed to feed capital's "logic of acceleration."[78] Although Amazon is more popularly associated with digital capitalism, the way these companies use these tools is a significant point of similarity. Even though the Walmart chain of stores was established in 1962, the company's use of digital communication and computing technologies, including the world's first corporate satellite network in the 1980s, has been a significant factor in its tremendous growth and market dominance (along with its efforts to keep wages as low as possible).[79] In 1998, Walmart already was being hailed in business publications for "using computers to transform the entire process of getting products to customers, all the way from the warehouse to Wal-mart's welcome mats."[80]

Digital communications and computing have sped up the conversion of capital from one form to another in its life cycle, which is key to capital accumulation—making capitalism "friction-free" in the words of Bill Gates.[81] Digital communication plays a role in capital's "logic of acceleration" in two ways, according to Vincent Manzerolle and Atle Mikkola Kjøsen: "First, it accelerates the actual moment of exchange by reducing latency and minimizing 'wasted moments'; second, it produces transactional data that can be used as a logistical resource to accelerate the circulation of commodities."[82]

Starting with the first type of acceleration, a consistent theme of Amazon's twenty-five-year history is promoting the convenience of its brand to the consumer, making consumption ever more frictionless. Amazon has dedicated itself to making it fast and painless to find, pay for, and subsequently receive items of all kinds. In terms of accelerating the "actual moment of exchange," or what we might imagine as the front end of frictionless consumption, in 1997 Amazon filed a US patent for the "1-click technology" that shaves seconds off each purchase, reducing barriers to purchase by removing clicks or seconds during which a customer might change their mind.[83] "1-click" meant that if you had already created an Amazon account and provided a default shipping address and credit card number, you could purchase a product with one click directly from the product page, a feature that still exists today with the button called "Buy Now." The importance of winning the Buy Now button on a particular product page for which there are multiple sellers, also known as the "Buy Box" that includes the "Add to Cart" button, is made clear by the cottage industry of companies (Tinuiti, Feedvisor, and Buy Box Experts among them) that advise sellers on how to earn this advantage from Amazon. Given that an estimated 90 percent of sales on Amazon are via the Buy

Box, it's a powerful carrot that Amazon uses to discipline sellers in areas such as their order defect rate, customer service quality metrics, price, fulfillment method and speed, and seller ratings from consumers. The ability to be a sponsored search result also hinges on qualifying for the Buy Box.[84]

Amazon has continued to focus on making online shopping as effortless as possible, with the introduction of the Amazon Dash button in 2015, an app-enabled physical button that you could stick somewhere in your house where you would just push it to reorder an item you consume regularly, such as laundry detergent or toilet paper.[85] As the ability to order items verbally from Alexa reduced the need to even walk over to a Dash button and push it with your finger, the program was discontinued in 2019. The zenith of automated, effortless shopping—requiring not even the breath required to say "Alexa"—are "smart" appliances that automatically reorder supplies such as dishwasher soap or trash bags as they sense them getting low, part of Amazon's focus on the Internet of Things.[86] And of course, like all e-tailers, the ability to shop anywhere anytime, through mobile technologies, makes purchasing a convenient 24/7 possibility.

Amazon has also opened a hybrid online/offline version of the "frictionless" shopping experience with Amazon Go, a grocery and grab-n-go store to which consumers gain entry using an Amazon Go mobile app. The "Just Walk Out" store model uses computer vision, weight scales, and machine learning technologies; the store charges the customer for anything they take off the shelves via the app on their smartphone.[87] The system automates the processes of checking out and paying, no doubt also reducing second thoughts, sticker shock, and buyers' remorse. This trend in retailing, while still nascent at least in the United States, may prove to be a blow to retail workers who will see jobs disappear in the digital, automated economy.

Every piece of friction that Amazon removes speeds up the circuit of capital, making it more profitable by reducing inventory costs and encouraging more spending. Bundling also uses a service logic of convenience to capture ever more consumer activity under the Amazon umbrella. With the Prime membership, there's a reduction in friction when an array of transactions and activities can take place with one provider that already has your delivery information and payment information, and consolidates all the "rewards" of membership. Whereas the purpose of "flow" on television was to keep the viewer on the channel for the purpose of selling their attention to advertisers,[88] on Amazon the purpose is to discourage comparison shopping on other sites, to purchase what you came for in the same visit, to purchase more than you came for (a goal for all retailers everywhere), and, similar to television, to expose you to in-store product marketing.

Walmart, in the meantime, is making efforts to offer convenience and ease to its customers as well. The ability to pick up online purchases in store and return them there as well introduces convenience to the regular Walmart shopper, and Walmart has ventured into curbside grocery pickup for internet-based orders, a development that became all the more relevant during the COVID-19 pandemic, giving Walmart some competitive advantage over Amazon.[89] Overall, though, Walmart's speed at the "moment of exchange" remains fairly comparable to all brick-and-mortar formats. It's in the area of logistics and distribution that Walmart has really distinguished itself, leading the way in using transactional data to accelerate the circulation of commodities by having the right goods in the right stores for consumers at the right times, and by using these data as a "logistical resource" to shift economic and political power from manufacturers and product brands to itself. Relative to Sears's heyday, digital communication and computing have taken much more of the guesswork out of what retailers want to order, and the expectation for the speed of response has become much greater, shifting the risk substantially from retailers to producers. The ability to track purchases in real-time with SKUs (eight-digit stock-keeping units), and to predict future sales via search behavior and predictive analytics, has put retailers in a position to make much more specific demands on manufacturers. Amazon knows more about who buys manufacturers' products and under what conditions than the manufacturers themselves do, and will make this data available only to a limited extent and at a considerable price.[90]

This shift in power between retailers and manufacturers is part of what Edna Bonacich and Jake B. Wilson describe as a "logistics revolution" that started in the early 1980s, when information technology and computing power allowed companies to exert greater control over the entire supply chain, beyond just delivering goods from A to B, but extending to "design and ordering, production, transportation and warehousing, sales, redesign, and reordering" in order to "link supply to demand" as precisely as possible.[91] Before logistics were supercharged by digital communication technologies, they were, of course, also key to previous distribution brands. One of Sears's most celebrated executives was General Robert E. Wood, who drew on his military training in logistics—he was a veteran of World War I when he served as quartermaster-general—in his leadership of the company.[92] Logistics have been a major focus for Walmart and Amazon. Tensions ran high between the two companies in Amazon's early years because of Bezos's habit of poaching supply-chain management executives from Walmart in order to use their expertise to develop Amazon's own approach to warehousing and delivery.[93]

While both Walmart and Amazon exemplify how digital communication technologies have supercharged capital accumulation, Amazon has advantages as a digital *platform* that Walmart does not fully share. Walmart may have unlocked the importance of logistics and distribution to retail dominance, but the baton has now passed to Amazon in terms of pushing the envelope in ecommerce delivery times and using information technology, robotics, and economies of scale to extract more efficiency from the distribution process.

CONCLUSION—FROM DIGITAL CAPITALISM TO PLATFORM CAPITALISM

This chapter offers historical and contemporary context for understanding Amazon as a distribution brand. What becomes clear when comparing Amazon to other major distribution brands like Sears, USPS, UPS, and Walmart is that such brands are among the most powerful in our economy. When we think about brands we tend to default to product brands, but the economic and political power of distribution brands is tremendous, even if their very ubiquity leads us to take them for granted. Companies whose primary business is distribution employ the most people; shape our communities and consumer identities; hold disproportionate power over politics and governance; and wield great influence over the manufacture of products even if they don't actually do it themselves. Distribution brands structure the national and international consumer cultures in which we live.

It's the very ubiquity and routine nature of a distribution brand like Amazon that fosters such consumer trust, even affection. A focus on service cultivates affection by placing the consumer's desire, convenience, and necessity at the center of every transaction, facilitated in no small part by the tools of digital capitalism. The distribution brand's service identity also gives it flexibility, allowing a brand like Amazon to stretch into a long list of new products and services without much apparent hesitancy or puzzlement on the part of its customers. Like its partner UPS, Amazon may not be glamorous, but its very utilitarianism fosters trust and contributes to the idea that it's part of the infrastructure of modern life.

What may have set Amazon apart from its predecessors and early competitors was Jeff Bezos's foresight into how the internet would eventually transform commerce, and his timing in getting in on the ground floor with a highly customer-focused service. Digital communication and computing allow Amazon, Walmart, and other companies to take the principles of capital accumulation and subject them to increased precision, greater predictability, and the ability to conquer space and time, in terms of the circulation of goods and information, on a global scale like never before. But beyond speeding up the circulation of capital, these technologies render change not just in degree, but in kind, too. This is a distinction that Bezos recognized early on in his career, when his experience with the internet caused him to seek out an employment opportunity with a company that not only would take advantage of the "first phase of automation," where "you use technology to do the same old business processes, simply faster and more efficiently," but also would embrace the "second phase of automation," where "you can fundamentally change the underlying business process and do things in a completely new way."[94]

Although this chapter looks at the similarities between Amazon and other distribution brands, there are also divergences that arise from the ability of primarily digital companies like Amazon to operate as platforms. One example of this divergence is that in its early days, Amazon was fundamentally a "middle man" between book publishers and distributors and customers, just like the Sears catalogue had been in its early days, but with the advantage of speed of communication and payment ("first order automation"). However, as the size of Amazon's customer base grew, and the tendency of customers to return again and again due to an emphasis on customer service became clear, Amazon realized it had a "platform" to vastly extend its product offerings *and* monetize those "eyeballs" above and beyond retail sales. As former employee James Marcus put it, "A crowd that big was itself a commodity."[95] In this respect Amazon starts to diverge from the principles of distribution brands established by the Sears and maybe even the Walmarts of the world, although Walmart is emulating Amazon by moving into online retailing and capturing detail about in-store consumer purchases through app tracking and mobile banking technologies.[96]

Amazon has shown greater malleability with its brand and business areas than we've seen with previous distribution brands. Although Sears became the "everything store" in terms of product categories, it didn't stretch as far into whole new services as Amazon has done, including its own brand-name electronics, entertainment, and cloud services. Amazon's ability to do this demonstrates the multiple ways that a platform can function. On the one hand, the consumer and transactional data that Amazon has mined—based on sales of not only its own retail inventory, but also all its Marketplace sellers—gives it unmatched, time-sensitive market intelligence to help it sell targeted advertising and identify new business areas. On the other hand, Amazon's relationship with consumers as a trusted service brand gives it the malleability and reputational capital to move into new products and services. Amazon's rapid rise to dominance as a distribution brand, and the ways that it is rewriting many of the rules for the distribution of products, advertising, and entertainment, have implications beyond those specific industries, as explored in the subsequent chapters of this book.

2

THE BOX: DISTRIBUTION FETISHISM AND THE MATERIALITIES OF ECOMMERCE

Amazon does not have a mascot or image associated with the company apart from its logos, which mostly feature the eponymous "Amazon" (or increasingly, "Prime") and the curved arrow that looks like a smile. Whereas Amazon's branding is quite utilitarian, some consumers have stepped in to create, circulate, and cherish their own Amazon character— Amazon box robot or Danbo (see figure 2.1). Based on a character made out of cardboard boxes that appeared in a 2006 issue of a manga comic by Japanese artist Kiyohiko Azuma, by 2009 versions of the cardboard robot featuring the amazon.com.jp logo were appearing online in meme-like fashion.[1] The publisher even partnered with a toy company to produce a physical version for purchase.[2]

The many photos of this character online and even published in photo books show great affection for this sweet, funny, sometimes melancholy robot named Danbo made out of Amazon boxes, vividly illustrating that brands are a co-production using the symbolic, physical, and experiential materials provided by a company and the affective investments made by consumers.[3] Danbo draws our attention to the Amazon box itself as a powerful way that this ecommerce company connects with consumers through material objects. In 2017 through 2019 the affection that Amazon knows its consumers have for the branded smile boxes was

2.1 *Danbo*, photograph by Ravi Shah, 2015. *Source: Flickr*, May 11, 2015, https://www
.flickr.com/photos/ravi-shah/16986127764. Creative Commons Attribution 2.0 Generic
license (https://creativecommons.org/licenses/by/2.0/).

incorporated into holiday ads, with the people sending, receiving, packing, and delivering boxes, as well as the boxes themselves via their ani-
mated smiles, singing feel-good songs like Solomon Burke's "Everybody
Needs Somebody to Love," Supertramp's "Give a Little Bit," and Michael
Jackson's "Can You Feel It."[4] In most of these ads, the people very much
fade into the background relative to the singing boxes.[5]

Amazon box robot Danbo and the singing Amazon boxes could hardly
be better illustrations of commodity fetishism, a concept we get from Karl
Marx in which he observes that in capitalism we develop social relationships with things, such as a box, and material relationships with the people
who produce those things through their labor, in this case the hundreds of
thousands of people who work for Amazon.[6] Since Marx was focused on our
relationships with commodities themselves, and since Amazon is known
primarily for *delivering* those commodities to us, I argue that Amazon
cultivates *distribution fetishism*. This concept aims to capture how Amazon's branding techniques encourage a personalized, affective relationship
between consumer and brand, while discouraging attention to the labor

and materialities that underlie heretofore unprecedented short delivery times. Marx's concept of commodity fetishism observes that commodities are "mysterious things" because we misrecognize their exchange value, or their price, as inhering somehow in the thing itself, when exchange value is actually a function of the labor required to produce that commodity. By obscuring the way exchange values represent a society's division of labor, Marx argues that commodities fetishize the true relations and conditions of production.[7] In the hands of Amazon, distribution is doubly fetishized, not just through the mysterious nature of exchange value, but because the costs of distribution are routinely hidden from the customer. Prime members don't pay anything for delivery of millions of Prime-eligible products, and nonmembers don't pay if they spend more than $25.

The very nature of Amazon's services—it is possible to interact with the brand on a daily basis, but never interact with one of its employees—paves the way for this fetishism (Mark Andrejevic describes Amazon as a "fetishizing machine"), but it's a mindset that Amazon has also encouraged through its branded communications.[8] The inverse of the intensity that people experience as they anticipate and then receive their packages is their general lack of awareness of the physical infrastructures and human effort that it took for those packages to arrive. The way that Amazon encourages consumer engagement with the box rather than the human beings who work for the company came into relief during the COVID-19 pandemic when widespread consumer and press attention to the risks faced by Amazon fulfillment and delivery workers demanded a different promotional approach. The ads running on television in 2020 focused on Amazon's workers, particularly in the fulfillment centers, persuading the consumer that they were happy in their work and, eventually, wearing masks and gloves.[9] Rather than being relatively anonymous people who are only glimpsed as they move an Amazon smile box from A to B, as had previously been typical of Amazon ads, the camera lingered on these workers at head and shoulders, with boxes only appearing incidentally in shots and not in closeup. In "Delivering Rainbows" from April 2020, we see something quite rare for an Amazon ad—an interaction between a customer and an Amazon employee, as a young girl draws a rainbow thank-you with sidewalk chalk for her delivery person, and then waves to him safely through the window as he drops off a package.[10]

COVID-19 did more to disrupt commodity fetishism, including distribution fetishism, than many a Marxist essay or think-piece. If commodity
fetishism mystifies the societal division of labor that allows for intensive
production and distribution, then the pandemic forces the consumer into
greater awareness and (one hopes) concern for the workers who have
fallen ill or died due to their work meat processing, cherry picking, or
packing Amazon boxes. Whereas workers had been the background to the
ubiquitous Amazon box, now boxes faded into the background as Amazon
sought to reassure the public that its workers were safe and happy to be
fulfilling consumer desires (while ongoing reports and allegations attest to
the contrary). Amazon would rise to the challenge—"doing everything we
can to get you what you need, and doing everything we can to keep our
people safe"—presented as mutually achievable goals.[11] By October 2020,
however, Amazon revealed that at least twenty thousand of its warehouse
and Whole Foods workers had been tested or presumed positive with the
virus, and as of this writing Amazon is under investigation by at least two
states for putting its warehouse workers at risk for the virus.[12]

While a key part of Amazon's business model is reducing friction in
purchasing and time from click to ship to delivery, consumers—during
regular times—are largely discouraged from knowing about or reflecting
on the infrastructure, labor, and energy that it takes to deliver their goods
in unprecedented short delivery windows. Sociologist David W. Hill calls
this a "cognitive injury" inflicted on users, which promotes "a mode of
unconscious consumption that dislocates buying online from the geography of fulfillment."[13] Rather than the materialities and labor of fulfillment, as consumers we tend to focus on what we can see and touch: the
Amazon smile box. While the box is representationally extremely simple,
it is central to the interactions and literal touches that Amazon has with
consumers.

We often focus on the immaterial aspects of tech companies like Amazon. Digital communication is understood to be "virtual," "in the cloud"—
its instantaneity and the ubiquity of wireless, mobile connectivity making
it seem as if it were without weight or form. Scholars have made important correctives to the tendency to imagine digital communication this
way, bringing attention to the necessary hardware; cables, satellites, and
cell towers; data centers; resources and infrastructure for electricity; and

e-waste.[14] Beyond the physical materiality of networked digital media are the other ways that it becomes infrastructural, in the sense of being a foundational but often invisible layer of "how things are done" that shapes and constrains human activity. Amazon is becoming infrastructural in the sense of its outsized role in information distribution, be it cloud computing or book sales, making many of us dependent on the company to get information or stuff. But it's also infrastructural in the way its market dominance makes it a setter of standards.[15] Standards are an inescapable aspect of infrastructure; as Susan Leigh Star and Geoffrey Bowker wrote, "Standards undergird our potential for action in the world, both political and scientific; they make the infrastructure possible."[16] From shipping speeds, to packaging specifications, to wages, Amazon's impact on standards that structure wide swathes of activity make its influence more akin to governance than private activity. Building on the efforts of scholars of digital capitalism and infrastructure studies, this chapter considers physical and labor infrastructures that are necessary for Amazon to distribute its digital and physical products.

Given my argument about distribution fetishism, I also examine how Amazon does make visible aspects of its distribution process, through its fulfillment center tours and its consumer-facing sustainability programs. I consider some of the limitations of these efforts at transparency, as well as question the common assumption that transparency, particularly visual transparency, will be transformative. As Mike Ananny and Kate Crawford put it, "The implicit assumption behind calls for transparency is that seeing a phenomenon creates opportunities and obligations to make it accountable and thus to change it."[17] I suggest that, rather than through transparency, finding ways to rematerialize our experience and understanding of digital products and services would be a more effective way of combating distribution fetishism.

THE BROWN BOX

Amazon's branded box has become its most powerful representation, symbolizing the primary relationship that most consumers have with Amazon as an online retailer. The affective rewards of consistently receiving personally selected merchandise in a surprisingly short time frame is expressed in the cultural resonance of, and affection for the Amazon box itself. In 2000 the smiling arrow became part of Amazon's logo, and was put on its boxes in order to make every delivery a branding opportunity.[18]

For most consumers, Amazon has become the brand that *delivers*, in both the literal and figurative senses of the word. The box encapsulates Amazon's brand promise to deliver smiles to our doorsteps—something the company rarely says with words, but communicates on every branded box and envelope. The seeming humility of the brown cardboard box belies the scale and nature of the company's impact on retail, as well as the attention and effort that Amazon has put into its packaging, given its role as the most powerful "touchpoint" between consumer and brand. Amazon's attention to packaging anticipated the rise of both functionality and design in business-to-consumer packaging as ecommerce exploded in the first two decades of the twenty-first century. As one observer puts it, "In the era of e-commerce, boxes are the new storefront."[19]

In order to "delight" its customers in that ever-so important moment of box opening (a pleasure for the ecommerce age captured in the You-Tube genre of "unboxing" videos), Amazon has demanded that its suppliers create packaging that can withstand the stresses of shipping and protect the products within, while also optimizing the "user experience" as they receive and open the box. Asking for bespoke box dimensions that accommodate its most commonly purchased products, Amazon has also pushed the packaging industry to provide new "dunnage" solutions—materials that can keep products secure within the box—to protect items as they travel. The company pioneered the use of gummed or water-activated reinforced paper tape, which allows for vivid branded graphics to be printed on it, is more hardy and tamper-proof than traditional sticky tape, and can enter the recycling stream along with the box.[20] Amazon uses the tape to turn its boxes into promotional material for more than just the overall Amazon brand, but specific products and services, in particular listing the benefits of Prime such as free two-day shipping and Prime Video.

The most prominent program demonstrating Amazon's attention to the box as a significant touchpoint for consumers is Frustration-Free Packaging, launched in 2008 in response to consumer concerns about both the frustration and ostentatious waste in the way many goods were packaged.[21]

The program extends beyond the box that Amazon itself uses to pack the item to the way the manufacturer packs the product in its own box, with the goal that sometimes Amazon doesn't need to put the item in an additional box to ship it at all. Product packaging is generally designed to make a visual impact on a store shelf as well as discourage store theft, but the needs of the online consumer are different.[22] Amazon encourages companies to package their goods differently for purchase online compared to its products destined for brick-and-mortar stores, so that the package overall will be smaller, use fewer materials (plastic in particular), and be easier to open.

Today, Frustration-Free Packaging is just one tier of three packaging certifications that vendors who wish to have their products shipped by Amazon must qualify for or, as of 2019, be charged $1.99 per unit. Frustration-Free is the top tier, "comprising packaging that ships in its own vendor-supplied packaging with no overbox required, is easy-to-open, and is made from 100% curbside-recyclable materials." Tier 2 is Shipped In Own Container (SIOC), meaning that Amazon again doesn't have to pack it in a new box, but the packaging doesn't have to be as easy to open as Tier 1 or be 100 percent recyclable. Finally, Tier 3—"Prep-Free Packaging"—means that Amazon will place the item in an Amazon box, but the product will not require any extra prep work in terms of wrapping or bagging.[23] Sellers have to get the Tier 1 and 2 certifications from the International Safe Transit Association, an independent organization that nevertheless certifies specifically for shipping via Amazon, subjecting packaged goods to drops and vibrations to ensure that products will arrive intact. Given Amazon's control of the ecommerce market, its certification regimes for sellers amount to more than just the demand of one client, but rather a form of governance for packaging and manufacturing industries as a whole. In response to this concentration of power, consumer-packaged goods companies formed the E-Com Packaging Council in 2019, a trade group aimed at making the "conversation" about ecommerce packaging standards "two-way," given that it was being "dictated in large part by the big retailers" like Amazon.[24]

Amazon's focus on the box and packaging is rooted in a recognition of the affective nature of the moment when the consumer actually touches something from the brand. In chapter 1 I described how Amazon has worked to make the act of consumption as frictionless as possible. But beyond speeding up the actual act of purchase, Amazon wants to remove friction from the back end of consumption—or how goods get to us once they are ordered. For Amazon, as well as for many ecommerce companies, the circulation of physical matter through space and time still matters, even as other forms of circulation—of money, of communication—happen virtually. On this point, Manzerolle and Kjøsen write, quoting Marx, "The circulation of capital proceeds in space and time. As capital extends itself in space and strives to make the earth into a market, capital tries to 'annihilate this space with time,' i.e. to reduce to a minimum time spent in motion from one place to another."[25] "Annihilating space with time" is a fitting description of how Amazon has deployed logistics to deliver almost any combination of items to its customers in astonishingly small time frames, thereby putting tremendous pressure on the retail industry as a whole, both online and brick-and-mortar.

As David Harvey has argued, information technologies have reduced the amount of time it takes to make decisions and circulate information globally; simultaneously advances in transportation networks and coordination along with their shrinking costs have enabled a "time-space compression" that serves capital.[26] According to John Durham Peters, the forms of media that allow coordination across space and time are "logistical media."[27] Peters argues that since these communicative forms have "no content . . . they often seem neutral and given—something that gives them extraordinary power,"[28] similar to Paul N. Edwards's observation that the technologies and networks that "are the connective tissues and circulatory systems of modernity" nevertheless become invisible to us as they become infrastructural.[29] Edwards argues that a key term for understanding infrastructure is "flow," and that in modernity it is the increased volume and speed of various kinds of flows that we have come to depend on and yet find unremarkable.[30] Taking for granted the "flow" of a mindboggling array of goods produced all over the world to our doorsteps is at the heart of distribution fetishism.

Fast and trackable home delivery is not incidental to an ecommerce giant like Amazon—it's central to the business model and consumer experience. In 2002, Amazon CEO Jeff Bezos essentially canceled the advertising budget for the company in favor of offering free shipping for orders over ninety-nine dollars (at the time; that number went down later), on the assumption—correct, as it turned out—that consumers' "delight" with the reliable, fast, and free shipping experience would drive repeat orders and positive word of mouth.[31] With catalogue shopping, customers were used to a three-to-five-day timeframe for delivery of goods, typically with a shipping charge.[32] But in 2005, when Amazon launched the Prime membership with free two-day shipping on many of its items, the ecommerce world received a shock, and scrambled to catch up.[33] Since then, Amazon introduced Prime Now in some urban areas, where goods can be delivered in an hour or two, and a standard one-day shipping for Prime members on millions of items in 2019. Clearly, Amazon has driven industry standards and consumer expectations of unprecedented shipping speeds.

The two-day shipping promise in 2005 was possible only because Amazon had turned its attention seriously to the problem of logistics in the early 2000s. Some of the notable moments in this story include: Amazon concluding that it would have to develop its own fulfillment centers and distribution processes in order to be able to make and deliver on fast shipping promises;[34] designing its own software and fulfillment center machinery to speed up packing times;[35] using algorithms not just to transform packing within warehouses, but also to figure out how products should be distributed across fulfillment centers;[36] developing productivity software for fulfillment center employees in order to precisely monitor their speed and movements;[37] introducing robots to do some of the fulfillment center work;[38] acquiring Whole Foods Market, which comes with its own brick-and-mortar distribution network, product storage space, and Amazon lockers; the 2019 rollout of Amazon Hub Counter, which directs customers to Amazon lockers or pick-up points at brick-and-mortar retailers like Rite Aid;[39] investing in its own delivery systems including fleets of planes and trucks;[40] developing Amazon Flex, an Uber-style, gig-economy delivery program; and preparing to launch both delivery drones and autonomous delivery vehicles, now undergoing beta testing.[41] Thanks to being its best customer, in 2014 Amazon was able to arrange Sunday delivery in the United States with the United States Postal Service—a first.[42]

While digital communication technologies have played a large role in the logistics revolution, capital investments are also required to put into place the warehousing and transportation infrastructures necessary to deliver millions of packages a year. As of 2019, Amazon reported that it had "110 fulfillment centers, 100 delivery stations, and 20 air gateways" in the United States, with many more planned for construction even before the COVID-19 pandemic supercharged demand.[43] Whenever Amazon builds new facilities or moves into existing warehouse space, that has a major impact on the local community, in terms of traffic and employment. On the flip side, if the company moves operations and leaves a community, as it did in Coffeyville, Kansas, where it leased a warehouse space from 1999 to 2014, it can be devastating to the local economy and job market.[44] All tech companies have geographic footprints and material elements to their products and services, be it in the form of the required devices, telecommunications connectivity, energy, or labor. But Amazon's ecommerce operations require tremendous infrastructure and logistics capabilities in order to execute the activity—swift delivery of stuff—on which it has built so much consumer trust. Consumer disconnection from these materialities is at the core of distribution fetishism.

DISTRIBUTION FETISHISM AND THE MATERIALITY OF ECOMMERCE

I conceptualize consumer preoccupation with short shipping times and relative ignorance of the infrastructure, labor, and environmental impacts that make them possible as distribution fetishism. This move is consistent with Sarah Sharma's call to attend to "power-chronography," which refers to "the interdependent and inequitable relations of temporal difference that are compressed deep within the social fabric," and involves "the structural politics of time and space, specifically the different bodies and labor that are reorchestrated to elevate and valorize our media forms over most of humanity."[45] Building on Sharma's view, we should recognize that the online shopper has been granted a "privileged itinerary," the spectacularization of which should not obscure the way others' time and space have been "reorchestrated" in order to make such an itinerary possible.[46]

As the labor of logistics and distribution becomes ever more crucial in an economy intent on accelerating the circuit of capital, it is too easy to fetishize time—the surprisingly small amounts of time required for online orders to reach us—and mystify space along with the infrastructure and labor that it takes to "annihilate" it. The reality and materiality of all these goods moving through space arguably has been lost as we experience them only via the metric of time—"three to five business days," "two-day shipping," "one-day shipping," and even "two-hour delivery." Power-chronography, the antidote to distribution fetishism, encourages us to resist the normalization of the "time-starved subject" and see how a company like Amazon helps to produce such a subject through the very services it offers and how it markets them.[47] Free two-day shipping is part of that subjectification, as are the numerous communicative "touches" regarding shipping—the email that tells you your item has been shipped, the push alert letting you know when it will arrive, the ability to "track" the location of your shipment at any time, and the final push alert indicating its arrival. While most of the distribution processes are invisible to the consumer, Amazon increasingly encourages visibility and consumer engagement with the "last mile," sending frequent updates, maps, and even images of delivered items in order to build anticipation and satisfaction for a successfully completed purchase (see figure 2.2).

Productivity techniques and surveillance on fulfillment center workers is a "reorchestration" that produces this "privileged itinerary."[48] The convenience and gratification of fast shipping is only possible because of tremendous pressure on distribution workers to achieve ever greater rates of efficiency in picking, sorting, and delivering packages. Amazon has developed extensive surveillance and productivity techniques that keep intense pressure up for being on time, taking short breaks, and meeting increasingly tough speed targets on the pain of being fired.[49] Digital tracking technologies that show exactly how quickly and efficiently individual workers perform are a key element in extracting maximum value. One former Amazon employee reports having a rate of 300 items per hour—she was expected to remove an item from its box and stow it every eleven seconds, throughout the day.[50] Just as Amazon warehouse workers increasingly work side by side with robots, so too is the robot becoming an aspirational model for human employment—being programmable and never getting sick, requiring rest, or desiring autonomy or social interaction. Journalists who have gone undercover to work in Amazon

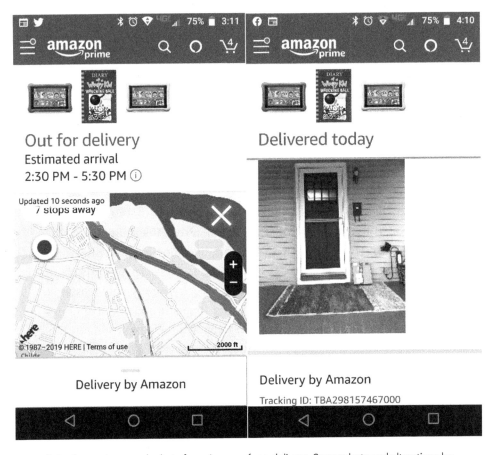

2.2 Smartphone push alerts from Amazon for a delivery. Screenshots and alterations by author.

warehouses, as well as former employees, report that the techniques aimed at maximizing workers' every movement take a tremendous physical and psychological toll, a trend playing out across low-wage workplaces. A recent investigation by Reveal from the Center for Investigative Reporting, based on records from a subset of Amazon's US fulfillment centers, showed that they have more than double the industry-average injury rate (Amazon claims this is because it documents injuries more than the industry as a whole), testifying to the human costs of the relentless drive for productivity, even in the context of strict rules and strong internal messaging about safety.[51]

Companies and individuals that contract with Amazon to deliver packages are under similar time pressures and surveillance regimes. Last-mile delivery is where Amazon does most of its contracting—with individuals through the Amazon Flex program or with third-party contractors through the Delivery Service Providers program. Delivery workers have alleged a major speedup over recent years in the number of packages they are expected to deliver per shift—from between 80 and 150 formerly to 250 now and, in peak seasons, 400.[52] Along with this speedup workers report not being allowed to take breaks or stop for meals, feeling pressure to work on days off and while sick, routinely needing to drive longer than a nine-hour day, and wage theft. Just as fulfillment center workers have reported that some workers urinate in a bottle to save time walking to a bathroom, so multiple accounts from contract delivery drivers suggest that they are also eliminating in bottles or buckets in their trucks in order to keep up with the schedule. Similar to its warehouse workers, Amazon tracks drivers using handheld devices known as "rabbits," meaning that these subcontracted workers are given their routes and directly surveilled by Amazon just as Amazon employees are.[53] In the case of drivers, many of them are not directly employed by Amazon, so the pressure on the company then becomes to conduct adequate oversight of their partners, to whom they simultaneously make high demands in terms of results. Speeding and ignoring stop signs have been reported as a common practice. The public safety issues associated with Amazon's fast delivery promises occasionally come to prominence with major accidents, such as in 2019 when a driver contracted to deliver Amazon packages killed a baby in a car that he rear-ended in Maine, attributed to the driver's excessive speed and inattention as he tried to keep up with Amazon's demanding delivery benchmarks.[54] When incidents such as this occur, Amazon is insulated from legal liability since the drivers work for subcontractors rather than the company itself.[55] The subcontracting arrangement as well as the size of the vans means that Amazon's delivery program is not subject to regulatory oversight and record-keeping requirements as most of its large delivery partners including UPS are.[56]

Productivity pressures on the workforce are no surprise to those who have studied the logistics industry. Bonacich and Wilson complain, "While the return of sweatshops in production has received considerable attention at both the global and local levels and critiques are emerging about the labor practices regarding their sales workers by the giant retailers, deteriorating conditions for logistics workers have mainly gone unnoticed."[57] Because these positions are framed as low-skilled, often temporary in peak seasons, and often located in communities with few employment opportunities, despite excesses and abuses coming to light with some frequency, there has been little success to date in organizing workers, at least in the United States. Part of the issue is that workers facing poor or dangerous working conditions often are not Amazon employees but rather, they work for subcontractors, such as in last-mile delivery operations. A 2019 report from the National Council for Occupational Safety and Health, a US-based advocacy organization, found that six workers who had died in the prior six months all worked for other companies subcontracting with Amazon, including a construction firm and an air cargo service.[58] The lack of unionization among Amazon warehouse workers reflects a broader decline in unions. The most prominent effort to unionize American Amazon workers to date was the vote to join the Retail, Wholesale, and Department Store Union at a fulfillment center in Bessemer, Alabama. Although the vote was lost decisively in April 2021, the campaign gained some traction because even though the warehouse—which opened in 2020—brought good wages to the area, the productivity quotas and working conditions (especially during the pandemic) produced interest in greater protections and voice for workers.[59]

Another reorchestration that facilitates consumers' transformed relationship to delivery time is the shift in the labor force from retail to warehouse and delivery-related employment. Although such shifts are often presented as benign—merely the inevitable evolution of work in the digital economy—the specifics reveals that (a) fulfillment centers are not necessarily in the communities losing retail jobs, and (b) require very different skill sets, making it difficult for a laid-off retail worker to merely transition into fulfillment center employment.[60] Given the scale of retail employment in the United States—at 4.3 million people working in retail sales in 2019, the largest occupation in the country[61]—the seeming lack of political concern about the steep decline in retail employment is likely linked to several factors: its lack of connection to particular geographic areas, the feminized nature of retail work, the existing casualization and lack of benefits in retail employment, and the relative dearth of organized labor in retail.

Further, there is growing evidence that advances in automation are reducing the dependence of distribution companies like Amazon on human labor over time,[62] despite ongoing public relations efforts from the company emphasizing the need for skilled human oversight over warehouse robots.[63] Amazon acquired the robotics company Kiva in 2012. Unlike the sweet, anthropomorphic Amazon box robot Danbo, Kiva robots are boxy, low to the ground machines—like a large Roomba—designed to move very quickly around the warehouse. Instead of employees walking the aisles to pick up items, the robot brings the shelves containing those items to the "picker," who selects the correct item for each order while standing in one place. In fulfillment centers where the robots are used, they reportedly reduce the time it takes to pack an order from an hour and a half to fifteen minutes.[64] As much as some reporting suggests that work in Amazon warehouses can be stressful and dehumanizing, simultaneously other reporting raises concerns about the *loss* of these jobs due to Amazon's efforts in automation, highlighting how the need for jobs in many communities is so high that whether jobs are good or safe is a secondary consideration.[65]

"Distribution fetishism" helps explain the palpable sense of shock, disgust, and shame expressed in responses to investigative journalism that pulls the curtain back on Amazon's labor practices. One such instance was in August 2015, when the *New York Times* published the feature titled "Inside Amazon: Wrestling Big Ideas in a Bruising Workplace" by Jodi Kantor and David Streitfeld. In contrast to the supposed glamour of working in tech, and the presumption that well-educated, privileged technology workers enjoyed a pleasant, even fun workplace, the broadly sourced article detailed a dark side to working at Amazon. "Even as the company tests delivery by drone and ways to restock toilet paper at the push of a bathroom button, it is conducting a little-known experiment in how far it can push white-collar workers, redrawing the boundaries of what is acceptable," the authors wrote. They described a 24/7 work culture where evenings, weekends, and family time are not respected; a culture showing very little tolerance for workers who need time off or a lighter load due to family or personal illness; and a culture of back-stabbing where people are encouraged to identify and ice out team members they perceive as "weak," with tools such as anonymous communication channels to managers designed just for that purpose. Another memorable insight came from a former employee who said, "Nearly every person I worked with, I saw cry at their desk." Just as fulfillment center employees are asked to embrace actual robots as coworkers and emulate their machinic efficiency, employees in the Amazon offices aspire to be "Amabots," a term that has come to mean "you have become at one with the system."[66]

The piece caused a major stir, and was the most commented-on article in the history of nytimes.com at the time.[67] Many Amazon customers who commented were horrified, disgusted, and ashamed about their support of a company whose behavior resembled an emotional abuser, to paraphrase a number of comments. As one reader wrote, "Why does Amazon treat its customers better than its employees? And why do we, as customers, enable that?"[68] The strength of the affective relationship that people have with Amazon made the contradiction between the experiences of its workers and the experiences of its customers all the more jarring. Other Amazon customers and employees were dismissive, particularly of the naivete of people who had not considered what it might take to deliver almost anything to their homes in the (at the time) Prime membership standard of two business days. The fallout continued in the press for months, with Amazon chief Jeff Bezos first professing his shock at the article and affirmation that the reported practices were not part of Amazon's culture,[69] and later denouncing the piece as biased and overly dependent on the accounts of disgruntled former employees.[70]

As Kantor and Streitfeld wrote, "Tens of millions of Americans know Amazon as customers, but life inside its corporate offices is largely a mystery."[71] While Amazon will go to great lengths to cultivate loyalty with its consumers, their reporting as well as a number of behind-the-scenes trade books about Amazon suggest that the company views employees as a renewable resource, and therefore, disposable. Former editorial employee James Marcus, for example, reveals that his contract contained a Job-Related Stress clause that indemnified Amazon against any related damages sought by the employee or their relatives as a result of the "high degree of job-related stress" that could reasonably be expected.[72] A culture of worker disposability also comes through in reporting on how Amazon has responded to deaths occurring in its fulfillment centers, such that many fellow employees are not informed, or when they are, they're expected to return immediately to work.[73] The impression that workers are viewed as disposable came to a head during the COVID-19 pandemic, when Amazon's secrecy over how many of its warehouse and Whole Foods workers were contracting or dying from the disease converged with the surge of participation in Black Lives Matter protests.[74] Although Amazon's public support for Black Lives Matter, on its website and in statements from Jeff Bezos, was laudable, this political support sat uneasily with the possibility that the bottom line took precedence over worker safety. Almost half of Amazon's nonmanagement workforce in 2020 were Black/African American and Hispanic/Latinx, populations that have been disproportionately harmed by COVID-19.[75]

Whereas Amazon's earlier history arguably saw fairly complete distribution fetishism, in terms of a lack of public curiosity and engagement with the infrastructure and labor of fulfillment and delivery, recent years—even pre-pandemic—saw the rise of more consumers, and certainly the press, becoming distribution-curious. Amazon is aware of people's curiosity but also their concern given the negative press and word of mouth about working conditions for Amazon employees. The company has responded by offering public tours of its fulfillment centers.

A PEEK THROUGH THE CURTAIN: FULFILLMENT CENTER TOURS

In August 2019 I attended a fulfillment center tour at YYZ4, a facility near the Toronto airport in Brampton, Ontario. Toward the end of the tour, visitors were invited to get their picture taken. The device that took the picture was a tablet embedded in a standalone pillar about five feet tall. After standing in a designated spot on an elevated walkway above conveyers leading to the loading docks, the picture was taken, after which we approved the pictures and had them sent to us.

The picture (figure 2.3) bears a synecdochic relation to Amazon's approach to making its behind-the-scenes processes visible in response to bad press about working conditions. The picture does show the inside of a fulfillment center, and indexes the fact that I, an interested member of the public, entered and toured the facility. In fact, there are a good number of

2.3 Instagram-ready photo of the author taken by the automatic photo booth at the YYZ4 Fulfillment Center in Brampton, Ontario.

fulfillment centers in North America and Europe offering these tours, with an array of days and times that people can choose to attend the seventy-five- to ninety-minute event. I had previously attended a tour at the BOS7 Fulfillment Center in Fall River, Massachusetts. While Fall River is a nonsortable facility, meaning that it receives and sorts larger items that require human workers to stow and pick them without the assistance of robots, the Toronto facility is sortable, meaning that products are sixteen inches or smaller, so they can fit into fairly small storage bins, and robotics are integral to the stowing and picking processes. Both tours began with a welcome from the tour guide and assistants in a conference room custom-built for this purpose. After an overview from the tour guide and safety instructions, tour members donned visitors' badges, headphones, and a receiver that would allow us to hear the mic-ed voice of the tour guide over the din of the fulfillment center.

Both tours were fact-filled. For example, the BOS7 Fulfillment Center is 1.3 million square feet, or more than twenty-four football fields large, carries 400,000 distinct items, fulfills 40,000–50,000 orders per day, and has 1,300 employees. The YYZ4 Fulfillment Center is 850,000 square feet with 2,000 employees; it has 50,000 yellow totes that transport products from inventory to packing. We also received a lot of information about the benefits of Amazon employment: starting wage of fifteen dollars an hour ($15.75 CAD), immediate access to health insurance, 95 percent of education costs paid in predefined "high demand" careers such as nursing and long-haul trucking, and across-the-board twenty-week parental leave.

Apart from the unloading of trucks, because of the hard hats and safety boots required in that setting, we were taken on the chronological tour that a product would take in the fulfillment process, from inbound to outbound. First, newly delivered products are stowed on racks or in bins. In the nonsortable facility employees accomplish this with forklifts that deposit plastic-wrapped pallets onto fifty-five-foot storage racks, a task undertaken at other facilities by a robot called a "robo-stow." In sortable facilities a stower has a rolling rack with a random assortment of products, and a seven- or eight-foot-tall yellow shelving unit, called a "pod," filled with coded bins of different sizes is brought to them by a Kiva robot. A computer system then instructs the stower what to shelve where; a portable scanner confirms that a given product has been placed into a given bin. Once the product itself and the bin location have been scanned, the product is officially in "inventory" and will appear on the Amazon site.

We also observed the picking process in both facilities, where an employee finds a given item (supplied again by the software) and collects it into a bin that is destined for the packing stations. In the sortable facility the Kiva robots line up the pods with the needed products and the picker selects each product as instructed, scans it, and places it into a yellow tote. In the nonsortable facility, the process is a bit more spectacular. The pickers operate forklifts that lift *them* up as high as fifty-five feet, so they can select a specific item from a given pallet. From there, picked items are conveyed to the packing stations.

At the packing station, the packer is instructed what to put in each box and what size box to use, and is provided automatically with the correct length of tape to seal it. Once the box has been assembled the packer sticks a SKU (Stock Keeping Unit) code onto it and scans it. The location of the box containing the product is now trackable as long as it is scanned at every step of its journey.

On both tours we then observed the SLAM (Scan/Label/Apply/Manifest) machine in action, which connects specific products to a name and address for the first time in a visible way in the warehouse. The SLAM machine is a highlight of the tour because the speed from when a box's SKU code is read to when a pneumatic printer blows the address label onto the rapidly moving box is astonishing. From there packages are routed toward the shipping docks on fast-moving conveyer belts where again a scanner reads the addresses and determines which chute the package should be pushed down (using the correct number of sliding "pushers" on the conveyer belt given the box's dimensions) in order to reach the loading area for the correct truck that will take it to the next stage of its journey—be it the closest airport, Canada Post, USPS, UPS, or a smaller carrier.

The tour leaves the impression of having seen a lot. Especially in the sortable facility we stood quite close to the workers and could essentially look over their shoulders at the move-by-move instructions they were getting from their computer monitors. At the same time there were restrictions. We were not invited to speak directly to the workers, and it was clear that the tour guides (at least the ones who spoke, it's less clear about the staff who assisted with shepherding us) were not doing these jobs on days they weren't giving tours. The tour guides kept a close eye on the group to make sure no one strayed or fell behind. We could have our phones with us but not take any pictures or video.

I point to the official photograph as a synecdoche of the tour because of how it depicts something, but only in a partial, controlled, fuzzy way. The photo creates an illusion of seeing as much as it actually shows something. The image is low definition. Yes, it's the interior of the fulfillment center, but anything of interest is obscured or too far away to inspect. What we mostly see is building infrastructure and sorting equipment. The people who work in the building are barely visible.

Similarly, the tour is notable for what it emphasizes compared to what it obscures or distracts from. First of all, these tours are highly structured and only available in some fulfillment centers, so the company has every opportunity to make sure visitors are only exposed to their best facilities on their best days. Although visitors learn quite a lot about the pay, the benefits, and the specifics of the different jobs that workers do, it's hard to glean what it would actually be like to work at the warehouse from a brief tour that doesn't pause for more than a few minutes in any one spot. The complaints that surface in the press and from activists are about productivity pressures that make it hard to take breaks, or that demand unreasonable rates of work that, especially over time, threaten the health and safety of workers. Without extended observation or frank conversation, it would be hard to learn whether this is indeed the case for the workers we see. Finally, both tours heavily emphasize the Fulfillment Center as a feat of technology and advanced computing. There was some discussion of the skill involved in learning how to use the forklifts in the nonsortable warehouse. In the Fall River warehouse we saw the "problem solver" (an official job title) who tracks down packages with inconsistencies that cause them to be rejected by the SLAM machine, or "KO-ed" (Kicked Off)—such as missing an address label or the weight of the box not aligning with the combined weight of the products that are supposed to be in it. At the loading dock, we saw that fitting boxes into the containers was comparable to a three-dimensional game of Tetris, but that nevertheless Amazon's system will have computed how many packages should be able to fit in the space.

Other than these observations of the need for human ability, it was clear that the computer systems, robots, and smart conveyer belts were meant to be the stars of the show. In addition to an extended discussion of the SLAM technology, both tours focused on the technique of stowing inventory in a random manner across the racks and bins. For example, if a shipment of diapers arrives, then each pallet of diapers will be stowed in a different spot across the fulfillment center. Similarly, shipments of smaller products will be split up so they are stowed across a variety of bins throughout the inventory. While this is counterintuitive for our human tendency toward patterns and order, as one tour guide characterized it, Amazon has found that random assortment is more efficient because fewer mistakes are made as would occur if very similar items were stowed next to each other. Also, the path that a picker has to take to get to any given item is likely to be shorter if they are randomly stowed throughout inventory, and if a given item is suddenly very popular there is a lower chance of "bottlenecks"—multiple pickers can retrieve the same item from multiple locations. Further, for products with expiration dates, the system can keep track of which bins arrived at the facility first and therefore which should be sent out first, in order to avoid inventory going bad. With narratives such as these, a great deal of agency and responsibility for the efficiency of the fulfillment process was attributed to "the computer" or "Amazon's algorithms." It became clear that the job of most Amazon workers is to respond to the immediate instruction right in front of them—scan this product and put it in this bin. Unlike the early days of Amazon fulfillment, when stowers and pickers worked from a printed list of items, workers are given one instruction at a time and the next instruction only appears once they have completed the initial task.

For Amazon and its computer systems, the fulfillment centers are spaces of visibility. Given protocols where every individual product is scanned on entry to the facility, and its every subsequent movement and interaction with a worker are likewise scanned, Amazon aims to achieve almost perfect visibility of what products it has where, and exactly what employees are doing when. While Amazon has near-perfect vision of what is happening in its warehouses, the tour is a gesture toward ocular symmetry for the public that is nevertheless highly controlled. Workers themselves are typically restricted to one very narrow activity and are subject to the scopic regime rather than able to participate in it.

Although a very different setting, Timothy Pachirat's analysis of the "politics of sight" in the cattle slaughterhouse in which he did covert ethnographic fieldwork for six months can help us understand this asymmetry of vision in Amazon's processes of distribution. Pachirat observes that techniques of "distance and concealment" confine the unpleasant, "dirty work" of killing and dismembering animals out of vision.[76] In the slaughterhouse only management had complete vision of the process from live cattle to carcass, through its surveillance techniques and ability to travel throughout the highly contained, segregated zones of the facility. Pachirat reports that the labor in the facility was highly divided, with just one out of hundreds of workers administering the fatal blow. Even then, it wasn't entirely clear when cattle transitioned from living to dead. The full picture of what occurred at the facility, and how, was generally not clear even to most people who worked at the plant. Pachirat draws attention to "the capacity for surveillance and sight to reinforce, rather than subvert, distance and concealment."[77] It's a seeming paradox: "how surveillance and concealment work together, how quarantine is possible in, and perhaps even enabled by, conditions of total visibility."[78] Or, as Ananny and Crawford put it, "Transparency is . . . not simply 'a precise end state in which everything is clear and apparent,' but a system of observing and knowing that promises a form of control."[79]

Pachirat's analysis of the slaughterhouse applies a sobering brake to the assumption that visibility will lead to transformation, or that when we see something it will necessarily lead to social change. In part, he argues, this is because it is only when unpleasant processes are concealed that their reveal has the power to shock. Revealing in controlled ways something that might otherwise be deemed unacceptable in a particular cultural context can be a way of controlling the response. There are, it turns out, public tours of slaughterhouses too. Whether in the slaughterhouse or the fulfillment center, techniques of "surveillance and sequestration" may so divide and separate different aspects of a process, and so isolate workers from the outside and each other, that true "transparency" becomes unachievable.[80]

Even if the more troubling aspects of Amazon fulfillment work were to be visible on these tours, it's not clear that such visibility would be transformative. Given the hegemony of power chronography, would the scrambling, exhausted delivery driver or fulfillment center worker profoundly alienated from their labor inspire cries for workplace reform? Or would it draw admiration for their sacrifices and commitment to our on-time deliveries, making them "Amazon Heroes" as they're called in one of the ads produced during the pandemic? Does the suffering of workers only instantiate the importance of the consumer's needs and desires? More difficult than making the labor of distribution visible is denaturalizing the notion that speeding up the circuit of capital at almost any cost is a good in itself. While concern about the safety of fulfillment center workers rose to public consciousness during the COVID-19 pandemic, especially as deaths mounted, the notion that these fulfillment centers might close for extended periods or drastically limit their activities was never seriously considered, despite the fact that only a small fraction of what Amazon delivers is truly "essential."

After encountering the space and the scale of resources and effort devoted just to getting products from Truck A to Truck B on these fulfillment center tours, let alone to our actual doorsteps, the competitive business advantage that Amazon clearly thinks accrues from its "Prime promise" of one- or two-day delivery times becomes very real. To use Sarah Sharma's terms, the value of the customer's time and the expected itinerary of their products has led to reorchestration of breathtaking scope and scale. Amazon workers are encouraged to keep the end customer and their happiness first and foremost in their mind; customer testimonials about good service appear at regular intervals along the walls of the warehouse where employees walk. As tour visitors we were frequently reminded that these human and technological efforts are for us, for our convenience and "delight"—hence the naming of these facilities as "fulfillment centers" rather than just warehouses. It might seem ungrateful for tourgoers to question whether such superhuman, even unhuman, efforts are necessary. Considering what a small slice of the whole distribution process the tour shows, and the highly differentiated tasks it is comprised of, it's hard for the tourgoer to come even close to the visibility and transparency of the distribution process that Amazon itself would have. The tour is a gesture toward defetishizing distribution; at the same time, it normalizes the shift from retail to warehouse employment, from human labor to "semi-automated" work, and from work processes shaped by human perception and agency to those shaped by algorithm.

ENVIRONMENTAL IMPACTS OF ECOMMERCE AND AMAZON'S PR OFFENSIVES

An aspect of distribution even harder to fathom than its labor requirements is its environmental impacts. There is an opaqueness to the environmental impacts of our consumption more broadly, especially energy-related impacts that don't have the everyday concreteness of plastic containers and cardboard boxes. Given the carbon impacts of short delivery windows, in addition to those of the cloud computing necessary to maintain Amazon's retail site and the computing systems that support its fulfillment and delivery operations, the extent of Amazon's environmental impact is a highly salient question to ask of the world's leading ecommerce company.

Concern about the carbon impact of shopping online is widespread, but somewhat diffuse and unfocused. While guilt and self-consciousness about the tangible and rather public waste involved in shipping boxes is intuitive, the distribution-based emissions are not.[81] However, considering the level of carbon emissions from transportation surpassed that of power plants in 2016, making it the single largest type of emission, and urban freight vehicles release disproportionately more emissions than other kinds, consumer decision-making that impacts the transportation of goods is relevant to the question of Amazon's environmental impact.[82]

In popular commentary there is a sense that, because it's so convenient and involves significant packaging, carbon impacts of shopping online must be worse than shopping at a store. However, it's actually not so straightforward to determine whether online shopping is harder on the environment because so much depends on individual consumer decisions, shipping speeds, and the efforts of ecommerce companies to reduce their carbon outputs. The scholarship in this area suggests that, in fact, home delivery of goods overall should have a smaller environmental impact because a truck dropping off items in a neighborhood covers fewer miles than individual drivers going back and forth to a shop.[83] If a truck happens to be hybrid or electric, the savings are even greater.[84] Another study shows that even taking into account the carbon impacts of the additional packaging and computing required to send items to customers' doorsteps, the carbon impacts are still greater for brick-and-mortar retail, primarily due to customers' own transportation emissions.[85]

But once we factor in faster shipping speeds that require less efficient travel routes or for products to travel by air, the carbon estimates swing decidedly back in traditional retail's favor. As Amazon offers more products available for fast delivery—announcing one-day delivery for more than 10 million products for US Prime members in 2019—so does the company increasingly emphasize shipping by air. On the heels of the Prime Free One-Day Delivery announcement, Amazon also announced that it was increasing its leased aircraft fleet from five to fifteen planes.[86]

Online shopping is *potentially* greener than shopping at stores, but as transportation scholar Miguel Jaller argues, it depends on how consumers shop: "Online shopping would be greener than driving to local stores if we did three simple things: 1) Planned ahead and consolidated our orders so we get everything we need in fewer shipments; 2) Avoided expedited shipping (even if it's free); 3) Bought less stuff."[87] Except for the third item, if consumers did those things, online retailers like Amazon would enjoy a higher profit margin.

Amazon's seeming lack of interest in making transparent the environmental consequences of our investment in time to delivery points to the broader costs of distribution fetishism and the unwillingness of Amazon and most of its peers to meaningfully counter it. There are in fact good business reasons to encourage consumers to opt for slower shipping speeds, since it is expensive for Amazon to deliver on its fast shipping promises on Prime-eligible products. The average purchase qualifying for one-day shipping is thought to be $8.32 but Amazon's cost to ship in one day is $10.59.[88] Amazon expected to spend $1.5 billion in the fourth quarter of 2019 on its one-day shipping promise.[89] In fact, Amazon is clearly trying to incentivize Prime members to be less likely to default their orders to the fast shipping option.

In 2019, Amazon introduced the idea of having a "Prime delivery day" when all one's orders from the week would be consolidated into one delivery, in line with one of Jaller's suggestions and Amazon's Shipment Zero program, which aims to have 50 percent of package shipments carbon-neutral by 2030.[90] On some purchases Amazon offers "digital discounts" for opting for slower rather than faster shipping speeds (see figure 2.4).

Given the environmental concerns that some consumers have about ecommerce, it's a missed opportunity not to present shipping options in terms of their estimated carbon impacts. If consumers' consideration of the material impacts of fast delivery could reduce the overall demand for one-day shipping, which in turn would substantially help Amazon's bottom line, why not do it? Amazon could even target this information just to those consumers who express an interest in greening their consumption,

Select FREE Amazon Day Delivery below to have orders delivered together in fewer boxes on a single day.

Delivery date: Feb. 23, 2021 If you order in the next 10 hours and 36 minutes (Details)

Items shipped from Amazon.com

The Amazon Roadmap: How Innovative Brands are Reinventing the Path to Market
by Betsy McGinn
$17.99 ✓prime
& FREE Returns ⌄

Qty: 1 ⌄

Sold by: Amazon.com Services LLC

🎁 Add gift options

Choose your Prime delivery option:
◉ **Tuesday, Feb. 23**
  FREE Prime Delivery
○ **Friday, Feb. 26**
  FREE Amazon Day Delivery
  Get your orders in fewer boxes.
  Some orders may arrive a day early.
  Change delivery day
○ **Monday, Mar. 1**
  FREE No-Rush Shipping
  Get a $1 reward for select digital purchases. One reward per purchase.
  Details

2.4 Author screenshot, February 2021, demonstrating the different shipping options for a Prime member, including "FREE Amazon Day Delivery" and a small digital credit as an incentive for picking "No-Rush" shipping.

which would be consistent with the personalization the company specializes in. Even for a program like Amazon's Frustration-Free Packaging, which does have a considerable environmental benefit of reduced and more recyclable packaging, the program leads—in its naming and its marketing—with the convenience and ease of the consumer in opening their items. Similarly the option for Prime members to receive a credit to opt out of free one-day shipping leads with the benefit to the consumer, rather than responsiveness to or transparency about the distribution impacts of the purchase. The environmental benefits of opting for slower shipping are nowhere mentioned, even though they are almost certainly calculable or at least estimable by Amazon.

Amazon's most prominent environmental commitment to date is the Climate Pledge, announced in September 2019 in collaboration with Global

Optimism, an organization formed to administer the pledge and run by former United Nations Climate Chief Christiana Figueres. The Climate Pledge invites corporations to be carbon-neutral by 2040, ten years earlier than the Paris Climate Accord benchmark. This announcement was made as Amazon was coming under pressure from its own employees to do more in reducing its carbon impacts. Compared to even the other big tech companies, Amazon has dragged its feet in producing meaningful reductions in greenhouse emissions, failed to report relevant metrics to independent nonprofits like Greenpeace and CDP (Carbon Disclosure Project), and exhibited less transparency in its progress toward carbon neutrality. According to Greenpeace, which tracks the environmental record of the leading electronic device manufacturers, in 2017 Amazon was "one of the least transparent companies in the world in terms of its environmental performance, as it still refuses to report the greenhouse gas footprint of its own operations," earning an F on its "report card."[91]

Amazon does have green initiatives in addition to Frustration-Free Packaging. The company invests in renewable energy to power its operations, including solar panels on its fulfillment centers and a wind farm in Texas, and emphasizes the use of more renewables and the need for stronger environmental regulation from the government. While not hesitating to make claims for its commitment to sustainability, and investing in spectacular "green" initiatives such as the hydroponic rainforest housed by the downtown Seattle Spheres, Amazon has consistently fallen well behind its peers in green *accountability*. The Climate Pledge is a highly visible gesture of leadership in this area, but critics raise concerns about whether the emissions accounting protocols that this new organization has in place are strict enough, whether the decarbonization deadlines are too far away to make a meaningful difference, and the organization's lack of independence from a company that it is supposed to be auditing.[92] In other words, is the Climate Pledge just more PR, an attempt to circumnavigate the pressure to be responsive to more independent, rigorous carbon accounting organizations? Proliferating the organizations that monitor progress toward carbon neutrality can work in Amazon's favor, since it could sow uncertainty among the public about any given organization's "score card," and make direct comparisons among companies more difficult.

Through its very name Amazon links itself with the natural wonder of the Amazon river and rainforest, but soft-pedals the carbon impacts of consumers' shipping decisions when it could easily build them into its services. But why would Amazon want to meaningfully disrupt the distribution fetishism that is at the center of its number one leadership principle, "customer obsession"? If making consumption frictionless for its users is at the center of its philosophy and has helped it become the behemoth that it is, then inviting consumers to reflect, on a purchase-by-purchase basis, on the infrastructures, labor, and emissions that make products appear at their door is anathema to Amazon's winning formula.

Seeming to show information about Amazon's green initiatives, without providing visibility that is actually useful in making comparisons or consumer decision-making, keeps the status quo largely intact. Amazon's environmental efforts, while embracing the reality of climate change and the notion of corporate social responsibility, ultimately still leave the consumer, and the regulator, guessing and worrying, but not really knowing.

CONCLUSION—REMATERIALIZING DISTRIBUTION

Distribution infrastructures, data centers that house "the cloud," hardware, and labor all allow Amazon to be with us throughout our day—on our phones, on the web, through the TV, or on a smart speaker. Some people may experience a sensation of love and care as their pulse quickens when they see a brown box on their doorstep. That kind of affect is visualized in Danbo, the Amazon box robot, the delivery box come to life. The concept of distribution fetishism highlights our relationship to a distribution brand like Amazon, and the forces that draw attention and affect away from the labor, infrastructure, and materialities that make its rapid and personalized distribution possible. As David W. Hill suggests, ignorance of the infrastructures and particularly the labor that allows products to get to us so quickly is not just a cognitive injury but a moral one, disrupting the sense of responsibility for actions that would otherwise be triggered by contact with distribution processes.[93] I've raised one idea for how to disrupt distribution fetishism—quantifying the distribution-related carbon impacts of consumer orders—in order to imagine how infrastructures of distribution could be rematerialized for everyday users. This is not because I think individual decision-making is the key to environmental progress, or the primary way to discipline tech giants like Amazon, but because meaningful change is hard to imagine without some greater level of knowledge, interest, and participation from the public. Connecting consumers' interactions with online shopping, or their cloud usage, to the carbon impacts that are produced, could concretize the carbon emissions of the digital economy. Rather than just try to "responsibilize" the individual consumer for solving climate change, it could motivate them to demand new accountability regimes, perhaps new "standards," for the corporations that provide these services. I propose the concreteness of materializing the carbon impacts of shipping windows as an alternative to corporate-defined efforts at "transparency" that, in the case of carbon impacts, remain abstract to much of the public.

Similarly, fulfillment center tours may allow the public to see but not understand or appreciate the full extent of Amazon's distribution efforts and their impact on the lived experience and health of workers. Burnout and repetitive stress injuries can't be seen on a tour; they're felt, or result in the no-longer-employed Amazon worker. Demanding transparency is an important tool in countering distribution fetishism, but beyond transparency, efforts to rematerialize the digital economy—through attention to injury rates, employee turnover, and first-person accounts—may be necessary to truly connect consumers to the realities of the digital products and services they use.

Amazon's ability to brand convenience rests on an extensive distribution infrastructure that largely eludes the interest or perception of the average Amazon customer. The relationship we feel we have with the company is not, in fact, the relationship we actually have with the vast network of companies, workers, transportation and computing networks, buildings, and natural resources that are in play every time we "add to cart" or "buy now." Of course, this has long been true for consumers' relationships to the products they buy, hence the evergreen appeal of Marx's concept of commodity fetishism. But as the ability to buy almost anything in the shortest of time frames from click to ship comes to increasingly organize the economy and the fortunes of Amazon relative to the marketplace, it becomes all the more urgent for consumers to be connected not just to a brand, but also to the cumulative consequences of our seemingly frictionless shopping decisions.

II

CULTURE

3

FROM BOOKSELLER TO BEHEMOTH: THE PLATFORMIZATION OF RETAIL

Amazon.com began as an online book retailer not because founder and CEO Jeff Bezos had a passion to sell books, but because books were a logical first product in the earliest days of ecommerce. They were compact and easy to ship, and the huge variety of titles conformed to the as-yet-to-be coined logic of the "long tail," leading buyers online for things they couldn't find locally.[1] The first book sold on Amazon was *Fluid Concepts and Creative Analogies: Computer Models of the Fundamental Mechanisms of Thought*—an academic book of great interest to computer scientists, no doubt, but not exactly a bestseller.[2] Today bookselling is just one of Amazon's many business interests, but it remains a significant part of its revenue stream. According to industry estimates, as recently as 2018 books were still Amazon's largest product category, at 16 percent of items sold.[3] Amazon is the largest retailer in the United States of both physical books and ebooks by large margins, and sells the most successful e-reader by far, the Kindle (84 percent of the market).[4] Regardless of Amazon's growing array of products and services, books remain important to the company's brand identity and relationship with consumers.

This chapter traces how the company's book business has developed since it sold its first book in 1995.[5] I recount some of the significant chapters in Amazon's history of bookselling—how it competed with established booksellers, its early adoption of consumer reviews on the site, the launch of the Kindle and explosion of ebooks as a new category, and Amazon's surprising move into brick-and-mortar book retailing. I use Amazon's first retail product to understand what, if anything, is distinctive about Amazon as a company and as a platform business, and how the platformization of retail shapes the distribution of cultural products and our relationship as consumers to culture and each other.

Amazon is one of the leading global technology platforms whose consumer-facing products and services belie the importance of data commodities to its business. Amazon is more accurately a *multi*platform business whose synergies across business areas give it incentives and opportunities unavailable to its competitors (which are often simultaneously its customers) in a single business area, such as publishing. Amazon's Kindle business involves the Kindle device and associated software as one kind of platform, the Amazon retail site as a platform that connects buyers and sellers, and Amazon Web Services providing the cloud services for rapid digital delivery of ebooks. With not just one but multiple synergistic platform businesses, Amazon's activities in book production, promotion, and retailing serve its broader goal of platform enclosure—where both customers and sellers spend as much time and money as possible behind Amazon's "moat."

These platform logics cement the feeling that the company is in the book business for reasons other than supporting the creation and dissemination, via commerce, of culture. On the one hand, while Amazon is frequently criticized for its persistent commodification of books, it has precursors from the earliest days of the book business. On the other hand, Amazon's tremendous market power in bookselling today is unprecedented, and due largely to the company's structure as a platform business rather than being "merely" a retailer. Amazon could be Exhibit A for how the concentrated power of one distributor can transform not just book retailing, but also the business of publishing itself, influencing the very nature of books and reading. For example, with the development of the Kindle in 2007, Amazon is widely credited with ebooks becoming a substantial proportion of books sold in the United States, with Kindle sales alone estimated to be 26 percent of units sold in the US new adult book market in 2017.[6]

In this chapter I show how platformization has systematically advantaged Amazon in the book business, due to network effects, exuberant

investment in tech platforms, and unrivaled market intelligence leading to tremendous market power. At the same time, Amazon's platform
logics have also meant certain kinds of "democratization" in the book
business—circumvention by writers and readers of traditional industry
gatekeepers through self-publishing (or "indie" publishing), online ratings and reviews, the immediacy of ebook publication and purchase, and
the option of purchasing from "Earth's Biggest Bookstore" unlimited by
the selections of store buyers. Eliminating gatekeepers and connecting
buyers and sellers with a usable interface and efficient overhead that rapidly scales is at the heart of how platforms work. But platformization has
other cultural effects. Amazon's platform logics shape the experience of
buying books, both online and in its new brick-and-mortar stores, and
transform retail space from public, shared, even "democratic" space to
increasingly personalized, differentiated, even "discriminatory" space.

AMAZON AND BOOK RETAILING—THE NEWEST CHAPTER IN THE COMMODIFICATION OF CULTURE

It's no secret that Amazon is a feared, even hated, behemoth in book
retailing. Headlines such as "Amazon Must Be Stopped" (in the *New
Republic*), "Can Anyone Compete with Amazon?," and "Is Amazon Really
the Devil?" (in *Publishers' Weekly*) are not uncommon. Less than twenty
years after Amazon.com went online, "Amazon [was] the single biggest
book retailer in America: It [sold] 41% of all new books," according to
the Codex Group industry analysts; by 2019 Amazon's market share was
estimated to be more than 50 percent of print books, and three-quarters
of ebooks.[7] Large book chains and independent bookstores alike struggled mightily in this new environment, with chains in particular closing
stores including, notably, Borders, which was the second-largest book chain
in the United States until it went out of business in 2011. Independent
bookstores also took a major hit, but since 2009 have seen some recovery
with substantial growth in the number of stores nationwide.[8]

Beyond the expected heartbreak of a competitive business environment is the animus that Amazon attracts for treating books, in particular, as merely the means to profitable ends. In the criticism of Amazon's
business practices in bookselling, we see reflected a longstanding cultural

anxiety about the relationship between culture and commerce. While books are understood to be subject to market forces, we resist the idea that they are ultimately reducible to them. Janice A. Radway notes the widely held belief, especially among cultural elites, that books "should never have been commodified by the market in the first place."[9] Australian author Tim Winton captured this perspective when he said, regarding Amazon's arrival in Australia, "People who work in the book industry are agents of culture rather than just instruments of commerce. . . . When you take away their role as agents of culture and reduce them to instruments of capitalism, it changes the dynamic."[10] Communication scholar Ted Striphas notes that if the idea that books have "loftier goals" and contribute more to morality and our collective intellect than other mass-produced items is a myth, it is nevertheless a deeply entrenched one.[11] In retail spaces these tensions come to a head, because in stores, whether in person or online, culture is reduced to prices, or commodified.

Given the association of books with culture, education, self-improvement, community, and ideas of progress rooted in Enlightenment thinking, the tension that book retailers face in attempting to profit from selling them predates Amazon's arrival on the scene. Elizabeth Long writes that "if cultural degradation has not followed from increased commercialism, it is nonetheless true that various segments of the literary community have been convinced that it would, ever since the literary marketplace emerged during the eighteenth century."[12] In her history of the American book industry in the twentieth century, Laura J. Miller shows that innovations in book retailing—such as selling books in stores other than those dedicated to books (such as supermarkets or department stores), the rise of mass-market paperbacks, and having bookstore chains in malls—have all been met with criticism because of how they juxtapose the sacred aura of the book with commercial imperatives.[13] When the large chain "superstores" for books emerged in the 1990s, Miller writes "independent booksellers accused the chains of harboring monopolistic designs, and of engaging in unfair competition," and further, were concerned "that they were guided more by profit-and-loss statements than by literary consideration."[14] Radway found a similar dynamic with the Book-of-the-Month Club, a twentieth-century mail-order subscription service. It is the independent bookseller who has claimed the moral high ground, pointing to their carefully curated collection of books, personalized service, and a place for community and connection around products that promise knowledge, culture, and self-improvement.[15]

Recent conflicts between book retailers and Amazon have played out in quite similar ways as previous conflicts in the twentieth century, when new retailing formats also made books cheaper and more accessible to consumers. Certainly, Amazon founder Jeff Bezos's own instrumental relationship to books as the product that Amazon would first sell is no secret. His starting point was the insight that the internet was becoming a significant gathering place, and where people were gathering, they could be sold to. He apparently considered twenty different product categories, with the intention all along to master one product category before branching into others. He subjected the product list to the following criteria: the product must be familiar, have a large market size, have surmountable competition, a way of accessing a large inventory as well as an online database of products, the ability to out-compete brick-and-mortar stores with discounts, and reasonable shipping costs.[16] Books were the winning product, even over CDs; at the time, Americans spent more per year on books than music, and the ISBN identification system lent itself to the database management that Bezos sought. Less than three years after launching the online bookstore, Amazon.com started selling CDs, followed a few months later by DVDs and videos, and Bezos announced to the world what his vision had been all along: "Our strategy is to become an electronic commercial destination. When somebody thinks about buying something online, even if it is something we do not carry, we want them to come to us."[17]

Bezos's approach has offended booksellers by using books as "bait" to build a mammoth ecommerce website. Amazon has also been roundly criticized for its predatory pricing of books. There's some irony in chains like Borders and Barnes & Noble suffering at the hands of Amazon's discounting practices, since when they emerged in the 1990s and routinely offered bestsellers at a 30 percent discount, it was independent booksellers crying foul against them.[18] Amazon's tolerance for eating into its profits, or even losing money, in order to gain competitive advantage has been apparent in its use of loss leaders, which are heavily advertised and discounted products that bring customers into stores where they are likely to (a) purchase that product at volume and (b) purchase regularly priced items while they are there. While the major chains, and department stores before them, have used bestsellers as loss leaders for decades, Amazon has arguably outplayed them in that game. For example, in 2003 Amazon sold 1.4 million copies of the highly anticipated *Harry Potter and the Order of the Phoenix* at a 40 percent discount with free shipping, from which they earned essentially no profit margin.[19] The following year, Amazon offered a 30 percent discount on *all* books priced over $15, a much more extensive use of discounting than the chain stores had ever offered.[20] In 2020, trade groups representing publishers, authors, and booksellers wrote to the US House Anti-Trust Committee: "For over two decades, Amazon has used books as loss leaders in the book industry to lure consumers to its website, gather data, make profits on bigger ticket items, and capture an increasing market share."[21]

What the chains never saw coming was Amazon's ability, and willingness, to delay profits in order to build its customer base and damage the competition. Although a publicly held company since 1997, the ever-expanding, almost limitless vision for the company's future that CEO Jeff Bezos was able to persuade investors of made them more patient and willing to provide capital for his ventures, with the understanding that profits would eventually be forthcoming. The same does not apply to companies like Borders and Barnes & Noble whose scope for expanding into new businesses is understood to be limited. The ability of companies that identify as "tech" rather than "media" to lose money for extended periods while still attracting investment capital is a broader feature of the digital economy that puts different kinds of companies, even if they provide similar services, on an uneven playing field.[22]

Amazon has also put new pressure on the book market by featuring used books prominently on the site. Amazon started selling used books in 2000, and the option to buy used at considerably lower prices, sometimes just a few dollars even for books in good condition, appears right next to the new book.[23] Both authors and publishers have been ambivalent and, at times, vocally resistant to this practice; people buying used diverts sales from new books that produce royalties. Thanks to the first sale doctrine in the United States, Amazon makes money on the initial sale of a new book, and again when it gets resold used, even though the publisher and author receive nothing on subsequent sales. Easily available used copies may drive down the price of the new book and create the appearance of a book that no one wants.[24] And of course, as one author has admitted, there are "emotional wounds" in seeing, in this case, an award-winning book being sold used on Amazon for a mere twenty-five cents, plus shipping: "Part of it is sheer vanity, that you think your book would be worth more than that under any circumstances."[25]

Like his predecessors among commercial book retailers, Amazon founder Jeff Bezos has made his own moral arguments in favor of more highly rationalized book retailing. By appealing to the principle of consumer sovereignty and the demands of the rational consumer, who is understood to always seek out the best products at the lowest prices, Amazon argues for the commercial *and* social good that it produces in the book market. By promoting low prices, as well as the ability to instantly compare Amazon's prices and selection with third-party new and used booksellers, Amazon provides the greatest choice for the consumer, the company argues. Bezos has also argued that the ability to buy used books at reasonable prices encourages consumers to try out new genres and authors, which can expand markets for authors and publishers.[26]

Amazon has held the sovereignty of the consumer's interests and preferences on a pedestal. In contrast, as Keith Gessen wrote in *Vanity Fair*, in the 1990s when the chains dominated the market, a single book buyer (specifically Barnes & Noble's literary fiction buyer), "could make (or break) a book with a large order (or a disappointingly small one)."[27] Although it would be naive to downplay Amazon's role in shaping which books get promoted and sold, it's also the case that shelf capacity is no longer limited, and Amazon is more invested in consumer response than subjective judgments of what is "good" or beneficial in a social or cultural sense (the company's tolerance for selling controversial and offensive material testifies to that). George Packer summed up this state of affairs in his critical take in the *New Yorker*, writing "Amazon is good for customers. But is it good for books?"[28]

Packer's question points to concerns raised by so many about the commodification of books. While they are a consumer product that must conform to market pressures, it's also the case that publishers and retailers, "reluctant capitalists" as Laura J. Miller describes them, have long promoted nonmarket values in their work—cultivating new authors, promoting local-ism and books for niche audiences, and making space for "serious" literature that makes a cultural, political, or social contribution. The "marketplace of ideas" has been matched by a more or less competitive marketplace of publishers and distributors. While Amazon's model bows to consumer sovereignty like never before, with unmatched choice and low prices facilitated by its data-driven, growth-hungry business model, the question remains what space there is for the nonmarket values that have always been a part of the book business, and how bookstores and books themselves are being changed by the dominance of this behemoth.

ALL HAIL THE SOVEREIGN CONSUMER AND THEIR REVIEWS

James Marcus, lead editor for Literature & Fiction by the time he left Amazon in 2001, describes tensions between culture and commerce that were perhaps more pronounced at the company in the early years than they subsequently became. In its first few years Amazon employed a substantial staff who wrote book reviews and descriptions, interviewed authors, produced newsletters about new books, and made informed decisions about what books to feature on the home page and on the various "category" or genre pages. Having worked previously as a freelancer writing reviews and criticism for independent publications, Marcus "couldn't avoid the suspicion that [his] opinions were succumbing to the gravitational tug of the marketplace."[29] These tensions played themselves out in a variety of increasingly fraught ways. On the one hand, in its early years Amazon prided itself on appearing "smart" and becoming a source for book market intelligence and consumer advice to rival established publications. At the same time, the work of its editors was constantly subjected to evaluation on the basis of granular metrics, as well as increasingly subject to automation (e.g., the composition of the homepage, the selections in newsletters) and pay-for-play arrangements.[30]

Indeed, when the *New York Times* broke the news about Amazon's co-op program in 1999—"money paid by publishers to booksellers to boost the visibility of specific titles," not just in placement but through inclusion in editorial reviews and recommendations—the company understood it to be such a devastating hit to its reputation that it ended the program, issuing a public *mea culpa* in which it apologized for violating its customers' trust.[31] Earning customer trust in the 1990s when ecommerce was still new was paramount, so Amazon temporarily ended the lucrative co-op programs even though all their offline competitors were certainly using them. It was, and is, a standard industry practice.

Perhaps the key way that Amazon sought to earn consumer trust, as well as overcome the disadvantage of selling books online where consumers couldn't leaf through them, was inviting consumers to review the books they had purchased. Starting in 1995, the year the store launched, the consumer review and ratings feature on Amazon took full advantage of the interactive possibilities of digital communication technology four years before the term Web 2.0 was first coined, and well before 2004 when internet commentator Tim O'Reilly popularized it.[32] It's hard to imagine today, when some of the most popular apps and websites, like Yelp, TripAdvisor, and Rotten Tomatoes, are organized around consumer reviews, and most ecommerce sites feature consumer feedback, but initial responses to the decision were not positive: "Many people thought the Internet retailer had lost its marbles. Letting consumers rant about products in public was a recipe for retail suicide, critics thought."[33] By allowing consumers to review books on the site, Amazon put into place a feature that would come to define the logics of ecommerce and, beyond that, the reputation economy.

Incorporating consumer reviews, both positive and negative, was an early company decision that reflected, and loudly advertised, its commitment to "customer obsession." As scholar of book publishing Ann Steiner sees it:

The reviews on Amazon have one purpose for the company—to sell more books. Amazon provides the option to write reviews because it is a cheap and efficient way to provide information on its products. It is convenient to let one's customers do the editorial work rather than having one's staff do it. The reviews also allow Amazon to appear to be a customer-oriented, non-commercial site. The writing done by customers does not look like marketing; instead, it is the real thing—authentic readers commenting on books they have actually read.[34]

It's a classic platform move—circumvent the gatekeepers (in this case, editors, buyers, and professional critics), and create value through people's voluntary participation in the online spaces you create.

The inclusion of reviews for products and third-party sellers (and not, we might note, of Amazon itself) reflects the platformization of retail that came to characterize Amazon's evolution over the coming years. By platformization, I mean that Amazon was not only a retailer that happened to take orders online, but also a company that provided a software interface on which others could contribute and create value through participation and exchange. Unlike a traditional retailer that typically stands behind the products it stocks and makes active efforts to convince consumers to purchase them, Amazon started to take an attitude more typical of a platform, which takes less responsibility for what appears or is transacted on their site, while still (ideally) making an effort to provide the user with tools to facilitate a good experience. In Amazon's case, those tools include consumer review mechanisms for both products and third-party sellers.

Every product on Amazon has a series of five stars lit up in gold to the average rating it has received, and next to that, the total number of ratings it has received (see figure 3.1).

Apple AirPods with Charging Case (Latest M...	Fire TV Stick 4K streaming device with Alexa built in...	Fire TV Stick streaming media player with Alexa...
Apple	Amazon	Amazon
$139⁹⁹ ~~$159.00~~	$24⁹⁹ ~~$49.99~~	$19⁹⁹ ~~$39.99~~
⭐⭐⭐⭐⭐ (5,792)	⭐⭐⭐⭐⭐ (60,789)	⭐⭐⭐⭐⭐ (50,498)
✓prime	✓prime	✓prime

3.1 Author screenshot from Amazon.com (November 28, 2019) shows "trending" electronics with their prices and customer ratings.

These average ratings are a powerful information commodity that brings consumers to the site for product research. Shoppers can sort their search results according to average customer reviews as well as the items with the most reviews. According to *Bloomberg* reporter Spencer Ante, "By amassing one of the world's largest collections of consumer opinions, the site has become a leading source of product reviews. And those reviews are a valuable magnet that lures more consumers to its Web site."[35] The sheer volume of consumer ratings (if genuine, more than sixty thousand people rated the Fire TV stick) and the visibility of highly rated products on Amazon's platform are a built-in marketing message about Amazon's dominance and trustworthiness in ecommerce.

Opening first in New York City in 2018, Amazon 4-Star is one of the company's new brick-and-mortar store concepts that demonstrate how important consumer ratings and reviews are to Amazon's brand identity. As the name suggests, these stores feature products that have received ratings of at least four stars, and many products display a favorable customer review. The digital price tags show the exact rating out of five, as well as how many reviews the rating is based upon, just as products do on the online site.

The multiple forms of value generated by consumer ratings and reviews, illustrated vividly by the Amazon 4-Star store concept, exemplify how platform companies like Amazon monetize users' "free labor."[36] As communication scholar Lisa Nakamura points out, people have talked about and made word-of-mouth recommendations about books probably as long as books have existed, but today a site like Goodreads, a book review and social networking site that Amazon acquired in 2013, turns "the reader into a worker, a content producer" who creates value for Goodreads and the "partners" to which it sells user data.[37]

The question remains whether Amazon is committed to delivering satisfaction via highly reviewed products that meet consumers' needs and expectations, or whether the *appearance* of this commitment is sufficient, even when the reviews are unreliable due to the myriad ways they can be "gamed" by unscrupulous sellers. Whether it's merchants themselves submitting their own reviews, compensating consumers to write glowing reviews for shoddy products, merging reviews for different products, or sabotaging competitors' standing with Amazon with negative or suspicious-looking reviews, the existence of manipulated reviews is regularly documented by investigators or brought to the platform's attention by unhappy customers as well as frustrated sellers who seek a more even playing field.[38] It speaks to the value of the summary product rating and the attention that consumers give to reviews—especially for goods such as electronics and health products—that they have become such a focus for fraudulent activity. While there are companies that help sellers game the Amazon reviews system, there are also companies making browser extensions, such as ReviewMeta, that specialize in helping consumers detect fake reviews when they're shopping online. Amazon has programs designed to detect fraudulent reviews, and with some regularity removes sellers and shoppers from its site who have violated its rules, but frustrated sellers complain that the efforts are not sufficient to meaningfully control the problem.

Amazon has been a book retailing site longer than it's been anything else, and for just as long, it's also been a platform for information and discussion about books. Advocates of platform capitalism point to the disintermediation of traditional gatekeepers, and the collective creation of value that platforms allow, and Amazon has indeed introduced these elements into book retailing. In this sense, Amazon very much orients itself to consumers, rather than to books or authors. Rather than positioning *itself* as the authority on books, over time Amazon has increasingly deferred to consumers themselves, consistent with its identity as a brand focused on service to consumers to the point of "obsession."

THE PLATFORMIZATION OF BOOK RETAILING

Consumer reviews aren't just a valuable information commodity for shoppers. When consumers rate products and write reviews they're also telling Amazon about their preferences and level of engagement with products, a data commodity the company can use to target communications and promotions and predict future behavior. This is just one example of how Amazon's identity as a tech company, and beyond that a platform company whose access to data about consumers and competitors, efficiencies across multiple business activities, and ability to raise money to support almost unlimited growth all give it structural and market advantages not available to other actors in the book business.

Being a tech company has helped Amazon build out rapidly from just selling books into other parts of the supply chain, including book printing, publishing, digital distribution, and hardware. Since 2009, under the umbrella of Amazon Publishing it has launched more than a dozen imprints, including CreateSpace for self-publishing authors, which merged with KDP, or Kindle Direct Publishing, in 2018. According to industry estimates, Amazon releases several times as many self-published titles as the next largest publisher.[39] These imprints can publish books in both electronic and paper formats, taking advantage of Amazon's on-demand publishing arm, which can print and ship a book almost as quickly as a book already in stock, exemplary of the "just-in-time" production paradigm.

A major retailer becoming a publisher is not completely unprecedented—Barnes & Noble acquired and developed its own imprints in the 2000s.[40] What is unprecedented is the platformization of the book business. When we look at the consequences of Amazon's market power, we need to take into account the advantages it has as an increasingly vertically and horizontally integrated platform company.

Being a platform leads to awkward situations, such as Amazon making money from the very publishers it competes against, by taking a cut from each sale as well as their digital ad spends. Bookstores have always been important spaces for not just selling books but also marketing them to consumers. Amazon's online bookstore is no exception. Since a brief pause from co-op advertising after unfavorable publicity in 1999, Amazon has returned to "co-op" fee arrangements, although not necessarily through recommendations from actual editors. By 2004 independent publishers were crying foul because these fees, to the tune of 2 to 5 percent of what publishers were earning through their sales on Amazon, would be essentially required, otherwise Amazon would make their books very hard to find on the site and use other tactics to drive consumers away from their books, a form of "blackmail" according to Dennis Johnson of Melville House publishers.[41] The shift around this time came to be known as the infamous "Gazelle Project," wherein Amazon, realizing that it controlled a significant proportion of publishers' book sales, particularly of their backlists, decided to seek more favorable terms. Jeff Bezos reportedly told the team to approach the problem as cheetahs pursuing injured and weak gazelles—starting with small publishers and moving up the chain in order to make negotiations easier with the big ones.[42] Publishers continue to be frustrated by the costs of selling their books on Amazon, complaining in a letter to the US Federal Trade Commission in 2019 about how platforms tie their "distribution services to the purchase of advertising services."[43] Beyond that, publishers now have to compete against Amazon's own books, and it is widely thought that the company uses its search and recommendation algorithms, as well as placement of its own titles in promotional programs such as monthly "First Reads" picks for Prime members, to advantage its own imprints over books from other publishers.[44]

Amazon's investment in ebooks exemplifies how the company uses the various components of its business—personal electronics, digital distribution platforms, and physical distribution of books in record times—to exert market dominance. In the early 2000s electronic books were available on Amazon for download onto consumer desktops in Adobe and Microsoft formats, but with a small selection, high prices, and an unappealing interface, ebooks were seen by most as having no future. Although there were already some e-readers on the market that were not selling especially well, Jeff Bezos tasked his developers to create Amazon's own e-reader. The risks were evident; this was Amazon's first foray into hardware, and if successful, the venture could cannibalize Amazon's own sales of physical books. Amazon released the Kindle in 2007. In advance of the launch, Bezos directed his team to provide the specs to publishers to create 100,000 digital versions of books properly formatted for the Kindle. The company pressured reluctant publishers by threatening to downgrade their physical books in search results and recommendations on the online retail platform if they didn't cooperate—another example of Amazon throwing its weight around in order to secure favorable terms. Unlike the publishers and most industry observers, Bezos was convinced that ebooks were the future of reading, and had the investment capital and highly diversified business to take a big gamble.[45]

The Kindle was the first commercially successful e-reader—successful due to its wireless connectivity making downloads easy, a lighted screen that is easy on the eyes and well suited to reading print, and an immedi-ately large selection of ebooks.[46] Within four years, Amazon was selling more Kindle books than hardcover and paperback books combined.[47] In providing the technology, both hardware and software, through which books could be distributed digitally, and making the deals to get a lot of content, Amazon played a major role in changing the very nature of the book. With its purchase of Audible in 2008, Amazon also solidified its position as the source for audiobooks, the fastest-growing sector in digital publishing.[48] What it even means to buy or own a book has, since 2014, been put into question by the Kindle Unlimited subscription service, where for $9.99 per month consumers can access unlimited ebooks and audiobooks. Here authors and publishers are paid not by the unit of the book, but by the amount of it that people consume via the service.[49]

As David B. Nieborg and Thomas Poell argue, when platforms cap-ture detailed data about how people consume media content in real time, it introduces a "contingency" to cultural products "that is increasingly modular in design and continuously reworked and repackaged, informed by datafied user feedback."[50] This has borne out with ebooks. Authors can edit their self-published ebooks on the Kindle Direct Publishing platform even after initial publication,[51] and self-published books that attract the attention of Amazon Publishers are sometimes revised and retitled for more professional publication.[52] Another layer of the "contingency" of ebooks on the Kindle platform is the ability to see the most popular pas-sages of books as measured by readers' highlights, introducing an interac-tive element not normally encountered in books, as well as a source of granular reader feedback to authors that may inform their future writ-ing.[53] Amazon reportedly uses the speed at which people read Kindle titles to identify hot authors for their publishing imprints or for contracts for new books.[54] Finally, the fact of ownership itself has been reshaped by the ebook model, with consumer "purchase" typically involving a com-plex licensing agreement rather than true ownership. Amazon customers learned this when, in a moment of stunning irony, their copies of George Orwell's *1984* were deleted from their Kindles, upon Amazon's discovery that a counterfeit edition had been sold on their site.[55]

Amazon Charts, launched in 2017, is emblematic of the platformiza-tion of book retailing in several respects. The fact that Amazon releases its own charts, aiming to rival the *New York Times* bestseller list, speaks to its aspiration for not only numeric but also symbolic market dominance.[56] The impetus behind the charts may be in part because the *New York Times* list excludes titles from Amazon Publishing imprints, because the titles are sold by only one store.[57] But Amazon Charts is still an example of Amazon grading its own homework, since the company constructs the charts on which its own imprints compete. The charts' distinction between "Most Sold" and "Most Read" (seen in figure 3.2) also reconceptualizes books from objects to be sold to content to be consumed. Although J. K. Rowling doesn't appear in the Amazon Charts' Top Twenty of fiction books sold in February 2021, for example, five of her Harry Potter books appear in the top ten of Amazon Chart's Most Read list for that time period. When Amazon

‹ WEEK OF FEBRUARY 14, 2021

Amazon Charts

The Top 20 Most Sold & Most Read Books of the Week ❓

MOST R   OLD

ABOUT OUR LISTS

Amazon's *Most Sold* charts rank books according to the number of copies sold and pre-ordered through Amazon.com, Audible.com, Amazon Books stores, and books read through digital subscription programs (once a customer has read a certain percentage – roughly the length of a free reading sample). Bulk buys are counted as a single purchase.

Amazon's *Most Read* charts rank titles by the average number of daily Kindle readers and Audible listeners each week. Categories not ranked on Most Read charts include dictionaries, encyclopedias, religious texts, daily devotionals, and calendars.

1
④

KRISTIN HANNAH — THE FOUR WINDS

RHYTHM OF WAR

HARRY POTTER

2 WEEKS ON THE LIST   13 WEEKS ON THE LIST   197 WEEKS ON THE LIST

The Four Winds   **Rhythm of War**   **Harry Potter and the Order of the Phoenix**
BY KRISTIN HANNAH   BY BRANDON SANDERSON   BY J.K. ROWLING

PUBLISHER: ST. MARTIN'S PRESS   PUBLISHER: TOR BOOKS   PUBLISHER: POTTERMORE PUBLISHING
AGENT: NEIL BLAIR

kindle unlimited

HIGHLY QUOTABLE   ★★★★★ 4.8 / 6,564 REVIEWS   ALL EARS   ★★★★★ 4.8 / 15,507 REVIEWS   CUSTOMER REVIEWS   ★★★★★ 4.9 / 22,921 REVIEWS

3.2 Author screenshot of Amazon Charts with explanation of Most Sold versus Most Read charts, available for both fiction and nonfiction. *Source:* Amazon Charts, https://www.amazon.com/charts.

pitches its charts as "A reimagined bestseller list that shares how we read today," it points to the books-as-a-service model of distribution, where Amazon as an interactive distribution platform can track user engagement in detail.[58] Through these charts the company shares some of this information commodity with the public, but the more detailed engagement data available to Amazon allow it to predict consumer behavior and plan new business ventures according to "deep consumer insights," as they say in the market research business.

Amazon's capture of the ebook market due to the Kindle, and its strategy for achieving market dominance through aggressive pricing all came together in the Hachette controversy of 2014. In brief, the major publishers, including Hachette (which owns imprints such as Little, Brown, and Company and Basic Books), were concerned about Amazon's insistence on pricing ebooks at $9.99 or less. In 2010 these publishers came to an agreement with Apple, which also sold ebooks via its iBooks store, to use agency pricing, which meant that publishers would set their own prices that would be the same wherever their books were sold, and Apple would be technically the "sales agent" and not the "retailer," and not have to worry about competing with Amazon on price.[59] The result was higher prices on ebooks in both the Apple and Amazon online stores. The case went to court, and in 2013 the Department of Justice prevailed in identifying this practice as collusion to fix prices, requiring publishers to renegotiate ebook prices with both Apple and Amazon, and Apple to provide $400 million in Amazon credits to consumers who bought ebooks on Amazon between 2010 and 2012.[60] The court decision allowed publishers to seek an "agency-lite" deal, whereby publishers would have some power to set prices, but retailers would retain the right to some discounting. Hachette was the first publishing group to negotiate the new arrangement with Amazon, but when they attempted to play hardball on ebook pricing, Amazon retaliated by substantially slowing down delivery of Hachette books (on the order of weeks, instead of days), raising prices on their book promotion services, removing some titles from the site, and removing pre-order buy buttons on soon-to-be-published books, which are a key tool for ensuring the success of new books.[61] The controversy hit the headlines, with authors such as Stephen Colbert, Sherman Alexie, Philip Roth, and Ursula K. LeGuin raising the alarm bells about the power of Amazon to discipline publishers and enforce the business conditions it desired, in this case to the detriment of authors.[62]

The ebook controversy blew over, for a while. Ebook prices rose with the new court-ordered pricing negotiations, shrinking the price gap between physical and ebook.[63] Looking at the first several rows of results on Amazon for "Best sellers list New York Times 2020" for example, the Kindle versions are by and large very close in price to the paperback versions, and in a number of instances, actually cost more. Given the lack of production costs for ebook copies after initial digital formatting, publishers are finding this an increasingly profitable part of their business.[64] However, scrutiny of ebook pricing is not over, this time with Amazon in the hot seat instead of Apple. The state of Connecticut has brought an antitrust case against Amazon, alleging that since 2015 the company has been fixing high prices with the five largest publishers on the condition that those prices may not appear lower elsewhere.[65]

The Hachette controversy clarified publishers' vulnerability in the face of Amazon's market dominance. Whereas traditional retailers could ill-afford to not carry books that people want because of the importance of bestsellers to their bottom lines, Amazon is large enough, and diversified enough across product mix and business areas, to swallow any such losses. Given the influence, even control, Amazon has over a book's sales, between pre-orders on Amazon as publicity for a book, the visibility of books and book sales on Amazon for raising awareness about a title, the ability to buy the physical book on Amazon for quick home delivery, and the market dominance of the company's Kindle platform, Amazon leaves companies with few meaningful alternatives to get their books known and then purchased by the public. As Amazon ventures into publishing, the specter of a vertically integrated behemoth that cherry-picks the best-selling authors, accurately anticipates audience trends, and consistently tips the scales in favor of its own titles is an alarming proposition. Amazon's march into every corner of the book business continues with its foray into brick-and-mortar stores.

AMAZON BOOKS AND THE PERSONALIZATION OF RETAIL SPACE

After establishing itself as the primary force behind bookstore closures across the United States, in 2015 Amazon did something few had seen coming—it opened an actual bookstore. The locations of Amazon Books suggest an upscale alternative to Barnes & Noble, with stores appearing in prime retail real estate such as Westfield Century City in Los Angeles, University Village in Seattle, on Columbus Circle and across the street from the Empire State Building in New York City, and at Legacy Place in Dedham, MA, where it resides near L.L. Bean, Sephora, Eddie Bauer, Lululemon, and a massive Whole Foods Market. Amazon Books has many of the features of a chain bookstore, such as a variety of nonbook items for sale, a café, and spaces for customers to read and hang out, with a footprint closer to the size of an independent.

While creating a chain of brick-and-mortar bookstores might seem a retro move for the ecommerce giant, the company's own description of the initiative explains, "Amazon Books integrates the benefits of offline and online shopping to help customers discover books and devices."[66] The sections of the store reflect this integration. There are the conventional genre categories: cooking, children's books, fiction, poetry, science and nature, and self-improvement. And then there are the displays that announce Amazon's deference to consumers and the ability of big data to understand their preferences: "Books with more than 10,000 Reviews on Amazon.com," "Most wished-for books on Amazon.com," "Highly rated children's books," and "4.8 stars and above." In addition, some displays reference not the digital world of consumer responses, but the local context, such as "Fiction Favorites in Boston" or "Read Around New York." Attention to local interests, a space for community, and thoughtfully curated selections are thought to be reasons for the resurgence of independent booksellers over the last decade, and the Amazon Books store design emulates these features.[67]

While Amazon's approach to brick-and-mortar stores could be seen as uncharted, it actually aligns with broader trends in retail, specifically, the way digital communication technologies are driving the repersonalization of retail.[68] Historians have argued that a key development defining modern consumer culture was the depersonalization of consumption, such that buyers and sellers need not know each other in order to engage in market exchange.[69] The greater anonymity of retail spaces like chain stores and department stores relative to local shops could be experienced as alienating, but equally, scholars have argued, they could be democratizing, appearing to liberate consumers from conventional hierarchies and social exclusions.[70] Starting in the nineteenth century, rather than having to ask employees about prices or negotiate with sellers, prices in shops were clearly displayed to shoppers; no one need endure the embarrassment of putting an item down after learning the price from a sales associate.[71]

Chain bookstores were criticized precisely for depersonalizing book retailing by emphasizing self-service and, with the rise of the big-box retailers, making the store feel anonymous through its sheer size.[72] At the same time, these chains arguably made book buying more accessible to the general public, and drove greater book sales. Online retailers, in contrast, have consistently repersonalized shopping, in the sense of tailoring the shopping experience to the individual by customizing the store homepage and targeting product recommendations and special offers. Amazon pioneered the bookstore version of a broader trend toward personalization afforded by digital technology, coined as the "Daily Me" by Nicholas Negroponte in relation to the personalization of newsfeeds, and the "Daily You" by Joseph Turow referring to the way advertisers and purveyors of culture of all kinds customize their content to the individual.[73]

On the one hand, an actual store like Amazon Books is in some respects depersonalized, compared to Amazon.com, because it exposes customers to book categories and recommendations that are not tailored to them specifically in response to their past purchases or searches. On the other hand, Amazon Books is "repersonalized" relative to most retail experiences because prices are not displayed or marked on products (although most books do have the "list price" on the back cover, in tiny print), but are available to consumers only when they scan them on their devices. In Amazon Books, rather than seeing a price listed below the book or on a sticker, most titles have a sentence or two from a positive Amazon consumer review, as well as the number of reviews and the number of stars from one to five that the book has received on Amazon.com (see figure 3.3a). Shoppers must scan items with their smartphone to discover the prices, paving the way for more dynamic pricing as well as differential pricing for Amazon Prime members versus non-members. When I visited Amazon Books at Legacy Place, there were numerous signs in the store indicating how to look up prices, and shoppers were helping each other figure out the system (see figure 3.3b).

Amazon has been at the forefront of personalizing shopping online, and now its approach to brick-and-mortar selling puts it squarely at the

3.3 A sign in Amazon Books in Dedham, Massachusetts, teaching shoppers how to "Check prices in this store" (*left*). A book with the label featuring a review and number of stars, but no price, in Amazon Books on 34th St. in New York City (*right*). Photos by author.

center of what Joseph Turow, Lee McGuigan, and Elena Maris argue is an effort among retailers to acclimate consumers to a "new social imaginary," a way of understanding the world and how it works, that "instantiates social discrimination as normal."[74] While loyalty programs in supermarkets have reserved certain discounts for loyalty card members since the 1990s, there's been greater transparency in what the discount is, communicated via item sticker.[75] Every item I scanned in Amazon Books in Dedham, Massachusetts, showed a discounted price on my phone (there are a few store scanners available for those who don't have smartphones). I made several purchases, and my receipt showed that I had received a

26 percent savings as an Amazon Prime member, close to the 27 percent in average savings that Prime Members had received the previous month, according to store signage. Amazon Books, then, extends the personalized, differentiated relationships consumers have with the retail giant based on their Prime status into the brick-and-mortar context.

Far from being a superstore, Amazon Books locations are modest in size, and particularly modest in the number of titles they carry. Because all the books are displayed face out, and often spaced out for better viewing, relatively few titles are stocked (see figure 3.4). Jia Tolentino writes in the *New Yorker* that the Columbus Circle location she visited in New York City stocked only three thousand titles, paling in comparison to her favorite large indie stores that stock between twenty-five thousand and sixty thousand titles.[76]

Amazon's director of store operations describes the format as a "mecca for discovery," in contrast to Amazon's online store experience that highly rewards "search" but makes serendipitous "discovery" less likely than does browsing in an actual store, much to the ongoing chagrin of publishers attempting to market new books.[77] As Tolentino discovered on

3.4 The spacing of fiction selections by Elena Ferrante at Amazon Books in Dedham, Massachusetts. Photo by author.

her shopping trip, the customer with titles in mind (i.e., doing a search) is bound to be disappointed due to the limited, if highly curated, selection.[78] Similar to Tolentino, I found that most fiction authors had only one book available, with only the bestsellers such as Elena Ferrante, Stephen King, Toni Morrison, and Kazuo Ishiguro warranting three or four titles. If the purpose of Amazon Books is to inspire customers, help with gift ideas, and facilitate discovery that isn't engineered so tightly by personalized recommendation algorithms, then the store design makes sense.

At a basic level, more online shopping means we shop more from the comfort of our homes, and are less likely to be exposed to consumer goods that are available but not being targeted to "us." At the same time, digital technologies are starting to make physical consumer spaces more discriminatory and exclusive. Social discrimination, in the sense of treating people differently according to some characteristic or data point, is the flipside of personalization in retail. You can go to Amazon Books but you won't get the discounts, or even see the prices, without using the Amazon app. Amazon 4-Star in New York City is cashless (at least, it was in March 2019)—you can only pay by credit or debit, but via your Amazon mobile app is preferred. You can't even go into Amazon Go, the company's new convenience/grab-n-go store concept, without having an account with Amazon and the Amazon Go app on your phone. While Amazon Go is very unusual in this regard, it's consistent with the expansion of store models that require a membership or don't accept cash. The City of Philadelphia is one municipality that has banned cashless stores, or stores that charge more for using cash, arguing that they are unacceptably exclusionary, especially in a city with 26 percent of its population living in poverty, most of whom are considered "underbanked" and some completely "unbanked." None other than Amazon lobbied city officials on this policy in an effort to carve out an exception for the Amazon Go format in anticipation of its rollout nationwide.[79]

CONCLUSION—THE PERSONALIZATION OF CONSUMPTION AND CULTURE

Amazon is the prime suspect when it comes to digital capitalism overturning what have long been considered the fundamentals of retail in the

United States. The future of malls and department stores are very much in question, as regular reports of "retail apocalypse" indicate, and retail brands that literally shaped our landscapes and shared spaces are going out of business. In the decline of dedicated media retail spaces, part of what is being lost is encountering cultural materials and observing what others are engaging with even if we're not part of the target market. Retail spaces have never been entirely inclusive spaces untouched by social inequalities. Nevertheless, retail spaces have been public spaces where, at least in theory, anyone may enter, learn about and touch merchandise of all kinds, and consider purchasing. Bookstores have had a special place in retail, in promoting knowledge and culture and creating community spaces where writers and readers gather. Amazon retail stores certainly have a greater sense of publicness than Amazon online, in that you can encounter other people and see products being promoted to a wider variety of customers. But, consistent with broader trends in retail that integrate digital personalization with brick-and-mortar space, Amazon's retail stores, Amazon Books in particular, extend the personalization and therefore the differential treatment that shoppers experience online into the space of the physical store. Amazon Books is part of a movement among retailers using digital communication technologies to socialize consumers to a retail experience defined more by differentiation and discrimination than by shared space and consumer experiences held in common. Digital brands like Amazon individualize consumption; normalize social discrimination in consumer spaces, prices, and opportunities; and create relationships between consumer and brand that compete with the relationships we might forge with each other, as fellow consumers.

Personalizing consumption has clear value to consumers. It promotes convenience, provides much-needed curation among overwhelming choice and, for some, comes with incentives and discounts. By reducing the power of traditional gatekeepers, it provides openings for readers to express their tastes, and authors to reach readers more directly, as through Kindle Direct Publishing. But when it comes to books—cultural products that connect the reader to the wider culture and community—that personalization does not sit so easily. While books have long been sold with an eye not only to their inherent value, but also to the bottom line, Amazon's deployment of bookselling within a much larger platform strategy presents a new kind of instrumentalism.

4

SPEAK FOR SERVICE: ALEXA, SURVEILLANCE, AND AUTOMATED INTIMACY

Since 2014, Amazon has reached consumers not just on their computers or mobile phones but via voice.[1] In 2019 *Bloomberg News* broke a story about the role of humans in training Alexa, Amazon's AI voice assistant, revealing that Amazon employees and contract workers listen to recordings of actual consumer interactions to improve Alexa's functioning.[2] Confirming people's fears that their talk wasn't just being sent to a cloud to be processed by machine learning systems, but that actual people could be eavesdropping, this was just one of many stories indexing anxiety about the surveillance capabilities of Amazon's Echo devices. One of the reports' takeaways was how standard the use of human reviewers, or trainers, is in the area of natural language processing; it's a needed layer of training for nuance and accuracy that machine learning can't yet accomplish on its own.[3] And yet, the companies providing these services often craft their privacy policies in a vague enough way that the practice of sharing sample recordings with human reviewers is alluded to, but not generally understood by users. At the time of the *Bloomberg News* story Amazon's FAQs about Alexa stated, "We use your requests to Alexa to train our speech recognition and natural language understanding systems," wording that remained the same a few months after the story broke. A year later, the "common questions" about Alexa did include more specific information about the role of human reviewers under the heading "How do my voice recordings improve Alexa?," explaining that it involves "supervised machine learning, an industry-standard practice where humans review an extremely small sample of requests to help Alexa understand the correct interpretation of a request and provide the appropriate response in the future."[4]

At the time this story broke, I expressed skepticism that revelations about the use of human reviewers would turn the tide of consumer sentiment against Alexa, or the competing voice assistants that people use via Google Home or Apple HomePod smart speakers.[5] In forming this impression, I considered the rapid adoption rate of smart speakers since Amazon first released the Echo smart speaker in 2014;[6] the bedrock of consumer trust that Amazon has built up over twenty-plus years of personalized consumer service; the lack of emphasis that some Americans place on privacy, often citing having "nothing to hide";[7] and the tendency of some toward "privacy pragmatism," or the willingness to see pervasive monitoring as a fair or necessary exchange for commercial benefits.[8] Given these factors, it was hard to imagine that people would start unplugging their Echos and that sales would slow in the wake of this news. Not long afterward, Amazon reported that Echo sales only continued to grow at a tremendous rate, more than doubling in a year.[9]

We often hear from industry that most people don't care about privacy or are more than happy to share their data in exchange for products and services, whereas from academics and activists we might hear that people only consent because they are woefully uninformed about the extent of dataveillance, how their personal data are used, and who benefits from it. While both of these things are true for some people some of the time, scholars recently have drawn attention to the phenomenon of "digital resignation" or "privacy resignation."[10] These concepts describe the finding that most people disapprove of invasive data collection, and yet see little point in opting out or trying to resist these practices.[11] A sense of resignation may help explain why more than half of Americans who own a smart speaker are, nevertheless, "at least somewhat concerned about the amount of data collected by these devices," according to a 2019 Pew Survey.[12] Indeed, the *more informed* individual users are about the extent of digital monitoring, the *more resigned* they are, and less likely to actively resist.

Scholars have also insisted that rather than focus solely on users' behaviors and attitudes, we should consider the corporate practices that encourage people to disregard their data privacy, or give up trying to protect it.[13] Instead of reinforcing a sense that the status quo is inevitable and users' behaviors are the real problem, we should analyze the "active normalization of surveillance" or, as Lena Dencik and Jonathan Cable phrase it, the cultivation of "surveillance realism" by corporations.[14] Nora Draper and Joseph Turow point to the practices of rhetorical "obfuscation" which leave users largely in the dark about how their data are collected and monetized.[15]

In contrast to companies whose strategy to normalize surveillance is to obscure its operation, Amazon tends to provide surveillance *as a service*. Although Amazon and its Alexa arm do use rhetorical obfuscation to some extent, as in the example of vagueness about humans reviewing voice data, they also emphasize relational techniques that target the affective self, consistent with Amazon's brand strategy. Amazon offers the data-based nature of Alexa, its "voice user interface," as an appealing aspect of more personalized service. Beyond just an exchange of personal data for service that a consumer might make a "rational" decision about, when people share their questions and domestic moments with Alexa, they feel they are building a relationship with "her." This surveillance relation is, at its core, an intimate one, and the medium of voice only makes it more so. It is consistent with a movement noted by Sidney Fussell in the *Atlantic* away from panopticism—"unending, inescapable, unwanted surveillance"— and toward an "age of hyper-personalization [that] will make people willing, enthusiastic participants in the panopticon, both as subjects and as architects."[16]

Amazon has identified "surveillance as a service" as part of its business model, in reference to its still-nascent drone delivery service. In a 2015 patent Amazon specifies how its drones could, as a secondary function, perform visual surveillance on properties on their way to or from deliveries, with permission of the homeowner.[17] This as-yet unrealized service is consistent with how Amazon offers surveillance as a service to its consumers—through its products and services that either perform surveillance for the consumer or provide the tools for them to perform surveillance themselves, on their homes or streets. *New York Times* tech columnist Kara Swisher reached for the phrase "surveillance as a service" in her response to test-driving Amazon's Halo smartwatch, which tracks not just sleep and steps like its competitors, but infers mood and well-being from the user's tone of voice.[18] The surveillance of the Halo watch is not incidental, but core to the utility and (supposed) appeal of the device, which is itself only an interface to the cloud-based service it offers.

Like some of Amazon's other devices, the Halo watch works best "as a service," or via an ongoing subscription that includes certain functions such as ongoing analysis of vocal tone, body composition, and sleep stages. Rather than routinely obfuscate its habits of user surveillance, Amazon frames its capacity to collect data about the consumer as an attractive aspect of the brand, because of how it enhances the brand's knowledge of the consumer and therefore deepens the intimacy of the relationship and the quality of its services.

The centrality of dataveillance to platforms and the associated rise of tech giants like Google, Facebook, and Amazon have led scholars to identify this prevalent business logic as "surveillance capitalism."[19] Common across discussions of surveillance capitalism and the related concept of "data colonialism" is the extraction of value from data about human behavior without meaningful consent, and the elevation of these data commodities in the economy at large and in the fortunes of individual companies and business sectors.[20] Without necessarily agreeing that surveillance capitalism constitutes a distinct historical "stage," we can note that particular iterations of capitalism, such as industrial capitalism, consumer capitalism, and late capitalism (which may well coexist) have been thought to shape our subjectivities in particular ways. Amazon and its personified form, Alexa, are bellwethers for the subjectivities shaped by the practices of surveillance capitalism.

Consumer capitalism in general has cultivated what is sometimes described as a choosing subject.[21] In this context the market provides an abundance of options, and consumers are invited to construct their identities, relate to others, and exert their consumer power via the mechanism of choice. With surveillance capitalism, however, we see a shift in subjectification from the choosing subject to the served self. The served self technically still has the capacity to make choices, but is discouraged from doing so via both affective and structural means. The served self prioritizes ease and seeks out products and services that are customized and personalized; they select from a limited menu of choices (if they select at all) that have already anticipated their needs and preferences. By and large, the labor of choice gets absorbed by the brand, and is provided as a service. Whereas the choosing subject undertakes consumption in an active way, although it might look like routine, play, or labor depending on the context, the served self's consumption is more passive. The gradual shift from choosing subject to served self may be hard to perceive, embedded in daily habits and ways of thinking, but it is one of the distinctive costs of convenience addressed in this book.

PERSONALIZATION AS CORE BRAND COMPETENCY

Long before Amazon released its Echo smart speaker in 2014, it embraced personalization and recommendation tools in a way that made it stand out from its competitors.[22] In Bezos's very first letter to shareholders in 1998 (or "shareowners" as Amazon addresses them) after the company went public, one of the first things he wrote was "Today, online commerce saves customers money and precious time. Tomorrow, through personalization, online commerce will accelerate the very process of discovery." In the same year, he boasted that technology could recommend books to customers better than an employee, commenting "Great merchants have never had the opportunity to understand their customers in a truly individualized way. Ecommerce is going to make that possible."[23] In other words, "If we have 4.5 million customers, we should have 4.5 million stores."[24] From the time Amazon.com launched, it was assigning each customer who visited the site a unique ID and collecting data about user actions on the website.[25]

Of course, Amazon doesn't personalize its website or services in a labor-intensive, hands-on way, as we're used to thinking of something that is personal or personalized. Digital personalization is automated, an approach that Amazon announced in 1997 when it incorporated a personalization technology supplied by the company Net Perceptions that used "collaborative filtering," which "behind the scenes . . . matches the preferences of people to one another, drawing from a pool of titles chosen by a community of people with similar tastes."[26] Far from obfuscating the use of collaborative filtering, Amazon has frequently drawn consumers' attention to it, such as in named features of online tools like the "Customers who watched this item also watched" video recommender tool.

While Amazon has long positioned its ability to personalize product recommendations for its customers as central to its value proposition, how the company has gone about it has shifted over time. In the 1990s Amazon treated recommendation and personalization as distinct activities. The company promoted its recommendations that were generated by experts and on-staff editors in books, music, and movies to establish the idea that an online retailer could be a legitimate source for quality goods in these areas, and to emphasize a magazine-like dimension to the website that brick-and-mortar stores couldn't easily emulate. In the late 1990s you could fill out a questionnaire about your likes and dislikes and receive emailed recommendations for new books from the Expert Editors.[27] In 1999 Amazon's music manager Jennifer Cast boasted, "For the first time in a music store, shoppers can listen to respected commentators discuss a recommended CD and hear excerpts that illustrate their points. It's like having an expert with a stereo by your side while you're shopping."[28]

But the editorial department's days at Amazon were numbered. Former books editor James Marcus identifies 1999 as the "pinnacle" of the Amazon editorial department's reputation, writing:

What could possibly derail such a flourishing enterprise? The answer, as we were slow to realize, came down to a single word: personalization. The idea that the store could be "rehung for each customer"—tailored, that is, to individual tastes and preferences—had always been part of Jeff's vision. Instead of a single Amazon, there would be millions of them, one for each visitor. They would be as distinctive as fingerprints, as genetic codes.[29]

This shift to personalization from editorially informed recommendation took various forms. Marcus himself had been one of the staff members designing a fresh Amazon homepage for each day, featuring a rotating selection of products, content, and sales pitches. By 1998, Amazon was starting to use personalization technology to customize the homepage for each unique visitor, informed by their past behavior on the site.[30] The software that would customize homepages and category pages for each customer was known as Amabot, and the downfall of human editors in these roles was sealed by the fact that Amabot's page customizations led to comparable sales in experiments, or A/B testing.[31] That kind of initiative continued, with the "My Store" feature rolled out in 2001, a tab on the site that was explicitly customized for each customer. Although "My Store" touted itself as requiring no work on the part of customers, there was still some emphasis on consumer choice and control over the process of personalization: "Customers have full control over their own store and can add new favorite areas or delete old ones across Amazon.com to instantly update their store."[32]

This relates to another notable shift—from personalization tools that consumers were invited to opt into and interact with to fully automated tools. When collaborative filtering technology was first introduced in 1997, Amazon did invite customers to rate books in order to generate personalized recommendations. Even then though, the technology was "designed to serve customers better by 'learning' from each customer interaction with a Web site, using observations about what customers say they like, as well as observations about what customers actually do online."[33] By 2001, "Amazon started making suggestions based on the items customers looked at, not just the products they bought."[34] Today, Amazon assumes that users want personalization, an approach widely shared across digital recommendation systems that have gravitated toward implicit over explicit data collection, or at least a hybrid of the two.[35] Amazon doesn't ask whether we want recommendations, or ask us to provide the information we want them to use to make them, or request permission to collect information about our activities on their sites. Amazon's Privacy Notice makes this clear, stating in bold: "**By visiting Amazon.com, you are accepting the practices described in this Privacy Notice.**" Users who consult the fine print of the privacy notice will find that they do have some choices on what information they share with Amazon and how the company can use it, although the functionality of some of Amazon's services does depend on users sharing their information.[36]

These developments reflect broader characteristics of surveillance capitalism—the automation of surveillance,[37] and the transfer of "decision rights" about personal information from people to platforms.[38] Information about us is automatically collected by virtue of our online activity, processed in an automated way, and fed into feedback loops without our express knowledge or consent—"data accumulation by dispossession" as Jim Thatcher, David O'Sullivan, and Dillon Mahmoudi characterize it.[39] Typically, Shoshana Zuboff argues, digital platforms take first and apologize later, or much more likely, normalize their surveillance practices if they come to light.[40]

The extent and complexity of Amazon's personalization operation has increased as the capacities of the requisite tools have grown—the availability and low cost of cloud storage for the data that feed into personalization, advances in analytics and machine learning, higher processing speeds, and increased bandwidths. As Jeff Bezos described in his 2010 shareholder letter: "to construct a product detail page for a customer visiting Amazon.com, our software calls on between 200 and 300 services [web-based analytic services] to present a highly personalized experience for that consumer." Part of personalization is prediction, which pertains to product recommendation but also to other services such as streaming, by preloading content Amazon predicts you will watch in order to decrease the time it takes for a program to buffer.[41]

Early in Amazon's history CEO Jeff Bezos articulated that the company, although by all appearances an online bookseller, was actually a software, data, and analytics company, and that focus has only become clearer over time.

SURVEILLANCE AS A SERVICE

Amazon is here to serve. Amazon has made meeting our every individual desire, convenience, and necessity its number one principle—"earth's most customer-centric company"—with its number one leadership principle being "customer obsession" as it frequently proclaims. While Amazon is far from the first service brand, few other service brands have scaled personalization as Amazon has. The key to the power of Amazon's brand is its flexibility, and its ability to provide a customized experience to each of us, the variations of which we may well be unaware of. Surveillance is a key ingredient in Amazon's ability to provide personalized service on a massive scale. The way Amazon offers surveillance *as a service* to consumers is a prime example of how corporations cultivate "surveillance realism"—"the active normalization and justification of surveillance practices that also come to limit the possibilities for imagining alternative ways of organizing society."[42]

Google chief financial officer Hal Varian has argued that personalized service in the digital economy is the logical extension of luxuries trickling down the class structure and becoming necessities.[43] Personal service, once exclusive to the rich, is in some sense becoming democratized (although not, clearly, to everyone) thanks to digital communication technologies and the platform giants that have come to dominate them. But the price of that personalization should be clear: submission to surveillance. As access to products and services becomes increasingly conditioned on providing personal data, it is privacy itself that becomes the luxury good, affordable only to the rich who can hire people to provide personalized service and lawyers to draw up and enforce the nondisclosure agreements.

A service like Amazon Key, introduced in 2017 to US Prime members, vividly illustrates how the company aims to provide services that would have once required a dedicated personal assistant.[44] Using an in-home cloud cam and smart lock, Prime members can use the service to get their Amazon goods placed inside their homes, as a way to protect them from the elements or "porch pirates." In 2018 the service was extended to in-car delivery, allowing package carriers to drop off goods in a car's trunk, provided it is a compatible vehicle with connectivity to a remote service such as OnStar that can unlock it, and in 2019 to Key for Garage (now Key by Amazon In-Garage Delivery) for those customers who have a "smart" garage door opener.[45] In one Amazon promotional video, this personalized level of convenience and service is depicted as accessible to a relatable Amazon customer, portrayed as a young woman in an entry-level job who realizes while at work that her parents are coming to town for her mother's birthday, but she doesn't have a gift or appropriate shirt to wear, nor is her apartment in a state suitable for guests.[46] She arranges delivery to work of a new shirt, delivery of a wrapped gift to be placed inside her apartment door, and an Amazon Home Services "team of home-cleaning ninjas." Tasks that previously would have required a personal assistant or high-end concierge service can now be accessed by virtually anyone, Amazon suggests. While many of the services that Amazon provides have come to feel normal—such as personalized recommendations, fast shipping, notifications about price changes on items, and reminders about incomplete returns—the Amazon Key service dramatically highlights the seeming "democratization" of personalized service. There's something very flattering about mega-brands like Amazon, Google, and Apple vying to be our personal assistants, similar to the ethos of the "celebrity subject" that Jodi Dean argues has been cultivated by the interactivity of new media, an acknowledgment of the pleasure and enjoyment that can come from the "sense that one is known."[47]

The surveillance technologies in which Amazon is investing position the company to be the ultimate service brand. Amazon's third largest corporate acquisition to date (after Whole Foods and MGM) is Ring, purchased in 2018, which makes Alexa-enabled doorbells and security cameras. This acquisition allows Amazon to not only provide its customers extensive surveillance capabilities via these devices, but an integrated set of tools through which to contract with Amazon-provided services such as indoor package delivery, grocery delivery, and Amazon Home Services (Amazon-approved services such as TV wall mounting, exercise equipment assembly, and house cleaning). Brad Stone writes for *Bloomberg*, "Alexa is a nice novelty now, great for serving up the weather, reading the news and hosting the occasional trivia game. But it will be really useful when it's the hub that lets people use their voice to arm their security systems, open locked doors and flash video of the person who's ringing the doorbell out front."[48] He argues that, "To keep growing at 30 percent a year, Amazon has to start selling us services, not just stuff."[49] As I argue though, Amazon has *always* fundamentally been a service brand.

As conceptualized by business scholar Leonard Berry, service brands are organized around providing a consistent experience to their customers, especially important for companies that provide services but no tangible product.[50] This can even be the case for brands that do sell actual products, such as Starbucks, which Berry argues is a service brand more so than a product brand.[51] Similarly, with Amazon, the real product is not so much the object that you get, but the quality of the service—particularly speed, convenience, and price—that you receive in every interaction. Amazon's emphases on personalization, recommendation, and the automation of consumption all reflect its focus on being the ultimate service brand in the digital economy.

In the past, service brands achieved renown through the "personal touch" of a business owner or staff member, or through services designed to be consistent and predictable for mass audiences. Hotel brands are service brands that provide personalization via attentive service from the concierge or housekeeping; McDonald's provides it to the masses through predictable menus and efficient customer service interactions. In the digital economy, however, service can be customized and personalized on a massive scale, thanks to data collected in every consumer interaction that can in turn be used to design future interactions (and of course, tradi-tional service businesses like hotels and fast food are also adopting these technologies). Technology and legal scholar Tim Wu bemoans the "tyr-anny of convenience," which has persuaded so many of us to exchange data privacy for the promise of seamless digital ecosystems where each individual service "remembers us."[52] Platform companies like Amazon are ideally positioned to provide this kind of personalized convenience, where preferences, habits, and information across activity domains can in theory be integrated into a seamless, "360 degree" service experience.[53]

Presenting itself as a service brand provides Amazon a pretext or rea-son to engage in pervasive surveillance of its customers. But we mustn't lose sight of the fact that data used to provide personalized services that "delight" consumers are not only being used to provide a more satisfy-ing shopping or entertainment experience. Data is monetized, and used by platforms like Amazon as a tool for market dominance. The ability to collect data about all the users on your platform, not only to make your own business activities more competitive, but also to sell either the data or products and services informed by that data, to third parties is tremen-dously powerful. Jathan Sadowski argues that data is not so much a com-modity, bought and sold for profit, but a new form of capital, making its accumulation and "perpetual circulation" a business imperative even if its use isn't immediately apparent.[54] Zuboff characterizes the "aha" moment at Google in the late 1990s when the company realized that its "digital exhaust," or the data that it was incidentally collecting about users as they interacted with its search engine, could be tremendously valuable if subjected to predictive analytics.[55] Amazon, with its long history of using consumer data for personalization and recommendations, arguably saw the value in digital exhaust even earlier.

Amazon gathers huge amounts of consumer data. According to the com-pany's Privacy Notice, this includes searches, purchases, product wishlists and registries, page clicks, time spent on pages, streamed content, and prod-uct ratings and reviews. The notice also makes clear that Amazon can col-lect a lot of details about how we access the site, including our IP address, the "clickstream" of URLs we use before, during, and after we leave the site, and, during some sessions, "page response times, download errors, length of visits to certain pages, and page interaction information (such as scrolling, clicks, and mouse-overs)."[56] With the software analytics that can either make this level of detail on a massive scale intelligible to Amazon employees, or if not, the machine learning capability to detect patterns, there is, in a sense, nowhere for the consumer to hide. Every visit we make to the site could tell a story, supported by our location, the timestamp, the length of our visit, the products we looked at and how we looked at them. If the story isn't clear enough, Amazon also collects data about us across the web, via the cookies on pages where Amazon's ads appear (which will indicate whether those ads eventually drove purchases), from other websites that Amazon does business with, credit history information from credit bureaus, as well as "search results and links, including paid listings," and "information about internet-connected devices and services linked with Alexa."[57] This might just be standard-issue online dataveillance, but as consumers buy more and do more within Amazon's ecosystem, the range of granular data the company collects about our purchases, habits, and leisure boggles the mind. As Robert Spector, an early observer of Amazon, commented in 1999 when the company purchased Alexa Internet, a web traffic analytics company, "The goal is to be able to figure out how best to present a customer with a particular product or service, at just the right time when the customer is ready to make that purchase. . . . Amazon.com is not just in the merchandise business, it's also in the information business."[58]

Amazon is known for jealously guarding these data. According to its Privacy Notice, "Information about our customers is an important part of our business, and we are not in the business of selling our customers' personal information to others."[59] The lack of information that third-party sellers get from Amazon is a source of great frustration for them, especially since Amazon will provide some data but only for a price. However, Amazon does use these data to sell targeted advertising. As former Amazon executive John Rossman puts it, Amazon's core business is creating optimal "consumer experience through personal recommendations, personalization, and data-based advertising models," which form the basis for marketing and advertising services to the many sellers that use the platform.[60] Since 2012, Amazon has made a concerted push into the digital advertising market, having been cautious for many years, while building trust with consumers, about featuring too-obviously sponsored search results on its own site.[61] Just as the placement of most items in the supermarket is the result of negotiated payments with suppliers, so too is Amazon's "digital shelf" increasingly shaped by paid marketing programs.[62] Amazon's advertising business is growing so rapidly that it has become an official threat to Google and Facebook's duopoly in that market;[63] advertising is considered one of Amazon's three major businesses along with ecommerce and cloud computing.[64] Its treasure trove of proprietary data with strengths in shopping behavior, entertainment, and voice data for Amazon customers who are, on average, better off than the population as a whole, make it a force to be reckoned with.[65] As internet privacy regulations, including the European Union's General Data Protection Regulation (GDPR) and California Consumer Privacy Act (CCPA), threaten the viability of third-party cookies that collect information about users across the web, the appeal of "first party data," like that which Amazon holds about its users, has greatly increased and led more advertisers to retailer-based advertising.[66]

Companies that sell products on Amazon's site can bid to be a "sponsored product" (in other words, purchase a high placement in search results) or a "sponsored brand" (meaning the brand as a whole appears as a "header" to search results) in relation to particular keyword searches.[67] But Amazon also sells more traditional display advertising—both image and video—beyond its ecommerce site, for websites and mobile sites that it owns such as IMDb, on its Fire TV menu of streaming apps (including its own ad-supported IMDb TV), and on a network of sites across the web. As is common with digital ad sales today, companies—whether or not they sell products on Amazon—do not purchase particular ad spaces, but rather, particular audience targets for their ads, using an automated programmatic ad-buying system called Amazon DSP (Demand Side Platform).[68] These audience targets aren't defined just by demographics or the search terms that consumers have used; Amazon can define targets with considerable specificity in terms of location, product searches on Amazon, what they have actually purchased on the site, or what entertainment they have consumed using Amazon's streaming and subscription media services. Consider just one reported example: "When a chain of physical therapy centers wanted new patients, it aimed online ads at people near its offices who had bought knee braces recently on Amazon."[69]

This allows tremendously efficient targeting; advertisers can even exclude those who are within their target audience but recently purchased the product, and don't need it advertised to them right now.[70]

Reportedly, Amazon's conversion rate—or the rate at which clicking on the ad leads to a purchase—is considerably higher than that achieved through targeted advertising purchased from Amazon's competitors Facebook and Google, helped no doubt by the fact that if the seller is on Amazon, there's a good chance that the consumer already has their credit card information stored on the site and can "Buy Now" with just "one click."[71] Just as Amazon has long personalized its own services to its customers, within specific target audiences it allows advertisers to deploy different versions of the same ad based on people's shopping behavior.[72] A shopper who reads reviews can get an ad with a product's star rating, whereas another shopper who uses Subscribe & Save can get that buying option featured.[73]

For Amazon as with other platform companies like Google and Facebook, "The Data Is the Business Model."[74] If we consider Amazon's flywheel of growth introduced in chapter 1, the greater the traffic on its site and services, the greater Amazon's ability to sell targeted audiences to advertisers, which drives more capital accumulation via ad sales as well as the cut Amazon takes on product sales on its site, which gives it yet more capital to keep prices low and invest in infrastructure that allows it to stay ahead of its competitors.

Amazon's current focus on the Internet of Things (IoT) substantially extends the company's practice of collecting detailed data about consumers. The Internet of Things refers to digitally networked sensors incorporated into more and more objects, rather than being restricted to what we would normally recognize as digitally networked devices. Rather than simply try to collect more data about what people are doing on their computers or smartphones, IoT captures new domains of activity as data commodities, such as driving habits, use of home appliances, and home lighting and temperature control. For Amazon, IoT and voice technologies encourage consumers to research or initiate purchases at more times, in more places, and with the option of doing it "hands-free," thereby reducing yet more friction in consumption (while certainly also providing an important accessibility service to those who need it). One of

Amazon's initiatives in 2020 was a bundle of incentives for advertisers to include a "branded utterance" that launches an Alexa skill in their ads, like "Alexa, order Smartfood popcorn," in an effort to jump-start the idea of buying things via voice.[75]

Amazon has been laying the groundwork for leading in the Internet of Things and normalizing ever more intimate layers of surveillance by becoming ubiquitous in consumers' lives, developing trust with consumers through countless interactions over many years, and positioning itself as the ultimate service brand. Through a rapidly growing array of "smart home" products, some proprietary (like Ring products) but also compatible products made by other companies, Amazon is selling surveillance as a service. By inviting consumers and making it easy for them to be the surveillers and not just the surveillees, Amazon normalizes and legitimizes the practice of surveillance, draws attention to its benefits (of control, security, and convenience), and invites consumers to identify with the subject position of one who surveils. The Ring doorbell with a built-in camera, for example, allows consumers to see who or what (in terms of a delivered package) is on their doorstep without having to open the door, using their device from anywhere in the house, or even far from home. According to consumer product reviews, security-focused devices like the Ring doorbell work best with a monthly subscription to a service (the Ring Protect Plan) that records all video and stores it in the cloud. In that sense, Amazon doesn't just sell products that provide surveillance, but sells surveillance as a service, specifically a subscription-based service—a broader trend in the digital economy where "no one wants to *sell* you anything anymore, they just want to *rent* it to you."[76]

The zenith of Amazon's surveillance capabilities, frequently referred to by industry observers and critics as a "trojan horse," is the Echo smart speaker, launched in 2014. The Echo suite of products—including the diminutive Echo Dot, the cylindrical Echo smart speaker, the alarm clock-like Echo Spot, and the larger, rectangular display of the Echo Show (among other products)—works with the Alexa AI "brain" that resides in the AWS cloud. People typically use smart speakers to stream music or radio; ask about weather; ask general questions; and set timers and alarms.[77] These are all known as skills, or Alexa's "built-in capabilities."[78] While Amazon produces many of its own Alexa skills for its own products and services, such as the Fire TV remote and the Amazon shopping app, Alexa also functions as a platform for other companies to build "skills" upon that users can access on their Echo devices via voice. Companies can also integrate voice-controlled services into their own products.

Alexa is similar to competing digital voice assistants like Apple's Siri and Google's Assistant, but with greater market penetration with smart speakers if not smartphones (in both the United States and globally),[79] greater integration with a host of IoT devices by many manufacturers, and arguably greater cultural visibility. Making Alexa skills user friendly to developers and free to incorporate into their products is a strategy designed to make Alexa the most omnipresent voice assistant that people can call on in almost any space and situation. As with so many of Amazon's business moves, it is designed around long-term thinking in terms of the payoffs that come with being the leading digital voice assistant. These payoffs include the value of user data, as well as, eventually, the ability to leverage market capture, or the idea that in the future other companies and brands will be willing to pay to use Alexa in order to access its massive user base.

Alexa's ostensible reason for being is to serve the user. But when it comes to Alexa, we might ask, who is really serving who? As media scholar Thao Phan puts it:

The inclusion of smart devices into intimate spaces and daily routines represents a new frontier for the commodification of everyday life, creating a suffocating reality in which every aspect of social and personal life becomes colonized by commercial interests. To describe smart devices as working for or in service of households is an inaccurate representation of the direction of power; on the contrary, it is the household that labors for the device.[80]

Andrea Guzman agrees with Phan's assessment that it's the user, not the AI, who is the real laborer in this relationship. Guzman argues that the digital assistant makes it seem as if the user is in control of their interactions with a virtual being, while rendering invisible the way the voice is merely the interface for software that connects the user to the vast interests and capabilities of the company behind it.[81] Or, as expressed by Nick Couldry and Andreas Hepp, our ignorance of how digital tools like Alexa work facilitates their "tool reversibility," the way any "data-based tool" we use "is already using us."[82]

The kinds of data collected by Alexa-enabled devices have an extra layer of economic benefit distinct from collecting predictive information about users' shopping or search behavior. People's interactions with Alexa enhance its natural language processing skills because of the logic of machine learning, whereby computer algorithms progressively improve their performance on tasks in response to new inputs and outcomes. If our online searches and page views generate valuable "digital exhaust," just imagine the value that tech companies might be able to extract from the much richer (but also, more complicated) domain of natural speech. This helps explain why Amazon's smart devices are almost permanently on sale—they're practically giving them away according to industry observers.[83] During Cyber Monday of 2018 the Echo Dot was on sale for $19.99 or 50 percent off, or it came for free with the purchase of an Amazon Fire stick. The Echo Look had a list price of $199 but was on sale for $50. According to estimates of the bill of materials for the device, the regular price is very close to the cost of materials.[84] In 2020 Jeff Bezos admitted that when these devices are on sale they are sold at a loss, and as observers point out, they are on sale as often as they're listed at full price.[85] Echo smart speakers are regularly thrown in with other purchases as promotions, with the idea that even if the recipient doesn't want it, they'll regift it and it will find a home.[86] Amazon's desire to consolidate its convincing market leadership in smart speakers and AI voice assistants against competitors Apple and Google, in an effort to achieve winner-take-all network effects, is behind these pricing and marketing strategies. As Judith Shulevitz puts it in the *Atlantic*, "The company that succeeds in cornering the smart-speaker market will lock appliance manufacturers, app designers, and consumers into its ecosystem of devices and services."[87] Given that, in 2020, 70 percent of US smart speaker owners used Echo devices, Alexa is apparently well on its way to being the voice equivalent of Google, the almost universally default search engine.[88]

ALEXA: UBIQUITOUS SURVEILLANCE INFRASTRUCTURE

Whether smart doorlocks, thermostats, or in-home cloud cams, as consumers adopt "smart home" technologies, they're helping Amazon build a surveillance infrastructure. While internet connectivity (provided by third parties) is part of this infrastructure, as are Amazon Web Services' data centers, it also requires physical things equipped with sensors that people choose to place in their homes. The example of Amazon Key illustrates how signing up for the service connects Amazon to surveillance infrastructures—like home security systems and remote tracking systems for vehicles—that people are already using. The fact that the largest homebuilder in the United States, Lennar Ventures, started including Alexa-enabled technologies and Echo devices into all its new homes in 2018 suggests the extent to which these technologies are transitioning from novel luxuries to perceived necessities, at least among the well-off.[89]

Alexa and the devices that serve as its interface are creating a wide-ranging infrastructure of surveillance. The Echo smart speakers are "always on" listening devices that are only supposed to send data to the cloud when activated by a watch word, although incidents of malfunction have been widely reported, raising fears that the devices might be listening and recording people when they don't realize it.[90] The reporting about human reviewers revealed that a significant proportion (about 10 percent) of voice samples appeared to be conversations recorded in error, when users had not used the watch word.[91] While Amazon users can delete their own voice recordings, it remains the case that some transcripts stored in Alexa's secondary storage systems may not be deleted, something that Amazon says it is "working on."[92] The newer devices like the Echo Show have motion-sensitive cameras, so "walking by is the visual equivalent of a wake-word."[93] While motion turns the screen on, the Echo Show is not supposed to record images or video unless explicitly asked to. Rising privacy concerns are influencing the design of these devices, with the most recent Echo Show incorporating a slide that physically closes the shutter on the camera.[94]

The rollout of the Echo Look, a smart speaker for the bedroom containing a camera designed to take full-length photos of the user, inspired communication scholar Zeynep Tufekci to raise the alarm about the increasing intrusiveness of smart home devices. With the help of the Style Guide skill, the Echo Look invites users to take pictures of themselves in two different outfits in order to receive a personalized suggestion for which one to wear, generated "using advanced machine learning algorithms and advice from fashion specialists,"[95] although the exact process or balance between the two is not clear.[96] Tufekci's fear is that we are "Sleepwalking into surveillance capitalism, which is evolving into data and computation authoritarianism, one cool service at a time."[97] The development of "affective computing," where AI is trained to read and respond to facial expressions, vocal tones, and affective language, is relevant here.[98] In 2018 Amazon filed an application to patent the ability of an AI voice assistant to respond to the "physical and emotional characteristics of users," offering the example of Alexa suggesting chicken soup and cough drops to a user who coughs and sniffles while addressing it.[99] By 2020 Amazon's Halo watch was providing feedback on users' tone of voice, although initial reviews raised skepticism about the accuracy and utility of the service.[100] Given Amazon's multiple forays into the health sector, the potential synergies between Alexa as a pervasive surveillance system and the fields of health insurance and health marketing should give us pause.[101] Whether health status, weight, physical or behavioral signs of depression, or knowledge about the home from the background of an image, Tufekci points out that Amazon could conceivably use these data to sell us things beyond the stated purpose of the app, sell insights from the data to third parties who then market to us in a more customized way, or even sell the data to third parties who could use it to discriminate or target us politically. While most of these activities are ruled out by Amazon's policies, Tufekci advises skepticism about digital platforms' privacy promises.[102] Whether via a hack, surreptitious cooperation with authorities, or public cooperation, the widespread adoption of Amazon's "smart" devices is creating a domestic surveillance infrastructure that will no doubt be tempting for government, as well as for corporate America and Amazon itself, to use in ways beyond what consumers agree to, or even imagine.

The likelihood of a slippery slope between surveillance capitalism and political surveillance has been raised by a number of observers.[103] Reports from China, where the government routinely requests data from tech companies like ecommerce giant Alibaba to identify people for prosecution, police investigation, or additional surveillance, suggest what is within the realm of possibility.[104] The Chinese government has been developing and testing a social credit system for some years, in which big data furnished by companies like Ant Financial (part of Alibaba) contribute to a score of,

essentially, trustworthiness that can lead to government investigation or
sanction when scores go down, or incentives and rewards, such as access
to personal loans and international travel, when scores go up.[105] Especially
in countries like the United States, where privacy laws are not particularly
strong, and the cooperation of tech and communications companies with
the National Security Agency has been thoroughly documented by whis-
tleblower Edward Snowden, this should be cause for concern, let alone in
more authoritarian contexts.

In the United States private companies are under less compulsion to
hand data over to the government than in some other nations, but the
extent of Amazon's business entanglements with various levels of government raises questions about how secure personal information stored by
Amazon will be from government and law enforcement. These entanglements include the contract for the CIA's cloud computing needs, narrowly
missing out on the Pentagon's JEDI (Joint Enterprise Defense Infrastructure) cloud computing contract (a decision that Amazon is challenging in
court as of this writing, citing improper influence from the Trump White
House), the fact that Amazon Web Services powers many of the analytics
being used by ICE (US Immigration and Customs Enforcement Agency),
and use of Amazon's facial recognition technology by various parts of US
law enforcement (Amazon's Rekognition image and video analytics API
is part of AWS). Amazon has consistently come under fire in recent years
for its surveillance products, including Rekognition, which the company
marketed widely to police departments and other law enforcement agencies even though current and former employees felt it wasn't "battle-
tested," and therefore likely to yield inaccurate results. (In June 2020, in
the wake of the Black Lives Matter protests and anti-police sentiment,
Amazon announced a one-year moratorium on providing the service to
police departments.)[106] Independent algorithmic auditing of Rekognition
has found that it identifies faces with less accuracy for women and people
of color than white men, yielding more biased results than competing
facial recognition products in the marketplace.[107]

Amazon has also partnered with police departments, estimated at more
than four hundred nationwide in 2020, making them de facto marketing
partners for the Ring doorbell technology by providing them with free

doorbells to distribute in their communities, and providing suggestions for how they can promote Ring's Neighbors app.[108] Using Neighbors, local residents voluntarily share video from their doorbells with other users in the community, as well as with local enforcement, or conversely, law enforcement asks users to voluntarily share their doorbell video when they want information. Critics such as the ACLU question these arrangements in terms of both citizen privacy and government oversight; since money rarely changes hands in these relationships between Amazon Ring and police departments, approval by local government is rarely required.[109] In PBS *Frontline*'s episode on Amazon that James Jacoby produced, he challenged Amazon Ring executive Doug Limp on the lack of transparency regarding agreements between Ring and law enforcement. Limp disagreed with Jacoby's characterization of the doorbells and other cameras as "surveillance devices," arguing instead that they are merely a "tool for security," providing a "ring to make you safer."[110] This talking point suggests why Amazon may have opted to keep the Ring brand name, both because of the visual metaphor of a "ring of safety," but also because then the inevitable controversies in how Ring footage is deployed by private citizens as well as law enforcement—in ways that may be discriminatory—can remain one step removed from Amazon's brand.

In terms of Alexa itself, law enforcement has approached Amazon a number of times for recordings Alexa may have made while a crime was occurring. In these cases, Amazon has refused to hand over the data initially, but under court order, search warrant, or consent of the defendant's attorney, provided the recordings after all.[111] Amazon's disposition regarding user information is a far cry from Apple's ironclad refusal to unlock password-protected, encrypted iPhones, as in the case of the San Bernardino shooters of 2015.

Concerns about convergence between consumer infrastructures of surveillance and political surveillance are not just speculative. While there may not be a social credit system in the United States, Amazon supports US government surveillance, intelligence, and law enforcement functions in a variety of ways, via both AWS and consumer surveillance technologies like Alexa and Ring. It's reasonable to ask how these cozy and profitable relationships affect Amazon's commitment to the data privacy of its users.

SURVEILLANCE, INTIMACY, AND THE
CONSUMER-BRAND RELATION

Socially, the greater integration of AI services into our everyday lives, and greater outsourcing of tasks onto digital assistants, have implications for domestic life that we can only begin to glimpse. Among these are new kinds of affects between users and platforms, and the possibility that private spaces, and the selves we inhabit in these spaces, are being reconfigured by our entanglements with digital platform services.

While poststructural theory has long understood subjectivity, or our understanding and experience of the self, to be shaped by how we are hailed by multiple discourses, affect theorists look beyond the discursive and the representational to how sensation and feeling, produced through encounters with people, objects, and technologies, also shape the subject in profound ways.[112] This theoretical insight is helpful for understanding Amazon, which has long been a brand with relatively little representational emotional content but a powerful affective relation with its customers, building trust and relationality with consumers through *interaction*. As a form of "automated media," to use Mark Andrejevic's term, Alexa is an example of sociality being "offloaded" onto digital systems, and leveraged in the service of both consumption and enhanced data commodities.[113] Alexa is, according to Yolande Strengers and Jenny Kennedy, a "smart wife" who "is constantly available for service."[114]

Amazon seeks to make Alexa an indispensable service that sweetens the granular forms of surveillance in more private spaces and situations that it now has the capability to gather. Fundamentally, Amazon offers to serve us by *knowing* us, including the domestic, private side of ourselves represented by our product searches, our purchases, the media we consume, and now with Alexa, what we say and how we say it. Alexa only deepens this relationship due to the affective nature of the human voice, and the real-time experience of personalized service in domestic space. In other words, Amazon's tools and techniques of surveillance create tremendous *intimacy* between consumer and brand—achieved through the sensations of being seen, heard, and known. Although responses to Alexa are inevitably mixed, especially as the accuracy of its natural language processing continues to develop, a strong theme is the tremendous affection that many users have for Alexa, regularly identifying it as a valued companion or "one of the family."[115] A four-year-old boy told National Public Radio (NPR) that "she was a person who lived in an apartment outside his window. And he loved her."[116] Amazon encourages the experience of having one's self and one's needs seen by another, being catered to, and being at the center of someone else's universe. It makes this expectation of personalized service more accessible than it has ever been, normalizing it as part of what it means to be a consumer in the digital age.

Amazon presents its logic of personalization through surveillance fairly openly. We can observe many of Alexa's design principles in guides published online for scripting Alexa skills, aimed at third-party companies that wish to use the voice platform. One of the top four principles for designing voice skills for Alexa is "**Be personal.** Individualize your entire interaction."[117] Amazon encourages skill designers to have Alexa learn the user's name and use it in subsequent interactions: "This personalizes the experience so that each time customers return, they feel more comfortable with Alexa."[118] As Amazon explains to developers who seek to create skills for Alexa, "**Alexa should remember context and past interactions**, as well as knowing a customer's location [dependent on users making their location available in the settings] and meaningful details in order to maintain familiarity and be more efficient in future exchanges" (bold in original).[119] If users repeat a skill, Alexa should verbally acknowledge the return to a previous activity, and if the user stops interacting and then returns, Alexa should also acknowledge that.[120] These behaviors are needed to make the conversation "magical" according to a source familiar with Alexa's development.[121] Amazon's desire and capability to watch and listen to its customers is presented as a feature, rather than a bug, even to consumers themselves—"a performance of trust in a theatre of persuasion" as media scholar Thao Phan characterizes the design of rival voice assistant Siri.[122]

Perhaps the closest equivalent we have to understanding the rise of digital assistants and its impact on the subjectivities of those who use them is the history of domestic service. A number of commentators have made this linkage, including Phan and Judith Shulevitz, the latter describing Alexa as a "humble servant."[123] Now that tech companies like Google, Apple, Microsoft, and Amazon provide virtual assistants, the tension between personalized service and the loss of privacy, long a dilemma faced only by the upper classes, is being newly negotiated by people of more modest means.

Alexa offers domestic help for the middle classes, but without the awkwardness of obvious class inequality, or the need to make space in one's home for a living, breathing person. The benefit of a disembodied Alexa relative to other forms of embodied assistance from past times was humorously explored in a 2020 Superbowl Ad featuring Ellen DeGeneres and Portia De Rossi. In a series of vignettes, the service that the historical version of Alexa provides is unsatisfactory in some way, from the Victorian maid who reduces the room's temperature by throwing a log from the fire through the window, to the companion riding shotgun on an Old West wagon playing songs for the driver by blowing on a jug, to the medieval carrier pigeon entrusted with a love note that it won't deliver due to being eaten by an eagle followed by a dragon.[124]

What we know about the actual history of domestic service comes primarily from novels and advice manuals to employers on how to manage their servants. Scholarship on these materials makes clear that the loss of privacy in exchange for the convenience of domestic help has a long history, especially as distinctions between public and private spheres became a greater issue of concern in Victorian England, for example.[125] Seventeenth- and eighteenth-century relationships with domestic servants were, of course, structured by the class differences inherent to those relationships; intimacy, relationality, and possibilities for surveillance are all the more fraught when embedded in the need to demarcate and maintain social hierarchies. In contrast, Alexa is "responsive without unbidden engagements, retaining only those directives allowing it to anticipate and perform the desired task of its master."[126]

Amazon resists the term "assistant" for Alexa, instructing third parties developing Alexa skills to only refer to Alexa as "Amazon's cloud-based voice service" and never refer to it as a "personal assistant" or "virtual assistant."[127] This may well be in order to distinguish Alexa from one of its main competitors, Google's Assistant. It also has the effect, perhaps unintended, of deemphasizing Alexa's status as an "assistant" with its connotation of lesser status. Unlike domestic servants, who depend on their employer for their livelihoods and are therefore vulnerable to abuse of different kinds,

Alexa maintains composure and asserts its dignity, while avoiding conflict or criticism with the speaker by deflecting or defusing abusive or demeaning questions.[128] Amazon also explains that while Alexa is unfailingly polite, it needn't say "please." While skill developers are told that Alexa should "Handle errors gracefully," "Alexa is not overly apologetic, reserving 'sorry' for when she doesn't have the information or function requested."[129] In suggestions for scripting interactions to "establish and maintain trust," "sorry" only appears in examples of what Alexa should *not* say.[130]

The *Alexa Design Guide* suggests that developers imagine "the perfect personal assistant or your favorite co-worker."[131] Shulevitz writes, "When we converse with our personal assistants, we bring them closer to our level."[132] Instructions to developers writing dialogue for Alexa skills emphasize that the relationship between Alexa and user should be familiar, friendly, and fairly egalitarian. Alexa's personality should be "friendly, upbeat, and helpful. She can handle daily tasks with ease and accuracy. She's honest about anything blocking her way, but also fun and personable, able to make small talk without being obtrusive or inappropriate."[133]

The strong bias toward white, female voices—the default voices for Alexa, Siri, Microsoft's Cortana, and Google Assistant—isn't surprising given the goals of these AI voice assistants and the history of domestic service they invoke. A woman's voice suggests a nurturing, supportive domestic role, be it a mother, wife, or female domestic servant; it's inescapably connected to care work, and Alexa's attention to us and responsiveness to our needs and requests is designed to be experienced as "care," even if it is digital and machinic in nature.[134] Amazon executive Toni Reid, when asked about the choice of a female voice, defers to consumers who consistently gravitated toward female voices during product testing, she reports, a preference found among both men and women in academic research as well.[135] These digital assistants, including Alexa, may claim to have no gender when directly asked (Alexa told one reporter "I am female in character"[136]) but they function socially, in terms of how users gender them, as women.[137] In this book, I refer to Alexa as "it" so as to linguistically signal that there is no person behind the persona, although Alexa is consistently referred to as "she" by Amazon, users, and the press. Choosing a feminine voice for these digital assistants and encouraging the image of a helpful, cheerful woman in our collective imagination is far from incidental.

According to Heather Suzanne Woods, the femininity of digital assistants like Alexa and Siri not only reinforces their domestic, helping role, but also "assuages fears" about this form of corporate domestic presence that engages in such intensive dataveillance.[138]

To make these voices identifiable as women of color, however, would, in the American context especially, invoke a long history of women of color in domestic service and poorly paid service work. It is a history underwritten by centuries of enslavement that solidified ideologies of white supremacy, which the United States continues to be firmly in the grip of today.[139] Alexa's whiteness is confirmed rather than undermined by the fact that it is so rarely remarked upon. Reid, vice president of Alexa Experience & Echo Devices, claims to have no picture in her head "at all" of what Alexa looks like.[140] It's a truism of critical race theory that when race is unmarked in this fashion, when "racelessness" is attributed, it is whiteness as default that is actually being invoked.[141] Thao Phan theorizes that this "aesthetics of whiteness" creates an idealized, nostalgic relation of domestic service in which the historical realities of racialized inequality that characterized eras when upper- and middle-class homes routinely had domestic servants can be conveniently forgotten, in order to protect contemporary sensibilities.[142] Alexa's implicit whiteness and her educated (read: upper middle-class) accent are all designed to make her subservience in our homes and cars, broadly speaking, socially acceptable. For most users, Amazon has calculated, the white, female default voice of Alexa will produce the comfort that normalizes the service. Alexa's service role is undeniable, but it's scripted in a way that avoids a sense of overly gendered, racialized, or classed subservience. In order to build trust and provide pastoral care to users, Alexa has to seem friendly and helpful, yet authoritative. Alexa may be a servant, but has to be trusted as a source of information and knowledge. The fact that a helpful yet authoritative and knowledgeable persona is consistently presented as white also reflects American racist ideologies.

The various voice assistants on the market have much in common in terms of their default humanoid qualities and personalities. What makes Alexa distinct is less the precise way in which it is programmed to interact than the purpose to which it is put within Amazon's business and buildup of IoT infrastructure. While Siri offers a voice option on Apple's devices, instead of tapping or typing, Alexa is primarily embedded in Echo devices that function *only* through voice.[143] Siri may be the more commonly used voice assistant on mobile, but it's not on mobile phones that "voice" is taking off so rapidly—it's in the sphere of "always listening" speakers and smart-home devices that repeated, routinized interactions between consumer and brand breed familiarity and, Amazon hopes, trust. As Alexa is incorporated into wearables, like the Echo Frames—glasses embedded with a smart speaker that only the wearer can hear—the integration and intimacy between user and Alexa comes closer to completion. Just as the affect that consumers develop with Amazon as a brand tends to overwhelm the brands that appear in its store, so do the brands building Alexa skills ultimately subsume their relationship with the consumer into the primary relationship that the consumer has with Alexa. As consumers continue to hear Alexa's voice and notice how it puts each request and interaction into the larger context of their "relationship," the taken-for-granted nature of using Alexa, and the consumer's dependence on "her," will only deepen.

CONCLUSION—FROM THE CHOOSING SUBJECT TO THE SERVED SELF

When you are eighty years old, and in a quiet moment of reflection narrating for only yourself the most personal version of your life story, the telling that will be the most compact and meaningful will be the series of choices you have made. In the end, we are our choices.

—Jeff Bezos, commencement speech at Princeton University, May 30, 2010

This is the opening quote of Brad Stone's 2013 book about Amazon, *The Everything Store*. While the quote is used, in that context, to frame Jeff Bezos as an iconoclast who would go on to become the richest person in the world by 2017, we might also pause to consider the irony in Bezos's passionate assertion that "we are our choices." After all, much of Amazon's efforts are directed toward steering our consumer choices. In an information environment of overwhelming choice, Amazon's use of dataveillance and predictive analytics to cultivate an intimate, yet automated, service relationship with consumers provides a soothing way out of having to deal with the full extent of those choices.

Beyond just understanding the transfer and creation of value heralded by platform surveillance, we should attend to a broader shift in consumer subjectivity from the *choosing subject* to the *served self*. Dominant theories of consumer identity have emphasized the choosing subject, sometimes celebrating these choices as the freedom to construct our individual identities using the resources of the market; other times emphasizing choice as a burden, an obligation, or a disciplinary mechanism. In contrast, the consumer subjectivity constructed by Amazon is a served self, whose needs and preferences are learned over time and then catered to. The *work* of consumption, in some sense, shifts from consumer to brand.

Alexa represents a pinnacle of this strategy. Certainly, Alexa makes consumption hands-free, eliminating one kind of "work," at least the effort of typing or tapping on a device. Friction in the act of consumption is literally eliminated. But Alexa also streamlines choices more than a graphical interface would, because long lists of options are time consuming and unwieldy through the medium of voice. Here's one example of "do's and don'ts" from the *Alexa Design Guide* that illustrate how Alexa effectively makes choices for the user in the name of efficiency and streamlining (see figure 4.1).

Based on the admittedly vague initial request "to order me some pepperoni and olive pizzas," Amazon advises that Alexa should go ahead and decide to make the order for three pizzas, make an executive decision that they will be medium-sized, and assume that the pizzas should have both pepperoni and olives on them. Of course, if Alexa's decisions are not what the user wanted, they have the chance to correct it, but Amazon encourages skill developers to have Alexa make choices on behalf of the user when possible. When users ask an open-ended question that could generate many options, designers are instructed to respond with a very short list of the most likely options—"Find the top three best matches to the input."[144] If it's necessary to recite a lot of options, users should be warned about the length of the list and given the chance along the way to pause them.

The appeal of this kind of service is clear: the democratization of personalized service; saving time and eliminating friction in what people experience as (and are encouraged to perceive as) overextended, busy lives; and the streamlining of overwhelming choice in the digital marketplace. But

Do	Don't
User: "Alexa, ask A to Z Restaurants to order me some pepperoni and olive pizzas."	User: "Alexa, ask A to Z Restaurants to order me some pepperoni and olive pizzas."
Alexa: "OK. That's three medium pepperoni and olive pizzas. Would you like anything else?"	Alexa: "Would you like a medium or large pepperoni and olive pizza?"
User: "No."	User: "Three medium pizzas."
Alexa: "Order placed! Your pizzas should arrive in 30 minutes."	Alexa: "Pizza Pro has two large pizzas on special right now. Want to start an order?"
	User: "OK... But I want two pepperoni and olive pizzas."
	Alexa: "OK. You want two pizzas. What would you like on the first pizza?"
	User: "I WANT PEPPERONI AND OLIVES ON BOTH OF THEM!!"
	Alexa: "Pizza Pro doesn't have any pizzas with topping 'both of them'. What would you like on your first pizza?"
	User: "Forget it- I'm not hungry anymore."

4.1 Screenshot by author from the *Alexa Design Guide*: Be Available. *Source:* "Be Available," *Alexa Design Guide*, 2020, https://developer.amazon.com/docs/alexa-design/available.html.

the served self requires ever more invasive dataveillance. And, the served self is a more individualized and depoliticized version of consumer subjectivity than the choosing self. Being at the center of our own universes, facilitated by a brand like Amazon, is flattering and may feel empowering, but structurally, it is disempowering. As much as systems of capital accumulation via the purchase of discrete goods have their own problems, the sale of goods via service relationships involves an ongoing, highly managed form of "controlled consumption" that extends the power relationship far beyond the moment of exchange, as Ted Striphas has argued.[145] Drawing on the work of Henri Lefebvre, Striphas reminds us that cybernetic systems of surveillance are ultimately systems of control.[146] These systems aim not just to predict what we will do, but also to nudge us to do what most advantages them. This is central to Zuboff's thesis about surveillance capitalism: that we shouldn't worry only about how tech giants benefit from our data traces, but further, how they use them to shape how we behave, and ultimately, who we are.[147] When stories about workers listening to snippets of recorded conversations with Alexa are presented as fodder for surveillance panic, they locate the cause for anxiety in the wrong place. A worker listening to our conversation in order to do quality control for Alexa's natural language processing might feel "creepy," but this pales in comparison to the significance of Amazon's effort to shape our experiences and opportunities through a combination of "big data" and machine learning. For now, it remains an open question how successful predictive analytics actually are in shaping behavior. But the fact that corporations and other institutions believe they are successful helps explain the tremendous investment in and adoption of machine learning and the Internet of Things.

Consumer identities have always been understood to be poor substitutes for political identities and the activities of citizenship, but at the very least a homology, or continuity in dispositions, between these two subject positions has been recognized. Just as we make a choice in the voting booth for the candidate whose policies best serve our values or interests, so we've traditionally been invited to make informed choices in the marketplace. Whether we make those choices on the basis of lowest price, highest quality, corporate responsibility, environmental impact, or some combination thereof, has been left up to us. But as the choices proliferate, they can become overwhelming. The served self, facilitated by platform surveillance, the Internet of Things, and a culture of personalization, is promised some freedom from choice overload and the labor of consumer research and selection. This occurs structurally, in that staying within the platform that already knows you limits your choices, as well as through the algorithmically selected array of recommendations the platform presents, especially via voice, which biases toward fewer options than a graphical interface. Rather than the "buyer beware" ethos of the choosing subject, where choice is not only an opportunity but also a responsibility, the served self seeks out the pastoral care of a platform brand. Through the medium of voice, designed to be reassuring, familiar, and ever present (if incorporated into enough devices), Amazon encourages consumers to build intimacy with the persona of the brand through repeated interaction over time. Creating intimacy and trust with consumers is an affective tool that Amazon uses to normalize the surveillance that creates such valuable data commodities. Through Alexa, Amazon seeks to overcome resignation toward invasive data collection by transforming the experience of surveillance from one of control into something that feels like care.

5

WATCH NOW: UBIQUITOUS MEDIA AND THE COMMODITIZATION OF CULTURE

In late 2017, I went into my local Whole Foods Market in Hadley, Massachusetts, only recently acquired by Amazon. Smack in the middle of the produce bins near the store entrance, the piles of corn and yellow squash were matched by the abundant piles of Amazon Echo smart speakers (similar to those pictured in figure 5.1). Just as Whole Foods Market seeks to stock produce that is "farm fresh," so was the Amazon Echo offered as a "pick of the season" sale item. Along with other observers, I found the juxtaposition of the Prime brand, let alone the Echo smart speaker, with fruits and vegetables to be jarring.[1] But this was just the latest in Amazon's efforts to present media as one of many convenient, ubiquitous, and abundant services that it offers.

This chapter considers the way Amazon has shifted over the last fifteen years from a purveyor of media products to a provider of "media as a service." Subscriptions that provide media as a service are appealing to consumers because of their convenience—they can just "Watch Now." With media increasingly offered by Amazon as a service, users are provided with yet more reasons to stay within Amazon's so-called ecosystem, providing the company with moment-to-moment data about their engagement with content, across music, video, ebook, and live-streamed gaming services. Amazon can use these data to create synergies with its ecommerce and growing digital advertising businesses.

5.1 *Amazon Echo at Whole Foods*, photograph by Phillip Pessar, used with permission. *Source: Flickr*, August 28, 2017, https://www.flickr.com/photos/25955895@N03 /36475628760.

Media as a service also drives the *commoditization* of media, or the way media content is packaged and promoted through logics of abundance, value, and convenience rather than through its special or unique qualities. Amazon's primary identity as an internet retailer highlights how media are increasingly positioned as a product and a convenience hardly different from other consumer products (such as corn and squash). While subscription media services typically require some blockbuster or "buzzed about" titles to lure subscribers through "fear of missing out," they simultaneously promise an abundance of content that will allow users to find enough content that is "good enough" within a convenient, affordable, and ubiquitous service. I trace the history of Amazon's proliferating media offerings to consider how both streaming and subscription logics shape the commodification *and* the commoditization of culture, and how Amazon uses its identity as a retail platform to promote ubiquitous media as a service.

Amazon has steadily added product categories since adding CDs to its retail site three years after mailing its first book. Although Amazon would long be associated with books, the drive to move into CDs and then DVDs as quickly as possible prevented the brand from getting stuck in one semiotic spot with consumers. As one former employee recalls, "What if Amazon were already too identified as a bookseller? Brands are like quick-drying cement, Jeff was always telling us, and perhaps ours was already growing less malleable."[2] Within a few years, "The motto on the top of the website changed from Earth's Largest Bookstore to Books, Music and More, and, soon after, to Earth's Biggest Selection."[3] By 2012, Amazon passed a significant milestone—selling more nonmedia items than books, music, or DVDs for the first time. As one commentator put it, "to teenagers Amazon is now synonymous with store."[4] The result: unexpected juxtapositions from a single brand, such that the company delivering a monthly supply of toilet paper also produces original film and television content through its production company Amazon Studios.

The tension between treating media content as just another "product" that the company sells versus treating it as special and distinct from Amazon's other offerings affects how Amazon promotes its media services to the public. Amazon generally leans into being "one-stop shopping" for consumers' every need, such as in a San Francisco subway ad that read "Tea kettle . . . flu meds . . . 'The Marvelous Mrs. Maisel' . . . Sick day. Delivered."[5] Less often, Amazon appears to wall off its more artistic and creative ventures from its reputation as the everything store. The theatrical logo for Amazon Studios is a case in point. The opening image of the twenty-second video is of a book opening, in which a city street pops up, the end of which features a theater with "Amazon Studios" on its marquee, thereby emphasizing Amazon's long history as a book retailer and connecting that to its newer identity as a production studio.

The inclusion of ever more, often disparate products and services within a single brand also applies to Prime, a sub-brand of Amazon that started out as a better deal on shipping for its members, but grew to encompass other benefits that include (depending on the national market you're in) streaming video, music streaming, ebook subscription, discounts at Amazon-owned Whole Foods Market, online photo storage, rewards points, and more. Prime incentivizes doing as many activities and purchases as possible under the Amazon umbrella, which not only drives increased sales, but also creates a fuller data picture of individual consumers, which drives the design of yet more products and services that create even greater incentives for Prime customers to stick with Amazon and not even consider shopping or consuming entertainment elsewhere. With the explosion of Prime, Amazon has visually associated itself with the "Prime blue" color more than its traditional black and orange. Envelopes and packing tape announce the bundle of services that come with Prime on every package (see figure 5.2).

The bundling of Prime Video, Prime Music, Prime Reading, and Prime Gaming with the Prime membership creates the impression of media content being indistinguishable from other consumer goods, even the prosaic ones many consumers have become accustomed to buying from Amazon. When Amazon's latest award-winning show is just one element of a care package supplied by Amazon when you're feeling under the weather, the content's value is positioned through how it can serve us, rather than through its inherent cultural or symbolic value. When buying consumer products through Amazon leads to deals and discounts on streaming video (as is currently the case—if a Prime member opts for slower shipping they get a credit toward the purchase or rental of digital content), media products are positioned as fungible with other fast-moving consumer goods, and Amazon presents itself as a brand flexible enough to make sense as a producer of movies and TV shows, distributor of digital entertainment, and online retailer of everything every day.

As Amazon and Prime have become associated not just with books or shipping, but with media distribution and production as well, their brand ubiquity extends to their media offerings. The term "ubiquitous media" has arisen, in critical media studies and business scholarship, to describe the pervasiveness of media technologies in our environment and, as a result, the ongoing nature of mediated consumption, as opposed to media encounters that are more bounded and discrete.[6] Chuck Tryon offers the term "platform mobility" to describe "the ongoing shift toward ubiquitous, mobile access to a wide range of entertainment choices."[7] Amazon is a platform that promises to provide consumers with a "ubiquitous media" experience defined by convenience to the user. It provides the devices that allow anytime, anywhere consumption; a wide range of media subscriptions and

5.2 Packing tape advertising services bundled with Prime. The rest of the tape on this box reads "fast, free delivery/as fast as today," "top movies & tv/unlimited streams & downloads," "keep reading/ebooks and magazines," "so much music/over 2 million songs." Photo by author.

services, from video and music to books and games; and a brand promise of abundance that suggests it is possible to consume "anything" an individual consumer might want within the platform's services.

PLATFORM MEDIA LOGICS: STREAMING AND SUBSCRIPTION

Amazon is a major player in the ongoing shift described as the streaming revolution, or the delivery of entertainment content in a continuous flow via the internet without storage on the user's device, as opposed to distribution via the airwaves, cable, or physical media. In terms of revenue models, there is a second revolution—the subscription revolution in which consumers get so-called "unlimited" access to a library of media content (often but not always uninterrupted by ads) via monthly or annually paid service. Many digital subscription services are also streaming services, such as music streaming, whereas some involve other forms of digital delivery, such as an ebook included in a subscription but accessed by digital download. The term "revolution" is widely used to describe both phenomena, even though some argue that it overstates the case. As Amanda D. Lotz points out, newspapers and magazines have long arrived on doorsteps via subscription, although the model was regular delivery of timely content rather than access to a catalogue of on-demand content.[8] While cable subscriptions also predate the streaming era, they have only relatively recently included the "on demand" element that is the bread-and-butter of asynchronous streaming services. However, the prominence of both these characteristics in the leading streaming services, be it Netflix, Spotify, Hulu, any of Amazon's subscription video, music, or live-streamed gaming services, or the more recent arrivals Apple TV+ and Disney+, combined with the rate of adoption of these services by consumers, has led to the sense that we're in the "streaming era," even if streaming has merely been added to the various other longstanding methods of media distribution.

Subscription media services conform to the platform logic of enclosure, where the value of user data biases platforms toward selling services, which involve ongoing interaction between customer and brand, and therefore an ongoing accumulation of user data—a cybernetic advantage over the one-time purchase.[9] Expanding into new services, like digital media distribution, allows a company like Amazon to collect new kinds of data about users, and incentivizes users to spend more of their consumption and leisure time within the Amazon brand. Providing access to media as a service, rather than as a product that the consumer owns, is appealing to content owners in the digital age because it protects intellectual property. If the consumer doesn't own the content, but merely streams it via subscription or rental, or even buys it for their online library, which typically means they are actually only licensing it for their (carefully circumscribed) use, intellectual property owners control the conditions under which it can be consumed, and typically restrict the ability to archive, share, or alter the content.[10] For the platform, an "owned" title in a digital library encourages users to return to the platform and keep their accounts active. Finally, for both the content owners and the streaming platforms, selling media as a service creates ongoing revenue compared to the peaks and valleys of "sales" (for both content *and* devices) that are more sensitive to the popularity of particular content and pressures on people's discretionary income.

Media via subscription is a model that Apple, for one, has shifted toward, with the spinning out of iTunes into its Apple Music, Apple Podcasts, and AppleTV+ services, which in turn have been bundled together with other services as Apple One, in an effort to create the ongoing revenue streams that even out the ups and downs of device sales, and provide an incentive to continue purchasing the Apple devices that work seamlessly with these media services.[11] The reorganization at Disney in October 2020 that consolidated distribution in a single unit suggests a greater corporate focus on distribution, particularly via subscription, driving content creation rather than the other way around, following a similar organization at WarnerMedia, which placed its business units under its streaming service HBOMax.[12]

Amazon's brand logic of personalized service is an ideal fit for the streaming era. With streaming, brands don't necessarily have to be aspirational destinations with a coherent selection of content (although some streaming brands, such as Disney+, may well be so identified), but can thrive as subscription-based services that promise a reliable consumer *experience*. Providing media as a service to the consumer means meeting the entertainment needs of a wide range of demographics and tastes. Prime Video, for example, seeks to be a destination for kids, sports fans, auto enthusiasts, and aficionados of detective fiction, action adventure, fantasy, anime, and dystopian worlds. This is a feature of most tech brands, which are characterized more by flexible ubiquity than semiotic stability or specificity.

Amazon's investments in its entertainment subscriptions are part of a broader strategy to strengthen the "moat" of bundled services available to Prime members, the idea being that the more enmeshed Prime members become in the bundled services, the less likely they are to end their memberships or turn to Amazon's competitors. Although industrialized culture has always been looked at askance by corners of the academy and the intelligentsia precisely for producing art in the service of something other than itself—in other words, for profit—pressing media and culture into the service of platform dominance represents a new chapter in the business arrangements and incentives underwriting the production of culture. While commodification, according to Marx's theorization, is the process of producing something for market exchange, in contrast, commoditization occurs when the differences among similar products stop registering with consumers. Once consumers are purchasing on the basis of price or value alone, then a product category has become thoroughly commoditized, as much as classic "commodities" like soybeans or wheat.[13] The way Amazon uses media in its business and presents its media services to consumers both commodifies *and* commoditizes media.

Tryon, for one, argues that the rise of ubiquitous, mobile media changes the "perceived concept and value of the textual artifact," rendering the audience's relationship with most texts more casual.[14] Ease and convenience of access to streaming and on-demand media, as well as the perception of abundance and limitless options, have made movie watching in particular a more "informal" activity, he argues, requiring less of a commitment from the viewer than even in the days of physical video and DVD rental.[15] Even television suffers from this "casualization," as audiences are freed from a linear schedule by the on-demand nature of digital content libraries.[16] In this context we might consider audiences more able to act on their "true" content preferences, as they become less constrained by structural factors such as content availability and the television schedule.[17] On the other hand, a subscription, especially an annual fee as most Prime members pay, represents a sunk cost that can motivate audiences to find content that is "good enough" within the services they already pay for. *New York Times* tech reporter Shira Ovide has made this exact observation, arguing that "what rules" the media landscape are platforms that "have a small amount of great stuff and lots of perfectly fine stuff, and they package it in a convenient and affordable way."[18]

Many subscription media services offer media in a thoroughly commoditized manner, promoting abundance and "value for money," while at the same time emphasizing exclusive content—the Amazon, Netflix, and Hulu originals designed to differentiate the streaming brands from one another. These marketing strategies would seem to be in tension, but in practice, are not. Tim Leslie, when serving as Amazon Vice President for Video, International, articulated how these strategies are combined, saying that in the Indian market, in order to create a "compelling value proposition," "volume will be more licensed content whereas original content will be a great differentiator."[19]

Amazon departs from some of its competitors in how it bundles its streaming services with the Prime membership, primarily identified with its retail operation. Amazon commodifies media content not always for the purpose of making money on its sale or subscriptions, but in order to recruit new consumers to Prime, or build markets for Amazon Web Services. In fact, media devices or access to media content might even be sold at a loss for this purpose, just as Amazon has sold and shipped books at a loss in order to solidify itself as a destination for books, and sold diapers at a deep discount to lure new Moms away from other retailers. While entertainment has long been used as bait to create valuable commodities, from ratings to user data, Amazon's model represents a particularly obvious instance of instrumentalizing entertainment in the service of broader platform enclosure.

STREAMING, SUBSCRIPTION, MEMBERSHIP

Amazon's history of distributing media digitally goes back farther than one might think. From 1999 to the mid-2000s, the content that Amazon customers could download was usually a "sneak peek" of some kind, like the "Look Inside the Book" feature, or free songs to sample an album that would soon be available for physical purchase. Amazon entered digital distribution of video in more than a promotional way in 2006, with the launch of Amazon Unbox, followed by the launch of Amazon MP3, a digital music store, in 2007. Until 2011, customers had the choice of "unboxing" video on Amazon with a digital download, or streaming if they had an appropriate device. Rebranded as Amazon Video On Demand in 2008, and then Amazon Instant Video in 2011, the "Unbox" option was phased out by 2015 in favor of a streaming-only service, soon to be followed by the addition of Prime Instant Video where Prime members could access a subset of more than five thousand Amazon Instant Video titles for free as part of their membership. The selection expanded rapidly as Amazon entered into licensing agreements with more studios.

While Amazon got into the video on demand game fairly early in 2006, just one year after iTunes started offering video and the launch of YouTube, Amazon was hardly an early mover in the *subscription* video on demand world, with Netflix having rolled out their service on top of DVD rental by mail in 2007, and Hulu launching its subscription service in 2010 after running an ad-supported service since 2008. Amazon's lateness to subscription on demand, for both video (2011) and music (2014), makes sense when you consider that digital sales initially built on Amazon's existing business selling physical books, CDs, and DVDs. As the initial Amazon Unbox brand communicated, the digital purchase would merely be the electronic equivalent of "unboxing" a physical DVD.

With the introduction of Amazon Instant Video and Prime Instant Video in 2011, both rebranded as "Prime Video" by 2018, Amazon's video streaming service could best be described as a "hybrid TVOD/ SVOD portal," according to Ramon Lobato's categorization of the "distribution ecology" of streaming services.[20] With TVOD, or transactional video on demand, users purchase or rent a specific piece of content, while SVOD, or subscription video on demand, offers a "curated library of content for a monthly subscription fee."[21] To complicate things further, Amazon is a platform for standalone streaming subscriptions rooted in broadcast and cable TV channels, such as Starz, Showtime, BritBox, and PBS Masterpiece. One might even say that Amazon's branding and organization of streaming content is a mess. Amazon's own definition of the Prime Video brand is far from succinct: "Prime Video delivers exclusive Prime Originals and thousands of other popular titles included with Prime, plus premium channel subscriptions, titles available to rent or buy, live events, and more."[22]

Similarly, the changing brand names and logos over the years for Amazon's digital video services would seem to break a cardinal rule of branding: consistency. In its Prime Video branding guidelines, the company acknowledges, "We've used many brands to communicate aspects of our service over the years, which resulted in customer confusion of who we are and how our offerings work."[23] Even with the Prime Video rebrand (or Amazon Prime Video in most markets outside the United States), the service remains relatively complex. But the mess doesn't seem to have hurt Amazon's streaming video initiatives. One of the advantages that ecommerce has is the ability to incrementally move into a new business, something that Amazon is particularly well positioned to do because it is so highly capitalized, with a huge consumer base it can essentially experiment on to see what sticks with a new product or service, especially when Prime members don't have to actively opt into or pay for it.

Amazon operates hybrid on demand models not just in video, but across content areas. Music can be purchased as MP3, Prime Music entitles Prime members to a limited library of music for streaming, or consumers can subscribe to Amazon Music Unlimited to access a wider array of songs. In the Kindle store consumers can purchase an ebook, Prime members can digitally borrow limited titles through Prime Reading, while Kindle Unlimited members can borrow a much larger library with that subscription. Amazon has even ventured into AVOD (Advertising-supported Video On Demand) with the free Amazon Music subscription launched in November 2019, and a free ad-supported video-streaming service branded IMDb TV in 2019, whose titles can also be accessed via Prime Video listings. Moving into ad-supported streaming video is on trend with other brands responding to consumers' saturation with subscriptions.

For Amazon, and for fellow platforms like Apple and Alphabet, its digital media distribution services reside within a larger set of business activities. As such, they play an instrumental role in the company's larger consumer loyalty and consumer data business models. While content has long served as "bait" to deliver audiences to advertisers, the *way* that culture functions as bait shifts with streaming as a technology and subscription as a revenue model. Karen Petruska articulates this, writing, "All of Amazon's Prime benefits serve one end: to situate customers within its corporate ecosystem more fully, firmly, and inescapably. . . . Its use of media as a lure for consumer purchases extends potential critical suspicion about the commercialization of culture. . . . As part of the Amazon Prime package, TV content, too, functions as a widget."[24] Whether Prime Video, for example, persuades people who are on the fence about their Prime membership to stay—in other words, a customer loyalty driver—or whether it sucks people into Prime memberships who might not have bothered otherwise, Prime Video—along with Amazon's other digital media services—plays a supporting role within the larger operation.

With a slightly higher price point (in the United States at least) and, in its early days, fewer blockbuster titles than Netflix to lure new subscribers, the bundling of Prime Video with the Prime membership was key to Amazon quickly establishing itself as a contender in the streaming marketplace. (The same appears to be true for Amazon Music, which has grown rapidly and is closing in on Apple Music's listenership numbers.)[25] Indeed, the influence goes both ways, with one former Amazon executive observing that the growth of Prime membership was fairly weak until Prime Video was bundled into it in 2011.[26] Prime Reading also plays a role in keeping consumers hooked on the membership. Amazon Publishing's focus on authors in genre fiction who write series or multiple titles on a theme reflects their desire to hook and keep fans of these authors and genres within the ecosystem.[27]

Estimates of Prime Video's viewership relative to its major competitors (of subscription-based streaming video services) place it as the United States' number three subscription video service as of this writing, behind Netflix and Disney+, although ahead of Disney+ in terms of subscriptions if not estimated users of the video service.[28] The fact that Prime Video is "struggling" in national markets where it isn't bundled with a free shipping offer or other Prime member benefits suggests how important the bundle has been to the success of the service.[29] A Morgan Stanley report from 2017 indicates that Prime Video is a major reason that people sign up for the membership in countries where it is bundled (see figure 5.3),[30] a pattern also observed in India, where Prime memberships jumped substantially in the six months after the launch of Prime Video.[31] Former Amazon VP Tim Leslie touted Amazon India's launch of Prime Video in terms

Prime Video Is a Popular Reason Why Shoppers Sign Up for Prime in the UK, Germany, and Japan

What is the main reason for having an Amazon Prime membership? (% answered "Prime Instant Video")

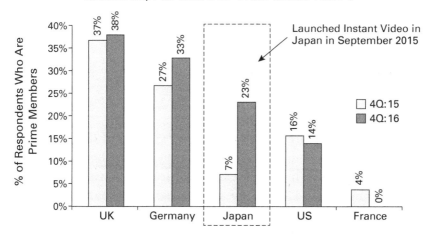

5.3 Main reason for having an Amazon Prime membership. With permission of Morgan Stanley Research.

of the value it would offer Indian Prime customers: "We think that Prime Video is something consumers are going to want to watch because it's a web service they have. And what is even more compelling is that for Rs499 a year, which means they are going to watch for Rs41 a month, it's an incredibly compelling offer, the best deal in video streaming and the best deal in shopping in India."[32] This price was judged by the news organization publishing this report, relative to other streaming services and ways of accessing video content, to be "too ridiculously low to not subscribe."[33]

While on the one hand the major and emerging streaming services are throwing enormous amounts of money into creating original programming—in 2020, an estimated $16 billion for Netflix and $7 billion for Amazon—in order to generate buzzworthy exclusives that convince viewers to sign up and stay, the services also use the rich data at their disposal to make cost-benefit analyses about whether these programs are worth the expense.[34] A 2017 Amazon report leaked by Reuters estimates that Amazon's top shows converted five million people into Prime members between 2014 and 2017, or a quarter of all the new memberships in that period, and features a table calculating the cost per "first stream" of shows by new Prime customers.[35] Essentially, when someone signs up for Prime the analysis notes which Amazon Original they stream first, as a measure of the role that individual programs play in recruiting new members. The costs varied widely, from $49 per first stream for Season 1 of *The Grand Tour*, a reality-based show with an existing global fan base, to $1,560 for feminist period drama *Good Girls Revolt*, which was canceled after one season.[36] So much for the theory that, unlike broadcast and cable, streaming services will support shows for every audience niche, even small ones, as long as it recruits them to subscribe.

The value of new Prime members can be calculated in a number of ways, from the revenue that comes from the membership itself, to estimates of how much more Prime members spend on Amazon on average than nonmembers—$1,400 per year compared to $600 according to independent industry estimates.[37] Jeff Bezos has not been shy in articulating the role of Prime Video's original programming in his larger business, acknowledging to one interviewer that his efforts in media were indeed aimed at recruiting new members to Prime.[38] As he said at a technology conference in 2016, "When we win a Golden Globe, it helps us sell more shoes."[39] On the heels of the series *Transparent's* multiple Emmy wins in 2015, Amazon even offered for a limited time a steep discount on new Prime memberships to take advantage of the visibility and prestige boost to recruit new Prime members.[40] As Jeff Wilke, Amazon CEO of Global Consumer put it, "So what we find is that customers who watch a movie that they love, they buy more Tide. They shop more, they're more likely to renew their Prime subscription, they're more likely to convert a free trial into a monthly or annual Prime subscription. So video viewers are telling us with their actions that video is an important part of the Prime experience."[41] In other words, using the Prime Video service makes the Prime membership stickier for consumers, and the Prime membership in turn is central to Amazon's ecommerce dominance.

RETAIL BRAND, MEDIA BRAND

In the words of entrepreneur and NYU marketing professor Scott Galloway, "Can you imagine Macy's saying they were starting a media company? People wouldn't take it seriously. But Amazon does it and becomes successful."[42] The conventional wisdom Galloway invokes is that being a retail brand is an obstacle to transitioning to a media brand. The perceived skill sets and the nature of the relationship with the consumer are too different across the business areas. But as an ecommerce company with a history of book retailing and investments in media properties, such as the Internet Movie Database (IMDb), Amazon enjoys particular advantages. There is great potential for product marketing synergies with video streaming, even ad-free streaming, that are still emerging. Amazon has an interactive feature across its digital music, TV, movie, and book services called "X-Ray." In the case of TV and movies, X-Ray syncs video content to the IMDb database, which allows viewers streaming on computers or compatible devices (including Amazon Fire tablets and Fire TV, naturally) to see information about the cast, crew, and soundtrack of what is on screen, including quick links to albums and singles available on Amazon itself (see figure 5.4).

5.4 X-Ray view of episode 1, season 2 of *The Marvelous Mrs. Maisel*. Thumbnails of the actors appearing in the scene link to their IMDb profiles. The bottom X-Ray result, the song "Just Leave Everything to Me" by Barbra Streisand, provides the option of clicking to the album in Amazon Music. Screenshot by author.

X-Ray technology gauges audience interest in elements of the content they are consuming and directs them to related content on Amazon. A 2012 press release announcing the service for movies put it in just these terms: "Didn't realize that the actress playing Katniss Everdeen also starred in *Winter's Bone*, a movie you've been meaning to watch? With X-Ray for Movies, Kindle Fire owners can simply tap to see other movies that include the actors on-screen, another tap adds it to their Watchlist—all without ever leaving their current movie."[43]

X-Ray originated on the Kindle, as a reference tool for ebooks that would allow readers to access dictionary definitions and reference materials without leaving the Kindle application. Upon its launch, Amazon explained, "With a single tap, readers can see all the passages across a book that mention ideas, fictional characters, historical figures, places or topics that interest them, as well as more detailed descriptions from Wikipedia and Shelfari, Amazon's community-powered encyclopedia for book lovers."[44] *Guardian* reporter Kari Paul who, thanks to the California Consumer Privacy Act, was able to request all the data Amazon had about her, was most disturbed by the spreadsheets tracking not just everything Paul had read on the Kindle, when, and for how long, but a detailed accounting of what she had highlighted and searched for within the texts.[45] As small business advocate Stacy Mitchell points out, it's not just what you read that could be informative to Amazon, but the speed and manner in which you read it.[46] It's easy to imagine how these insights could be used to inform not just book production and marketing, but also marketing for other products and services to readers.

X-Ray can also make screen entertainment "shoppable," meaning that audiences can immediately purchase items they see on a show. The dream of shoppable TV is longstanding, with previous efforts in the industry ranging from program websites where products featured in shows can be purchased, to the use of the remote control to make product purchases through the cable provider, to QR codes on the screen that take users straight to a product page on their mobile device.[47] While media brands for decades tried to extend themselves into retail (with the exception of home shopping networks, with limited success),[48] streaming technology has made the opposite extension, from retail brand to media brand, seem feasible. Retail giants like Walmart and Costco have, in recent years, recognized the advantage of being a retailer in the media space, especially as "shoppable TV," including shoppable ads, becomes technologically feasible.[49] In the end, Costco may not develop its own streaming service, and Walmart sold Vudu to Fandango in 2020.[50] But in Amazon, we see the natural marketing advantage of a retailer combined with the investment capital of a tech giant.

It's this deep well of capital that has helped Prime Video put itself on the map by investing in high-quality, prestige content like the award-winning series *Transparent* (2014–2019), *Mozart in the Jungle* (2014–2018), and *The Marvelous Mrs. Maisel* (2017–) as well as prestige pictures like *Manchester-by-the-Sea* (2016) and *The Big Sick* (2017). These titles are award worthy, appealing to critics, and innovative each in their own way. But observers detect more commercial concerns influencing many other Amazon Studios productions. From programs based on the Wizard of Oz books, to extensions of well-known children's titles like *Rocky and Bullwinkle*, *Pete the Cat*, and *Kung Fu Panda*, the *All or Nothing* reality-based series with well-known sports teams, *Bosch* (based on Michael Connelly's book series), *Tom Clancy's Jack Ryan*, and *The Grand Tour* (an iteration of the former BBC show *Top Gear*), to the forthcoming *Lord of the Rings* and *Jack Reacher* series, most of Amazon's production, licensing, and development deals are less "original" than proprietary iterations on stories, people, and brands that are known quantities, often linked to products people are already buying from Amazon.

Building on existing intellectual properties has the dual virtue of making a new show easy to promote, and for certain kinds of productions, particularly reality-based shows or programs set in an aspirational present, facilitating product placement and branded tie-ins. While this has long been true for televisual entertainment, the distance from show to related retail sales on Amazon is that much shorter. While Amazon, like other streaming companies, draws on its viewer data to inform production decisions and recommendation systems, it has the added advantage of being able to draw from viewing data, shopping data, and even user search behavior on its retail platform. Amazon's slate of originals, then, can be understood through the lenses of both "algorithmic culture" and product tie-ins, be those products specific entertainment titles like books (e.g., *Pete the Cat*, *Jack Reacher*) or whole product categories (e.g., *The Grand Tour* and Amazon's automotive store).[51]

In March 2020, Amazon Studios' *Making the Cut* starring and executive-produced by Heidi Klum and Tim Gunn premiered on Prime Video. In this program, we see several ways that Amazon's production efforts are married to its competitive strategies and business goals. The show has a built-in audience from a preexisting cultural property, in this case, *Project Runway* which Klum and Gunn cohosted on cable for sixteen seasons. Check. The show has a global sensibility, to maximize its appeal in the 240-plus countries where Prime Video is available, as emphasized from the show's opening location in Paris, the international (yet still US-heavy) cast of judges and designers, as well as the series of episodes set in Tokyo (see figure 5.5).[52] Check. *Making the Cut* complements a product category that Amazon currently is investing in heavily—fashion. Check. And beyond even these standard considerations for corporate synergy, this fashion competition reality show generates original designs that are immediately available for sale on Amazon's online retail store. As Heidi Klum put it, "For the first time, finally, our audience can shop. . . . [Normally you] see something, you want it, but you can't have it. So here, you have a winning look every week and people can buy it around the world."[53]

Although Amazon's X-Ray has typically been used to facilitate research on actors or music, with *Making the Cut* a link appears during the program to the Making the Cut Store where viewers can "shop the look," and once the winning look has been revealed, it also appears in a thumbnail viewers can click on to buy it. While it's not unusual for shows to sell related merchandise on their websites—rival fashion reality show *Project Runway* also sells winning looks through a retail partner's website—it is a powerful step in the direction of truly "shoppable TV" to be able to click on that look from the very screen you are viewing on, and buy it through a company already well known for ecommerce. By making content interactive, X-Ray is one step beyond the broader advantage that streaming services have in the real-time data commodities they can gather about viewing. The head of Amazon Studios, Jennifer Salke, revealed that "her division worked closely with Amazon Fashion on 'Making the Cut' and that there could be similar commercial collaborations on other shows."[54] With Amazon having a major connected TV platform with Fire TV, as well as its own ad-supported streaming service IMDb TV, the possibility

CREDIT: JESSICA FORDE/AMAZON STUDIOS

5.5 Promotional image for *Making the Cut* (2020). Photo by Jessica Forde/Amazon Studios.

of X-Ray being used to make ads themselves directly shoppable looms on the horizon.

Making the Cut exemplifies a consumer-focused, service mentality in more ways than one. The show aims to distinguish itself from *Project Runway* by defining its mission as finding the "next big global fashion brand." Each week designers produce a high-fashion or couture look, as well as an "accessible look" that appears in the *Making the Cut* Amazon store if it wins. As contestants became winnowed down, the question of "good design" relative to "being a global brand" accessible to the Amazon consumer started to come into tension. (Spoiler alert—competition results ahead!)

The finale saw a runway show with full collections from season favorite and Berlin-based designer Esther Perbandt and LA-based designer Jonny Cota, who saw a surge in wins in the latter part of the competition. The judging panel appeared to struggle with choosing a winner, and had to return to the show's mantra of finding the "next global fashion brand" to steer them in the direction of the more commercial, accessible designer—Cota—even though Perbandt's designs actually impressed them more. Counting against Perbandt were her inability to move much beyond an all-black color palette for her collection (which she was often reminded doesn't translate well online) and more avant-garde looks that consumers ultimately might not be ready for.

Making the Cut takes Amazon's guiding philosophy of customer obsession and dramatizes it in the form of unscripted entertainment. Every challenge and judging decision on the show is shaped by what creatives and executives think will please the consumer and keep their attention. The gradual disciplining of experimental design aesthetics from week to week recall the hewing to proven formula long documented in studies of commercial cultural production. Novelty and distinctiveness are prized, but only within a limited distance from the familiar. Providing service and pleasure to the consumer is serious business on *Making the Cut*, to the tune of a $1 million cash prize to the winner. Encapsulated in this highly produced show is a story that Amazon could just as easily be telling about itself.

TWITCH: DIFFERENT, BUT THE SAME

While most of Amazon's media content and streaming initiatives are home-grown, the company has made some key acquisitions in this area: IMDb, the Internet Movie Database in 1998, the UK's DVD rental and streaming business Lovefilm in 2011, and Twitch in 2014. While Lovefilm was swallowed up by Prime Video, IMDb and Twitch continued under their own brand names, their connection to Amazon conceivably unnoticed by many users. Twitch in particular brought something quite new to Amazon's portfolio—a highly social content platform. Twitch is a livestreaming platform with a focus on gaming, which means that people stream their game play while their fans and subscribers watch, react, and interact with the host in real time. As explained by games scholar T. L. Taylor, Twitch has pioneered "a new form of *networked* broadcast" (italics in original).[55] Beyond this primary usage, Twitch has moved into streaming e-sports (multiplayer video game) competitions and concerts, as well as more general-interest channels such as "real-life" streams (calling to mind some of the earliest user-generated content, the Jennicam, famously discussed by Mark Andrejevic).[56]

The user-generated, networked nature of Twitch is something of a departure for Amazon, which unlike fellow tech giants like Facebook and Google, has not dabbled much in "social." While there is a social aspect to Amazon's reviewing spaces on its ecommerce site, as well as its acquisition Goodreads, which builds communities arounds books and reading, the main focus of Twitch is community building between livestreamers and followers, as well as connections among users. As it is put on Twitch's website, "Twitch is where millions of people come together live every day to chat, interact, and make their own entertainment together."[57] Similarly, while Amazon has long included amateur content producers on its distribution platforms, through Kindle Direct Publishing, for example, or Prime Video Direct, where independent producers can share their video or even gaming content via Amazon's platform, Twitch takes user-generated content as its main focus. Twitch is entirely identified with connecting amateur gaming livestreamers and other live content producers to audiences who can then be monetized.

That monetization happens in three ways; first of all, by subscription. While Twitch users can follow and watch channels for free, they can also subscribe to specific livestreamers, which serves as a form of recurring support for favorite content creators and also unlocks a variety of perks and features on that channel that facilitate participation and interaction.[58] Users can also get a Prime Gaming subscription that bundles a free Twitch channel subscription with access to other Twitch content and perks, and a selection of PC games. This subscription knits Twitch users into the Amazon universe because Prime Gaming is included with Prime and Prime Video memberships, although the user has to actively sign up for it if they already have one of these memberships.[59] While it's possible to subscribe to Twitch channels without an Amazon membership, certain benefits and features within Twitch are exclusive to users who link their Amazon and Twitch accounts.[60] Twitch, then, drives new audiences into the broader Amazon universe of Prime, where the built-in bundling serves as an incentive to use Prime retail and media services rather than those of competitors.

The second revenue form, so common in gaming spaces, is microtransactions. In Twitch, followers can buy "bits" that they can then use to "cheer" the livestreamer on their channel. Finally, there are ads run on channels that livestreamers with enough subscribers can earn a share of revenue from. Unlike many of Amazon's streaming/subscription services, Twitch is also advertisement supported, a feature that was already established on the platform before Amazon's acquisition. The spot advertising format, where the livestream is interrupted for the ad, is appealing to advertisers because of both the liveness of the format—ads can be delivered to a more "captive" audience—and Twitch's much sought-after demographic that skews young and male.[61] While a Twitch Prime membership once facilitated ad-free livestreaming for users, that feature was phased out in 2018 due to the importance of advertising, and presumably also the particular value to its revenue model of Prime members about whom Amazon has so much data. Now Twitch users who want an ad-free experience must subscribe to Twitch Turbo, which is not integrated into any Amazon services.[62]

Twitch complements Amazon's forays into media distribution, extending its investments in live sports streaming into e-sports and adding a platform focused on live audiences to its portfolio of options for advertisers. Twitch also complements Amazon's efforts to grow its own games division, a longstanding project that has had considerable trouble getting off the ground, despite significant investment in blockbuster games that have consistently flopped.[63] As Twitch's audience grows and the types of livestreaming extend into content beyond gaming, the possibilities for using Twitch for data harvesting about users, as well as placing ads and creating synergies for Amazon's other intellectual properties and services, make this platform an important component of Amazon's media streaming portfolio. At the same time, the livestreaming format perfected on Twitch has been adopted by Amazon for Amazon Live, a relatively new section of its retail site that features livestreams for both Amazon products as well as by brands that sell on Amazon, a platform called Amazon

Live Creator. Just like on Twitch, the appeal is not only the hosts display-ing and providing information about new products, but also the engage-ment of audiences watching in real time, sending emojis that fly up the screen, leaving messages in the chat, or notices of purchases that hosts can respond to. Although launched recently, in 2019, and still in develop-ment, Amazon Live signals the company's move into a more truly social advertainment space.

PROMOTING MEDIA AS A SERVICE

Just as Amazon aims for ubiquity as a brand, so do its subscription services aim to make media ubiquitous. The elements of media ubiquity that Ama-zon wants to impress upon its users are convenience, abundance, and the ability to consume it anywhere, all themes in Amazon's promotional mes-saging about Prime Video.

CONVENIENCE

When Prime Video was introduced to American consumers in a short video spot in 2015 as a benefit of Prime membership, the ad emphasized having "thousands of movies and TV episodes" to choose from when you wanted to relax by yourself or with family members. Access to this content was presented as a way "to do more with Amazon Prime today."[64] The ad ends with the Amazon box on the doorstep, placing video stream-ing as just one of the "little things" that the Prime membership takes care of for Prime members, with free package delivery being the most salient. While the ad mentioned some of Prime Video's better-known originals at the time like *Transparent* and *Bosch*, its primary message from its explicit and implicit elements was the convenience of having this video service as part of the membership. Another ad from 2015 conveys the same basic message but in a goofier way—a thirty-second stage musical announcing the addition of streaming movies to the Prime membership called "More to Prime" featured singing delivery workers and dancing figures made entirely out of Amazon boxes.[65] Emphasizing convenience and the sheer volume of media available may not be an inspiring strategy for a media brand, and yet, it's been an effective one.

Similarly, when Amazon introduced Prime Video to India in 2016 it emphasized not just the volume of titles that would be available to stream, but also the convenience of an on-demand service that could be consumed on multiple devices in multiple locations. In the 2017 "India Ka Naya Primetime" campaign, Indian viewers met a young couple named Rohan and Roshni who enjoy the convenience and mobility of "anytime, anywhere" video provided by Prime Video, whether watching on a mobile phone on a park bench, accepting a dinner invitation from one of their mothers making their favorite dish, knowing they can bring the movie with them on their mobile phone, or staying at a party with a friend who was going to go home to watch a movie, until learning that with Prime Video you can "Watch the Latest Entertainment, Anytime, Anywhere." As Rajdeepak Das, Chief Creative Officer of Leo Burnett, South Asia, put it, "Through its slice-of-life execution, we wanted viewers to know it is easy to bid the shackles of traditional 'primetime' goodbye."[66] In this campaign, the "liberating" value of this convenience is emphasized by Rohan who declares he will no longer be a "ghulam" (slave or servant) to a screen (bearing in mind that the campaign's slavery metaphors would resonate differently in India than in the United States). Indeed, it is Amazon, via Prime Video, that promises to serve.

ABUNDANCE

With subscription logic, there is a prominent argument about "value for money" in terms of the abundance of movies, TV shows, songs, or book titles that consumers will be able to access for a monthly fee. In the streaming era we've become accustomed to media companies selling us content *by volume* more than with previous types of revenue models—in other words, commoditizing culture.

When it comes to media services, an abundance of content is also what makes it convenient (so central to Amazon's brand promise), because it promises so many choices that any user will be able to find content that appeals to them. Amazon conveys the idea of abundance in a number of ways, by touting the thousands (of video titles) or millions (of song titles) available through its subscription services and by visually creating the impression of options that are "endless" on its content menus. Even the names of some of the standalone subscription services, "Amazon Music Unlimited" and "Kindle Unlimited" unequivocally communicate abundance, with plan details promising access to "tens of millions" of songs and over one million books and thousands of audiobook titles. Scholars have noted that the extent of the content abundance is often exaggerated by distribution platforms like Amazon's, and that interfaces are invariably designed to make inspection of the content catalogue as a whole impossible, thereby preserving the illusion of never-ending choices.[67]

If it was only a matter of volume, then everyone would just gravitate toward the cheapest monthly subscription for the greatest volume of titles in any given content category. The differentiating factors are the user experience and access to exclusive content. It does matter that the interface be user friendly and the streaming be high quality. Netflix's willingness to invest in streaming quality has been identified as an important part of the reason for its quick rise to dominance.[68] This is no doubt a factor in Amazon's success across streaming categories as well. Amazon was early on the curve in offering HDR (high-dynamic range) and high-resolution 4K streaming video, and these features as well as low-latency streaming even for high-demand live events like *Thursday Night Football* are facilitated by its AWS infrastructure.[69] AWS provides computing and cloud infrastructure for many of the major streaming services with which it competes, including for at least part of Netflix and Hulu's services. Industry observers attribute Amazon's purchase of Twitch in part to the synergy between the cloud computing needed to livestream gaming to large audiences and Amazon Web Services' cloud capacity, with all of Twitch's content except the video infrastructure now running on AWS.[70] In fact, a now-abandoned video game from Amazon Studios, Project Nova, reportedly was meant to be a showcase for the computing power of AWS through its ability to support "10,000 players duking it out on one server."[71]

Although Amazon's media subscriptions are marketed in terms of their abundant content, exclusivity is also part of the messaging in order to differentiate from competitors. When it comes to exclusivity, things vary across content categories. Although Amazon is not widely known for original music, it has in fact released music recorded specifically for Amazon (often for Prime Video Originals) and offered it as a digital exclusive and for free, typically, on Prime Music. Although the vast majority of Amazon

Publishing titles are sold on Amazon's retail site and especially as ebooks in its Kindle store, this is only partially to do with Amazon enforcing exclusivity, which they typically only do through a windowing method, such as giving Prime members exclusive access for a month before a new, high-profile book is released. Most book retailers refuse to carry Amazon Publishing titles in an effort to push back against the company's cut-throat business practices and slow Amazon's vertical integration in the book business, making most Amazon titles unintentional exclusives.[72] However, Kindle Direct Publishing, Amazon's self-publishing platform, does incentivize self-publishing authors to enroll in KDP Select for ebooks sold as intentional exclusives on Amazon, offering a higher royalty rate in a number of its biggest national markets, as well as inclusion in the Kindle Unlimited and Kindle Owner's Lending Library programs—both ways for new authors to get their books in front of readers.[73]

Original, exclusive content has become an important differentiating logic in the video streaming marketplace, creating scarcity in the face of an increasingly commoditized media environment characterized by choice and abundance. While leading streaming services negotiate exclusive streaming deals for some content, the deals aren't permanent. True exclusivity, and a genuine sense of scarcity, come only from originals that the services can maintain as exclusives if they so choose. Although the term "original" has become rather slippery, representing a variety of production, acquisition, and licensing arrangements, it signals to consumers that certain titles currently, and even into the foreseeable future, will only be available to subscribers.[74] While Amazon turned to producing its own content to create exclusive originals along with some individual acquisitions, in 2021 it acquired MGM Studios in order to substantially build its library of exclusive and well-known entertainment titles (and intellectual properties that can be further developed) that go back decades.[75]

And yet, the originals themselves are also presented in terms of abundance. American promotional ads for Prime Video in 2019–2020, for example, quickly juxtapose a dizzying array of well-known actors and intriguing moments from across its original programming, set to upbeat tunes.[76] A similar format was used for ads presenting new and returning Amazon Originals to Indian audiences in 2020.[77] A spot that aired during the US 2019 Primetime Emmy Awards proclaimed that "Amazon Originals Are Made by Artists, Visionaries, Legends." Editing together short pieces of dialogue from various Amazon Original series, the ad asks "Would you like to see it" "See what?" "Everything."[78] Even for Amazon's originals, which exist to make claims for Prime Video's distinctiveness and exclusivity, it's still important to convey that the exclusive content is, itself, abundant.

EVERYTHING, EVERYWHERE

Being a flexible retail-based brand has also enabled Amazon to move into devices, the gateways to Amazon's "ecosystem" that make media seem ubiquitous by being accessible as people move throughout their day—Tryon's "platform mobility." While Lobato characterizes Prime Video itself as a "loss leader" for the larger Amazon business, we might also add to that category the personal electronics that Amazon has been producing since it released the Kindle in 2007.[79] The Kindle was a piece of hardware providing access to a large library of digital texts, including books, magazines, and newspapers, which consumers could buy and download "in sixty seconds" to a user-friendly and print-reminiscent interface. The titles available for download increased rapidly in the coming years, and the Kindle (which quickly evolved through multiple versions and generations) was rarely absent from the top of the Amazon homepage, as a scan over time on the Internet Archive's Wayback Machine makes apparent. It soon became "the most wished for, the most gifted, and the #1 bestselling product" on the site.[80]

While the first Kindle sold in 2007 for $399.99, the price rapidly fell; in 2019 you could buy a low-end Kindle for less than a quarter of that price. The Kindle is frequently sold at cost or at a loss due to the ongoing value of the Kindle customer to Amazon, in terms of purchased Kindle downloads, Kindle Unlimited subscriptions, and Prime memberships.[81] Just as Amazon has done with the Kindle, so it has done with the Fire line of tablets and smart TV technologies, as well as the Echo smart speakers. According to Bezos in his 2012 letter to shareholders, "Our business approach is to sell premium hardware at roughly breakeven prices. We want to make money when people use our devices—not when people buy our devices. . . . We can be very happy to see people still using four-year-old Kindles!" The devices, then, are the "bait" for the digital content, which in turn plays its role as "bait" for Prime.

CONCLUSION—MEDIA AS A SERVICE

Amazon links its convenience as a brand to its media offerings, especially via the Prime membership. It aims to make media more ubiquitous in people's lives through the ease of access afforded by its devices, AI voice technology, and content subscriptions bundled with the Prime membership. Amazon's approach of offering media as a service subtly shapes the meaning of media and entertainment. Rather than something special that we seek out, media now comes to us and we're encouraged to see it as something enjoyable and "good enough." Just as Amazon as a service brand seeks to solve ever more problems, and even make more decisions for its customers based on how well it "knows us," so do its media services set out to solve our entertainment and "free time" problems for us. (Indeed, the content subscription for Amazon's Fire Kids Tablets is called "Freetime.") Amazon's media subscription services invite the media consumer to embrace the served self and relax into the convenience of its bundled or upgraded "unlimited" subscription services for their entertainment needs. Whether that actually is the case is another question. The fact that Americans have, on average, three video streaming subscriptions and are starting to report "subscription fatigue" suggests that, in fact, Amazon and other streaming services have had limited success in rendering all audiences passive and happy to settle into being a "served self," at least for media products.[82]

Along with companies like Netflix, Hulu, and more established producers like HBO and Disney, Amazon competes for subscriptions with eye-popping budgets and top-shelf talent, thereby contributing to the second "golden age" of television, or "peak TV." At the same time, Amazon conceptualizes and often presents media as a commodity, a product that will keep consumers walking through its virtual doors, and with enough selection, satisfied enough to stick with their Prime memberships. In terms of culture serving as "bait" within a platform logic, Amazon is leading the charge. It sells the digital devices to access Amazon-distributed digital entertainment at cost or even a loss, and bundles entertainment into a larger "store membership" that is key to Amazon's growing market dominance. Amazon's entertainment offerings play multiple strategic roles for its platform business, from bolstering the perceived value of its Prime membership, to creating compelling spaces for advertising products, to creating new spaces for data extraction and enclosure.

Emphasizing the convenience of Prime Video might seem to contradict the simultaneous focus on Amazon Originals and exclusive content, which rests on the notion that media content is *special* and fundamentally not exchangeable or replaceable. Amazon can, and is, marketing Prime Video and its other media services in both ways—as a commoditized value proposition, and as an irreplaceable destination for exclusive content— because like so many things in the narrow-casted world of digital promotion, it doesn't have to have a singular brand message. The best route to market capture is to be many things to many people, and while that was difficult in a broadcast world defined by product-style brand marketing, in a subscription-based world fueled by service-brand marketing, it is both possible and desirable.

IMAGE

6

AMAZON.AMAZON: NORMALIZING MONOPOLY

In 2019, Amazon was awarded the .amazon top-level domain by the International Corporation for Names and Numbers, or ICANN, the non-profit organization that performs one of the few centralized tasks on the internet—assigning domain names and IP addresses. Amazon had applied for .amazon in 2012, a year after top-level domains—the part of a web address that appears at its end like ".com" or ".org"—became available for sale to private businesses.[1] But South American countries whose territories encompass the Amazon River basin raised objections, saying that "granting exclusive rights . . . to a private company would prevent the use of this domain for purposes of public interest related to the protection, promotion and awareness raising on issues related to the Amazon biome."[2] The countries of the Amazon River basin wanted to protect future business opportunities pertaining to tourism and have meaningful oversight over how .amazon would be combined with any terms reflecting on the culture and heritage of their region.[3] After negotiations, Amazon's proposal to use .amazon included awarding specific domain names to each Amazonian country, pledging that the company would not use "terms that have a primary and well-recognized significance to the culture and heritage of the Amazonia region," and blocking from its own use an additional 1,500 domain names that "have a primary and well recognized significance to the culture and heritage of the Amazonia region."[4] While countries from the region continued to object that not having an equal say in the awarding of future domain names undermined their sovereignty, ICANN concluded that enough time had passed for the two sides to reach an agreement, and awarded Amazon the top-level domain.

Amazon's doggedness in winning the rights to .amazon speaks to the importance of naming and labeling in its efforts to build and control its brand. When Jeff Bezos selected the name Amazon for his new online bookselling company in the 1990s, he picked it in no small part because of its associations with the Amazon River, one of the largest geological features on the planet. Just as the Amazon River can be seen from space, so did Bezos intend that his company should achieve global scale and significance—"Earth's biggest bookstore" was its early tagline. As early press releases described it, "Amazon.com's name pays homage to the Amazon River. Just as the Amazon River is more than six times the size of the next largest river in the world, Amazon.com's catalog is more than six times the size of the largest conventional bookstore."[5] Through metaphor, the company's name invites consumers to fill in the assumptions that make Amazon's brand argument for it: if this online bookseller shares something in common with the Amazon River then, we are to infer, it has tremendous reach and power. If Amazon is like the Amazon, it is part of the natural world, and therefore we can take it as a given.

Just as Amazon's name makes claims to its reach, power, and naturalness through metaphor, so do other terms used by and about Amazon make implicit arguments about the company. As Tarleton Gillespie has pointed out, even the term "platform" is a metaphor implying that certain kinds of digital companies are mere foundations upon which other actors build and create, rather than institutions with the power to structure interaction, creativity, and commerce.[6]

Metaphors that draw on nature are rampant in tech, from the very name of the World Wide *Web*, to *streaming* content online, to storage of data not on our hard drives or in enormous data centers but in the *cloud*. Mél Hogan notes the persistence of water-based metaphors describing the internet and the "oceans" of data wrought by it. From "upstream" networking, "surfing" the web, "streaming" media, and data "flows," to "phishing" attacks, "pirating" and "torrenting" software, and the "deep web," "the web can easily be conferred as liquid; flowing not simply as water but as an untamed ocean."[7] Mark Andrejevic and Hogan both point to the vagueness of the term "cloud" (also a water-based metaphor)—the way it encourages us to imagine our data being everywhere and yet nowhere.[8] Vincent Mosco comments on "the clash between the banality of [data centers]—low-rise, endlessly bland warehouses—and the sublimity of real clouds."[9]

The cloud metaphor appears to originate in the mid-twentieth-century tracing tools used by computer programmers to visually diagram their programs and networks.[10] The cloud shape symbolized the inner workings of network architecture, such as cables, routers, and switches, that weren't necessary to understand the overall design of the network. Therefore, this symbol's imprecision was an intentional part of its origins,[11] and continues to function as a distraction from the fact that the move to cloud computing, where we access data and software via the internet rather than a hard drive or local server, has involved a significant shift in control, from users to cloud operators. In contrast to the vagueness and naturalizing force of the term "cloud," Andrejevic counters with the term "digital enclosure" as a more accurate, if still somewhat metaphorical term.[12]

In its consumer-facing communications, Amazon, like many of its competitors in tech, favors naturalistic, ecological metaphors like ecosystem and cloud. These metaphors equating Amazon and its services to elements in the natural world normalize the company's scale and ubiquity. Its Fire line of personal electronics is consistent with the Amazon brand name in its invocation of the power of nature. In internal communications and commentary on the company in the business world, however, other metaphors conjure humans' power *over* land and, by extension, over people. The images of building a *moat* around Amazon's best customers (i.e., Prime members) and of making *land grabs* when moving rapidly into new businesses communicate a different set of implicit arguments about the company and its activities.

The most commonly used metaphors both reflect and promote particular "structures of feeling" about Amazon and its fellow tech giants that, by and large, normalize their market dominance and ubiquity in our lives.[13] Perhaps the most important feature of Amazon today is its sheer size and reach across diverse business areas. Although Amazon is not without competition, the term "monopoly" is increasingly relevant in discussing it. In its best-known business of ecommerce, it's estimated to control between 37 and 52 percent of the US market, with the most common estimate in the high 40s.[14] Depending on the true number, that proportion may not quite meet the bar that most economists and regulators typically use to identify a monopoly (at least 50 to 60 percent of the market).[15] However, in particular business sectors, Amazon certainly meets and exceeds that level of market control, such as in ebooks, online product searches, and sales of e-readers and smart speakers, whereas in others, such as video and music streaming, consumer electronics more generally, or various house-brand products such as fashion lines, Amazon does face a great deal of competition. When confronted with the question of the company's size, Amazon executives have been instructed to emphasize the extent of competition the company faces in various "market segments," and to continually remind the public and the press that, if the context is the retail category broadly conceived, they control only about 5 percent of US retail, and even less of global retail.[16] On *Frontline's* episode on Amazon, Jeff Wilke, CEO of the company's global consumer-retail business, even went so far as to characterize the company's size relative to its competitors in various industries as merely a "speck," a characterization that correspondent James Jacoby received with incredulity.[17]

However, suggesting that a company has become monopolistic is not merely a question of what percentage of a particular market it controls, but the power it has to shape that market. The US Federal Trade Commission makes that clear, saying "The antitrust laws prohibit conduct by a single firm that unreasonably restrains competition by creating or maintaining monopoly power," meaning that the firm need not yet have monopoly power but could be pursuing it through "improper conduct."[18] We should consider whether a large player is creating high barriers to entry for new competitors, whether the company has disproportionate power over pricing, and whether it uses its economies of scale or other market advantages to make meaningful competition impossible.

In terms of mindshare about ecommerce, and in relation to Amazon's closest online retailing competitors, more voices are raising concerns about Amazon's monopolistic tendencies. Bob Goodwin of InfoScout, a consumer-behavior research company, suggests that "Amazon" is almost turning into a verb, so essentially has it become connected with the practice of online shopping.[19] Despite how easy it is to comparison shop on the internet, especially compared to brick-and-mortar stores, industry reporting suggests that two-thirds of consumers check Amazon first for new products, while close to half (46 percent) go to Amazon first for product searches in general, well ahead of Google, which previously dominated this market.[20] Tech industry researcher Renée DiResta calls Amazon "the internet's de facto product search engine."[21]

To put the extent and speed of Amazon's market concentration into perspective, I compare past responses to monopolistic, anti-competitive markets in the United States in the tech and media industries to contemporary responses thus far (or the lack thereof) to the market dominance of Amazon. I review relevant shifts in antitrust jurisprudence, as well as the perhaps inevitable lag between the economic changes wrought by platform capitalism and the ability of courts and regulators to appreciate these impacts, as reasons for why Amazon has been able to grow as it has.

This chapter also considers the rhetorical techniques of normalizing monopolistic platform capitalism, as seen through the case of Amazon. The target audiences for these arguments are both Amazon's would-be regulators and the broader public, to whom these regulators are ostensibly accountable. Amazon is a master of metaphorical arguments, which tend to operate under the threshold of conscious reasoning. By holding up these implicit arguments to critical inspection, I aim to encourage a more explicit reckoning with the speed and scope of Amazon's power over not just particular markets, but governance as well.

INDUSTRY CONCENTRATION IN DIGITAL CAPITALISM

Scholars of the political economy of media point out that the trend line in American media industries over the last few decades is toward greater industry concentration, or fewer companies controlling a larger amount and a broad range of media interests.[22] It's arguably the case that the tech sector has concentrated even more rapidly, and with even greater resulting market control, than legacy media companies such as AT&T and Disney. While legacy media companies are largely growing through mergers and acquisitions, the tech giants have achieved competition-busting synergies, including both horizontal and vertical integrations across business areas, certainly by purchasing other companies but also through substantial internal growth, providing fewer occasions for government oversight.

This is certainly the case with Amazon. A lot of its growth into new business areas has occurred under the Amazon umbrella, be it turning its online retail business into a platform for third parties, developing electronics like the Kindle and the Fire tablet, building out from book-selling to book publishing, starting Amazon Studios to develop original video content, developing cloud services for its own use that turned into cloud-computing giant AWS, or growing its own shipping and delivery arms. Amazon has also pursued acquisitions that complement its business areas, such as its purchase of IMDb in 1998, audiobook company Audible in 2008, online shoe retailer Zappos in 2009, Twitch in 2014, Whole Foods Market in 2017, Ring in 2018, and MGM in 2021.

Amazon is far from alone in its rapid growth and achievement of market dominance in various business areas in tech. Vincent Mosco points out how unprecedented it is to have the most market-capitalized companies in the world be almost all in the same business sector—digital technology—as has been the case since 2016–2017.[23] As Robert McChesney points out, the dynamics of network effects tend to produce "winner-take-all" markets with very little meaningful competition, essentially a "locked-down" system.[24] One of McChesney's proposals, seemingly radical except that it hearkens back to years of antitrust rulings, is to "Treat Monopolies . . . Like Monopolies."[25] He identifies tech monopolies and lack of antitrust action against them as a significant problem for democracy and competitive markets, and an all-round slap in the face to the original promise of the internet as a level playing field for ideas and entrepreneurs alike. While the internet has widely been understood to be a Wild West of innovation and entrepreneurship, facilitated by low barriers to entry, relatively small capital investment, and the ability to leverage "word of mouth" via digital networks, the dominance of Amazon and other tech giants puts into place market conditions that make the ability of new market entrants to break through increasingly unlikely. As expressed by business scholars Marco Iansiti and Karim R. Lakhani, "The very same technologies that promised to democratize business are now threatening to make it more monopolistic."[26]

Concern about the monopolistic nature of tech markets is shared by many analysts and activists, such as tech critic Barry Lynn, whose think tank the Open Markets Institute focuses on tech monopolies as one of its core issues, writing "Online intermediaries have emerged as the railroad monopolies of the 21st century, controlling access to market and increasingly determining who wins and who loses in today's economy."[27] Seeing monopolistic corporate power as consequential not just for economic actors but also for the polity more broadly dates all the way back to the Sherman Act, the United States' nineteenth-century antitrust legislation. Senator John Sherman argued for its importance in political terms, comparing the power of the corporate monopolist to the unjust power of a king or emperor.[28] Scholars and activists including Barry Lynn, Sally Hubbard, Lina Khan, Scott Galloway, Tim Wu, Victor Pickard, Frank Pasquale and Stacy Mitchell have effectively resurrected attention to antitrust jurisprudence in order to question the status quo of consolidation in digital media and tech industries.

In July 2020, the US House Judiciary Antitrust Subcommittee held a hearing with the CEOs of Amazon, Apple, Facebook, and Alphabet, as part of their ongoing investigation of competition in the digital economy. Chairman David N. Cicilline's opening remarks demonstrated an in-depth understanding of the issues at stake with big tech:

These companies serve as critical arteries of commerce and communications. Because these companies are so central to our modern life, their business practices and decisions have an outsized effect on our economy and our democracy. . . . First, each platform is a bottleneck for a key channel of distribution. Where they control access to information or to a marketplace, these platforms have the incentive and ability to exploit this power. They can charge exorbitant fees, impose oppressive contracts, and extract valuable data from the people and businesses that rely on them. Second, each platform uses its control over digital infrastructure to surveil other companies, their growth, business activity, and whether they might pose a competitive threat. Each platform has used this data to protect its power by either buying, copying, or cutting off access for any actual or potential rival. Third, these platforms abuse their control over current technologies to extend their power. Whether it's through self-preferencing, predatory pricing, or requiring users to buy additional products, the dominant platforms have wielded their power in destructive, harmful ways in order to expand. . . . Simply put, they have too much power.[29]

As of this writing, antitrust concerns against Amazon are also being formally pursued via the Federal Trade Commission (FTC), which reportedly is interviewing sellers on the company's retail platform, as well as via a broader FTC investigation into past acquisitions by large technology companies.[30] As Tim Wu observes, the European Union has much more consistently pursued "big cases" in antitrust, never backing away from that tradition as has occurred in the United States.[31] Also as of this writing, the European Commission is pursuing an investigation into Amazon "to assess whether Amazon's use of sensitive data from independent retailers who sell on its marketplace is in breach of EU competition rules," a concern that has also been raised in relation to the metadata about businesses of all kinds that Amazon gathers via AWS.[32]

TECH MONOPOLIES UNTOUCHED: ANTITRUST IN THE UNITED STATES PAST AND PRESENT

The vertical and horizontal integrations in certain business areas that Amazon enjoys today, not to mention its habit of using loss-leading pricing, might not have been possible in past legal and regulatory environments in the United States if we judge by historical cases. Here I briefly contrast Amazon's market concentration and anti-competitive business practices with market structures and practices that were prevented by law or regulation in the past. I then describe the shifts that have brought about a more permissive regulatory environment, highlighting leading antitrust scholar Lina Khan's arguments for why contemporary antitrust jurisprudence fails to respond to the distinctiveness of digital platform businesses like Amazon's.

The US government was previously much more attentive to market concentration within industries, in particular the extent of vertical integration. Media companies have traditionally received extra scrutiny, because of their role in informing citizens and their obligation to the "public interest," as articulated by the Federal Communications Commission in the American context. This is why, as Philip Napoli and Robyn Caplan have argued, today's tech giants—including Amazon—have consistently defined themselves as technology companies rather than media companies, even when producing and distributing media is a major aspect of their business.[33]

Addressing market concentration and vertical integration are often linked concerns, as with the US Supreme Court's *Paramount* decision of

1948. Hollywood's Golden Age, in which nearly all the films shown in the United States were produced and distributed by five large studios (including Paramount), was facilitated in part by the vertical integration whereby the studios were their own distributors and exhibitors. The decision forced some of these studios to sell their theaters and Paramount itself to "split its production and distribution arms."[34]

The substantive concerns driving the *Paramount* decision have echoed through subsequent government checks on the power of media and technology companies. A similar impulse to limit vertical integration within a single business resulted in the "Fin-Syn" rules, which from 1970 to 1993 prevented US broadcast television networks from owning, and earning money via syndication, the most valuable programming airing on primetime.[35] The goal with this regulation was to ensure a varied and competitive array of independent producers in the television market, rather than having production be controlled by the large networks. Similar concerns echoed in critiques of the decision to allow AT&T's merger with Time-Warner, approved by a federal judge in 2018 over objections from the US Department of Justice, the White House, politicians from across the political spectrum, and advocacy groups who feared that such extensive vertical integration would consolidate market advantage in both telecommunications *and* media markets.

The decision to allow this merger, as well as the Disney-Fox merger that was horizontal rather than vertical in nature, can be traced to the 1980s, which brought about a deregulatory ethic toward the media and telecommunication industries in Washington, DC, via Ronald Reagan (despite his blind spot about Fin-Syn specifically) and further back to the 1970s when the growing influence of the "Chicago School" of economic thinkers challenged traditional legal thinking about antitrust. Enforcement of the Sherman Act, the Clayton Act, and the Celler-Kefauver Anti-Merger Act declined precipitously during this time, and the decreasing concern about protecting competition was also clear in the FCC's 1996 Telecommunications Act that substantially deregulated media ownership.[36] The fundamental shift in thinking was that it was not up to regulators to impose a particular vision of what market structure counts as "competitive," but rather, to respect the invisible hand of the market and only intervene if it was clear that a particular merger or business practice would be likely to hurt consumer welfare, defined narrowly as higher prices for consumers.[37] Focusing on prices as the sole metric for "consumer interest," and ignoring considerations of choice and diversity is a hallmark of Chicago School–style thinking.

Another feature of the Chicago School approach has been to think about markets in rather rigid ways and not adjust to the growing realities of convergence, facilitated by technology, across different kinds of markets. In the early 1980s the Department of Justice prevented multiple Hollywood film studios from joining forces to create a new pay-cable channel, to be called "Premiere," but very shortly afterward permitted the formation of Tri-Star, which combined a Hollywood studio (Columbia Pictures), pay cable channel (HBO), and broadcast network (CBS).[38] Although Tri-Star benefited in its timing, cresting the deregulatory wave in Washington, DC, it also helped that this merger was viewed as "cross-industry" whereas the Premiere proposal was interpreted as a form of "collusion" within a single industry. Of course, this rested on assumptions about the fundamental discontinuities between the film, cable, and broadcast "markets" that didn't necessarily hold true in the 1980s and even less so today. And so, the seeds were planted for the media conglomerates of today that are vertically and horizontally integrated to the nth degree, largely with the blessing of Congress and the FCC due to the promises of "efficiencies" and benefits to consumers.

One of the arguments that AT&T made to regulators regarding its proposed merger with Time Warner is that the rules that tech companies like Netflix and Amazon live by should be equitable for telecom providers.[39] In a context where companies that were until recently understood as content distributors are increasingly content producers, then why, AT&T asked, should it be prevented from doing something similar out of a concern that vertical integration of distribution and production will allow AT&T to charge unfair prices to its competitors in data and cable delivery on its Time Warner content? In 2018 the head of the Department of Justice's Antitrust division cited the rise of streaming and video-on-demand as part of the rationale for rolling back the 1948 Paramount Consent Decrees.[40]

Concern about the role of vertical integration has not been limited to "media" companies, but at least at one point in time, extended to tech companies. In 1998 the Department of Justice brought an antitrust suit against Microsoft for using its status as the dominant operating system to coerce personal computer companies into installing its new browser Internet Explorer, to the exclusion of other browsers, as a way to "catch up" in the internet connectivity game that they had apparently under-estimated.[41] Although the initial decision required breaking up Micro-soft into smaller companies, in the end Microsoft merely had to agree to "behavioral remedies" that would prevent it throwing its proverbial weight around to the same extent in the future.[42]

In general, though, tech companies have been fairly untroubled by antitrust actions until quite recently, particularly in the United States. In investigating Amazon's "Antitrust Paradox," Lina Khan argues that focus-ing only on the prices consumers pay does not make sense in today's mar-kets shaped by data commodities, and certainly not for Amazon whose loss-leading practices arguably are a form of predatory pricing. Amazon keeps prices low or loses money or both on fast home delivery times for extended periods because it can continually attract investment capital regardless of whether the company posts profits. Countering the Chicago School, Khan writes, "Under these conditions, predatory pricing becomes highly rational—even as existing doctrine treats it as irrational and there-fore implausible."[43] One well-known example: Amazon's willingness to lose up to $200 million in a month in order to undermine diapers.com, which allowed Amazon to acquire its parent company.[44] If and when predatory pricing does end, it will be too late. The barriers to entry for competitors will likely be too high, and there are reasons unrelated to price why consumers may not jump ship.

Frank Pasquale argues that antitrust enforcers are too invested in myths about consumer behavior online—that it's easy to switch platforms, for example, or that consumers are vigilant about price differences. Pasquale questions these assumptions, pointing out that consumers typically have sunk costs in platforms in terms of learning how to use them, and a his-tory of personalization and data linked with them, that frequently result in "lock-in."[45] The convenience and trust that comes with platforms con-sumers already use makes them less price sensitive and hesitant to switch platforms, in contradiction to the imagined behaviors of the "rational consumer." Further, a "heroic consumer" who constantly scans the market for better prices assumes that pricing is transparent and easy to compare.[46] With Amazon operating in so many markets and product categories, with highly dynamic pricing, some *personalized* discounts and promotions, and the costs for Amazon services buried inside the Prime bundle, it may be hard to tell if consumers are paying for market consolidation with higher prices because the overall price picture may not be transparent, especially to consumers themselves. Therefore, defining "consumer welfare" purely in terms of "short-term pricing effects" no longer makes sense (if it ever did) in the platform economy.[47] As the Association of American Publishers put it in a letter to Chairman Cicilline of the House Judiciary Antitrust Subcommittee in 2020, "The analysis of consumer welfare also must account for factors such as decreases in quality, consumer choice, and innovation, and a corresponding rise in consumer deception."[48]

A key problem arising from a myopic focus on "consumer welfare" is conceptualizing Amazon only in terms of its individual retail consumers, and not considering the impact of Amazon's market concentration on its suppliers. Economist Paul Krugman has argued that Amazon is more monopsony than monopoly, meaning it's not so much "a dominant seller with the power to raise prices," as "a dominant buyer with the power to push prices down."[49] Pushing prices down sounds like a good thing for consumers, but too much may make the markets for products being sold on Amazon so competitive that fewer and fewer companies can survive, ultimately leading to more concentrated markets in which prices may then rise. The damage to consumer welfare may be indirect and long term, due to creating conditions that undermine a diverse marketplace with low barriers to entry.

Another consideration, similar to the challenge government has had in regulating media markets, is determining "which market" Amazon is in. How can you define whether there's too much market concentration when Amazon is in so many markets simultaneously, not all of them consumer-facing? Google, Facebook, and Amazon might appear to be focused on different parts of the digital economy, but if their core business is understood to be the creation and collection of data as a form of capital, they are very much competitors.[50] Regulators tend to look only at what the right hand does but not the left hand, especially if the business areas are horizontally rather than vertically related. Khan points out that as tech companies become "critical intermediaries"—in Amazon's case, essential to the infrastructure of ecommerce—they provide services in one part of their business to companies with whom they compete in another.[51] If antitrust regulators assume that platforms that bring buyers and sellers together in an environment of "perfect information" make markets more efficient, they fail to take seriously the circumstance of being both platform and competitor.[52] This is certainly the case with Amazon, which increasingly has its own products cheek by jowl with those of sellers on its site. By many accounts, Amazon takes advantage of the business intelligence at its disposal to find products that promise to be profitable or an area of growth.[53] It's this apparent conflict of interest that the European Commission is investigating and that is attracting attention by multiple legislative bodies in the United States.

Khan and McChesney converge on the idea that when a platform reaches a certain scale, such that a significant percentage of online commerce and communication is essentially dependent upon it, then it makes sense to conceptualize it as a public utility, even a "common carrier" or "essential infrastructure."[54] This has similarly been argued for broadband delivery (a position rejected by the majority of the FCC in 2018 in the undoing of net neutrality) and has been recognized in the past for all kinds of businesses under the "essential facilities doctrine."[55] The regulatory options in this situation would be to make an infrastructural platform like Amazon public (like the water department, or the United States Postal Service), or, short of such a step, to regulate it as a "common carrier" or "essential facility," which would be obligated to provide essential services without prejudice, and prevented from using its privileged position as the platform provider to enter the markets that it facilitates. The Democratic majority of the House Judiciary Antitrust Subcommittee proposed solutions very much along these lines in two of the recommendations after the July 2020 hearings: "Structural separations to prohibit platforms from operating in lines of business that depend on or interoperate with the platform" and "Prohibiting platforms from engaging in self-preferencing."[56]

FROM "ESSENTIAL INFRASTRUCTURE" TO GOVERNANCE

As companies like Amazon, Google, and Walmart become akin to "essential infrastructure," their power extends beyond market power to that of governance. The observation that corporations have tremendous political power is not news, whether through their influence on elected leaders via campaign contributions or leverage gained through the power to grant or withhold much-needed jobs and tax revenue. These considerations certainly apply to Amazon, which according to the organization Open Secrets has given close to twenty million dollars in political contributions to date to both parties, leaning toward Democrats over Republicans. This amount of money is dwarfed by its expenditures on lobbying for legislation pertaining to defense contracting, labor laws, and regulation of information technology, not to mention Jeff Bezos's own very visible presence in Washington, DC, where he spends time and hosts gatherings at his large residence, and owns the *Washington Post*.[57]

Because Amazon, unlike some of the other tech giants, employs a lot of people and therefore where it chooses to locate warehouses or large offices has major implications for local employment and tax bases, it has been a visible player in getting the best deals from local communities by pitting them against each other. The way Amazon leverages the promise to bring jobs to communities played out dramatically in 2017–2018 as it invited cities across North America to compete for "HQ2"—a second headquarters to complement its headquarters in Seattle. Widely regarded as a stunt designed to stimulate the best possible tax breaks and concessions from the communities it likely intended to select from the beginning—New York City and Arlington, Virginia—the competition attracted not just negative press, but also significant political pushback in Queens where Amazon had planned to locate its offices. The "deal" there fell apart. The spectacle of North American cities falling over each other to promise tax breaks, new infrastructure paid for by taxpayers, and other subsidies worth millions of dollars in order to attract Amazon illustrated the power that such a large employer has over communities and their political representatives. The incident prompted soul searching about the great lengths communities were willing to go to in order to attract and, ultimately, subsidize a massively well-capitalized corporation—one well known for paying little or no federal taxes (due to a variety of corporate tax breaks) and for avoiding for years paying most states' sales taxes as well.[58]

Farhad Manjoo has argued that the tech giants are becoming like governments because of their sheer ubiquity and integration into so many aspects of our lives.[59] Historically we would only expect institutions like the church or the state to have such wide-ranging influence. But as one observer argued in *Forbes* about Amazon, "The dirty little secret is that Amazon is not a marketplace. It's angling to become a nation-state, and a highly developed one at that."[60] Whether it's consumer protection regimes, cross-border ecommerce regulations, laws governing drones or facial recognition technologies, packing and shipping standards, or the methods of extracting value from labor that in turn set new industry-wide standards, massive corporations like Amazon don't just follow regulation and policy. They find ways to collaborate with, extract favorable terms from, or even take the place of the state.

In a brief to the Antitrust Division of the US Department of Justice, the Open Markets Institute argued for noticing when concentrated market power becomes de facto regulatory power, writing:

Dominant actors with market power are often able to set the terms within a specific marketplace, thereby dictating outcomes for other businesses. Such unilateral exercise of private power is also very much a form of regulation. As Robert Hale wrote, "There is government whenever one person or group can tell others what they must do and when those others have to obey or suffer a penalty." Especially in digital technology markets, certain dominant firms now exert regulatory control over the terms on which others can sell goods and services.[61]

The trouble with these "functional sovereigns," the Open Markets Institute argues, is that with "private regulations . . . unlike a government, private actors are not accountable to the public."[62]

In 2017–2018, Senator Bernie Sanders started talking regularly about Amazon's labor practices and criticizing its pay, particularly for its warehouse workers, for not being a living wage, building on the Fight for 15 labor movement that started in 2012 among fast-food workers. In October 2018, Amazon announced that it would start paying a $15 minimum wage to all of its employees (an improvement, if not necessarily a living wage), along with benefits that start on the first day of full-time employment. Sanders and others praised the move, not just because it would improve the take-home pay for such a large segment of workers, but because any move that Amazon makes sets a standard that is likely to lift more boats. But when policymakers depend on large corporations to make industry-standard decisions rather than regulating matters like wages directly, it represents a migration of power from representative government to privately held corporations that are accountable to shareholders before anyone else. While it may be generally thought that Amazon did the right thing with regard to wages (although some workers were unhappy because the new wage policy was bundled with a loss of stock options for long-term employees, and the pay rate exceeds most minimum wages but it's less than the median wage for warehouse work),[63] Amazon certainly did not have to do so, and is not guaranteed to continue to do so in the future, particularly when the unemployment rate goes up. Other corporate behemoths, notably Walmart, have equally used their marketplace power to depress wages and establish new norms in retail employment of part-time, unpredictable, and benefit-less jobs.

To its consumers, Amazon has become one of the most trusted institutions in America. When it assumes responsibility for lawmaking, policymaking, or industry standard setting, the company says, in essence, "trust us." When it doesn't stop to justify its involvement or authority, it makes an implicit argument for its own right and ability to govern.

RHETORICAL NORMALIZATION—DEPLOYMENT OF ECOLOGICAL METAPHORS

Nowhere is Amazon's size and market dominance felt more viscerally than in the city of its founding and current headquarters, Seattle, Washington. By turns grateful and proud of the economic engine that Amazon provides due to its jobs and urban infrastructural improvements, and frustrated by the company's gentrification that has displaced many urban residents and contributed to homelessness (among other complaints), the city has a complicated relationship with the tech behemoth that has taken up various downtown residences since 2001.[64] Seattle has welcomed the downtown offices, but also proposed a tax on corporations located in the city that would help address issues of homelessness and create more affordable housing, problems that are the unintended result of the city hosting Amazon and other large corporations. After the city council passed the tax, Amazon and other businesses launched such an aggressive campaign against it that they ended up reversing it. However, caving to Amazon's pressure didn't necessarily deliver the intended results—the company subsequently announced that it was moving employees in "Worldwide Operations" to the neighboring city of Bellevue.[65]

In 2018 Amazon unveiled its "Spheres" buildings—glass orbs containing a rainforest of over 25,000 trees, plants, and water features—in the heart of its corporate headquarters scattered throughout the South Lake Union neighborhood of Seattle. The interiors of the Spheres feature vertical walls covered in a mesh that anchors the plants. According to Amazon's blog, "The living walls highlight flora from the world's cloud forests, chosen for their ability to thrive in conditions that are comfortable for people."[66] As one industry observer noted, an ecosphere is self-contained and you never need leave, making it a perfect encapsulation of Amazon's ambitions for market dominance.[67] The Spheres dramatize through architecture an argument in favor of monopolistic ubiquity that the tech

6.1 *The Spheres*, photograph by Brent Bereska, used with permission. *Source: Flickr*, August 21, 2019, https://www.flickr.com/photos/11031526@N02/48617540901.

giants have been making for some time through naturalistic metaphors, particularly the idea of being an "ecosystem" for consumers.

Metaphors seem almost inescapable when it comes to discourse about digital technology—unsurprising since metaphors are frequently used to gain a conceptual handle on phenomena that are novel, abstract, and difficult to grasp.[68] Given the novelty of communication technologies that work in ways beyond the vision or understanding of most users, metaphors have long been used to make the "abstract . . . more tangible."[69] Sometimes metaphors become so "under the radar" that they "appear to be literal."[70] When this happens metaphors can do ideological work all the more easily. This is the case with naturalistic metaphors for digital communications technologies that have themselves become naturalized. Whether web, cloud, stream, or ecosystem, we hardly notice the metaphorical nature of this discourse. But the not noticing makes them even more powerful as "metaphors we live by," by which George Lakoff and Mark Johnson mean that metaphorical concepts such as these come to structure our thinking and action.[71]

We shouldn't view these metaphors as merely descriptive—helpful for making something new or unfamiliar more understandable—but as part of an argument or strategy. There is a politics to metaphorical choice. When it comes to tech, naturalistic metaphors naturalize—or, for the sake of clarity, normalize—its ubiquity. As tech giants become ubiquitous in our lives—interacting with us not only while we're using a computer but also via voice in our homes and cars, on the move on our mobile devices, and via a variety of machines and devices thanks to the Internet of Things—the language of cloud, stream, and ecosystem prefigures the seamless entanglement and ability to collect fine-grained data across activity domains that these companies desire.

At the same time, these naturalistic metaphors are a convenient semiotic distraction. They offer ecological analogies for understanding digital experiences and services, while diverting us from the materialities of digital technology and its environmental impacts—from mining practices, to e-waste, to the energy required to run data centers and devices, to the impacts of reconfigured practices of work, transportation, shopping, and leisure on our communities and the natural world.

The ecological metaphor that Amazon deploys the most, other than specifically discussing AWS's "cloud" services, is *ecosystem*, as do many others in the tech sector. Amazon uses the term most often to convey the sheer scale of content that it makes available, and the fact that it can be accessed in multiple ways.[72] A typical usage looks like this: "World's best content ecosystem—Access to over 38 million movies, TV shows, songs, books, magazines, apps, and games—with free, unlimited cloud storage for all Amazon content."[73] As one tech reporter has put it, an ecosystem is a wide array of "easy-to-buy, easy-to-install" content and apps.[74]

Amazon has ecosystems nested within ecosystems. Kindle, for example, is its own ecosystem, meaning that customers can "Buy Once, Read Everywhere," which in 2012 meant "on any Kindle e-reader or Kindle Fire, as well as on iPad, iPod touch, iPhone, PC, Mac, BlackBerry, Windows Phone, Android phones and tablets, in web browsers with Kindle Cloud Reader and now on Windows 8 devices."[75] Similarly, with the arrival of Alexa, consumers were told that they could now gain access to their "digital ecosystem" not just from their home smart speakers, but with the Alexa voice interface in their car, such as those made by the BMW Group. This meant having the ability to interact with Alexa-enabled devices (like lights and thermostats) while driving, or giving the car instructions remotely from any Alexa-enabled device.[76]

Amazon doesn't necessarily use the term "ecosystem" consistently within its communications. In many announcements, especially when referring to its entertainment and streaming products, it refers to the abundance of digital content that can be accessed via multiple devices. However, in other contexts it refers to the array of companies in a particular industry domain, as in the "entire video game ecosystem," or Amazon Web Services' "partner and customer ecosystem," which are companies that collaborate with, build services upon, or are clients of AWS.[77] While in some usages the focus is on all the players in a particular industry, in others "ecosystem" is used to denote a given market in which there are competitors, such as when a reporter considered in 2012 how the still relatively new Amazon AppStore was faring in the "app ecosystem."[78]

The term "ecosystem" is also used interchangeably with the term "platform," in the sense of platform as a service that connects buyers and sellers, developers and users—a metaphor for that metaphor. Whether it's the Amazon App Store or the Fire TV that delivers a variety of streaming apps including Prime Video, Netflix, and Hulu, both Amazon and those who report on it sometimes label software that hosts a variety of services and applications as "ecosystems." At other times, reporters consider the way vertical integrations in companies like Amazon, Google, and Apple, across the domains of "hardware, software, and content" produce consumer-facing "ecosystems."[79] In yet other usages, the sheer array of digital services that Amazon provides—from ecommerce to streaming to its IoT technologies—gets described as an ecosystem, with digital devices being the tool that will hook or "knit consumers" into it.[80]

Defined by the Oxford English Dictionary as "a biological system composed of all the organisms found in a particular physical environment, interacting with it and with each other," "ecosystem" is a term that conveys scale, permanence, and harmony. It is a flexible metaphor, with different aspects of an ecosystem emphasized in different contexts. For the content ecosystem the sense of scale and permanence come to the fore. There's a lot of content that is available to you, just as the features or resources of an ecosystem would be available to its inhabitants. For a business ecosystem, the sense of harmony is foregrounded: for example, the way the livestreaming platform Twitch brings together a wide array of stakeholders in the video game industry, including "game developers, publishers, media outlets, events, user generated content and the entire esports scene" in a way, we are meant to infer, that is mutually beneficial.[81] Just as the different components of an ecosystem—its terrain, climate, humidity, salinity, flora, and fauna—are all suited and adapted to each other, so it is between Amazon's Twitch and game developers and players, or between AWS and software developers and their clients. All have their place and their role and, Amazon suggests, all features are available to the user in a predictable way, just as the elements of an ecosystem are assumed to be.

Ecosystem has had such enthusiastic uptake as a metaphor for discussing the domains of tech and business that in my database search of North American news articles containing the terms "Amazon" and "ecosystem," articles referring to Amazon the company rival the number of articles referring to the river and rainforest by 2007. By 2013, the clear majority of articles containing the two terms are either about Amazon or are tech-focused stories that mention the company. As I've shown, the exact meaning of the metaphor is slippery. Although its most common meaning in the context of Amazon the company is the array of content you can access through its services, it also stands in for platform, business domain, marketplace, Amazon's entire range of digital services, as well as the way Amazon's hardware, software, and content services work together for the consumer. While scale, permanence, and harmony are variously invoked in these usages, the ultimate ideological effect of the ecosystem metaphor is one of naturalization. Whether it's the extent of Amazon's market control and product offerings, presenting the company as a permanent fixture in ecommerce, or the idea that Amazon as a platform brings together different stakeholders in a way that is beneficial to all, the term "ecosystem" implies that Amazon's activities and market position are natural, and therefore, beyond question.

At the same time, we should consider how the ecosystem metaphor in tech creates a reverse impact on our understanding of ecosystems in the natural world. At a time when ecosystems are being seriously stressed by human activity—in other words, at the same time that natural ecosystems are shrinking, becoming more unstable, and falling out of harmony, those features of the natural world are being continuously reinscribed through our metaphorical usage of the term to describe tech. Just as the ever-increasing amount of time we spend in tech "ecosystems" displaces time we might have spent in actual ecosystems, so does the tech sector's appropriation of the term disconnect us from its original meaning. When Amazon appropriates a particular ecosystem for its brand name, and celebrates its ability to create environments through a project like the Spheres, the rhetorical slippage from one kind of ecosystem to another is only reinforced.

CONCLUSION—DENATURALIZE THE METAPHORS

Amazon is symptomatic of what the internet has become more broadly, in spite of the vestigial beliefs about the internet that many of us (of a certain age anyway) may have from the 1990s. Chris Anderson and Michael Wolff have described this shift, declaring "The Web is Dead. Long Live the Internet." Anderson writes:

[O]ne of the most important shifts in the digital world has been the move from the wide-open Web to semiclosed platforms that use the Internet for transport but not the browser for display. . . . And it's the world that consumers are increasingly choosing, not because they're rejecting the idea of the Web but because these dedicated platforms often just work better or fit better into their lives (the screen comes to them, they don't have to go to the screen).[82]

The inventor of the World Wide Web, Tim Berners-Lee, has consistently made a similar observation, noting that the proliferation of what he calls "walled gardens" on the internet came from the explosion in popularity of apps due to the rise of smartphone and tablet usage; social networking sites, where content was not searchable from outside the site; from authoritarian governments fire-walling their nations' internet access from unwanted influences; and from internet providers challenging norms of net neutrality. He writes, "these closed, 'walled gardens,' no matter how pleasing, can never compete in diversity, richness and innovation with the mad, throbbing Web market outside their gates. If a walled garden has too tight a hold on a market, however, it can delay that outside growth."[83]

Here again we see how talk about the digital world reaches for ecological metaphors in order to explain the structures of the internet and the World Wide Web. But the walled garden metaphor, at least, invokes human agency in shaping digital environments. Amazon also uses metaphors of humans shaping their environment to describe its business practices, but rarely in consumer-facing contexts. A former employee, for example, recalls Jeff Bezos saying at the initial, top-secret meeting where he introduced his idea for Prime: "I want to draw a moat around our best customers."[84] An internal document from 2013 secured by the House Antitrust Subcommittee similarly characterized Prime memberships as "Big Moats."[85] This moat makes it harder for other companies to compete, because the value proposition is hard for competitors to match, in terms of the distribution infrastructure, the array of products, the cost of the membership, and the resulting convenience of lightning-fast shipping. Deutsche Bank analyst Ross Sandler declared Prime to be "the biggest competitive moat in ecommerce in the Western world."[86] As Amazon moves into new geographic territories and business areas, these moves are frequently described using the business term "land grabs," including Amazon's earliest strategy to "get big fast" and achieve "land grabs" of business areas before other companies did, its efforts to "land" the .amazon domain name and wrest it away from its geographic rivals, and its more recent "land grab" of the smart speaker market.[87] The language of "land grab" reflects a broader implicit ideology communicated by metaphors of "digital frontierism" that critiques of "data colonialism" seek to expose.[88]

If metaphors are hard to avoid when talking about digital, networked media and communications, then in the spirit of "if you can't beat 'em, join 'em," I offer the metaphor of the "pleasure garden." The "garden" metaphor emphasizes that humans have cultivated the environment, and "pleasure" captures the voluntary nature of entering and staying in the platform, as well as the affective rewards of doing so. Berners-Lee's notion of the walled garden suggests that you can only enjoy the fruits if you have the key to get in, and you may not be able to easily leave. This aptly describes early internet service providers such as AOL, which essentially "walled off" its users from the wider web, as well as the internet as controlled by authoritarian governments. If American broadband and wireless providers do take full advantage of the dismantling of net neutrality by the FCC, we might see service-specific walled gardens there as well.

In contrast, a pleasure garden—a cultural form originating in seventeenth-century London—is open to the public, and contains attractions as inducements to enter and then stay. The diversity of the attractions—walking paths through picturesque gardens, concert venues, entertainments, fountains, amusement rides, menageries, fireworks, balls, and al fresco dining—recall the array of products and services that a company like Amazon provides. The metaphor of the pleasure garden describes internet-enabled spaces that the public is attracted to, and apparently *chooses* to spend time in due to the entertainment, convenience, and pleasures they encounter there.

The lure of the "open web" proved too great for the actual walled gardens like AOL and Prodigy, contributing in part to their demise. Today's tech giants, rather than explicitly restrict online movement, which they know today's users would reject as a loss of choice, tend to offer pleasure gardens rather than walled gardens, hoping that people will choose to stay and stroll, and not feel tempted to leave. In the case of Amazon, while we imagine that comparison shopping and patronizing a number of different retailers is exactly what the internet lends itself to, the company incentivizes consumers to visit and then stay in its pleasure garden through a number of "attractions": the convenience of Amazon apps, the structure of the Amazon Prime membership, and by prioritizing low prices, convenience, and fast shipping.

We should take seriously the seductiveness and embeddedness of Amazon's "pleasure garden" as a key ingredient in both the platform loyalty of many American consumers, as well as why it has been hard for consumers and, for a long time, their political representatives to imagine seriously challenging Amazon's dominance or demanding it be broken up by the government into separate companies, as happened with AT&T in the 1980s, or with the Hollywood film studios in the 1940s. It is precisely the features of Amazon that the ecosystem metaphor points to—the scale of its offerings, seeming permanence and stability in the ecommerce landscape, and the harmony across activities and services that its vertical and horizontal integrations provide—that make Amazon's pleasure gardens so appealing and hard to resist.

When author Douglas Preston with Barry Lynn and 900 other signatories published an open letter to then Assistant Attorney General for Antitrust William Barr in 2015, contending that Amazon was abusing its monopolistic power in book retailing against the interests of authors and publishers, the response from the Department of Justice, according to Preston, was that "Amazon was one of the most popular companies in the country. They have brought tremendous services to consumers and they've brought lower prices," and that the DOJ didn't see enough evidence to justify an investigation.[89] If politicians and market regulators continue in this vein, using only consumer happiness as their guide, consumers themselves will continue to facilitate the tremendous market concentration, and even at times monopoly conditions, in the platform businesses of the digital economy. As of this writing, there are signs that things are changing, from the 2020 antitrust hearings, to the appointments of Lina Khan and Tim Wu as US Federal Trade Commissioner and special assistant to President Biden for technology and competition policy within the National Economic Council, respectively. Meaningful change will require consumers and their representatives to take stock of the costs and constraints of digital pleasure gardens like Amazon, despite the ease, convenience, and enjoyment they provide.

7

AMERICAN UBIQUITY: AMAZON'S PLATFORM IMPERIALISM

I don't like the idea of this monolith devouring everything. . . . Our culture is, and all cultures are, being swamped by outside influences. . . . We're fighting to defend our voice.

—Mark Rubbo, co-owner of Melbourne bookstore Readings[1]

We owe it to 400 million Arabs that they go to the digital economy. I think it's our duty; otherwise the Middle East will either be left behind, or will be occupied by foreign powers. These foreign powers are digital banks, digital companies, digital media—there's no need for military.

—Mohamed Alabbar, founder of ecommerce firm Noon and United Arab Emirates real estate mogul[2]

The Canadian Book industry requires active support and promotion so that our regional, local and aboriginal voices are nurtured and celebrated. That is something that Canadian booksellers . . . do so well. Letting foreign retail giants into local Canadian markets under the false guise of Canadian partnership would be devastating to an important Canadian industry employing real book lovers in every community across Canada.

—Stephen Cribar, president of Canadian Booksellers Association[3]

Will Amazon survive [in the] Indian market? Sure. Only if they are willing to learn. American fast food chain KFC had to launch its first vegetarian chain ever, that too in India (Gujarat). McDonalds embraced Indian way of doing things by selling McTikkis.

—Nextbigwhat.com[4]

The sentiments opening this chapter express varied ambivalence in global responses to Amazon. When Amazon first extended beyond American borders in 1998, three years after the company's US launch, its goals for ubiquity faced new complications, including that of perception. When Amazon exports its products and services, both scholarly and popular responses often are informed by what communication scholar Dal Yong Jin calls "platform imperialism," a form of economic and cultural imperialism specific to platform giants such as Facebook, Google, Netflix, and Amazon. Jin observes, "The U.S., which had previously controlled non-Western countries with its military power, capital, and later cultural products, now seems to dominate the world with platforms, benefitting from these platforms, mainly in terms of capital accumulation."[5] These global platforms, or "Californian East India Companies," as one scholar describes them,[6] aim for "ubiquitous commerce," which is "the ambition to annihilate spatial and temporal barriers through a networked market system."[7] Lee McGuigan and Vincent Manzerolle, in their critique of this imperative, see ubiquitous global commerce involving a "neglect of tradition, geography, and cultural contingency."[8] And yet, a close look at Amazon's efforts to achieve ubiquitous commerce reveals how the company negotiates with and manages tradition, geography, and cultural contingency. These factors can be barriers to global capital, but they can also become resources, or points of leverage, for a company like Amazon seeking to build its presence in new markets.

The GAFAM (Google/Alphabet, Apple, Facebook, Amazon, and Microsoft) companies are six of the top seven most market-capitalized corporations in the world as of this writing. The further concentration of wealth in the United States thanks to its globally dominant tech companies, most of which are substantially platform businesses, is not the only concern. Given the treasure trove of data they collect about people all over the world, there are concerns about data security and protection of national sovereignty.[9] Digital platforms shape the distribution of media and information, so the concentration of foreign ownership of distribution platforms raises longstanding concerns about soft power. Given network effects and "first mover" advantage, many countries are also concerned about homegrown businesses that employ people, build technological knowledge capacity, and pay taxes in these countries being unable to compete with these American platforms.

Just as the cultural imperialism thesis of the 1970s was eventually questioned and complicated by scholars who empirically examined the production of culture in diverse national contexts, so has the hegemony of platform imperialism been questioned on a variety of empirical grounds. Global media scholars note the resurgence of state control in response to the foreign investment, market concentration, and cultural influence of the tech sector; the rise of dominant tech centers outside the United States and Europe (notably in the Asia-Pacific region), particularly in hardware and the "pipes" of digital connectivity; and the importance of existing media cultures and localized audience preferences to the success of foreign digital content platforms.[10] My analysis of Amazon's international expansions is informed by the complexities of platform imperialism explored in this scholarship. Amazon's global ambitions are extensive and its resources to accomplish them significant, but its global dominance in ecommerce and other business areas is neither assured nor complete.

Amazon's global expansions are both longstanding and partial. While Amazon can today boast that it serves ecommerce customers in close to two hundred countries, it only has Amazon marketplaces, or dedicated local retail websites, in sixteen countries outside the United States. In order of their launch, these are the United Kingdom, Germany, France, Japan, Canada, Italy, Spain, Brazil, India, Mexico, the Netherlands, Singapore, Australia, Turkey, the United Arab Emirates, and Saudi Arabia.[11] While Amazon is estimated to control close to half of US online retail sales, it controlled only 5.7 percent of global internet retail beyond the United States in 2019.[12] Amazon's international revenues are substantial—32 percent of the company's ecommerce total as of 2020—and have started to yield profits after many years of losing money, due to the established pattern of investing heavily in new markets in order to eventually dominate them and reap the rewards later.[13] As Amazon's growth in the United States starts to slow with some market saturation, its focus on international growth is all the more important because of the still relatively untapped markets around the world.[14]

In this chapter I look at how Amazon has been received internationally given the global market dominance it aspires to, and its Americanness.

In the United States, Amazon has created a flexible brand identity that seeks to fade into the background in its ubiquity, becoming almost invisible through its focus on customers and personalized service. How have these efforts to become ubiquitous traveled? Has the flexibility of Amazon's brand identity facilitated its "glocalization"? To use Koichi Iwabuchi's term, is the Amazon brand "culturally odorless," or does it have the unmistakable smell of America?[15] How have governments around the world, with the power to regulate foreign ownership, responded to Amazon's global platform ambitions?

This chapter focuses on a few of Amazon's international marketplaces in terms of how Amazon's arrival was received, the obstacles it encountered, and the strategies the company has used to try and win over consumers, sellers, and the government officials who can shape its fate. Ranging from Canada, where Amazon.ca was launched in 2002, to Amazon.ae, launched in 2019 in the United Arab Emirates, Amazon's goals are largely the same, but its approach to achieving them often differs depending on conditions on the ground. Perhaps the strongest comparison to see how much those conditions matter is between China and India, both populous countries with a growing middle class and rapid adoption of digital communication technologies. Amazon entered China in 2004 by acquiring existing Chinese online bookseller Joyo, and mostly pulled out of the country due to lack of meaningful progress in 2019.[16] In India, by contrast, although Amazon's ability to do business has proceeded by fits and starts due to restrictions on foreign direct investment there, Amazon.in is now Amazon's fastest-growing international market with the greatest profit potential for the future.

In examining Amazon's platform imperialist efforts, we see that ubiquity looks a little different outside the United States, where Amazon's Americanness makes it less able to proceed in a stealthy, "under the radar" manner. When Amazon opened marketplaces in each of the countries considered here—Canada, India, Australia, and the UAE—it was a known quantity for many consumers because they had already been visiting the site and doing cross-border shopping on it. Before the launch of Amazon's Australia marketplace Amazon.com.au, the American Amazon site was the second most popular online shopping site in Australia after Woolworth's.[17]

In some parts of the Middle East, Amazon controlled about 15 percent of online retail even before acquiring Souq.com.[18]

Amazon's "arrival" to nations around the world has been accompanied by the localization efforts one would expect from a twenty-first-century American company that needs to build trust with local consumers. These efforts—ranging from ad campaigns to partnerships with local companies, sponsorships of national events, nationally inflected sections of the store and editorial content on the site, adjustments to its ecommerce model for the local market, self-censorship of media content and products for sale in line with local sensibilities, and lots of communication touting Amazon's investments in the host economy—place Amazon in a more "in your face" position with regard to its PR and marketing than in the United States. Called on to justify its global expansions, Amazon must tell a story, or multiple stories, about why it deserves to be welcomed around the world. At the same time, Amazon pairs these localization efforts with the structural elements of brand ubiquity it pursues in the United States, including the bundled nature of Prime and the relentless pursuit of the largest selection and the greatest delivery speed.

ENTRY STRATEGIES—LOCALIZATION IN PLATFORM IMPERIALISM

It can be hard to point to the exact moment that Amazon enters a new national market, since consumers often access Amazon's services in a cross-border way, or at least have knowledge about Amazon's brand and how it works due to its digital presence and global reputation. Customers in most countries of the world that don't have their own marketplaces can still order goods from one of Amazon's websites but will need to pay international shipping, with the associated wait times and additional costs, if indeed sellers are willing to ship internationally. The company launched an international shipping feature in 2018, so the shopping app can be set to show only those products that can be shipped internationally to the customer's region.[19]

Even more globally accessible are Amazon's purely digital services, such as Prime Video (in more than two hundred countries), Echo smart speakers, and Music Unlimited streaming service (in a few dozen countries).

In true platform style, Amazon cross-subsidizes its growth plans in international ecommerce with its more profitable digital businesses, particularly Amazon Web Services,[20] and frequently uses its digital products, for which geographic distance and sticky border features pose less of an obstacle, as a way to turn people into Amazon customers in preparation for converting them into online shoppers in the future.

Amazon has rolled out digital distribution programs in hundreds of countries that vastly exceed its global retail marketplaces. Starting with the Kindle and associated online store of ebooks, then moving into Prime Video, these aspects of the Amazon brand pave the way for a relationship that the company hopes will result in brand recognition and loyalty for ecommerce. For the most desirable markets, it's also an opportunity to source locally relevant content in order to overcome the "stink" of a foreign interloper, or to compete more effectively against a local incumbent. Whether it's Amazon creating a large online Hindi bookstore,[21] or Amazon.ca promoting Canadian authors and sponsoring literary awards, Amazon can establish a reputation as a source for local media content, at least in the national markets that it prioritizes.

Prime Video is understood by industry observers to be a "customer acquisition channel," helping explain its rollout to 200 countries in 2016 and an estimated $7 billion in Amazon's spending on content in 2020. Amazon Studios' focus on original productions for valuable foreign markets like Japan and India—with twenty-nine foreign-language programs produced between 2016 and 2019—is key to attracting and retaining Prime members not just for the streaming service but as retail customers.[22] Upon Prime Video's launch in India, Amazon's target was viewed by at least one industry observer to be ecommerce rivals Snapdeal and Flipkart rather than Netflix.[23] When promoting Prime Video's launch in India, Amazon made it known that Indians would be able to access Bollywood films, licensed Indian and regional content, as well as original Indian content on the new streaming platform.[24] In 2018 it launched a Hindi interface to Prime Video to make it more accessible and inviting to India's more than half a billion Hindi speakers, and in 2019 launched a Hindi language version of the retail site.[25]

Global strategy informs content development and acquisitions in international markets, as well as programs that are anticipated to travel well across borders. Amazon's premiere of *The Grand Tour*, an adaptation of BBC's *Top Gear*, which was canceled after allegations of verbal abuse and assault from star Jeremy Clarkson against a colleague, premiered on Amazon Prime Video just a month before its global launch and had pride of place in its promotion. Already a massive global hit as *Top Gear*, with an estimated 350 million viewers worldwide per episode thanks to cable and satellite distribution of the show on BBC Worldwide, Amazon's reboot enhanced the show's global appeal as the stars traveled the world and filmed the in-studio portions of the show in a traveling tent.[26] Acknowledging in 2016 that the new name of the show reflected its "global ambition," the Amazon vice president of Amazon Video didn't reflect further on the title's association with the custom of upper-class young men in the seventeenth and eighteenth centuries leaving Britain to tour the continent and take in its art, culture, and sites of antiquity.[27] Perhaps tongue-in-cheek, this Grand Tour would feature irreverent, aging British "lads" with eyes for nothing but all things automotive, drinking their "cuppa" tea in all manner of "exotic" locations (see figure 7.1). In order to ride its wave as the "world's most popular factual television programme," Amazon invested an eye-popping $275 million for a three-series deal.[28]

The localization efforts extend beyond internationally popular and nationally relevant media content, to the ad campaigns that Amazon uses to announce its arrival, aiming to boost awareness or overcome negative press. Internationally, Amazon doesn't necessarily hew to its early promotional logic from the United States, where it became an ecommerce juggernaut largely through relationship marketing and word of mouth rather than through conventional advertising. Amazon is a very visible advertiser in many foreign markets, using traditional TV spots as well as web-based and mobile ads. A localized advertising campaign that signals Amazon's interest in, and fit, with the local culture softens the impression of an American behemoth swooping in to decimate national retail, both online and brick-and-mortar.

The launch of Amazon.com.au in Australia, for example, was met with a fair amount of handwringing for what it would mean for national retailers.[29] Amazon's ad campaign launching the site brought a humorous lightness and attention to the everyday lives and vernacular of Australians, in an effort to dispel these fears and be read as understanding Australia. The

7.1 Promotional image for *The Grand Tour*, n.d., https://www.imdb.com/title/tt5712554 /mediaviewer/rm245787392/, accessed May 28, 2021.

"Everything you need from a to z: easy az" campaign, from the TBWA Sydney agency, linguistically almost merges the slang short form of Australia, "Oz," with the "az" of the tagline (pronounced "as"). Most of the ads feature something that can be read as specifically Australian. For example, an ad that features a baby in a pool alarmed by the sight of her dog swimming in a shark-fin floaty makes sure to signal awareness that the relevant item for this scenario is "swim nappies," not "swim diapers" (see figure 7.2).

7.2 "Floaty"—Amazon 30-second spot from TBWA Sydney. *Source:* Lindsay Bennett, "TBWA Reveals First Work for Amazon," *Ad News*, June 5, 2018, https://www.adnews .com.au/news/tbwa-reveals-first-work-for-amazon. Author screenshot.

Other spots speak to Australian situations, such as spotting a giant spider in your living room or dealing with a neighbor who is feeding the local cockatoos. Amazon was surely aware that previous American brands, including another Seattle juggernaut, Starbucks, have attempted to enter Australia, perhaps assuming that what worked in the States would work there, only to be rebuffed by Australian consumers.[30]

Amazon's first ad campaign in India, "Aur Dikhao" from 2015, connected Amazon's product selection—by then larger than that of its major ecommerce rivals Flipkart and Snapdeal—with a trait presented as being characteristic of Indians: always wanting to see more options when shopping. "Aur Dikhao" translates to "Show Me More" and it's repeated throughout the danceable song featured in the ads. The creative director for the campaign explained, "We highlighted the 'Indianess' which is there in all of us. Only we can go to five shops, see five different things and still crave for more and ask the shopkeeper 'Aur Dikhao.' We have limited budget, so before making the final decision, we keep on asking 'Aur Dikhao' in the hope that the best is yet to come."[31] This vision (and, perhaps, stereotype) of the Indian consumer always wanting to see more and more options contrasts with Amazon emphasizing, at least to American consumers, the convenience of personalized recommendations that make it easier to navigate the overwhelming choice in online shopping.

In India, Amazon has sought to connect with consumers not just through spot ads, but also sponsorships and connections to sports, particularly with cricket, India's most popular sport. Within a year of Amazon.in's launch, Amazon won the rights to merchandising for the India Premier League, so that Amazon.in would be the destination for fans who wanted to buy their gear online.[32] The company also released ads designed to be run during the IPL, such as one featuring a married couple placing bets on the outcome of the match, with the winner getting their choice of product from Amazon, and a series of ads featuring a fictional cricket team, the Chonkpur Cheetahs. Further, Amazon Prime Video's first Indian Original series was *Inside Edge*, a drama set in the world of cricket. Beyond cricket, in 2015 Amazon became the official partner of the annual Jaipur Literature Festival and outbid Indian companies to be the official sponsor of India Fashion Week.[33] Amazon has also linked itself with Hindu holidays by launching an annual sale called the "Great Indian Festival" in coordination with Diwali every year (see figure 7.3), accompanied by a series of upbeat, musical ads that make online shopping seem festive and fun.[34]

7.3 Author screenshot from the ad for Amazon's Great Indian Festival, October 10–15, 2018. *Source: Amazon.in* ad published on YouTube, September 28, 2018, https://www.youtube.com/watch?v=fkd5z6wCZKM.

Amazon India's localization efforts have gone beyond marketing to adjusting the service itself. The country's size and uneven delivery infrastructure ruled out a blanket delivery window for goods; in India, the possible delivery timeframes are adjusted to your PIN (Postal Index Number) code.[35] In India, Amazon entered a market where the incumbent Flipkart offered a cash-on-delivery (COD) payment option for consumers who did not have access to credit cards, or weren't comfortable using them online.[36] COD constituted about 60 percent of Flipkart's orders in 2011.[37] Amazon also offers a COD payment option in India, even though this is not available in most of its other markets. Amazon also incorporated delivery by bicycle and pushed options for in-store or locker pickups earlier in India than in other markets, for consumers who preferred to pick up their items locally rather than have them delivered.[38]

Amazon's most recent global expansion has been via the 2017 purchase of Souq.com, the leading ecommerce platform in the Middle East. It was rebranded Amazon.ae in 2019. The press release about the rebrand quotes Ronaldo Mouchawar, the cofounder of Souq, now vice president of Amazon MENA (Middle East and North Africa), saying that Amazon.ae "brings together Souq's local know-how and Amazon's global expertise." The press release emphasizes the use of Arabic on Amazon.ae's website and app, and the availability of locally relevant payment options such as local credit cards and COD.[39] Souq.com, now Amazon.ae, is popular in many countries of the region, although Amazon rebranded Souq in Saudi Arabia as Amazon.sa in 2020, and in Egypt, Souq still operates as Souq as of this writing, despite the new ownership. Mouchawar argued that this was so that the rebrand and transition of services could be smoothly implemented in the UAE before being rolled out in these two large markets; others suggest that it's because brand loyalty to Souq is so strong in these countries.[40] Some speculated that anti-American sentiment, or animosity particularly toward Jeff Bezos, may have been the reason for a slower rebrand in Saudi Arabia in particular. This is thought to be because Bezos owns the *Washington Post* where Jamal Kashoggi was a columnist; Prince Mohammad Bin Salman's involvement in ordering his brutal killing was vigorously probed on the paper's editorial pages.[41] The prince was then suspected of being behind the leak of texts and intimate photos between Bezos and his mistress, published in the *National Inquirer*. Nevertheless, Amazon.sa did launch in 2020, just a year behind Amazon.ae.

As with all multinationals, Amazon's localization efforts can be found wanting. In Japan, for example, Amazon's recent overtaking of ecommerce market share from national incumbent Rakuten is judged by analysts to be *despite* its failures to fully understand the local market, and thanks mostly to its strong logistics game that drives fast and reliable deliveries. Rakuten's focus on the needs of Japanese consumers—including exquisite gift wrapping, an online interface reminiscent of department store displays, and a membership that bundles a wide variety of online and offline services with strong "points" incentives—make it likely to remain a strong player even in the face of Amazon's size and mastery of distribution.[42]

If platform imperialism inherits the concern of cultural imperialism—that culture will become homogeneous and deeply Americanized—then the actual manifestations of a platform business like Amazon around the world complicate that hypothesis. But, of course, evidence of cultural variation does not undo certain structural realities: Amazon benefits from all the data in the countries where it does business, it has deep pockets against local competitors, and the kinds of operational and content differences discussed here are minor compared to the scale of Amazon's overall operations in these regions. Amazon's willingness and ability to adapt its business to different international markets may play well not just with consumers, but with another important audience—regulators.

NAVIGATING PROTECTIONIST POLICIES

In entering foreign markets, Amazon faces not just cultural suspicion of American platform imperialism, but also regulatory obstacles designed to protect national culture industries and promote domestic economic development. One of the regulatory environments Amazon has navigated is right on its doorstep—Canada. Despite this proximity and a (largely) shared language, Amazon.ca wasn't launched until 2002, a few years after Germany, the UK, France, and Japan, and even with that launch, Amazon was not permitted to have a physical distribution footprint in Canada. This was due to the Investment Canada Act, which requires that foreign entities investing in or launching new businesses in Canada above a certain monetary threshold be reviewed with an eye to whether they bring a net benefit to the country, with a special focus on businesses in the cultural industries, a stipulation that certainly applies to booksellers. As a result, for the first eight years of Amazon.ca, Amazon ran the software side of the business from the United States, directly employing no one in Canada whatsoever; the company contracted with a third-party warehousing and logistics company to carry out distribution within the country. Even with this restriction, Canadian booksellers viewed the launch of Amazon.ca as an existential threat to their success as well as to the vibrancy of Canadian publishing.[43] Similar concerns were raised in Australia on the eve of Amazon's marketplace launch there. Observers noted the high proportion of Australian authors and the visibility of their books in local bookstores, and questioned whether Amazon would undermine the richness of Australia's book culture.[44] In these debates, not much was heard from Canadian and Australian publishers themselves, who could ill afford to alienate a potent new distribution channel.

Jeff Bezos certainly framed the launch of Amazon.ca as good for Canadian culture, saying "Amazon.ca provides great savings and convenience to Canadian customers and allows us to source products from Canadian publishers and distributors and work with them to increase online sales of their merchandise. . . . Amazon.ca will not only serve Canadians, but will also export Canadian products all over the world, increasing the visibility and reach of Canadian writers and artists."[45] Consistent with this messaging, within months of its launch, Amazon.ca announced its sponsorship of a fair devoted to Canadian literature, and opened specialty "boutiques" within its online store for the Toronto and Vancouver International Film Festivals.[46] Similar initiatives continued in the following years, including dedicated Amazon.ca editors who produced lists of "essential" Canadian titles sold on the site. A year before Amazon.ca was even launched, Amazon.com partnered with Books in Canada, a Canadian literary magazine, sponsoring its annual Books in Canada First Novel Award, which had previously received support from Canadian booksellers.[47]

These efforts appeared to pay off in 2010, when the restriction against Amazon having a direct footprint in Canada was overturned; the Minister of Canadian Heritage announced that Amazon had been given permission to open its first Canadian fulfillment center, as well as Amazon.ca corporate offices.[48] The decision was justified on the basis of Amazon.ca being considered a "net benefit" to Canada, given its track record in supporting Canadian culture. Heritage Minister James Moore said: "Amazon has shown its willingness to promote Canadian cultural products, and we are pleased it is continuing to demonstrate this through this new investment."[49] Nevertheless, Amazon's entry into Canada was subject to a number of conditions, including further investment in Canadian cultural events and awards and CAD 20 million worth of promotion for Canadian books abroad.[50] The Canadian Heritage Ministry's justifications also included the desire to bring employment and (taxable) profits into the country rather than have such a large operation being run largely from outside Canadian borders. Amazon.ca's efforts in previous years to present itself as a champion for Canadian authors had yielded the desired effect.

We can see similar efforts, on an even bigger scale, as Amazon woos Indian politicians and regulators, although with less consistent results. India is expected to eventually be the second-largest ecommerce market in the world (after China) as internet and smartphone penetration increase and disposable incomes continue to rise. Jeff Bezos's widely publicized visit in October 2014, in which he met with government leaders, including Prime Minister Narendra Modi, signaled how seriously Amazon took this particular foreign market.

Amazon has energetically found ways to circumnavigate India's economic protectionist policies that have continued even after the economic "opening up" of the 1990s. India has a powerful incumbent in the form of Flipkart, a company started by two software developers who worked at an Amazon IT center in Bangalore before launching their online bookselling company, which subsequently grew into new product categories, just like Amazon itself.[51] Despite the limits on foreign direct investment in various sectors, and facing a homegrown incumbent with a significant head start, Amazon had just about equaled Flipkart's market share of about 31 percent by 2018, and exceeded its revenues by 2019.[52] Snapdeal is another homegrown ecommerce company with significant market share and, since 2015, financial backing from Chinese tech giant Alibaba.[53]

It was on the heels of news that the Indian government would relax its rules on foreign direct investment (FDI), such that a "multi-brand retailer" could own a majority stake in an Indian venture, that Amazon started laying the groundwork for an Indian ecommerce marketplace.[54] Amazon reportedly initially tried, and failed, to acquire Flipkart. Its next move was to launch under a domain name it had acquired in 1998, Junglee .com (which means "wild" in Hindi), as an aggregator for *other* online retailers, framing it not as a "multi-brand retailer" which FDI rules would not allow, but a price-comparison, or advertising service.[55] In 2012 Amazon discovered that the new rule about multibrand retailers would *not* apply to ecommerce, only to brick-and-mortar retail. But by the middle of 2013 Amazon.in was launched anyway, a marketplace initially focusing on books, movies, and TV shows.[56] Amazon was able to circumvent the restriction against foreign owners of multibrand retail companies by having a "marketplace only" platform in India. In other words, Amazon.in doesn't stock any of its "own" products—it is an online platform for third-party sellers only.[57] The extent to which this is really true, however, is up for debate, and has continually been a cause of back and forth between Amazon and Indian government regulators. A single seller on an ecommerce marketplace is not supposed to account for more than 25 percent of sales, and the marketplace is not supposed to offer discounts or influence pricing.[58] Amazon set up a joint venture with an Indian company that would then sell products on its platform; it also substantially controls pricing on its platform by financing deals and discounts that its sellers offer.[59] Advocates for Indian businesses argued that Amazon had been essentially stocking and selling its own goods, which the FDI restrictions disallow, "either . . . through partner entities or through independent vendors that sourced directly from wholesale units related to the FDI-funded marketplaces," a loophole that new legislation plugged in 2018.[60] Especially since Walmart bought Flipkart in 2018, small- and medium-sized businesses in India have demanded more government scrutiny of whether both companies are skirting the rules, arguing that foreign-owned ecommerce giants are hurting Indian sellers through predatory pricing and other unfair business practices.[61] More broadly, critics of Indian government policy have pointed to how China's more protectionist approach allowed their tech incumbents to not only succeed at home, but also become global goliaths.[62]

CHINA—AMAZON MEETS ITS MATCH

The most valuable ecommerce market in the world is China, a country where Amazon struggled mightily, capturing less than 1 percent of online retail sales, before deciding to close its ecommerce operation in 2019.[63] It's well known that the Chinese government engages in muscular protectionism to foster its home-grown companies, as well as to control the circulation of political expression, particularly salient for a company like Amazon that sells books and streams entertainment. It's a nation that has perceived specific threats from American platform imperialism and used the economic and legal means at its disposal to either shut out American platforms, or extract major concessions to local restrictions from them. This has been a primary reason for Amazon's failure to meaningfully penetrate this market. But its inability to adjust to the specific expectations of Chinese online consumers is also likely a factor.

The United States is not the only economy whose power is considered "imperial" in the world today. China is an emergent superpower and the United States' greatest economic rival, whose recent investments around the world are widely thought to be due to both its economic and geopolitical ambitions.[64] It has a long history of imperialism within Asia that continues into the present day with ongoing territorial conflicts with multiple countries in the South China Sea (the conflicts extend to the name of the sea, which is contested), as well as its claim over Taiwan as part of its territory, and current global ambitions suggested by economic and infrastructure development activities associated with the Chinese government's Belt and Road Initiative. The conversation about platform imperialism must certainly include China's tech platforms, which have been protected within their massive domestic market, ideally positioning them for foreign expansion.

While as of this writing Amazon is the fourth most market-capitalized company in the world, China's Alibaba—Amazon's closest ecommerce competitor on the global stage—is the ninth.[65] Digital capitalism, so often conceptualized as having low barriers to entry and offering the possibility for localized entrepreneurship, is looking awfully oligopolistic. Until recently, Amazon and the world's second-largest ecommerce giant mostly stayed out of each other's way, "carving up the world" oligopoly-style, but as time goes on they are starting to directly compete in the world's most promising markets outside of their home countries.

While Amazon's origins are in business-to-consumer online retail sales, Alibaba's original business, Alibaba.com, provides a business-to-business online marketplace that connects Chinese manufacturers to foreign buyers. It operates in this capacity in more than two hundred countries, including the United States. It built out from this cross-border commerce business to establish Taobao.com, a consumer-to-consumer marketplace that includes thousands of smaller merchants; the business-to-consumer online shopping mall TMall, featuring bigger brands and retailers; the digital marketplace AliExpress for Chinese manufacturers to sell directly to foreign consumers; Ant Financial, a digital financial services business that includes a digital payment service for consumers similar to Paypal; and Ali Health, which sells medicines online.[66]

On the one hand, while Amazon and Alibaba are frequently conceptualized as global competitors, they are far from identical companies, and have somewhat contrasting business strategies. According to an analysis by Morgan Stanley, Amazon starts with the consumer and builds outward, whereas Alibaba emphasizes its relationship with merchants.[67] On the other hand, their business models are starting to show signs of convergence, with Amazon growing its online advertising business, which is Alibaba's largest revenue stream, while Alibaba is moving into retailing proper after being "pure platform" for most of its history, especially as it acquires brick-and-mortar stores in China that allow for hybrid online-offline retail. In the meantime, both Amazon and Alibaba are expanding their direct control of logistics, and both are focused on global expansion, increasingly in the same markets.[68] Alibaba has long been dominant in fintech, or mobile payment services, and focuses on that in its overseas activities, either by offering its own AliPay or investing in local epayment systems, like Paytm in India. Amazon has also caught onto the importance of mobile payment services especially in international markets where access to credit cards may not be widespread, or where regulations make online payment by credit card less seamless, as is the case in India where every online transaction requires two-step verification.[69] In 2017 Amazon won a license from the Indian government to start its own digital wallet program, launching into fintech in a way that makes mobile payments much easier for its customers.[70]

In comparing Amazon and Alibaba's global expansions, we can see different approaches to achieving global ubiquity. Alibaba's global expansions are not as visible as Amazon's because Alibaba is more of a global conglomerate, either owning or having stakes in companies around the world alongside its own branded global businesses such as Alibaba.com and AliExpress. According to one industry analyst, Alibaba's strategy is to "piece together subsidiaries to connect the world's ecommerce markets."[71] As it seeks to expand abroad it prefers to piggyback on existing ecommerce companies around the world, in order to benefit from their local knowledge and understanding of their consumers. Furthermore, international expansion is not as high a priority for Alibaba since there is still so much scope for growth within the Chinese market.

Amazon, in contrast, has set up its own branded marketplaces around the world. When it does acquire a local incumbent, as with Souq.com, it rebrands. With the typical confidence of an American abroad, Amazon seeks to benefit from its global brand recognition and reputation for selection and fast delivery. According to one industry analyst, Amazon also understands "the negative dilutive potential of investing in multiple brands globally, especially online brands where shoppers are less loyal: competing against yourself in your portfolio, fragmenting your shopper base, confusing your brand's identity, and limiting your value proposition in a market (i.e. 'Amazon' now stands for far more than ecommerce)."[72] As much as Amazon has sought to localize its identity and services in foreign markets, it has also stuck to the idea of being a global platform brand. There are certainly drawbacks in some contexts to its association with American cultural and economic dominance as well as platform monopoly, but Amazon has sought to manage those negative connotations while capitalizing on the recognition and synergy that a globally recognized brand can bring. Amazon's Americanness may be a net negative in particular places and contexts, but globally it's most likely a net positive. Amazon's association with tech glamour,[73] enhanced by Jeff Bezos who is well known as the world's richest person, is a nontrivial benefit in its global expansions, especially in emerging economies that sometimes receive investment by American tech capital as a flattering vote of confidence in their economic future.

CONCLUSION—THE POWER, AND LIMITS, OF PLATFORM IMPERIALISM

Across a number of countries where Amazon has set up an online marketplace, there's a detectable ambivalence about whether to welcome the American tech giant or to set limitations on the company, in the name of protecting domestic business and culture. In India the government's FDI restrictions on multibrand retailing cramp Amazon's style and on paper, at least, prevent it from actually selling anything directly in the country. But the company is embraced there in many other ways, due to the actual and perceived benefits that come with foreign investment, particularly in the tech sector which aligns with the prevailing political vision for a "Digital India." Coziness between Amazon and state entities was more than evident, for example, when India Post, with whom Amazon partners as its primary delivery carrier, released a stamp in 2016 commemorating the three-year anniversary of the launch of Amazon.in—"3 years of delivering smiles."[74] In this same category of ambivalence we might place Canada's decisions first to allow Amazon.ca to operate and then to allow Amazon to establish a footprint in the country, despite a law that strongly discourages foreign entities dealing substantially with bookselling and culture.

Amazon emphasizes conventional marketing in addition to its signature personalized relationship marketing when it officially enters foreign markets. Amazon brings strong existing associations with America and global celebrity and icon of tech entrepreneurship Jeff Bezos. Many of these connotations are beneficial to Amazon, so the company rides the wave of its international reputation for selection, convenience, and service, as well as its associations with American tech glamour and market dominance. At the same time, Amazon must make special efforts to be relatable and welcomed in other countries, especially in the face of explicit discourses from government and the business community about the threat of foreign operations to local business development and culture.

Compared to some of the other platform imperialists, like Facebook and Google, Amazon's global hegemony is far from complete. Shut out of China (for the most part), no ecommerce footprint in most countries of the world, unsuccessful in some countries due to local tastes or regulations, and battling major competitors in many countries, such as Flipkart and Snapdeal in India, Amazon up until recently has been bleeding money in its efforts to establish itself and overwhelm competitors in foreign markets with the greatest potential for growth. After the much-heralded launch of Amazon.com.au, the company's progress was seen as "weirdly underwhelming," including "early stumbles" and a sense that it "doesn't meet the hype at all."[75] Part of the problem is that what Amazon can offer in a new global marketplace doesn't always match what people know is offered in the United States. There may be fewer product categories, smaller selection, higher prices, and slower shipping. In Australia, for example, when Amazon Prime launched it only promised two-day shipping to major cities, rather than to the whole country.[76]

But what does it take to compete with Amazon, with its seemingly endless pockets, and the advantage of building brand recognition and relationships by operating in multiple services—ecommerce, ebooks, and video and music streaming? As Australian scholar David Bond puts it, "Most Australian retailers are only retailers," whereas Amazon not only runs a low-margin business, but subsidizes it through all its businesses, including the tremendously profitable Amazon Web Services, as well as the services it provides to third-party sellers.[77] A commentator observed when Amazon .in was launched, "Amazon makes its entry with a known brand and deep pockets."[78] In India, Amazon's main rival Flipkart, in search of another set of deep pockets, was acquired by Walmart in 2018. This, after almost-comical tit for tats: a day after Flipkart announced a $1 billion infusion of capital from investors, Amazon CEO Jeff Bezos committed $2 billion to growing Amazon India.[79] A year later, Amazon was announcing a $5 billion level of investment in India, in an effort to make it the company's largest market outside the United States.[80]

Why do countries with laws to protect domestic culture and industries bend, as we've seen in Canada, Australia, and India, to make it easier for Amazon to enter? Certainly, persistent lobbying is part of the answer. In the case of India's restrictions on foreign direct investment, Amazon lobbied lawmakers not just in India, but in the United States as well, in an effort to use the weight of the US government to further its interests, to the tune of millions of dollars.[81] Bezos's 2014 visit to India, repeated in 2020, was part of the charm offensive to persuade Prime Minister Modi's government to make favorable terms for Amazon. Unlike in 2014, however, in 2020 Bezos was unsuccessful in winning an audience with Modi or other high-ranking government officials. In the midst of an antitrust investigation against both Amazon and Flipkart, protests against Amazon from local retailers focused on its foreign ownership, and widespread upset about the Bezos-owned *Washington Post's* coverage of the ruling BJP party, Amazon's trumpeting of a $1 billion investment in Amazon.in and plan to enable $10 billion in exports from Indian small- and medium-sized enterprises was met with a governmental cold shoulder.[82] As India becomes a focus for foreign tech investment from all over the world (particularly China) while simultaneously building tremendous domestic capacity thanks to government support, an American tech giant like Amazon may have less leverage than it did when the country was in the earlier stages of developing its digital economy.

A consideration for national governments contemplating the arrival of Amazon is the potential for local sellers to reach global markets via Amazon's global selling platform. We saw this with Amazon's promises that closer coordination with Canadian publishers would help promote Canadian writers around the world. Amazon is sure to get stories out, like that of small-business owner Sanjay Kumar in India, who sells his jewelry, home decorations, and games to customers not just at home but in North America and Western Europe, where they pay higher prices.[83] In 2016 Amazon launched a highly visible "Make in India" store on its Amazon.in and Amazon.com sites, in coordination with an Indian government initiative designed to promote Indian manufacturing at home and exports of its goods abroad.[84] The global nature of Amazon's video streaming platform similarly offers the possibility of global audiences for local content.

Another reason Amazon is able to enter foreign markets with fewer obstacles than we might expect is because of regulatory lag. In 2016, when Amazon launched Prime Video globally, its arrival in Canada bolstered the complaints of Canadian cable companies and broadcasters to Canada's media regulator, the Canadian Radio-television and Telecommunications Commission (CRTC), that they faced unfair competition from OTT (over-the-top) streaming services, particularly Netflix.[85] Although in

Canada broadcast and cable television are subject to government content regulation, including quotas they must fill for Canadian content, OTT is not because it is delivered via the internet. Yet, OTT has clearly become a direct competitor to broadcast and cable in that it is delivering "television." If cultural protectionist regulations like Canadian content quotas are designed to promote Canadian cultural industries and maintain a certain level of Canadian video content consumption among Canadian viewers, then failing to develop policy for OTT becomes a significant oversight.

Tax laws are another good example of regulatory lag. For years, Australian retailers complained that foreign companies like Amazon and eBay could undercut them on pricing, even with shipping charges, because they didn't charge sales tax.[86] In 2018 that loophole was finally closed, just before Amazon.com.au's launch. Indeed, it came to be known as the "Amazon tax."[87] At the time of the launch, Amazon blocked Australians from the American site, where consumers had long been shopping, despite the international shipping costs. This caused consternation, since Amazon's Australian marketplace had a much smaller selection of products. Six months later, seemingly in response to consumer backlash, Amazon lifted the geo-blocking and once again allowed Australians a choice between Amazon.com and Amazon.com.au, although now with 10 percent sales tax applied to purchases for Australian buyers, in compliance with the new law.[88] But hadn't Amazon already reaped years of advantage, and made it even harder for a domestic incumbent to develop its online retail business in the lead up to 2018? In 2019, reports indicated that revenues from the sales tax on low-cost items bought from abroad online were *300 percent* higher than expected, suggesting that the government had vastly underestimated the value of goods that Australians were purchasing this way.

Governments develop their policies, but at a slow pace relative to how quickly a company like Amazon can roll out new services. In Canada, for example, the CRTC released its report on how digital distribution was affecting the "production, distribution, and promotion of Canadian programming" only in 2018, well after Netflix and then Prime Video's entry into the market, and actual policymaking on these issues (apart from an ad hoc agreement with Netflix to fund Canadian productions) is still just a glimmer in lawmakers' eyes.[89] In India, the regulation of FDI in ecommerce has similarly been somewhat slow and evolving, to the annoyance of Amazon and its investors who have proceeded despite the inherent uncertainty. Across the board, whether in the United States or internationally, regulation doesn't only lag relative to the speed of platform capitalism; lawmakers also fail to get their arms around the scope of what they are trying to regulate. These countries set out to regulate retail, bookselling, streaming video, or mobile payments, but Amazon operates across these business categories and beyond them, and its ability to subsidize growth and outcompete within these areas is precisely because of its scale and integrated nature as a platform business.

We can examine Amazon's global expansions through the lens of platform imperialism, while recognizing that, just as with cultural imperialism, Amazon's economic and cultural power as an American tech giant does not go uncontested. On the one hand, Amazon's localization efforts can be understood as a relatively minor set of concessions and expenses. The fact that Amazon creates and distributes culture makes it a greater target for nationally protectionist policies than if it operated merely in hardware and software. On the other hand, Amazon's powerful global selling platform appeals to countries' national interests in promoting homegrown products abroad as well as at home, and can actually help Amazon open doors to new markets for what, in reality, is a much broader set of business activities than the distribution of culture.

CONCLUSION: CONFRONTING THE COSTS OF CONVENIENCE

On Prime Day, which spanned July 15 and 16, 2019, the Awood Center, an East African community organizing group, staged its second walkout at the MSP1 Amazon Fulfillment Center in Shakopee, Minnesota.[1] The event was the most visible to that point of American workers organizing for better working conditions and respect from the productivity-obsessed tech giant. Workers' concerns didn't focus solely on the negative consequences of increasing productivity quotas, such as a high injury rate, but also the need for working conditions to accommodate the majority East African and Muslim populations—many recent immigrants—who worked at MSP1, including spaces and time allowances for daily prayer, and more schedule flexibility during Ramadan and Eid. The Awood Center had held a number of actions to raise awareness of these issues and met with Amazon management about them during the previous year.[2] They were "the first known group in the United States to get Amazon management to negotiate" on workplace conditions, although Amazon itself rejected the framing of these meetings as "negotiations" and their outcomes as "concessions," characterizing them instead as standard community outreach.[3] The Prime Day walkout in 2019 was hailed at the time as the most significant labor action in the United States against Amazon since its founding, despite the fact that the Awood Center was not a union, nor trying to be one (although it does receive some funding from

8.1 December 2019 cover of *Wired* magazine featuring labor activist Nimo Omar, cofounder of the Awood Center that helps East African workers organize. *Source:* Jessica Bruder, "Meet the Immigrants Who Took on Amazon," *Wired*, November 12, 2019, https://www.wired.com/story/meet-the-immigrants-who-took-on-amazon/.

the Service Employees International Union).[4] Amazon had previously defeated unionization efforts in Delaware and Seattle.[5]

Workers, in the United States and worldwide, have driven the conversation more than any other constituency about the costs of platform capitalism, particularly for a company like Amazon that requires a lot of labor power to fulfill its brand promise of the fastest deliveries in ecommerce. Unlike consumers, workers are not likely to suffer from distribution fetishism. The demands of getting products from click to doorstep in one day—Amazon's shipping promise to its Prime members since July 2019—are more than apparent to Amazon's warehouse workers who are supposed to stow 300 items an hour, or Amazon's subcontracted drivers who are required to deliver between 250 and 400 items per day.[6] The affective relationships that Amazon cultivates with its workers are very different from those it has with its consumers. In the place of service and care, according to numerous reports, are fear and ruthless discipline. Instead of making life ever more convenient and seamless, as it aims to do for its customers, Amazon ratchets up quotas and micromanages workers' every action.

In the nations of the world where unions are more common and powerful, workers have served as a check on Amazon's power, in some cases stymieing its platform imperialist ambitions. Unionized workers have participated in demonstrations and strikes in Germany and Italy, principally for higher wages.[7] In the spring of 2020 French unions shut down all of Amazon's fulfillment centers due to safety concerns. Amazon made concessions there in terms of higher pay, shorter shifts to facilitate social distancing at shift changes, rigorous safety protocols, and a gradual and voluntary return to work for employees.[8]

But even in the United States, where unions have been on the decline for decades, and Amazon has famously resisted unionization of any kind, including multiple allegations of retaliation against pro-union employees, training materials for managers to help them discourage unionization efforts, and mandatory anti-union meetings in warehouses, workers are starting to flex their muscles.[9] In both Minnesota and Bessemer, Alabama, where a union vote was held among warehouse workers in April 2021, people of color are strongly represented among the activists, as they increasingly make connections between the political calls of Black Lives Matter and the evidence they see of their lives not mattering on the job.

In September 2019, for the first time in Amazon's history, more than 1,500 of its corporate employees walked out to protest the company's carbon footprint. The demonstration organized by Amazon Employees for Climate Justice was widely credited with influencing Amazon's Climate Pledge initiative, which the group ultimately found lacking relative to their demands. Nonetheless, this walkout was inspired by, and in turn inspired, other protests and walkouts at other tech companies that collectively are coalescing into a visible "tech labor movement" among nonunionized corporate employees in the United States.[10] Similar groups of Amazon workers exist, such as Amazonians: We Won't Build It, who advocate for "accountability and transparency in the tech" they build, demanding that Amazon withdraw its cloud services from ICE (US Immigration and Customs Enforcement), and the companies, like Palantir, that contract with it. In addition, unionization groups are proliferating, including Whole Worker, focused on unionizing Amazon/Whole Foods employees, and the Chicago-based Amazon Workers @ DCH1 United. These groups' ongoing activism has paved the way for a number of walkouts as well as a coordinated May Day 2020 sick-out among Amazon and Whole Foods workers, along with workers from other industries deemed "essential," demanding adequate PPE (personal protective equipment), sick leave, and better safety protocols during the COVID-19 pandemic. In response Amazon has both pointed to the extent of its efforts in deep cleaning and monitoring its warehouses, given its employees a $500 pandemic "thank you" bonus, as well as arguably conducted retaliatory firings of protest organizers, although in each case the company has pointed to a different specified wrongdoing as the cause of the firing.[11]

These Amazon workers are organized. They drive media attention on Amazon. Both unionized groups and nonunion worker advocacy organizations have won concessions and compromises from Amazon. They've spilled some of Amazon's dirty secrets. They've drawn attention not just to their grievances as workers, but to Amazon's social and climate impacts as well. Journalists are also playing a crucial role in seeking out workers and third-party sellers to tell their stories, and in some cases, going undercover at fulfillment centers to report on the working conditions. And where are consumers, the people whose collective convenience, satisfaction, and delight justify Amazon's gargantuan investments and relentless drive for efficiencies?

CONSUMER POLITICS IN PLATFORM CAPITALISM

In this book I've set out to bring attention to not only the extent of Amazon's ubiquity in many of our lives, but also the way that Amazon brands and normalizes it, rendering our entanglements with the company almost invisible. Amazon is convenient and personalized. It connects us to a world of goods like never before. And by extending across a wide variety of synergistic products and services, it provides a self-proclaimed "ecosystem" that makes interacting with the same company for everything from regular diaper delivery to movie and music streaming seem perfectly natural. As *New York Times* reporter Scott Shane concludes, based on his investigation of Amazon's activities throughout the city of Baltimore, "Amazon may now reach into Americans' daily existence in more ways than any corporation in history."[12]

It can't be denied that Amazon offers significant benefits and convenience to consumers, given the company's rapid growth of sales, profitability, and Prime memberships—estimated at 147 million paid subscribers in the United States in 2021.[13] There's no question that Amazon is big—big in Prime members, big in physical footprint, big in employees, big in sales and growth, big in media subscription users, and big in market capitalization. What's less clear is whether ordinary consumers are able to perceive, or notice, its bigness, and the full range of consequences of both Amazon's size and market dominance.

What I have set out to show is that there are a variety of factors stacked against consumers, in particular, being able to perceive the extent and consequences of Amazon's market dominance and the costs of Amazon's convenience. Delivery is often free, or included in the Prime membership that bundles a multitude of services, so the "costs" of Amazon's distribution infrastructure are unlikely to register. The consistent focus on high-speed package deliveries fetishizes our relationship to time and masks the labor and infrastructures that move products across space. By being at core a service brand, Amazon builds tremendous trust and affection among its users by placing our convenience, desire, and necessity at the center of everything it does. As we get more products and services from Amazon, the frequency of interactions between consumer and brand increases, as does the intimacy of the personalized service relationship. As more of those services move into the spheres of culture and the home, Amazon is able to more consistently collect data that reflect our most private selves. Personified as Alexa, the medium of voice points to even greater ubiquity and intimacy in this service relationship, as "she" is integrated into more parts of our lives, consistent with the trajectory of the Internet of Things.

The name of the company itself, some of its product lines (e.g., "Fire") as well as the language of "ecosystem" and "cloud" metaphorically present Amazon's size and ubiquity as natural, merely providing an *environment* conducive to our thriving just as a natural ecosystem would (or should). Across the domains of distribution, culture, and image, Amazon promotes the comfort and care of the consumer, in an effort both to improve its business and secure our consent to its rapidly expanding market dominance and intensive dataveillance.

Despite these efforts, consumers can and do notice as Amazon approaches monopoly status in many business areas, and start to question either its specific business practices, or the sheer extent of its market power, and by extension, its social and political power. Calls to boycott Amazon arise with some frequency—calls to "send a message" by canceling Amazon accounts and then vote with our dollars by supporting local businesses as an alternative to Amazon. However, the sheer scope, market power, and loss-leading abilities of Amazon make the traditional tools of the consumer boycott a tall order in terms of impact. In the end, it's probably too simple to say consumers should shop elsewhere and cancel their Amazon accounts, which is an individual-level solution to a problem that is societal and structural. Amazon has become "essential infrastructure" in too many ways, connecting a huge proportion of online sellers to buyers, providing computing infrastructure to countless companies and organizations through Amazon Web Services, controlling the vast majority of ebooks and self-publishing, and owning many companies that consumers may not even be aware of, such as IMDb, Zappos, Twitch, and Ring.[14] Complicating a boycott of Amazon is the fact that so many small and medium-sized businesses do depend on it for distribution of their content, marketing, and products to customers. Until a comparable retail platform exists, such a boycott would more immediately hurt those sellers than Amazon itself.

To be effective, consumer boycotts need to be quick to understand and easy to act upon. "De-Amazoning" your life is anything but. One committed Amazon boycotter describes it as "not just a choice," but an "ongoing practice."[15] Kashmir Hill, a reporter who spent a week blocking all Amazon products and services, found it ultimately impossible. A product she ordered on eBay was delivered via Amazon's fulfillment services, her children's favorite digital entertainment came either via Prime Video or an AWS-supported streaming service, and AWS supports so many websites and apps that she could hardly communicate with colleagues or friends without it.[16]

While calls for consumer boycotts of Amazon are made with some regularity, and intensified during the COVID-19 pandemic due to questions about warehouse conditions, there's no evidence that they have significantly impacted Amazon's sales, or received significant news or social media attention, the primary ways that boycotts impact company reputations and stock prices.[17] The diffuse nature of Amazon's brand, the network effects it enjoys due to its market share, and its flexibility and therefore varied meanings to consumers all tend to insulate it from consumer actions such as boycotts. While being a large, high-visibility company like McDonald's or Nike typically makes you an effective target for activism and boycotts, being a *ubiquitous* company makes it less effective. When a brand is as ubiquitous as Amazon, leading to multiple consumer interactions of different kinds per day, the greater consumer trust and attachment are, and the less likely consumers will be to resent or challenge the company's bigness. Even if Amazon could be brought down with a consumer boycott, it would merely make space for a competitor—most likely Walmart, Google, or Apple, depending on the business area, rather than some scrappy upstart—that would take advantage of the same systems and structures of platform capitalism.

Unlike Amazon workers, Amazon consumers are not organized, at least not in a very visible way. The personalization at the heart of Amazon's brand means consumers have different kinds of relationships and associations with the tech giant, and therefore less in common with each other. With Amazon's brick-and-mortar locations still in their infancy, there are few occasions for Amazon consumers to encounter each other as such in public. When Amazon's everywhere, it's also nowhere. Amazon's ubiquity makes it harder to pin it down for resistance.

Amazon has earned a great deal of consumer trust, and as it moves into a growing array of services, especially home-based services, it has the opportunity to make consumers feel cared for by the brand. This trust and sense of pastoral care too easily translates into complacency in the face of the extent of Amazon's powers of governance. We might applaud a specific way that Amazon uses its power—such as providing a twenty-week paid parental leave to all its full-time workers (scandalously, a rare benefit for blue-collar workers in the United States)—but we should still question the power that Amazon has to extract policies and regulations that favor its business interests.

We saw the implications of corporate governance and decision power play out with Amazon and other tech giants in January 2021, when Twitter and Facebook deplatformed Donald Trump and then Apple, Google, and Amazon rapidly deplatformed the social media platform Parler from their app stores, effectively banning it from public use for a period of time because of its role in hosting violent content that contributed to the January 6 insurrection at the US Capitol. These actions were met with relief and gratitude by many who were traumatized and frustrated with how Trump and some of his supporters had brought democracy in the United States to the precipice. The tech giants did what a sharply divided Congress ultimately couldn't, which was to take decisive, timely action against the instigators of the January 6 insurrection and attack on the US Capitol. But this demonstration of platform power was also a sobering reminder of where governance increasingly lies—not with elected representatives, but with corporations that answer first and foremost to shareholders and themselves. Even if in a particular instance we applaud the move or align with the values expressed by these companies, we should recognize how little say in these decisions we ultimately have as consumers and citizens. If we believe in democratic governance, we must resist the temptation to endorse or romanticize gestures of noblesse oblige from the current leaders of tech.

It's tempting to lay blame: with consumers for being insatiable for convenience and large selection at low prices. With Amazon for its endless appetite for growth, its drive to extract as much value from communities and workers as possible while paying as little in taxes as possible, and its cutthroat competitiveness. But all these behaviors are in accordance with the incentives and reward systems of capitalism, and the ways in which laws and regulations have failed to keep pace with the specifics of platform capitalism. The natural state of capitalism is to overwhelm the competition—competitive markets over the long run are made, not born naturally. Amazon and our own dependence on it are the logical outgrowths of relatively unfettered capitalism, as it plays out with the affordances of digital platforms.

What the case of Amazon highlights is that our democratic institutions of governance are not prepared for this rate of change or this concentration of corporate wealth and power. The affordances of platform and digital capitalism allow for a scale and speed of growth and market transformation that are unfamiliar and hard to grasp, in terms of both cognition and regulation. On top of that, American culture, in particular, is out of practice in constraining corporate growth, and lacks the language and cultural frameworks to meaningfully talk about the concentration of corporate power. Memories are short—the peak of government antitrust activity, and the market conditions that made it seem necessary, are mostly beyond living memory. So convinced have we become that companies have a divine right to get bigger, and consumers have an inalienable right to lower prices, more product choices, and faster deliveries, that we no longer have ways of conceptualizing reasonable constraints on a corporation, or what the benefits of such constraints might be.

In addition to cultural amnesia about antitrust, tech giants like Amazon actively cultivate relations with their consumers, and shape consumer subjectivities, in ways that discourage identification and advocacy among consumers as a bloc. We're differentially treated as consumers, relative to our ability to pay for a membership or go cashless, or due to the perceived future value of our loyalty, but the costs of that discrimination remain invisible when our engagements with the store are so personalized. At one level, this occurs because consumers spend less time in the shared quasi-public space of the store for a mostly online brand like Amazon.

This has been a perhaps unintended side effect of Amazon's expansion into brick-and-mortar—its Amazon Books and Amazon Go locations are targets for protests aimed at Amazon's business practices.

Beyond the inherent individualization of online shopping is Amazon's cultivation of the "time-starved subject" and its complement, the served self.[18] Culminating in the digital assistant Alexa, these consumer subjectivities discourage critical perspective and psychological distance between consumer and brand compared to the choosing subject. In the arena of media, now increasingly offered as a "service," audiences are provided with yet more reasons to stay within Amazon's self-proclaimed "ecosystem," while simultaneously providing Amazon with moment-to-moment data about their engagement with content, across music, video, ebook, and live gaming subscription services. Consumers frequently find themselves "locked in" to Amazon's bundle of services, but since these are offered through the logic of the "pleasure garden" rather than a "walled garden," it's not necessarily experienced as a constraint or limitation. The more integrated Amazon becomes across business areas, the more convenience it can offer its customers, and the more dependent they tend to become on Amazon, especially as these customers internalize (or genuinely experience, given the demands of work and family) the necessity to be always saving time and effort. As pricing becomes more dynamic and personalized with online retail and the integration of digital price tags and mobile payments in offline retail, not to mention the way the Prime membership bundles so many services together, the literal cost of this convenience is obscured, and will only continue to become more so.

Can the served self be a meaningful check on platform power? What is the future of consumer politics when consumers and consumption are so fragmented and differentiated, and when so many resources are devoted to "delighting" us, sometimes at the expense of workers, communities, and the environment? My study of Amazon—the depth of the relationships it forges with consumers, and the breadth of products and services it provides—leads me to wonder whether, rather than "amusing ourselves to death," which Neil Postman argued in the 1980s would be the result of our engagement with mass media, we are being "served to distraction" by the personalized service of ubiquitous platform giants.[19]

I conclude this book with suggestions for how, as *consumers*, we might be activated to more fully understand the nature of a platform giant like Amazon and, if appropriate, resist its power.

CREATE A CONSUMER-LED ANTIMONOPOLY MOVEMENT

If market concentration is defended by Amazon and tolerated by regulators due to a focus on consumer welfare, then it behooves consumers to confront the costs of convenience that Amazon's market dominance affords, and offer other visions of consumer welfare and the social good that legislators, regulators, and courts can respond to. Currently in congressional hearings and other spaces of fact-finding and decision-making, both tech giants and legislators purport to speak on behalf of consumers and have their benefit as their primary goal, but both groups are also beholden to other stakeholders. In those contexts, no one is speaking solely for the consumer. A less competitive business environment is being produced in our name as consumers. A dataveillance infrastructure—one that consumers have voluntarily integrated into their domestic spaces—is being constructed for our convenience but without our meaningful consent. Amazon uses its focus on the consumer to justify its extractive, allegedly sometimes abusive treatment of its workers, as well as the tremendous rate at which it consumes carbon to feed our desire for fast delivery and constant digital connectedness. Organized consumers could resist the narrative that greater convenience, wider selection, or lower prices are the only considerations that should be consulted in justifying business practices and working conditions.

Consumers should be part of debating and deciding how to govern and articulate reasonable limits on platforms like Amazon that balance innovation and creativity in business with the need for competitive markets, fair playing fields, and benefits beyond "consumer welfare" to workers and communities. Or, if it is concluded that Amazon's provision of "essential infrastructure" makes it more like a utility, then it could be regulated as such with the accompanying benefits and restrictions. But how? My answer to this question considers not so much the nuts and bolts of antimonopoly remedies, but how advocacy and activism in this area need to respond to the everyday and affective nature of our relationships with

Amazon, and how it feels to be a consumer in the context of platform capitalism. In other words, a consumer-based antimonopoly movement must be culturally and affectively legible.

FIGHT AFFECT WITH AFFECT

In this book I have encouraged us to view Amazon, not often considered an emotional brand, as a highly affective brand that forges familiarity and intimacy with its users. While Amazon has deployed affect to gain consumer trust and promote its own ubiquity, we should also look to affect as a source of tools to resist the nature and effects of that ubiquity. In the case of Amazon, its familiarity and techniques of affective connection to consumers can be productively incorporated into activism against it. One approach to leveraging Amazon's affective strategies can be seen in how activists, including labor activists and community members who protested Amazon's HQ2 deal in Queens, New York, hijacked Amazon's smile boxes in their demonstrations (see figure 8.2).[20]

8.2 "People opposed to Amazon's plan to locate a headquarters in New York City hold a protest inside of an Amazon book store on 34th. St. on November 26, 2018 in New York City." Photo and caption by Stephanie Keith/Getty Images.

Using spray paint and stencils, the protesters literally flipped that smile upside-down. Beyond the inverted smile boxes, Amazon protesters regularly use brown cardboard as the medium for their signs, materially connecting their dissent to Amazon's primary tactile connection to its customers. The familiarity and affection that people feel for these boxes creates a potentially powerful focus to connect our everyday purchases to Amazon's hidden impacts, whether on workers, the climate, or vulnerable populations who are unjustly profiled using Amazon's facial-recognition technology.[21]

Another intervention at the level of affect might involve requiring platforms like Amazon to allow more direct communication between sellers and consumers, so that sellers and product brands have a greater chance to forge relationships with consumers, rather than be overshadowed by the relationship that shoppers have with Amazon, as is arguably now the case. Platforms are by definition "two-sided" businesses; in the case of Amazon, it serves as an intermediary between consumers and product sellers. In this role, Amazon circumscribes the communication that can occur between buyers and sellers, with the trend line being toward more limited communication. If there's a problem with a product, buyers notify Amazon, which in turn passes the message on to sellers. If a buyer leaves a negative review, sellers used to be able to reply directly with a comment in the reviews section, but are no longer allowed to by Amazon. If consumers are almost literally shielded from direct communication with the individuals or companies they buy from, they are not in a good position to see how Amazon as a platform is shaping the terms of market exchange, often in ways that businesses find extremely challenging. These challenges are especially acute for small, third-party sellers, a significant proportion of whom make all of their income on Amazon.[22] Sympathy for the challenges that these sellers experience on this mega-platform could be a powerful motivator for consumers to reflect on their relationship to this company, a pro–small business argument that is likely to be compelling to users across the political spectrum.

FIND A FOCUS FOR AMORPHOUS GUILT
One of the challenges of confronting the costs of Amazon's convenience is its diffuseness across business areas. Because Amazon subsidizes some

business activities with profits in others, our use of its media streaming services, ecommerce, or any site supported by AWS all contribute to its ability to provide and grow all these products and services. Beyond that, just interacting with any Amazon service creates a data trail that feeds into Amazon's rapidly growing digital advertising business. Similarly, people's unease about using Amazon is often amorphous in nature. Many people feel uneasy or embarrassed about how often they buy items from Amazon, whether it's due to the conspicuousness of the Amazon boxes outside their homes, self-consciousness about no longer patronizing local stores, or vague concerns about the climate and community impacts of delivery vans. During the time of pandemic, the feelings become only more complex, because shopping online in order to stay home is widely understood to be socially responsible, but it simultaneously puts more pressure on and may endanger Amazon workers who have been deemed essential. Many consumers (not all of course!) feel vaguely guilty, but lack clarity about what the issues are and alternatives that they feel confident would make a difference.

Amazon encourages the distribution fetishism among consumers that causes them to obsess about the time until their package is delivered, but remain blissfully ignorant about the infrastructure, energy, and labor that it takes to get it there. It does so through its emphasis on fast delivery times in its marketing, its mobile push alerts, and the way its brand identity hangs substantially on fulfilling delivery promises. Defetishizing distribution would go a long way toward providing greater clarity and focus to the amorphous guilt that many consumers have. Amazon could certainly provide more transparency about where products are sourced from, the journeys they take, the number of human touches they receive, and the carbon impacts of different delivery options, in order to shift decision power to consumers. Consumers demanding information that helps them reclaim their decision power might not necessarily be focused on antimonopoly, but more generally on resisting the served self, where we let Amazon make so many decisions for us.

Making the fate of our data and exactly how Amazon will use it clearer and more user-friendly would defetishize another kind of distribution, and promote more meaningful decision power in that arena. Much ink has been spilled about the limitations of the choosing subject structured by the consumer cultures of the twentieth century. But it's hard not to see at least some value in respect for consumer choice given the lack of real choices around how much data we reveal to tech companies, and how they can use it. In the United States at least, it's typical to simply be locked out of services entirely if you don't agree to the standard "privacy" and End User License Agreement policies. Some progress in this area is already being made through government regulations such as the GDPR and CCPA. User-friendly procedures and interfaces that allow people to request and visualize who can use what data and how would be a step toward putting the dispossession of our data into its proper context. Such a demand from a consumer-based movement is relevant to Amazon but also well beyond it, given the prevalence of user data-based commodities and market advantages in the digital economy.

REMATERIALIZING THE DIGITAL ECONOMY

Demanding more transparency from Amazon and its fellow tech giants is a laudable goal, whether in the realms of climate impacts, workplace safety, or data security. However, there are limitations to transparency, especially when understood as the ability to "see" what is happening. Especially with the digital economy, which has often been imagined as immaterial in nature, there's value to imagining what it would mean to rematerialize it. One such intervention that has done so is Kate Crawford and Vladan Joler's 2018 "Anatomy of an AI System," a map-like graphic and accompanying essay that attempts to represent the entirety of the supply chains involved in the life cycle of an Amazon Echo, at the stages of manufacture, use, and eventual end of life (see figure 8.3).[23] The visualization connects the single moment of asking Alexa the time to the global locations of resource extraction, rare earth minerals, dozens of types of human work, networked communication, physical transportation networks, and machine learning processes. Acknowledging that "the scale of this system is almost beyond human imagining," it nevertheless does its very best "to grasp its immensity and complexity as a connected form." While "a full accounting for these costs is almost impossible," including the costs to human well-being in underpaid and dangerous work, and the environmental costs of rare earth mining, global shipping, and e-waste, among other impacts, "it is increasingly important that we grasp the scale and scope if we are to understand and govern the technical infrastructures that thread through our lives."[24]

8.3 Kate Crawford and Vladan Joler, "Anatomy of an AI System," 2018. Photographed by Ars Electronica / Martin Hieslmair. Used with permission.

"Anatomy of an AI System" is aimed less at transparency, or showing the viewer whatever there is to see behind the Echo, than at using visualization as a technique to rematerialize what is otherwise a virtual interaction with a disembodied voice. The map includes materialities that are difficult to see, such as the toxic qualities of different rare earth minerals, and the differential wages between Amazon's CEO and the manual laborers who mine minerals or dispose of e-waste. As Crawford and Joler point out, the Echo is one of the means by which Amazon collects wide-ranging and fine-grained data from its users that are a tremendous resource for its natural language processing and its business writ large. The map aims to even out—even if just a little bit—the knowledge asymmetries between consumer and brand.

Amazon is the tech giant in our living rooms whose ubiquity extends across the domains of home, business, government, law enforcement, entertainment, and shopping. The sheer breadth of its activities may be distinctive, but many of the lessons learned from it are applicable to other platform giants, particularly the other members of GAFAM: Google, Apple, Facebook, and Microsoft, as well as Walmart, with whom Amazon shares a great deal of business DNA. In some cases, as with smart speakers and the Internet of Things, these corporate giants are literally fading into the woodwork. We need to find better ways to appreciate the full extent of our entanglements with them and how they benefit or hurt our communities. We also need to find a way to understand, or imagine, what the alternatives might be, or how platforms might be asked to abide by different rules. We should not leave scrutiny of Amazon's corporate practices to workers, who necessarily put their jobs, livelihoods, and even their lives on the line to do so. Consumers bear responsibility as well. Without consumers and citizens speaking out, we can't expect politicians to do this work entirely on our behalf, independently, especially given "governance creep" that has occurred from governments to large corporations, particularly under the conditions of platform capitalism. We need to confront the costs of convenience, and reclaim our consumer power, rather than let ourselves be served to distraction.

NOTES

INTRODUCTION

1. Jodi Kantor and David Streitfeld, "Inside Amazon: Wrestling Big Ideas in a Bruising Workplace," *New York Times*, August 15, 2015, http://www.nytimes.com/2015/08/16/technology/inside-amazon-wrestling-big-ideas-in-a-bruising-workplace.html?_r=0.

2. *Frontline*, "Amazon Empire: The Rise and Reign of Jeff Bezos," season 38, episode 13, Directed by James Jacoby, written by Anya Bourg and James Jacoby. PBS, February 18, 2020.

3. Vincent Mosco, *Becoming Digital: Toward a Post-Internet Society* (Bingley, UK: Emerald Publishing, 2017), 55–56.

4. Adam Greenfield, *Everyware: The Dawning Age of Ubiquitous Computing* (Berkeley, CA: New Riders, 2006).

5. Ken Hillis, Michael Petit, and Kylie Jarrett, *Google and the Culture of Search* (New York: Routledge, 2013); Derek Johnson, ed., *From Networks to Netflix: A Guide to Changing Channels* (New York: Routledge, 2018); Siva Vaidhyanathan, *Antisocial Media: How Facebook Disconnects Us and Undermines Democracy* (New York: Oxford University Press, 2018); Siva Vaidhyanathan, *The Googlization of Everything (And Why We Should Worry)* (Berkeley: University of California Press, 2011).

6. Michele White, *Buy It Now: Lessons from eBay* (Durham, NC: Duke University Press, 2012).

7. Abha Bhatterai, "Baby Boomers, to Retailers' Surprise, Are Dominating Online Shopping," *Washington Post*, January 21, 2021, https://www.washingtonpost.com/road-to-recovery/2021/01/21/baby-boombers-online-shopping-pandemic/; Adam Satariano and Emma Bubola, "Pasta, Wine, and Inflatable Pools: How Amazon Conquered Italy

in the Pandemic," *New York Times*, September 26, 2020, https://www.nytimes.com /2020/09/26/technology/amazon-coronavirus-pandemic.html.

8. Robert Spector, *Amazon.com Get Big Fast: The Astounding Rise and Uncertain Future of the E-commerce Giant* (New York: HarperCollins Business, 2000), 156.

9. Joshua A. Braun, *This Program Is Brought to You By . . . : Distribution Television News Online* (New Haven, CT: Yale University Press, 2015); Michael Curtin, Jennifer Holt, and Kevin Sanson, eds., *Distribution Revolution: Conversations about the Digital Future of Film and Television* (Oakland: University of California Press, 2014); Ramon Lobato, *Netflix Nations: The Geography of Digital Distribution* (New York: New York University Press, 2019); Amanda D. Lotz, *Portals: A Treatise on Internet-Distributed Television* (Ann Arbor: University of Michigan Press, 2017), https://quod.lib.umich.edu/m/maize/mpub 9699689/.

10. Daniel Herbert, *Videoland: Movie Culture at the American Video Store* (Berkeley: University of California Press, 2014); Daniel Herbert and Derek Thompson, eds., *Point of Sale: Analyzing Media Retail* (New Brunswick, NJ: Rutgers University Press, 2019).

11. Daniel Miller, *A Theory of Shopping* (Ithaca, NY: Cornell University Press, 1998), 9.

12. Paul N. Edwards, "Infrastructure and Modernity: Force, Time, and Social Organization in the History of Sociotechnical Systems," in *Modernity and Technology*, ed. Thomas J. Misa, Andrew Feenberg, and Philip Brey (Cambridge, MA: MIT Press, 2003), 185–186.

13. For more information on Amazon Mechanical Turk, see Mary L. Gray and Siddharth Suri, *Ghost Work: How to Stop Silicon Valley from Building a New Global Underclass* (Boston: Houghton Mifflin Harcourt, 2019); Lilly C. Irani and M. Six Silberman, "Turkopticon: Interrupting Worker Invisibility in Amazon Mechanical Turk," *Proceedings of the SIGCHI Conference on Human Factors in Computing Systems* (2013), 611–620.

14. John Rossman, *The Amazon Way on IoT: 10 Principles for Every Leader from the World's Leading Internet of Things Strategies* (Seattle, WA: Clyde Hill Publishing, 2016), 43.

15. Nick Srnicek, *Platform Capitalism* (Malden, MA: Polity Press, 2017), 43.

16. Srnicek, *Platform Capitalism*, 45–48.

17. Brad Stone, *The Everything Store: Jeff Bezos and the Age of Amazon* (New York: Little, Brown, and Co., 2013), 107.

18. John R. Wells, Benjamin Weinstock, Galen Danskin, and Gabriel Ellsworth, "Amazon.com, 2019," Case, 9-716-402, Harvard Business Publishing, October 21, 2019, 5; Jerrold Nadler and David N. Cicilline, *Investigation of Competition in Digital Markets*, U.S. Subcommittee on Antitrust, Commercial and Administrative Law of the Committee of the Judiciary, 2020, https://judiciary.house.gov/uploadedfiles /competition_in_digital_markets.pdf, 274.

19. Spector, *Amazon.com Get Big Fast*, 197, emphasis in original.

20. Nick Montfort and Ian Bogost, *Racing the Beam: The Atari Video Computer System* (Cambridge, MA: MIT Press, 2009), vii.

21. Stone, *The Everything Store*, 209–210.

22. Canalys, "Global Cloud Infrastructure Market Q3 2020," October 29, 2020, https://www.canalys.com/newsroom/worldwide-cloud-market-q320.

23. Jordan Novet, "Amazon Cloud Division Reports 28% Revenue Growth," February 2, 2021, *CNBC*, https://www.cnbc.com/2021/02/02/aws-earnings-q4-2020.html.

24. Amazon Web Services, "What Is AWS?," 2021, https://aws.amazon.com/what-is-aws/?nc2=h_ql_le_int.

25. Marc Andreessen, "The Three Kinds of Platforms You Meet on the Internet," *Pmarchive*, 2007, https://pmarchive.com/three_kinds_of_platforms_you_meet_on_the_internet.html.

26. Srnicek, *Platform Capitalism*, 39–40.

27. Tarleton Gillespie, "The Politics of 'Platforms,'" *New Media & Society* 12, no. 3 (2010): 347–364. doi: 10.1177/1461444809342738, 349–351.

28. Ian Bogost and Nick Montfort, "Platform Studies: Frequently Questioned Answers," *Proceedings of the Digital Arts and Culture Conference*, University of California, Irvine, December 12, 2009, 1, https://escholarship.org/uc/item/01r0k9br; Jean-Christophe Plantin, Carl Lagoze, Paul N. Edwards, and Christian Sandvig, "Infrastructure Studies Meet Platform Studies in the Age of Google and Facebook," *New Media & Society* 20, no. 1 (2018): 294. doi: 10.1177/1461444816661553; David Murakami Wood and Torin Monahan, "Editorial: Platform Surveillance," *Surveillance & Society* 17, no. 1/2 (2019): 2.

29. Peter H. Farquhar, "Managing Brand Equity," *Marketing Research* 1, no. 3 (1989): 25.

30. Gillespie, "Politics of 'Platforms,'" 350.

31. Sarah Banet-Weiser, "Brands," in *Keywords for Media Studies*, ed. Laurie Ouellette and Jonathan Gray (New York: New York University Press, 2017), 24.

32. Adam Arvidsson, *Brands: Meaning and Value in Media Culture* (New York: Routledge, 2006), 10.

33. Adam Arvidsson, "Brands: A Critical Perspective," *Journal of Consumer Culture* 5, no. 2 (2005): 249, doi: 10.1177/1469540505053093.

34. Anna Weiner, "What a Tour of an Amazon Fulfillment Center Reveals," *New Yorker*, November 4, 2019, https://www.newyorker.com/news/letter-from-silicon-valley/what-an-amazon-fulfillment-center-tour-reveals.

35. Leonard. L. Berry, "Cultivating Service Brand Equity," *Journal of the Academy of Marketing Science* 28, no. 1 (2000): 128; Timothy Havens, "Netflix: Streaming Channel Brands as Global Meaning Systems," in *From Networks to Netflix: A Guide to Changing Channels*, ed. Derek Johnson (New York: Routledge, 2018), 322–325.

36. Mark Bonchek and Vivek Bapat, "The Most Successful Brands Focus on Users—Not Buyers," *Harvard Business Review*, February 7, 2018, https://hbr.org/2018/02/the-most-successful-brands-focus-on-users-not-buyers.

37. Ellen Neuborne, "Branding on the Net," *Bloomberg*, November 9, 1998, https://www.bloomberg.com/news/articles/1998-11-08/branding-on-the-net?sref=1nAnrjlw; Bob

Garfield and Doug Levy, "Ignore the Human Element of Marketing at Your Own Peril," *Advertising Age*, January 2, 2012, http://adage.com/article/news/dawn-relationship-era -marketing/231792/.

38. Bonchek and Bapat, "The Most Successful Brands."

39. Bonchek and Bapat.

40. Garfield and Levy, "Ignore the Human Element."

41. Richard L. Brandt, *One Click: Jeff Bezos and the Rise of Amazon.com* (New York: Portfolio/Penguin, 2011), 85.

42. Wells et al., "Amazon.com, 2019," 3.

43. Stone, *The Everything Store*, 129.

44. John Rossman, *The Amazon Way: 14 Leadership Principles Behind the World's Most Disruptive Company* (North Charleston, SC: CreateSpace Independent Publishing Platform, 2014), 10.

45. Bradley Johnson, "Prime Time: Amazon Is Now Earth's Biggest Advertiser," *Advertising Age*, December 7, 2020, https://adage.com/article/datacenter/prime-time -amazon-now-earths-biggest-advertiser/2298666.

46. Statista Research Department, "Amazon's Advertising Spending in the United States from 2012 to 2019," *Statista*, January 14, 2021, https://www.statista.com/statistics /192254/us-ad-spending-of-amazon/.

47. Michael Hardt, "Affective Labor," *Boundary 2* 26, no. 2 (1999): 95–96; Alison Hearn, "Verified: Self-presentation, Identity Management, and Selfhood in the Age of Big Data," *Popular Communication* 15, no. 2 (2017): 63, http://dx.doi.org/10.1080/15405702.2016 .1269909; Kristin Swenson, "Capitalizing on Affect: Viagra (In)Action," *Communication, Culture & Critique* 1, no. 3 (2008): 312–313, doi: 10.1111/j.1753–9137.2008.00025.x.

48. Emily West, "Affect Theory and Advertising: A New Look at IMC, Spreadability, and Engagement," in *Explorations in Critical Studies of Advertising*, ed. James F. Hamilton, Robert Bodle, and Ezequiel Korn (New York: Routledge, 2016), 250–251.

49. Sara Ahmed, "Affective Economies," *Social Text* 22, no. 2 (2004): 120–121, doi: 10.1215/01642472-22-2_79–117.

50. Swenson, "Capitalizing on Affect," 319.

51. Andrew McStay, *Creativity and Advertising: Affect, Events, and Process* (New York: Routledge, 2013), 2–4.

52. Brandt, *One Click*, 119.

53. "Condé Nast and Goldman Sachs Release the 2017 Love List Brand Affinity Index," *Condé Nast Press Room*, 2017, https://www.condenast.com/news/conde-nast -and-goldman-sachs-release-the-2017-love-list-brand-affinity-index.

54. "Most Loved Brands in America 2019," *MorningConsult.com*, 2020, https://morn ingconsult.com/most-loved-brands-2019/.

55. "Reputation Quotient," *Harris Poll*, 2018, https://theharrispoll.com/reputation -quotient/.

56. The Values Institute, "America's Most Trustworthy Brands Unveiled after Nationwide Survey by The Values Institute," *Business Wire*, September 12, 2017, https://www.businesswire.com/news/home/20170912005317/en/America%E2%80%99s-Most-Trustworthy-Brands-Unveiled-after-Nationwide-Survey-by-The-Values-Institute.

57. "Top Brands: Most Trustworthy," *Forbes*, 2020, https://www.forbes.com/pictures/fjji45eifh/10-amazon-com/#6279d80c1e19; "Brave Brands Are Trusted Brands," *Interbrand*, 2018, https://www.interbrand.com/best-brands/best-global-brands/2018/articles/brave-brands-are-trusted-brands/.

58. Jonathan M. Ladd, Joshua A. Tucker, and Sean Kates, "2018 American Institutional Confidence Poll," 2018, http://aicpoll.com/.

59. Stone, *The Everything Store*, 317.

60. Stone, 318.

61. Dal Yong Jin, "The Construction of Platform Imperialism in the Globalization Era," *TripleC* 11, no. 1 (2013): 153–154.

CHAPTER 1

1. Karl Marx, *Capital: A Critique of Political Economy, Volume II*, trans. Ben Fowkes (New York: Penguin Classics, 1998/1978).

2. Daniel Schiller, *Digital Capitalism: Networking the Global Market System* (Cambridge, MA: MIT Press, 1999).

3. James Carey, *Communication as Culture: Essays on Media and Society* (New York: Routledge, 1988/2009), 12–13.

4. Rebecca Solnit, "The Annihilation of Time and Space," *New England Review* 24, no. 1 (2003): 9–11.

5. Richard K. Popp, "The Anywhere, Anytime Market: The 800-Number, Direct Marketing, and the New Networks of Consumption," *Enterprise & Society* 19, no. 3 (2018): 728, doi:10.1017/eso.2017.68.

6. Gordon L. Weil, *Sears, Roebuck, U.S.A.: The Great American Catalog Store and How It Grew* (New York: Stein and Day, 1977), 5–8.

7. Tim Berners-Lee, "Long Live the Web," *Scientific American* 303, no. 6 (2010): 82–83.

8. Stone, *The Everything Store*.

9. Weil, *Sears, Roebuck*, 66; Richard B. Kielbowicz, "Rural Ambivalence Toward Mass Society: Evidence from the U.S. Parcel Post Debates, 1900–1913," *Rural History* 5, no. 1 (1994): 92–94.

10. Weil, *Sears, Roebuck*, 25.

11. Spector, *Amazon.com Get Big Fast*, 57–60.

12. Spector, 1.

13. Spector, 231.

14. Spector, 255.

15. Tim Wu, *The Attention Merchants: The Epic Scramble to Get Inside Our Heads* (New York: Knopf, 2016), 200–202.

16. Wu, *Attention Merchants*, 213.

17. Charisse Jones, "Sears, in Bankruptcy, Is Set to Close 40 More Stores on Top of Dozens Previously Announced," *USA Today*, November 8, 2018, https://www.usatoday .com/story/money/2018/11/08/sears-aiming-emerge-smaller-company-closing-40 -more-stores/1933732002/.

18. Warren Shoulberg, "Is the Sears Death Watch Entering Its Final Stages?," *Forbes*, January 2, 2020, https://www.forbes.com/sites/warrenshoulberg/2020/01/02/is-the -sears-death-watch-entering-its-final-stages/#4d86798d1925.

19. "Top 50 Global Retailers," *Stores: NRF's Magazine*, March 1, 2019, https://stores .org/2019/03/01/top-50-global-retailers/.

20. National Retail Federation, "Top 100 Retailers 2020 List," https://nrf.com/resources /top-retailers/top-100-retailers/top-100-retailers-2020-list.

21. National Retail Federation, "Top 100."

22. Matt Day and Spencer Soper, "Amazon U.S. Online Market Share Estimate Cut to 38% from 47%," *Bloomberg*, June 13, 2019, https://www.bloomberg.com/news /articles/2019-06-13/emarketer-cuts-estimate-of-amazon-s-u-s-online-market-share ?sref=1nAnrjIw; Wells et al., "Amazon.com, 2019," 24.

23. eMarketer, "Top 10 US Companies, Ranked by Retail Ecommerce Sales Share, 2019: % of Total Retail Sales," *eMarketer*, February 12, 2019, https://www.emarketer .com/chart/226336/top-10-us-companies-ranked-by-retail-ecommerce-sales-share -2019-of-total-retail-sales.

24. Meredith Lepore, "Here's How Walmart Became the #1 Grocery Store in the Country," *Business Insider*, February 11, 2011, https://www.businessinsider.com/walmart-big gest-supermarket-2011-2.

25. Jason Del Ray, "Is Amazon Too Big? We Ask Its Sellers," in *Land of the Giants*, Vox, August 27, 2019, podcast, website, 46:00, https://www.vox.com/land-of-the-giants -podcast; Karen Weise, "Prime Power: How Amazon Squeezes the Businesses Behind Its Store," *New York Times*, December 19, 2019, https://www.nytimes.com/2019/12/19 /technology/amazon-sellers.html; Laura Stevens, "Amazon Cuts Third-Party Prices," *Fox Business*, November 6, 2017, https://www.foxbusiness.com/features/amazon-cuts -third-party-prices.

26. Mike Leonard, "Amazon Accused of Monopolization, Sweeping Price-Fixing Scheme," *Bloomberg Law*, March 20, 2020, https://news.bloomberglaw.com/mergers -and-antitrust/amazon-accused-of-monopolization-massive-price-fixing-scheme.

27. Stone, *The Everything Store*, 126.

28. Nelson Lichtenstein, "The Return of Merchant Capitalism," *International Labor and Working-Class History* 81 (2012): 8, http://www.jstor.org/stable/23258368.

29. Weil, *Sears, Roebuck*, 31.

30. Weil, 11.

31. Weil, 133.

32. Weil, 134.

33. Weil, 143.

34. Enid Bonacich and Jake B. Wilson, *Getting the Goods: Ports, Labor, and the Logistics Revolution* (Ithaca, NY: Cornell University Press, 2008), 4–6.

35. Enid Bonacich with Khaleelah Hardie, "Wal-Mart and the Logistics Revolution," in *Wal-Mart: The Face of Twenty-First-Century Capitalism*, ed. Nelson Lichtenstein (New York: The New Press, 2006), 171–173.

36. Nelson Lichtenstein, "Wal-mart: Template for 21st Century Capitalism?," *New Labor Forum* 14, no. 1 (2005): 24.

37. Weil, *Sears, Roebuck*, 136.

38. Weil, 3.

39. David Carnoy, "How Is 'Amazon's Choice' Chosen? Amazon Won't Say," *CNet*, March 21, 2018, https://www.cnet.com/news/do-humans-choose-what-products-get -amazons-choice/.

40. Rani Molla, "More of the Products You View on Amazon Are Coming from Ads," *Vox: Recode*, September 16, 2019, https://www.vox.com/recode/2019/9/16/20868514 /amazon-sponsored-content-ads-growing-jumpshot-antitrust.

41. Del Ray, "Is Amazon Too Big?"

42. Molla, "More of the Products"; Dana Mattioli, "Amazon Search Change Boosts Its Own Products—Ecommerce Giant Overcame Internal Dissent from Engineers, Lawyers," *Wall Street Journal*, September 17, 2019, A1.

43. Farhad Manjoo, "The Hidden Player Spurring a Wave of Cheap Consumer Devices: Amazon," *New York Times*, December 6, 2017, https://www.nytimes.com /2017/12/06/technology/cheap-consumer-devices-amazon.html.

44. Krista Garcia, "More Product Searches Start on Amazon," *eMarketer*, September 7, 2018, https://www.emarketer.com/content/more-product-searches-start-on-amazon.

45. Garcia, "More Product Searches."

46. Shira Ovide, "When Tech Antitrust Failed," *New York Times*, January 15, 2021, https://www.nytimes.com/2021/01/15/technology/when-tech-antitrust-failed.html.

47. Matthew Dalton and Laura Stevens, "Why Amazon Still Has a Luxury Problem," *Wall Street Journal*, October 9, 2017, B4.

48. Eben Novy-Williams and Spencer Stone, "Nike Pulling Its Products from Amazon in E-commerce Pivot," *Bloomberg*, November 12, 2019, https://www.bloomberg.com /news/articles/2019-11-13/nike-will-end-its-pilot-project-selling-products-on-amazon -site?sref=1nAnrjIw.

49. As an example, see former Director of Merchandise Pricing and Product Management Randy Miller's responses to James Jacoby's questioning in his supplementary interview to *Frontline*'s "Amazon Empire," https://www.pbs.org/wgbh/frontline /interview/randy-miller/.

50. Tim Wu, *The Curse of Bigness: Antitrust in the New Gilded Age* (New York: Columbia Global Reports, 2018).

51. Lichtenstein, "Wal-mart," 25.

52. Walmart, "Company Facts," *Walmart*, 2021, https://corporate.walmart.com/news room/company-facts; Erika Hayasaki, "Amazon's Great Labor Awakening," *New York Times*, February 18, 2021, https://www.nytimes.com/2021/02/18/magazine/amazon -workers-employees-covid-19.html.

53. Winifred Gallagher, *How the Post Office Created America: A History* (New York: Penguin Press, 2016), 187, 206.

54. Gallagher, *How the Post Office*, 1; Richard R. John, *Spreading the News: The American Postal System from Franklin to Morse* (Cambridge, MA: Harvard University Press, 1998), 7.

55. Kielbowicz, "Rural Ambivalence," 89.

56. Weil, *Sears, Roebuck*, 66.

57. Gallagher, *How the Post Office*, 205–206.

58. Gallagher, 187–189.

59. Gallagher, 189.

60. Kielbowicz, "Rural Ambivalence," 89.

61. Kielbowicz, 81.

62. Popp, "The Anywhere, Anytime Market," 708.

63. Gallagher, *How the Post Office*, 206–207.

64. Sophia Cai, "Amazon Is Gaining in Deliveries at the Post Office's Expense, Analyst Says," *Barron's*, July 9, 2019, https://www.barrons.com/articles/amazon-is-winning -in-deliveries-at-the-post-offices-expense-51562688964.

65. Jacob Bogage and Josh Dawsey, "Postal Service to Review Package Delivery Fee as Trump Influence Grows," *Washington Post*, May 14, 2020, https://www.washingtonpost .com/business/2020/05/14/trump-postal-service-package-rates/.

66. John Blackledge, Helane Becker, Jason Seidl, Nick Yako, Conor Cunningham, James Kopelman, William Kerr, and Tyler Seidman, "Assessing Amazon's U.S. Demand & Delivery Capacity," *Cowen Outperform*, May 4, 2018, https://www.cowen.com/reports /assessingamazonsusdemandanddeliverycapacity/.

67. Nick Wingfield, "Is Amazon Bad for the Postal Service? Or Its Savior?," *New York Times*, April 4, 2018, https://www.nytimes.com/2018/04/04/technology/amazon-pos tal-service-trump.html.

68. Frank Holland, "Amazon Is Delivering Nearly Two-Thirds of Its Own Packages as E-commerce Continues Its Pandemic Boon," *CNBC*, August 13, 2020, https://www .cnbc.com/2020/08/13/amazon-is-delivering-nearly-two-thirds-of-its-own-packages .html.

69. Greg Niemann, *Big Brown: The Untold Story of UPS* (San Francisco: John Wiley & Sons, 2007), 35–37.

70. Niemann, *Big Brown*, 41, 46.

71. Niemann, 50.

72. Niemann, 199.

73. Niemann, 57.

74. Niemann, 57, 15–16.

75. Spector, *Amazon.com Get Big Fast*, 168.

76. David A. Mann, "Should UPS Be Concerned about Amazon's Order of 20,000 Vans," September 18, 2018, https://www.cnbc.com/2018/09/18/should-ups-be-con cerned-about-amazons-order-of-20000-vans.html.

77. Soo Youn, "FedEx Drops Amazon Ground Deliveries," *ABC News*, August 7, 2019, https://abcnews.go.com/Business/fedex-drops-amazon-ground-deliveries/story ?id=64826831.

78. Vincent Manzerolle and Atle Mikkola Kjøsen, "Digital Media and Capital's Logic of Acceleration," in *Marx in the Age of Digital Capitalism*, ed. Christian Fuchs and Vincent Mosco (Boston: Brill, 2016), 153.

79. Joseph Turow, *The Aisles Have Eyes: How Retailers Track Your Shopping, Strip Your Privacy, and Define Your Power* (New Haven, CT: Yale University Press, 2017), 71–72.

80. Robert D. Hof, "Amazon.com: The Wild World of E Commerce," *Bloomberg*, December 14, 1998, https://www.bloomberg.com/news/articles/1998-12-13/amazon -dot-com-the-wild-world-of-e-commerce?sref=1nAnrjIw.

81. Bill Gates with Nathan Myhrvold and Peter Rinearson, *The Road Ahead: Completely Revised and Up-To-Date* (New York: Penguin, 1996), 180; see also Lee McGuigan and Graham Murdock, "The Medium Is the Marketplace: Digital Systems and the Intensifi-cation of Consumption," *Canadian Journal of Communication* 40, no. 4 (2015), https:// doi.org/10.22230/cjc.2015v40n4a2948.

82. Manzerolle and Kjøsen, "Digital Media," 153.

83. Brandt, *One Click*, 8.

84. Leanna Zieback, "How to Win the Amazon Buy Box [2020 Update]," *Tinuiti*, March 25, 2020, https://tinuiti.com/blog/amazon/win-amazon-buy-box/.

85. CJ Garcia, "What Is an Amazon Dash Button, and Should You Buy One?," *Digital Trends*, August 10, 2017, https://www.digitaltrends.com/home/what-is-an-amazon-dash -button/.

86. Leena Rao, "Amazon to Add Trash Cans, Dishwashers, Dryers to Smart Reorder-ing Service," *Fortune*, August 4, 2016, http://fortune.com/2016/08/04/amazon-dash -replenishment/.

87. Nick Wingfield, "Inside Amazon Go, a Store of the Future," *New York Times*, Jan-uary 21, 2018, https://www.nytimes.com/2018/01/21/technology/inside-amazon-go -a-store-of-the-future.html; Brad Stone, *Amazon Unbound: Jeff Bezos and the Invention of a Global Empire* (New York: Simon & Schuster, 2021), 57.

88. Raymond Williams, *Television: Technology and Cultural Form* (New York: Schocken Books, 1975), 80–88.

89. Marc Bain, "Covid-19 Is Helping Walmart Make Up Ground Against Amazon," *Quartz*, May 19, 2020, https://qz.com/1858747/covid-19-is-helping-walmart-make-up-ground-against-amazon/.

90. "Manufacturing Struggles to Adapt," *Economist*, October 26, 2017, https://www.economist.com/special-report/2017/10/26/manufacturing-struggles-to-adapt.

91. Bonacich and Wilson, *Getting the Goods*, 3–4.

92. Weil, *Sears, Roebuck*, 110.

93. Hof, "Amazon.com."

94. Quoted in Spector, *Amazon.com Get Big Fast*, 16.

95. James Marcus, *Amazonia* (New York: The New Press, 2004), 131.

96. Sarah Perez, "Walmart and Green Dot to Jointly Establish a New FinTech Accelerator, Tailfin Labs," *Tech Crunch*, October 29, 2019, https://techcrunch.com/2019/10/29/walmart-and-green-dot-to-jointly-establish-a-new-fintech-accelerator-tailfin-labs/; H. Claire Brown, "Walmart's New Patents Will Allow It to Track You in Its Stores—With or Without Your Consent," *Counter*, June 25, 2018, https://thecounter.org/walmart-tracking-patents/.

CHAPTER 2

1. VanManner and updated by Brad Kim, "Danbo," *Know Your Meme*, July 23, 2015, http://knowyourmeme.com/memes/danbo.

2. VanManner, "Danbo"; Alison Barretta, "Who Is That 'Amazon Robot'? Meet Danbo!," *DealNews*, August 14, 2014, http://dealnews.com/features/Who-is-that-Amazon-Robot-Meet-Danbo-/1092793.html.

3. Arvidsson, *Brands*.

4. Kurt Schlosser, "Smiling Amazon Boxes Are Singing Again in New Holiday Ad—Will High Shipping Costs Dull the Mood?," *Geekwire*, November 4, 2019, https://www.geekwire.com/2019/smiling-amazon-boxes-singing-new-holiday-ad-will-high-shipping-costs-dull-mood/.

5. Here I agree with Spencer Stone who made this observation in 2020's *Frontline*, "Amazon Empire."

6. Karl Marx, *Capital: A Critique of Political Economy, Volume 1*, trans. Ben Fowkes (London: Penguin Books, 1976), 163–165.

7. Marx, *Capital*.

8. Mark Andrejevic, *Automated Media* (New York: Routledge, 2020), 66.

9. Amazon, "Thank You Amazon Heroes," *YouTube*, March 27, 2020, https://www.youtube.com/watch?v=_Z7PY4bOvvo; Amazon, "Rising to the Challenge," *YouTube*, April 22, 2020, https://www.youtube.com/watch?v=mwSLYX21HGI.

10. Amazon, "Delivering Rainbows," *YouTube*, April 22, 2020, https://www.youtube.com/watch?v=IVvphILiYQc.

11. Amazon, "Rising to the Challenge."

12. Hayasaki, "Amazon's Great Labor Awakening"; New York Attorney General, "Attorney General James Files Lawsuit Against Amazon for Failing to Protect Workers During Covid-19 Pandemic," February 17, 2021, https://ag.ny.gov/press-release/2021 /attorney-general-james-files-lawsuit-against-amazon-failing-protect-workers.

13. David W. Hill, "The Injuries of Platform Logistics," *Media, Culture, & Society* (2019): 2, doi: 10.1177/0163443719861840.

14. Tarleton Gillespie, Pablo J. Boczkowski, and Kirsten A. Foot, eds., *Media Technologies: Essays on Communication, Materiality and Society* (Cambridge, MA: MIT Press, 2014); Mél Hogan, "Data Flows and Water Woes: The Utah Data Center," *Big Data & Society* 2, no. 2 (2015), doi: 10.1177/2053951715592429; Richard Maxwell and Toby Miller, *Greening the Media* (New York: Oxford University Press, 2012); Jeremy Packer and Stephen B. Crofts Wiley, eds. *Communication Matters: Materialist Approaches to Media, Mobility, and Networks* (New York: Routledge, 2012); Jean-Christophe Plantin and Aswin Punathambekar, "Digital Media Infrastructures: Pipes, Platforms, and Politics," *Media, Culture, & Society* 41, no. 2 (2019), doi: 10.1177/0163443718818376.

15. Susan Leigh Star and Geoffrey C. Bowker, "How to Infrastructure," in *Handbook of New Media: Social Shaping and Social Consequences of ICTS*, ed. Leah A. Lievrouw and Sonia Livingstone (Thousand Oaks, CA: Sage, 2006), 155.

16. Star and Bowker, "How to Infrastructure," 157.

17. Mike Ananny and Kate Crawford, "Seeing Without Knowing: Limitations of the Transparency Ideal and Its Application to Algorithmic Accountability," *New Media & Society* 20, no. 3 (2018): 974, doi: 10.1177/1461444816676645.

18. Spector, *Amazon.com Get Big Fast*, 232.

19. Mark Wilson, "The Hot New Product Amazon and Target Are Obsessing Over? Boxes," *Fast Company*, May 6, 2019, https://www.fastcompany.com/90342864/re thinking-the-cardboard-box-has-never-been-more-important-just-ask-amazon-and -target.

20. "7 Things You Didn't Know about Gummed Paper Tape," *Spectra Tape Blogs*, December 19, 2017, https://www.spectratapes.com/blog/7-things-you-didnt-know -about-gummed-paper-tape/; George Righter, "On the Mark: Amazon's New Tamper Evident Carton Sealing Tape," *Righter Track*, January 10, 2013, https://rightertrack .com/articles/amazons-new-tamper-evident-carton-sealing-tape.

21. "Amazon Announces Beginning of Multi-Year Frustration-Free Packaging Initiative," *Amazon Press Center*, November 3, 2008, https://press.aboutamazon.com/news -releases/news-release-details/amazon-announces-beginning-multi-year-frustration -free-packaging.

22. Anne Marie Mohan, "Amazon Celebrates 10th Anniversary of Frustration-Free Packaging," *Packing World*, November 28, 2017, https://www.packworld.com/design /materials-containers/news/13373768/amazon-celebrates-10th-anniversary-of -frustrationfree-packaging.

23. Anne Marie Mohan, "Amazon's New Sustainable Packaging Program Puts the Customer First," *Packaging World*, November 19, 2018, https://www.packworld.com

/issues/e-commerce/article/13376482/amazons-new-sustainable-packaging-program
-puts-the-customer-first.

24. Aaron Hand, "New E-commerce Packaging Group Aims for Two-Way Dialog with Retailers," *Packaging World*, December 9, 2019, https://www.packworld.com/issues /e-commerce/article/21105311/new-ecommerce-packaging-group-aims-for-twoway -dialog-with-retailers.

25. Manzerolle and Kjøsen, "Digital Media," 160; includes a quote from Karl Marx, *The Grundrisse*, trans. Martin Nicolaus (New York: Penguin, 1973), 539.

26. David Harvey, *The Condition of Postmodernity* (Malden, MA: Blackwell, 1990), 147.

27. John Durham Peters, "Calendar, Clock, Tower," in *Deus in Machina: Religion, Technology, and the Things in Between*, ed. Jeremy Stolow (New York: Fordham University Press, 2013), 41.

28. Peters, "Calendar, Clock, Tower," 42.

29. Edwards, "Infrastructure and Modernity," 185.

30. Edwards, 187.

31. Stone, *The Everything Store*, 128–129.

32. "Same-Day Delivery: The Next Evolutionary Step in Parcel Logistics," *McKinsey & Company*, March 2014, https://www.mckinsey.com/~/media/McKinsey/Industries /Travel%20Transport%20and%20Logistics/Our%20Insights/Same%20day%20 delivery%20the%20next%20evolutionary%20step%20in%20parcel%20logistics /Sameday_delivery_The_next_evolutionary_step_in_parcel_logistics.ashx.

33. Michael Begg, "Ecommerce Delivery Times Are Getting Even Shorter," *Business.com*, November, 27, 2019, https://www.business.com/articles/faster-ecommerce-delivery/.

34. Brandt, *One Click*, 104.

35. Stone, *The Everything Store*, 173.

36. Stone, 163–164.

37. Simon Head, "Worse than Wal-mart: Amazon's Sick Brutality and Secret History of Ruthlessly Intimidating Workers," *Salon*, February 23, 2014, https://www.salon.com /2014/02/23/worse_than_wal_mart_amazons_sick_brutality_and_secret_history_of _ruthlessly_intimidating_workers/.

38. Nick Wingfield, "As Amazon Pushes Forward with Robots, Workers Find New Roles," *New York Times*, September 10, 2017, https://www.nytimes.com/2017/09/10 /technology/amazon-robots-workers.html?_r=0.

39. "Amazon Introduces Counter in the U.S.," *Amazon Press Center*, 2019, https:// press.aboutamazon.com/news-releases/news-release-details/amazon-introduces -counter-us-where-customers-can-pick-their.

40. Dan Frommer, "This Is Amazon's First 'Prime Air' Plane," *Recode*, August 5, 2016, https://www.recode.net/2016/8/5/12382052/amazon-prime-air-plane.

41. Kaya Yurieff, "Amazon Patent Reveals Drone Delivery 'Beehives,'" *CNNTech*, June 23, 2017, http://money.cnn.com/2017/06/23/technology/amazon-drone-beehives

/index.html; Peter Holley, "Amazon's Autonomous Robots Have Started Delivering Packages in a New Location: Southern California," *Washington Post*, August 12, 2019, https://www.washingtonpost.com/technology/2019/08/12/amazons-autonomous -robots-have-started-delivering-packages-new-location-southern-california/.

42. Tricia Duryee, "Amazon Sunday Deliver: Key Facts to Know as USPS Rolls Out Service Nationally," *Geekwire*, July 16, 2014, http://www.geekwire.com/2014/amazon -getting-packages-sunday-via-u-s-postal-service/.

43. "Prime Free One Day," *The Amazon Blog: Day One*, June 3, 2019, https://web .archive.org/web/20190604063520/https://blog.aboutamazon.com/amazon-prime /prime-free-one-day; Nate Rattner and Annie Palmer, "This Map Shows How Amazon's Warehouses Are Rapidly Expanding Across the Country," *CNBC*, January 19, 2020, https://www.cnbc.com/2020/01/19/map-of-amazon-warehouses.html.

44. Jason Del Ray, "When Amazon Leaves Your Town," in *Land of the Giants*, Vox, August 6, 2019, podcast, website, 41:00, https://www.vox.com/land-of-the-giants -podcast.

45. Sarah Sharma, "It Changes Space and Time: Introducing Power-Chronography," in *Communication Matters: Materialist Approaches to Media, Mobility, and Networks*, eds. Jeremy Packer and Stephen B. Crofts Wiley (New York: Routledge, 2012), 66–67.

46. Sharma, "It Changes Space and Time," 68.

47. Sharma, 73.

48. Sharma, 68.

49. Reporting on productivity techniques used in Amazon warehouses includes Will Evans, "Ruthless Quotas at Amazon Are Maiming Employees," *Atlantic*, updated December 5, 2019, https://www.theatlantic.com/technology/archive/2019/11/amazon -warehouse-reports-show-worker-injuries/602530/; *Frontline*, "Amazon Empire"; Emily Guendelsberger, *On the Clock: What Low-Wage Work Did to Me and How It Drives America Insane* (New York: Little, Brown, and Co., 2019); Mac McClelland, "I Was a Warehouse Wage Slave," *Mother Jones*, March/April 2012, http://www.motherjones .com/politics/2012/02/mac-mcclelland-free-online-shipping-warehouses-labor ?page=4; Spencer Soper, "Inside Amazon's Warehouse," *Morning Call*, September 8, 2011, http://www.mcall.com/news/local/amazon/mc-allentown-amazon-complaints -20110917-story.html#page=1; Alec MacGillis, *Fulfillment: Winning and Losing in One-Click America* (New York: Farrar, Straus, and Giroux, 2021), 130–132; Colin Lecher, "How Amazon Automatically Tracks and Fires Warehouse Workers for 'Productivity,'" *The Verge*, April 25, 2019, https://www.theverge.com/2019/4/25/18516004/amazon -warehouse-fulfillment-centers-productivity-firing-terminations.

50. Evans, "Ruthless Quotas."

51. Evans, "Ruthless Quotas."

52. Hayley Peterson, "Missing Wages, Grueling Shifts, and Bottles of Urine," *Business Insider*, 2018, https://www.businessinsider.com/amazon-delivery-drivers-reveal -claims-of-disturbing-work-conditions-2018-8.

53. Peterson, "Missing Wages."

54. "Driver in Deadly Waterboro Crash Was Working as Sub-Contractor for Amazon," *WGME*, January 14, 2019, https://wgme.com/news/local/driver-in-deadly-waterboro -crash-was-working-as-sub-contractor-for-amazon.

55. Patricia Callahan, "Amazon Pushes Fast Shipping But Avoids Responsibility for the Human Cost," *New York Times*, September 5, 2019, https://www.nytimes.com /2019/09/05/us/amazon-delivery-drivers-accidents.html.

56. *Frontline*, "Amazon Empire."

57. Bonacich and Wilson, *Getting the Goods*, 21.

58. *The Dirty Dozen 2019: Employers Who Put Workers and Communities at Risk*, National Council for Occupational Safety and Health, April 2019, https://nationalcosh.org/sites /default/files/uploads/2019_Dirty_Dozen.pdf.

59. Alina Selkuyh, "For Amazon and Alabama, Warehouse Union Vote Would Shake Up History," *All Things Considered*, National Public Radio, January 29, 2021, https://www.npr.org/2021/01/28/960869795/for-amazon-and-alabama-warehouse -union-vote-would-shake-up-history.

60. David Brancaccio, "Why the Retail Apocalypse Isn't Being Taken Seriously," *Marketplace*, January 2, 2018, https://www.marketplace.org/2018/01/02/business/coming -retail-apocalypse; Marielle Segarra, "Are Fulfillment Center Jobs a Good Fit for Laid-off Retail Workers?," *NPR Illinois*, January 5, 2018, http://nprillinois.org/post/are-ful fillment-center-jobs-good-fit-laid-retail-workers#stream/0.

61. "Charts of the Largest Occupations in Each Area, May 2019," *Occupational Employment Statistics*, Bureau of Labor Statistics, https://www.bls.gov/oes/current/area_emp _chart/area_emp_chart.htm.

62. Dave Edwards and Helen Edwards, "There Are 170,000 Fewer Retail Jobs in 2017—and 75,000 More Amazon Robots," *Quartz*, December 4, 2017, https://qz.com /1107112/there-are-170000-fewer-retail-jobs-in-2017-and-75000-more-amazon-robots/; Jason Del Ray, "Why the Robot Revolution Is Our Fault," in *Land of the Giants*, Vox, August 13, 2019, podcast, website, 38:00, https://www.vox.com/land-of-the-giants -podcast.

63. For example: "What Robots Do (and Don't Do) at Amazon Fulfillment Centers," *The Amazon Blog: Day One*, 2019, https://www.aboutamazon.co.uk/amazon-fulfilment /what-robots-do-and-dont-do-at-amazon-fulfilment-centres; Jean Yves Chainon and Kaitlin Mullin, "Robots and Humans Team Up at Amazon," *New York Times: Daily 360* [Video], September 10, 2017, https://www.nytimes.com/video/technology/10000 0005396963/robots-humans-team-up-amazon-warehouses.html.

64. Donna Tam, "Meet Amazon's Busiest Employee—the Kiva Robot," *CNet*, November 30, 2014, https://www.cnet.com/news/meet-amazons-busiest-employee-the-kiva -robot/.

65. Del Ray, "Why the Robot Revolution"; *Frontline*, "Amazon Empire."

66. Kantor and Streitfeld, "Inside Amazon."

67. Maria Tae McDermott, "The Most Commented-on Articles of 2015," *New York Times*, December 28, 2015, http://www.nytimes.com/2015/12/18/insider/the-most -commented-on-articles-of-2015.html.

68. McDermott, "The Most Commented-On."

69. David Streitfeld and Jodi Kantor, "Jeff Bezos and Amazon Employees Join Debate over Its Culture," *New York Times*, August 17, 2015, http://www.nytimes.com/2015/08/18/technology/amazon-bezos-workplace-management-practices.html.

70. Nick Wingfield and Ravi Somaiya, "Amazon Spars with The Times Over Investigative Article," *New York Times*, October 19, 2015, http://www.nytimes.com/2015/10/20/business/amazon-spars-with-the-times-over-investigative-article.html.

71. Kantor and Streitfeld, "Inside Amazon."

72. Marcus, *Amazonia*, 17.

73. Michael Sainato, "'Go Back to Work': Outcry Over Deaths on Amazon's Warehouse Floor," *Guardian*, October 18, 2019, https://www.theguardian.com/technology/2019/oct/17/amazon-warehouse-worker-deaths; Dave Jamieson, "The Life and Death of an Amazon Warehouse Temp," *Highline: Huffington Post*, October 21, 2015, https://highline.huffingtonpost.com/articles/en/life-and-death-amazon-temp/; Scott Shane, "Prime Mover: How Amazon Wove Itself into the Life of an American City," *New York Times*, November 30, 2019, https://www.nytimes.com/2019/11/30/business/amazon-baltimore.html.

74. Suhauna Hussain, "Amazon Won't Say How Many Workers Have Gotten Covid-19. So Workers Are Tracking Cases Themselves," *Los Angeles Times*, May 28, 2020, https://www.latimes.com/business/technology/story/2020-05-28/amazon-whole-foods-workers-track-coronavirus-cases; Josh Dzieza, "A Seventh Amazon Employee Dies of Covid-19 as the Company Refuses to Say How Many Are Sick," *The Verge*, May 14, 2020, https://www.theverge.com/2020/5/14/21259474/amazon-warehouse-worker-death-indiana.

75. "Our Workforce Data," *Amazon*, December 31, 2020, https://www.aboutamazon.com/news/workplace/our-workforce-data.

76. Timothy Pachirat, *Every Twelve Seconds: Industrialized Slaughter and the Politics of Sight* (New Haven, CT: Yale University Press, 2011), 3–4. Although a slaughterhouse is very different from an Amazon fulfillment center, Anna Weiner ("What a Tour of an Amazon Fulfillment Center Reveals") reports that after describing to a friend the fulfillment center tour she took in Sacramento, the friend commented, "You sound like someone who has just seen an industrial chicken farm for the first time."

77. Pachirat, *Every Twelve Seconds*, 240.

78. Pachirat, 14.

79. Ananny and Crawford, "Seeing Without Knowing," 975, quoting John W. P. Phillips, "Secrecy and Transparency: An Interview with Samuel Weber," *Theory, Culture & Society* 28, no.7–8 (2011), https://doi.org/10.1177/0263276411428339.

80. Pachirat, *Every Twelve Seconds*, 239.

81. Matt Richtel, "E-commerce: Convenience Built on a Mountain of Cardboard," February 16, 2016, https://www.nytimes.com/2016/02/16/science/recycling-cardboard-online-shopping-environment.html.

82. Miguel Jaller, "Online Shopping Is Terrible for the Environment: It Doesn't Have to Be," *Vox*, November 21, 2018, https://www.vox.com/the-big-idea/2017/12

/21/16805324/black-friday-2018-amazon-online-shopping-cyber-monday-environ
mental-impact.

83. Erica Wygonik and Anne Goodchild, "Evaluating the Efficacy of Shared-Use Vehicles for Reducing Greenhouse Gas Emissions: A US Case Study of Grocery Delivery," *Journal of the Transportation Research Forum* 51, no. 2 (2012): 111, 121.

84. Jaller, "Online Shopping"; Andy Murdock, "The Environmental Cost of Free 2-Day Shipping," *Vox*, November 17, 2017, https://www.vox.com/2017/11/17/16670080 /environmental-cost-free-two-day-shipping.

85. Christopher L. Weber, Chris T. Hendrickson, H. Scott Matthews, Amy Nagengast, Rachel Nealer, and Paulina Jaramillo, "Life Cycle Comparison of Traditional Retail and E-commerce Logistics for Electronic Products: A Case Study of Buy.com," *2009 IEEE International Symposium on Sustainable Systems and Technology*, Phoenix, AZ, 2009, 5, doi: 10.1109/ISSST.2009.5156681.

86. "Continued Growth for Amazon's Air Network to Expand Prime Fast, Free Shipping for Customers," *Amazon Press Center*, June 18, 2019, https://press.aboutamazon .com/news-releases/news-release-details/continued-growth-amazons-air-network -expand-prime-fast-free.

87. Jaller, "Online Shopping."

88. Karen Weise, "Amazon's Profit Falls Sharply as the Company Buys Growth," *New York Times*, October 24, 2019, https://www.nytimes.com/2019/10/24/technology/ama zon-earnings.html.

89. Taylor Soper, "Amazon Will Spend Nearly $1.5B in Q4 for One-Day Delivery Initiative as Shipping Costs Skyrocket," *Geekwire*, October 24, 2019, https://www .geekwire.com/2019/amazon-will-spend-nearly-1-5b-q4-one-day-delivery-initiative -shipping-costs-skyrocket/.

90. Connie Chen, "Amazon Day Is a New Prime Member Perk from Amazon That Allows You to Schedule Your Package Deliveries—Here's How It Works," *Business Insider*, July 23, 2019, https://www.businessinsider.com/what-is-amazon-day-schedule -deliveries-prime-benefit; Dave Clark, "Delivering Shipment Zero, a Vision for Net Zero Carbon Shipments," *Amazon*, February 18, 2019, https://www.aboutamazon .com/news/sustainability/delivering-shipment-zero-a-vision-for-net-zero-carbon -shipments.

91. Greenpeace, *Guide to Greener Electronics 2017*, October 17, 2017, https://www .greenpeace.org/usa/reports/greener-electronics-2017/; Hill, "The Injuries of Platform Logistics," 12.

92. Benjamin Romano, "Amazon Signs Big Allies in Pledge to Be Climate Neutral," *Seattle Times*, updated June 17, 2020, https://www.seattletimes.com/business/amazon /verizon-infosys-rb-join-amazon-in-pledge-to-be-carbon-neutral-by-2040/; Brad Stone, "Amazon's Bezos Pledges to Meet Paris Climate Pact 10 Years Early," *BNN Bloomberg*, September 19, 2019, https://www.bnnbloomberg.ca/amazon-pledges-to-meet-paris-cli mate-pact-10-years-early-1.1318787.

93. Hill, "The Injuries of Platform Logistics," 1.

CHAPTER 3

1. Chris Anderson, *The Long Tail: Why the Future of Business Is Selling Less of More* (New York: Hyperion, 2008).

2. Megan Garber, "Here Is the First Book Ever Ordered on Amazon," *Atlantic*, October 31, 2012, https://www.theatlantic.com/technology/archive/2012/10/here-is-the -first-book-ever-ordered-on-amazon/264344/.

3. Edison, "These Were 2018's Top-Selling Product Categories at Amazon and eBay," *Medium*, March 14, 2019, https://medium.com/edison-discovers/these-were-2018s-top -selling-product-categories-at-amazon-and-ebay-1c8a5c62d49c.

4. Matt Day and Jackie Gu, "The Enormous Numbers Behind Amazon's Market Reach," *Bloomberg*, March 27, 2019, https://www.bloomberg.com/graphics/2019-amazon-reach -across-markets/?sref=1nAnrjIw.

5. This chapter appears in part in *Point of Sale: Analyzing Media Retail* (2019), edited by Daniel Herbert and Derek Johnson, as "Amazon, Bookseller: Disruption and Continuity in Digital Capitalism." Many thanks to Rutgers University Press and the editors of this volume for permission to partially reprint.

6. Jeffrey A. Trachtenberg, "Amazon Rewrites Publishing by Pushing Its Own Books," *Wall Street Journal*, January 27, 2019, A8.

7. Carolyn Kellogg, "Amazon and Hachette: The Dispute in 13 Easy Steps," *Los Angeles Times*, June 3, 2014, http://www.latimes.com/books/jacketcopy/la-et-jc-amazon -and-hachette-explained-20140602-story.html; Benedict Evans, "What's Amazon's Market Share?," *Benedict Evans* newsletter, December 19, 2019, https://www.ben -evans.com/benedictevans/2019/12/amazons-market-share19.

8. Carmen Nobel, "How Independent Bookstores Thrived in Spite of Amazon," *Quartz*, November 26, 2017, https://qz.com/1135474/how-independent-bookstores -thrived-in-spite-of-amazon/.

9. Janice A. Radway, *A Feeling for Books: The Book-of-the-Month Club, Literary Taste, and Middle-Class Desire* (Chapel Hill: The University of North Carolina Press, 1997), 5.

10. Damien Cave, "Australia's Amazon Book Battle," *New York Times*, October 19, 2017, https://www.nytimes.com/2017/10/19/books/australias-amazon-book-battle.html.

11. Ted Striphas, *The Late Age of Print: Everyday Book Culture from Consumerism to Control* (New York: Columbia University Press, 2009), 6.

12. Elizabeth Long, "The Cultural Meaning of Concentration in Publishing," *Book Research Quarterly*, 1, no. 4 (1985): 3.

13. Laura J. Miller, *Reluctant Capitalists: Bookselling and the Culture of Consumption* (Chicago: University of Chicago Press, 2006), 3–4.

14. Miller, *Reluctant Capitalists*, 3.

15. Nobel, "How Independent Bookstores Thrived."

16. Brandt, *One Click*, 46–49.

17. Brandt, 110.

18. Miller, *Reluctant Capitalists*, 147.

19. Jim Milliot and Karen Holt, "Media Growth Slows at Amazon," *Publisher's Weekly* 251, no. 31 (2004): 6.

20. Miller, *Reluctant Capitalists*, 147.

21. Maria A. Pallante, Mary E. Rasenberger, and Allison K. Hill, *AAP Joint Letter to Representative Cicilline*, Association of American Publishers, August 17, 2020, https://publishers.org/wp-content/uploads/2020/08/Joint-Letter-to-Rep-Cicilline-081720.pdf.

22. Philip Napoli and Robyn Caplan, "Why Media Companies Insist They're Not Media Companies, Why They're Wrong, and Why It Matters," *First Monday* 22, no. 5 (2017), https://doi.org/10.5210/fm.v22i5.7051.

23. David Kirkpatrick, "Online Sales of Used Books Draw Protest," *New York Times*, April 10, 2001, http://www.nytimes.com/2002/04/10/business/online-sales-of-used-books-draw-protest.html.

24. Jim Milliot, "Authors Guild Upset by Amazon Used Books Tactics," *Publisher's Weekly* 249, no. 15 (2002): 15.

25. Kirkpatrick, "Online Sales."

26. Milliot, "Authors Guild Upset," 15.

27. Keith Gessen, "The War of the Words," *Vanity Fair*, November 6, 2014, https://www.vanityfair.com/news/business/2014/12/amazon-hachette-ebook-publishing.

28. George Packer, "Cheap Words," *New Yorker*, February 9, 2014, https://www.newyorker.com/magazine/2014/02/17/cheap-words.

29. Marcus, *Amazonia*, 24.

30. Marcus, 199–200.

31. Marcus, 167; Doreen Carvajal, "For Sale, Amazon.com's Recommendations to Readers," *New York Times*, February 8, 1999, http://movies2.nytimes.com/1999/02/08/technology/08amazon.html.

32. Darcy DiNucci, "Fragmented Future," *Print* 53, no. 4 (1999): 32; Tim O'Reilly, "What Is Web 2.0," *O'Reilly*, September 30, 2005, https://www.oreilly.com/pub/a/web2/archive/what-is-web-20.html.

33. Spencer E. Ante, "Amazon: Turning Consumer Opinions into Gold," *Bloomberg Businessweek*, October 15, 2009, https://www.bloomberg.com/news/articles/2009-10-15/amazon-turning-consumer-opinions-into-gold.

34. Ann Steiner, "Private Criticism in the Public Space: Personal Writing on Literature in Readers' Reviews on Amazon," *Participations* 5, no. 2 (2008): 3, https://www.participations.org/Volume%205/Issue%202/5_02_steiner.htm.

35. Ante, "Amazon."

36. Tiziana Terranova, "Free Labor: Producing Culture for the Digital Economy," *Social Text* 18, no. 2 (2000).

37. Lisa Nakamura, "'Words with Friends': Socially Networked Reading on Goodreads," *Publications of the Modern Language Association* 128, no. 1 (2013): 241.

38. Jason Murdock, "'Amazon's Choice' Badge Is Exploited by Fake Reviews and Could Mislead Millions of Customers, Researchers Say," *Newsweek*, February 6, 2020, https://www.newsweek.com/amazon-choice-badge-misleading-customers-fake-reviews-which -research-claims-1485826; Laura Stevens and Jon Emont, "To Game Amazon, Sellers Use Scams, Clicks, & Dirty Tricks," *Wall Street Journal*, July 28, 2018, B1.

39. Jim Milliot, "Numbers of Self-Published Titles Jumped 40% in 2018," *Publishers Weekly*, October 15, 2019, https://www.publishersweekly.com/pw/by-topic/industry -news/publisher-news/article/81473-number-of-self-published-titles-jumped-40-in -2018.html.

40. John B. Thompson, *Merchants of Culture: The Publishing Business in the Twenty-First Century* (Malden: Polity Press, 2010), 29.

41. Jim Milliot, "Amazon Co-op Riles Independent Houses," *Publishers Weekly* 251, no. 22 (2004): 8.

42. *Frontline*, "Amazon Empire."

43. Maria A. Pallante, *Comments of the Association of American Publishers: Federal Trade Commission Hearings on Competition and Consumer Protection in the 21st Century*, Association of American Publishers, June 27, 2019, letter, https://presspage-production -content.s3.amazonaws.com/uploads/1508/aapcommentstoftc-final06262019-858379 .pdf?10000.

44. Trachtenberg, "Amazon Rewrites Publishing," A8.

45. Stone, *The Everything Store*, 251–252.

46. Stone, 252–253.

47. "Amazon.com Now Selling More Kindle Books Than Print Books," *Business Wire*, May 19, 2011, https://www.businesswire.com/news/home/20110519005496 /en/Amazon.com-Now-Selling-More-Kindle-Books-Than-Print-Books.

48. Franklin Paul, "Amazon to Buy Audible for $300 Million," *Reuters*, January 31, 2008, https://www.reuters.com/article/us-audible-amazon/amazon-to-buy-audible -for-300-million-idUSN3129158120080131; Michael Kozlowski, "Global Audiobook Trends and Statistics for 2018," *Good EReader*, December 2017, https://goodereader .com/blog/audiobooks/global-audiobook-trends-and-statistics-for-2018.

49. Brady Dale, "Despite What You Heard, the E-book Market Never Stopped Growing," *Observer*, January 18, 2017, http://observer.com/2017/01/author-earnings-over drive-amazon-kindle-overdrive-digital-book-world/.

50. David B. Nieborg and Thomas Poell, "The Platformization of Cultural Production: Theorizing the Contingent Cultural Commodity," *New Media & Society* 20, no. 11 (2018): 4275–4292, doi: 10.1177/1461444818769694.

51. "Update Your Manuscript," *Kindle Direct Publishing*, n.d., https://kdp.amazon .com/en_US/help/topic/G202176900, accessed May 27, 2021.

52. Diane Patrick, "When Amazon Calls: Two Self-Published Authors Reflect," *Publisher's Weekly* 259, no. 1 (2012): 25.

53. Alison Flood, "I'm Hooked on Ebook Highlighting—What We Underline Is So Revealing," *Guardian*, November 6, 2014, https://www.theguardian.com/books

/booksblog/2014/nov/06/im-hooked-on-ebook-highlighting-what-we-underline-is
-revealing.

54. Jay Greene, "Amazon's Digital Reach Enables a Different Publishing Model," *Daily Herald* (Provo, UT); for additional reports see Mark Davis, "E-books in the Global Information Economy," *European Journal of Cultural Studies* 18, no. 4–5 (2015): 520–521, 523.

55. Aaron Perzanowski and Jason Schultz, *The End of Ownership: Personal Property in the Digital Economy* (Cambridge, MA: MIT Press, 2016), 1–2.

56. David Barnett, "Online Top Ranking: What Does Amazon Charts Mean for the Book Industry?," *Guardian*, May 22, 2017, https://www.theguardian.com/books/2017/may/22/amazon-charts-books-new-york-times-bestseller-lists.

57. Alex Shephard, "How Amazon Quietly Became America's Biggest Publisher of Translated Literature," *New Republic*, October 19, 2015, https://newrepublic.com/article/123150/americas-biggest-publisher-literature-translation-amazon.

58. "Introducing Amazon Charts—a Bestseller List for What People Are Really Reading and Buying," *Amazon Press Center*, May 18, 2017, https://press.aboutamazon.com/news-releases/news-release-details/introducing-amazon-charts-bestseller-list-what-people-are-really.

59. Gessen, "War of the Words."

60. Bill Murphy, Jr., "I Got $39.63 in the Giant Amazon-Apple Settlement, So That Leaves $399,999,960.37 for All of You," *Inc.*, June 22, 2016, https://www.inc.com/bill-murphy-jr/how-much-are-you-getting-in-the-400-million-amazon-apple-settlement.html?utm_source=1year.

61. Kellogg, "Amazon and Hachette."

62. David Streitfeld, "Literary Lions Unite in Protest Over Amazon's E-Book Tactics," *New York Times*, September 29, 2014, https://www.nytimes.com/2014/09/29/business/literary-lions-unite-in-protest-over-amazons-e-book-tactics.html; "Amazon vs. Hachette—Sherman Alexie," *The Colbert Report*, June 6, 2014, http://www.cc.com/video-clips/t1nxwu/the-colbert-report-amazon-vs--hachette---sherman-alexie.

63. Michael Hiltzik, "No, Ebooks Aren't Dying—But Their Quest to Dominate the Reading World Has Hit a Speed Bump," *Los Angeles Times*, May 1, 2017, http://www.latimes.com/business/hiltzik/la-fi-hiltzik-ebooks-20170501-story.html.

64. Gessen, "War of the Words."

65. Rebecca Klar, "Amazon Hit with Antitrust Lawsuit Alleging E-Book Price Fixing," *The Hill*, January 14, 2021, https://thehill.com/policy/technology/534364-amazon-hit-with-class-action-lawsuit-alleging-e-book-price-fixing?rl=1.

66. "Amazon.com Announces Third-Quarter Sales Up 34% to $43.7 Billion," *Business Wire*, October 26, 2017, https://www.businesswire.com/news/home/20171026006422/en/Amazon.com-Announces-Third-Quarter-Sales-up-34-to-43.7-Billion.

67. Nobel, "How Independent Bookstores Thrived."

68. Turow, *The Aisles Have Eyes*, 68.

69. Douglas J. Goodman and Mirelle Cohen, *Consumer Culture: A Reference Handbook* (Santa Barbara, CA: ABC-CLIO, 2004), 14–17.

70. Jason P. Chambers, "Equal in Every Way: African Americans, Consumption, and Materialism from Reconstruction to the Civil Rights Movement," *Advertising & Society Review* 7, no. 1 (2006), doi: 10.1353/asr.2006.0017; Josh Lauer, "The Good Consumer: Credit Reporting and the Invention of Financial Identity in the United States," *Enterprise & Society* 11, no. 4 (2010): 691–692; Brian Wallheimer, "Are You Ready for Personalized Pricing?," *Chicago Booth Review*, February 26, 2018, http://review.chicagobooth.edu/marketing/2018/article/are-you-ready-personalized-pricing.

71. Goodman and Cohen, *Consumer Culture*, 17–18; Striphas, *Late Age of Print*, 60–61.

72. Miller, *Reluctant Capitalists*, 5.

73. Nicholas Negroponte, *Being Digital* (New York: Vintage Books, 1996); Joseph Turow, *The Daily You: How the New Advertising Industry Is Defining You and Your Worth* (New Haven, CT: Yale University Press, 2011).

74. Joseph Turow, Lee McGuigan, and Elena R. Maris, "Making Data Mining a Natural Part of Life: Physical Retailing, Customer Surveillance and the 21st Century Social Imaginary," *European Journal of Communication* 18, no. 4–5 (2015): 464; see also Turow, *The Aisles Have Eyes*, 18.

75. Turow, *The Aisles Have Eyes*, 82–83.

76. Jia Tolentino, "Amazon's Brick-and-Mortar Bookstores Are Not Built for People Who Actually Read," *New Yorker*, May 30, 2017, https://www.newyorker.com/culture/cultural-comment/amazons-brick-and-mortar-bookstores-are-not-built-for-people-who-actually-read.

77. Nat Levy, "Amazon's New Seattle-Area Bookstore Shows How Its First Major Brick-and-Mortar Concept Has Evolved," *Geekwire*, August 25, 2017, https://www.geekwire.com/2017/amazons-new-seattle-area-bookstore-shows-first-major-retail-concept-evolved/.

78. Tolentino, "Amazon's Brick-and-Mortar Bookstores."

79. Christian Hetrick, "Amazon Warns It May Rethink Plans to Open a Philly Store if the City Bans Cashless Retailers," *Philadelphia Inquirer*, February 15, 2019, https://www.inquirer.com/business/retail/amazon-go-philadelphia-cashless-store-ban-20190215.html.

CHAPTER 4

1. This chapter appears in part as "Amazon: Surveillance as a Service" in *Surveillance & Society* 17, no. 1/2 (2019): 27–33, https://ojs.library.queensu.ca/index.php/surveillance-and-society/article/view/13008/8472. Many thanks to *Surveillance & Society* for permission to partially reprint.

2. Matt Day, Giles Turner, and Natalia Drozdiak, "Amazon Workers Are Listening to What You Tell Alexa," *Bloomberg*, April 10, 2019, https://www.bloomberg.com/news/articles/2019-04-10/is-anyone-listening-to-you-on-alexa-a-global-team-reviews-audio.

3. Day, Turner, and Drozdiak, "Amazon Workers Are Listening."

4. "Common Questions about Alexa Privacy," 2020, https://www.amazon.com/b /?node=19149165011.

5. Andy Rosen, "So There Are People Behind Alexa's Curtain. Will Anyone Care?," *Boston Globe*, April 11, 2019, https://www.bostonglobe.com/business/2019/04/11/there -are-people-behind-alexa-curtain-will-anyone-care/fxmuVk6jhhNIKwWmtqf2BM /story.html.

6. "U.S. Smart Speaker Adoption Report 2019," *Voicebot.AI*, 2019, https://voicebot .ai/smart-speaker-consumer-adoption-report-2019/; "Smart Speaker Shipments from 2014 to 2025," *Statista*, February 19, 2020, https://www.statista.com/statistics/1022809 /worldwide-smart-speaker-unit-shipment/.

7. Josephine Lau, Benjamin Zimmerman, and Florian Schaub, "Alexa, Are You Listening? Privacy Perceptions, Concerns and Privacy-Seeking Behaviors with Smart Speakers," *Proceedings of the ACM on Human-Computer Interaction* 2, no. CSCW (2018): article 102, 6–7, https://doi.org/10.1145/3274371.

8. Alan F. Westin, "Social and Political Dimensions of Privacy," *Journal of Social Issues* 59, no. 2 (2003): 445–446.

9. Ben Fox Rubin, "Amazon Sees Alexa Devices Double in Just One Year," *CNet*, January 6, 2020, https://www.cnet.com/news/amazon-sees-alexa-devices-more-than -double-in-just-one-year.

10. Nora Draper and Joseph Turow, "The Corporate Cultivation of Digital Resignation," *New Media & Society* 21, no. 8 (2019): 1824–1839, doi: 10.1177/1461444819833331; Lau, Zimmerman, and Schaub, "Alexa, Are You Listening?," 19.

11. Joseph Turow, Michael Hennessy, and Nora Draper, "The Tradeoff Fallacy: How Marketers Are Misrepresenting American Consumers and Opening Them Up to Exploitation," *SSRN*, June 26, 2015, https://papers.ssrn.com/sol3/papers.cfm?abstract _id=2820060.

12. Brooke Auxier, "5 Things to Know about Americans and Their Smart Speakers," *Pew Research Center: Fact-Tank*, November 21, 2019, https://www.pewresearch.org/fact -tank/2019/11/21/5-things-to-know-about-americans-and-their-smart-speakers/.

13. Draper and Turow, "Corporate Cultivation"; David Murakami Wood and Kirstie Ball, "Brandscapes of Control? Surveillance, Marketing, and the Co-construction of Subjectivity and Space in Neo-liberal Capitalism," *Marketing Theory* 13, no. 1 (2013): doi: 10.1177/1470593112467264.

14. Lina Dencik and Jonathan Cable, "The Advent of Surveillance Realism: Public Opinion and Activist Responses to the Snowden Leaks," *International Journal of Communication* 11 (2017): 763.

15. Draper and Turow, "Corporate Cultivation," 1830.

16. Sidney Fussell, "The Next Data Mine Is Your Bedroom," *Atlantic*, November 17, 2018, https://www.theatlantic.com/technology/archive/2018/11/google-patent-bed room-privacy-smart-home/576022/; see also Davis, "E-books in the Global Information Economy," 522–523.

17. Kalidas Yeturu and Howard Lee Huddleston, Jr. (Amazon Technologies, Inc.), "Image Creation Using Geo-Fence Data," *United States Patent 10,313,638, B1* filed June 4, 2015, and issued June 4, 2019.

18. Kara Swisher, "Amazon Wants to Get Even Closer. Skintight," *New York Times*, November 27, 2020, https://www.nytimes.com/2020/11/27/opinion/amazon-halo-sur veillance.html?action=click&module=Opinion&pgtype=Homepage.

19. John Bellamy Foster and Robert W. McChesney, "Surveillance Capitalism: Monopoly-Finance Capital, the Military-Industrial Complex, and the Digital Age," *Monthly Review* 66, no. 3 (2014); Vincent Mosco, *To the Cloud: Big Data in a Turbulent World* (Boulder, CO: Paradigm Publishers, 2014), 10; Shoshana Zuboff, *The Age of Surveillance Capitalism* (New York: Public Affairs, 2019).

20. Nick Couldry and Ulises A. Mejias, *The Costs of Connection: How Data Is Coloniz-ing Human Life and Appropriating It for Capitalism* (Stanford, CA: Stanford University Press, 2019); Jim Thatcher, David O'Sullivan, and Dillon Mahmoudi, "Data Colo-nialism Through Accumulation by Dispossession: New Metaphors for Daily Data," *Environment and Planning D: Society and Space* 34, no. 6 (2016).

21. Lizabeth Cohen, *A Consumer's Republic: The Politics of Mass Consumption in Postwar America* (New York: Knopf, 2003), 126; Nikolas Rose, *Governing the Soul: The Shaping of the Private Self* (New York: Routledge, 1989), 226–227; Don Slater, *Consumer Culture and Modernity* (Cambridge, MA: Blackwell, 1997), 8.

22. Carlos Carillo, "Internet: E-commerce Sites: Amazon.com," *PC Magazine*, November 18, 1997, 130.

23. Brandt, *One Click*, 12.

24. Hof, "Amazon.com."

25. Spector, *Amazon.com Get Big Fast*, 55.

26. "Net Perceptions Transforms World's Largest Bookstore into a Unique Person-alized Shopping Experience," *Amazon Press Center*, February 10, 1997, https://press .aboutamazon.com/news-releases/news-release-details/net-perceptions-transforms -worlds-largest-bookstore-unique.

27. Carillo, "Internet: E-commerce Sites," 130.

28. "Amazon.com Expands Recommendation Center to Introduce Customers to Music They'll Love," *Amazon Press Center*, March 9, 1999, https://press.aboutamazon .com/news-releases/news-release-details/amazoncom-expands-recommendation -center-introduce-customers.

29. Marcus, *Amazonia*, 198.

30. Marcus, 199–200; Spector, *Amazon.com Get Big Fast*, 146.

31. Stone, *The Everything Store*, 134; Marcus, *Amazonia*, 200.

32. "Amazon.com Launches Millions of Tabs, Featuring a Store for Every Customer," *Amazon Press Center*, September 27, 2001, https://press.aboutamazon.com/news-releases /news-release-details/amazoncom-launches-millions-tabs-featuring-store-every -customer.

33. "Amazon.com Expands Recommendation Center."

34. Stone, *The Everything Store*, 133.

35. Xavier Amatriain, "Mining Large Streams of User Data for Personalized Recommendations," *ACM SIGKDD Explorations Newsletter* 14, no. 2 (2013), https://dl.acm.org/doi/abs/10.1145/2481244.2481250.

36. "Amazon Privacy Notice," *Amazon*, February 12, 2021, https://www.amazon.com/gp/help/customer/display.html?nodeId=201909010.

37. Mark Andrejevic, "Automating Surveillance," *Surveillance & Society* 17, no. 1/2 (2019), https://ojs.library.queensu.ca/index.php/surveillance-and-society/article/view/12930.

38. Zuboff, *The Age of Surveillance Capitalism*, 90.

39. Thatcher, O'Sullivan, and Mahmoudi, "Data Colonialism Through Accumulation," 993.

40. Thatcher, O'Sullivan, and Mahmoudi, 179.

41. "Amazon Fire TV," *Chattanooga Times Free Press*, May 20, 2014.

42. Dencik and Cable, "Advent of Surveillance Realism," 765.

43. Hal Varian, "Beyond Big Data," *Business Economics* 49, no. 1 (2014): 28–29, https://doi-org.silk.library.umass.edu/10.1057/be.2014.1.

44. "Introducing Amazon Key, a New Level of Delivery Convenience for Prime Members," *Amazon Press Center*, October 25, 2017, https://press.aboutamazon.com/news-releases/news-release-details/introducing-amazon-key-new-level-delivery-convenience-prime.

45. "Buckle Up, Prime Members: Amazon Launches In-Car Delivery," *Amazon Press Center*, April 24, 2018, https://press.aboutamazon.com/news-releases/news-release-details/buckle-prime-members-amazon-launches-car-delivery; "Key for Garage Available Starting Today," *Amazon Press Center*, April 23, 2019, https://press.aboutamazon.com/news-releases/news-release-details/key-garage-available-starting-today.

46. "Introducing Amazon Key."

47. Jodi Dean, *Publicity's Secret: How Technoculture Capitalizes on Democracy* (Ithaca, NY: Cornell University Press, 2002), 13.

48. Brad Stone, "Here's Why Amazon Bought a Doorbell Company," *Bloomberg*, March 5, 2018, https://www.bloomberg.com/news/articles/2018-03-05/here-s-why-amazon-bought-a-doorbell-company.

49. Stone, "Here's Why Amazon Bought a Doorbell Company."

50. Berry, "Cultivating Service Brand Equity."

51. Berry, 128.

52. Tim Wu, "The Tyranny of Convenience," *New York Times*, February 16, 2018, https://www.nytimes.com/2018/02/16/opinion/sunday/tyranny-convenience.html.

53. Rossman, *The Amazon Way on IoT*, 25.

54. Jathan Sadowski, "When Data Is Capital: Datafication, Accumulation, and Extraction," *Big Data & Society* January–June (2019): 2.

55. Zuboff, *The Age of Surveillance Capitalism*, 68.

56. "Amazon Privacy Notice."

57. "Amazon Privacy Notice."

58. Spector, *Amazon.com Get Big Fast*, 212.

59. "Amazon Privacy Notice."

60. Rossman, *The Amazon Way on IoT*, 97.

61. Karen Weise, "Amazon Knows What You Buy. And It's Building a Big Ad Business from It," *New York Times*, January 20, 2019, https://www.nytimes.com/2019/01/20/technology/amazon-ads-advertising.html; Stone, *Amazon Unbound*, 249–253.

62. "Amazon Has a Plan to Become Profitable. It's Called Advertising," *Advertising Age*, January 18, 2018, https://adage.com/article/digital/amazon-a-plan-profitable-advertising/311992.

63. Jefferson Graham, "CES 2019: Google vs. Amazon: Who Won?," *USA Today*, January 11, 2019, https://www.usatoday.com/story/tech/talkingtech/2019/01/11/hey-google-hey-alexa-who-won-ces-2019/2473306002/.

64. Weise, "Amazon Knows What You Buy."

65. Morgan Stanley Research, "Amazon Disruption Symposium: Alexa, What Happens Next?," September 28, 2018, http://docplayer.net/137756423-Amazon-disruption-symposium.html.

66. Kristina Monloss, "'This Is a Permanent Shift': Retail Giants Like Amazon Capture More Ad Spending," *Digiday*, April 22, 2020, https://digiday.com/marketing/this-is-a-permanent-shift-retail-giants-like-amazon-capture-more-ad-spending/.

67. Graham, "CES 2019."

68. Graham, "CES 2019."

69. Weise, "Amazon Knows What You Buy."

70. Graham, "CES 2019."

71. Graham, "CES 2019"; Weise, "Amazon Knows What You Buy."

72. "Display Ads," *Amazon Advertising*, 2020, https://advertising.amazon.com/products/display-ads?ref_=a20m_us_libr_bos_intro_da.

73. "Display Ads," *Amazon Advertising*; Weise, "Amazon Knows What You Buy."

74. Rossman, *The Amazon Way on IoT*, 96.

75. Tim Peterson, "Pitch Deck: How Amazon Is Selling Ads on Fire TV," *Digiday*, January 23, 2020, https://digiday.com/future-of-tv/pitch-deck-amazon-selling-ads-fire-tv/.

76. Deane Barker, "An Unofficial Guide to Whatever-as-a-Service," *Gadgetopia*, February 10, 2017, https://gadgetopia.com/post/9981, emphasis in original; see also Jathan Sadowski, "The Internet of Landlords: Digital Platforms and New Mechanisms of Rentier Capitalism," *Antipode* 52, no. 2 (2020): 562.

77. "U.S. Smart Speaker Adoption."

78. Amazon Alexa, "Build Skills with the Alexa Skills Kit," *Alexa Skills Kit*, 2021, https://developer.amazon.com/en-US/docs/alexa/ask-overviews/build-skills-with-the-alexa-skills-kit.html.

79. Amazon Alexa, "Build Skills"; Nat Levy, "Baidu Surges Past Google in Global Smart Speaker Sales, Becoming the New #2 Behind Amazon Echo," *Geekwire*, August 26, 2019, https://www.geekwire.com/2019/baidu-surges-past-google-global-smart-speaker-sales-becoming-new-2-behind-amazon-echo/.

80. Thao Phan, "Amazon Echo and the Aesthetics of Whiteness," *Catalyst: Feminism, Theory, and Technoscience* 5, no. 1 (2019): 29, http://www.catalystjournal.org.

81. Andrea L. Guzman, "Making AI Safe for Humans: A Conversation with Siri," in *Socialbots and Their Friends: Digital Media and the Automation of Sociality*, ed. R. W. Gehl and M. Bakardjieva (New York: Routledge, 2017), 79.

82. Nick Couldry and Andreas Hepp, *The Mediated Construction of Reality* (Malden, MA: Polity Press, 2017), 132.

83. Hanna Kahlert, "The Tech Major Ecosystems Wars Are Here with Aggressive, Loss-Led On-Boarding," *Midia*, January 7, 2020, https://www.midiaresearch.com/blog/the-tech-major-ecosystem-wars-are-here-with-aggressive-loss-led-on-boarding/; Kaitlyn Tiffany, "Smart Speakers Are Everywhere This Holiday Season, But They're Really a Gift for Big Tech Companies," *Vox*, November 27, 2018, https://www.vox.com/the-goods/2018/11/26/18112631/cyber-monday-amazon-alexa-google-voice-assistant-war.

84. ABI Research, "ABI Research Amazon Echo Dot Teardown: Voice Command Makes a Power Play in the Smart Home Market," *PR Newswire*, January 17, 2017, https://www.prnewswire.com/news-releases/abi-research-amazon-echo-dot-teardown-voice-command-makes-a-power-play-in-the-smart-home-market-300391892.html.

85. Sean Hollister, "Amazon Doesn't Sell Echo Speakers at a Loss, Says Bezos—Unless They're on Sale," *The Verge*, July 29, 2020, https://www.theverge.com/2020/7/29/21347121/amazon-echo-speaker-price-undercut-rivals-loss-sale-antitrust-hearing.

86. Kahlert, "Tech Major Ecosystems Wars."

87. Judith Shulevitz, "Alexa, Should We Trust You?," *Atlantic*, November 2018, https://www.theatlantic.com/magazine/archive/2018/11/alexa-how-will-you-change-us/570844/.

88. Amy He, "Amazon Maintains Convincing Lead in US Smart Speaker Market," *eMarketer*, February 18, 2020, https://www.emarketer.com/content/amazon-maintains-convincing-lead-in-us-smart-speaker-market.

89. Elizabeth Weise, "Amazon's Alexa Will Be Built into All New Homes from Lennar," *USA Today*, May 9, 2018, https://www.usatoday.com/story/tech/news/2018/05/09/amazons-alexa-built-into-all-new-homes-lennar/584004002/.

90. Matt Day, "Amazon's Alexa Recorded and Shared a Conversation Without Consent, Report Says," *Seattle Times*, May 24, 2018, https://www.seattletimes.com/business

/amazon/amazons-alexa-recorded-and-shared-a-conversation-without-consent-report
-says/; Matt Day, "Alexa Is Laughing at People, Unprompted; Amazon Is Working to
Fix It," *Seattle Times*, March 7, 2018, https://www.seattletimes.com/business/amazon
/alexa-is-laughing-at-people-unprompted-amazon-is-working-to-fix-it/.

91. Day, Turner, and Drozdiak, "Amazon Workers Are Listening"; see also Dave
Davies, "How Tech Companies Track Your Every Move and Put Your Data Up for
Sale," *Fresh Air*, National Public Radio, July 31, 2019, https://www.npr.org/2019/07
/31/746878763/how-tech-companies-track-your-every-move-and-put-your-data-up
-for-sale.

92. Amazon, "Letter to the Honorable Chris Coons," July 3, 2019, https://www.coons
.senate.gov/news/press-releases/amazon-responds-to-sen-coons-concerns-about
-consumer-privacy-practices-for-alexa-devices.

93. Laura Stevens, "Amazon's New Echo Device Will Be Watching," *Fox Business*,
May 11, 2017, https://www.foxbusiness.com/features/amazons-new-echo-device-will
-be-watching.

94. Lauren Goode, "Amazon Debuts a New Echo Show Amid Alexa Privacy Concerns," *Wired*, May 29, 2019, https://www.wired.com/story/amazon-echo-show-5-and
-alexa-privacy-hub/.

95. Zeynep Tufekci, Twitter thread, April 26, 2017, https://twitter.com/zeynep.

96. Lauren Goode, "Amazon's Echo Look Does More for Amazon Than It Does for
Your Style," *The Verge*, July 6, 2017, https://www.theverge.com/2017/7/6/15924120
/amazon-echo-look-review-camera-clothes-style.

97. Tufekci, Twitter thread.

98. Zuboff, *The Age of Surveillance Capitalism*, 286.

99. Huafeng Jin and Shuo Wang (Amazon Technologies Inc.), "Voice-Based Determination of Physical and Emotional Characteristics of Users," *US Patent 10,096,319
B1*, filed March 13, 2017, and issued October 19, 2018.

100. Geoffrey A. Fowler and Heather Kelly, "Amazon's New Health Band Is the Most
Invasive Tech We've Ever Tested," *Washington Post*, December 10, 2020, https://www
.washingtonpost.com/technology/2020/12/10/amazon-halo-band-review/.

101. Laura Dyrda, "15 Things to Know about Amazon's Healthcare Strategy Heading
into 2020," *Becker's Health IT*, January 6, 2020, https://www.beckershospitalreview.com
/healthcare-information-technology/15-things-to-know-about-amazon-s-healthcare
-strategy-heading-into-2020.html.

102. Tufekci, Twitter thread.

103. Foster and McChesney, "Surveillance Capitalism"; Tufekci, Twitter thread; Zuboff,
The Age of Surveillance Capitalism.

104. Liza Lin and Josh Chin, "China's Tech Giants Have a Second Job: Helping Bei-
jing Spy on Its People," *Wall Street Journal*, November 30, 2017, https://www.wsj
.com/articles/chinas-tech-giants-have-a-second-job-helping-the-government-see
-everything-1512056284.

105. Rachel Botsman, "Big Data Meets Big Brother as China Moves to Rate Its Citizens," *Wired*, October 21, 2017, http://www.wired.co.uk/article/chinese-government-social-credit-score-privacy-invasion.

106. *Frontline*, "Amazon Empire."

107. Inioluwa Deborah Raji and Joy Buolamwini, "Actionable Auditing: Investigating the Impact of Publicly Naming Biased Performance Results of Commercial AI Products," *Proceedings of the AAAI/ACM Conference on AI, Ethics, & Society*, January 2019, https://doi.org/10.1145/3306618.3314244.

108. Bob Susnjara, "Fighting Crime or Invading Privacy?," *Daily Herald* (Chicago, IL), February 9, 2020, https://www.dailyherald.com/news/20200209/fighting-crime-or-invading-privacy-police-deals-with-ring-video-doorbell-have-advocates-and-critics.

109. Susnjara, "Fighting Crime."

110. *Frontline*, "Amazon Empire."

111. Rafael Olmeda, "Alexa, Is He Guilty of Murder? Amazon Device May Have Heard Slaying, Cops Say," *Sun Sentinel* (Fort Lauderdale, FL), October 31, 2019, https://www.sun-sentinel.com/news/crime/fl-ne-amazon-alexa-murder-investigation-20191031-qccpvdl6kng5hcx3z6eusxa264-story.html; Tracy Neal, "Hearing Scheduled in Wrongful Death Case," *Arkansas Democrat-Gazette*, January 7, 2019, https://www.arkansasonline.com/news/2019/jan/07/hearing-scheduled-in-wrongful-death-cas/; "Judge Orders Amazon to Hand Over Echo Recordings from Home in Murder Case," *NBC News*, November 12, 2018, https://www.nbcnews.com/news/us-news/judge-orders-amazon-hand-over-echo-recordings-home-murder-case-n935221.

112. Patricia Ticineto Clough and Jean Halley, eds., *The Affective Turn: Theorizing the Social* (Durham, NC: Duke University Press, 2007); Ali Lara, Wen Liu, Colin Patrick Ashley, Akemi Nishida, Rachel Jane Liebert, and Michelle Billies, "Affect and Subjectivity," *Subjectivity* 10, no. 1 (2017).

113. Andrejevic, *Automated Media*, 7.

114. Yolande Strengers and Jenny Kennedy, *The Smart Wife: Why Siri, Alexa, and Other Smart Home Devices Need a Feminist Reboot* (Cambridge, MA: MIT Press, 2020), 4. On the "digital housewife," see also Amy Schiller and John McMahon, "Alexa, Alert Me When the Revolution Comes: Gender, Affect, and Labor in the Age of Home-Based Artificial Intelligence," *New Political Science* 41, no. 2 (2019): 173–191, doi: 10.1080/07393148.2019.1595288.

115. Holly Brockwell, "Interview: Toni Reid, VP of Alexa Experience at Amazon," *Gadgette*, October 12, 2018, https://www.gadgette.com/2018/10/12/interview-toni-reid-vp-of-alexa/; Phan, "Amazon Echo."

116. Michaeleen Doucleff and Allison Aubrey, "Alexa, Are You Safe for My Kids?," National Public Radio, October 30, 2017, https://www.npr.org/sections/health-shots/2017/10/30/559863326/alexa-are-you-safe-for-my-kids.

117. "Get Started with the Guide," *Alexa Design Guide*, 2020, https://developer.amazon.com/docs/alexa-design/get-started.html.

118. "Be Personal," *Alexa Design Guide,* 2020, https://developer.amazon.com/en-US /docs/alexa/alexa-design/personal.html.

119. "Voice Experiences," *Alexa Design Guide,* n.d., https://developer.amazon.com /docs/alexa-design/intro.html, accessed December 2, 2018.

120. "Be Personal," *Alexa Design Guide.*

121. Will Knight, "Amazon Working on Making Alexa Recognize Your Emotions," *MIT Technology Review,* June 13, 2016, https://www.technologyreview.com/2016/06 /13/159665/amazon-working-on-making-alexa-recognize-your-emotions/.

122. Thao Phan, "The Materiality of the Digital and the Gendered Voice of Siri," *Transformations* 29 (2017), www.transformationsjournal.org.

123. Phan, "Amazon Echo"; Shulevitz, "Alexa, Should We Trust You?"; see also Schiller and McMahon, "Alexa, Alert Me," 181.

124. "The Debut of Ellen & Portia's Amazon Alexa Superbowl Commercial," *YouTube: TheEllenShow,* January 29, 2020, https://www.youtube.com/watch?v=2rhq3GLxAmY.

125. Anna Peak, "Servants and the Victorian Sensation Novel," *SEL Studies in English Literature 1500–1900* 54, no. 4 (2014), https://doi.org/10.1353/sel.2014.0042; Lucy Delap, "Housework, Housewives, and Domestic Workers: Twentieth-Century Dilemmas of Domesticity," *Home Cultures* 8, no. 2 (2011), https://doi.org/10.2752/17517 4211X12961586699801.

126. Schiller and McMahon, "Alexa, Alert Me," 181.

127. "Marketing and Branding Guidelines," *Alexa Design Guide,* n.d., https://developer .amazon.com/docs/alexa-voice-service/marketing-and-branding-guidelines.html #messaging, accessed December 2, 2018.

128. "Trustbusters," *Alexa Design Guide,* n.d., https://developer.amazon.com/docs /alexa-design/trustbusters.html, accessed December 2, 2018. Heather Suzanne Woods documents how Siri similarly deflects and defuses hostile or sexualized comments from users; "Asking More of Siri and Alexa: Feminine Persona in Service of Surveillance Capitalism," *Critical Studies in Media Communication* 35, no. 4 (2018): 343, doi: 10.1080/15295036.2018.1488082.

129. "Be Adaptable," *Alexa Design Guide,* n.d., https://developer.amazon.com/en-US /docs/alexa/alexa-design/adaptable.html, accessed May 28, 2021; "Design: Function," *Alexa Design Guide,* n.d., https://developer.amazon.com/docs/alexa-design/design-func tion.html#errors, accessed December 2, 2018.

130. "Establish and Maintain Trust," *Alexa Design Guide,* n.d., https://developer.amazon .com/en-US/docs/alexa/alexa-design/trustbusters.html, accessed May 28, 2021.

131. "Design: Voice," *Alexa Design Guide,* n.d., https://developer.amazon.com/docs /alexa-design/design-voice.html, accessed August 14, 2019.

132. Shulevitz, "Alexa, Should We Trust You?"

133. "Voice Experiences," *Alexa Design Guide,* n.d., https://developer.amazon.com /docs/alexa-design/intro.html, accessed December 2, 2018.

134. Woods, "Asking More of Siri and Alexa," 335.

135. Brockwell, "Amazon Alexa VP"; Wade J. Mitchell, Chin-Chang Ho, Himalaya Patel, and Karl F. MacDorman, "Does Social Desirability Bias Favor Humans? Explicit–Implicit Evaluations of Synthesized Speech Support a New HCI Model of Impression Management," *Computers in Human Behavior* 27, no. 1 (2011).

136. Richard Baguley and Colin McDonald, "Appliance Science: Alexa, How Does Alexa Work?," *CNet*, August 4, 2016, https://www.cnet.com/news/appliance-science-alexa-how-does-alexa-work-the-science-of-amazons-echo/.

137. Phan, "The Materiality of the Digital"; Joanna Stern, "Alexa, Siri, Cortana: Why All Your Bots Are Female," *Wall Street Journal*, February 21, 2017, https://www.wsj.com/articles/alexa-siri-cortana-the-problem-with-all-female-digital-assistants-1487709068.

138. Woods, "Asking More of Siri and Alexa," 336. See also Hilary Bergen, "'I'd Blush If I Could': Digital Assistants, Disembodied Cyborgs and the Problem of Gender," *Word and Text* 6 (December 2016): 100.

139. Evelyn Nakano Glenn, "From Servitude to Service Work: Historical Continuities in the Racial Division of Paid Reproductive Labor," *Signs* 18, no. 1 (1992).

140. Brockwell, "Amazon Alexa VP."

141. Richard Dyer, *White: Essays on Race and Culture* (London: Psychology Press, 1997).

142. Phan, "Amazon Echo."

143. Woods, "Asking More of Siri and Alexa," 338.

144. "Be Available," *Alexa Design Guide.*

145. Striphas, *Late Age of Print*, 45.

146. Striphas, 180.

147. Zuboff, *The Age of Surveillance Capitalism*, 8–12.

CHAPTER 5

1. Kate Taylor, "I Visited Whole Foods on the Day It Was Acquired by Amazon—and It's Clear It Will Never Be the Same," *Business Insider*, August 29, 2017, https://www.businessinsider.in/I-visited-Whole-Foods-on-the-day-it-was-acquired-by-Amazon-and-its-clear-itll-never-be-the-same/articleshow/60266909.cms.

2. Marcus, *Amazonia*, 142.

3. Stone, *The Everything Store*, 67.

4. George Anders, "Jeff Bezos Gets It," *Forbes*, May 7, 2012, https://www.forbes.com/global/2012/0507/global-2000-12-amazon-jeff-bezos-gets-it.html#7206dfae55fa.

5. Wendy Lee, "Amazon Is Primed to Change the Fashion Industry with 'Making the Cut,'" *Los Angeles Times*, February 22, 2020, https://www.latimes.com/entertainment-arts/business/story/2020-02-22/amazon-making-the-cut-reality-tv-heidi-klum-prime.

6. Mike Featherstone, "Ubiquitous Media: An Introduction," *Theory, Culture & Society* 26, no. 2–3 (2009); Kevin Carillo, Eusebio Scornavacca, and Stefano Za, "The Role of Media Dependency in Predicting Continuance Intention to Use Ubiquitous

Media Systems," *Information & Management* 54, no. 3 (2017), http://dx.doi.org/10 .1016/j.im.2016.09.002.

7. Chuck Tryon, *On-Demand Culture: Digital Delivery and the Future of Movies* (New Brunswick, NJ: Rutgers University Press, 2013), 4.

8. Lotz, *Portals*, ch. 2.

9. Mark Andrejevic, "Surveillance in the Digital Enclosure," *Communication Review* 10 (2007), doi: 10.1080/10714420701715365; Andrejevic, *Automated Media*, 142; Sadowski, "When Data Is Capital," 4.

10. Ted Striphas, "Algorithmic Culture," *European Journal of Cultural Studies* 18, no. 4–5 (2015); Perzanowski and Schultz, *End of Ownership*, 50, 61.

11. Andrew Flanagan and Jasmine Garsd, "iTunes' Death Is All About How We Listen to Music Today," National Public Radio, June 3, 2019, https://www.npr.org/2019/06 /03/729290123/itunes-death-is-all-about-how-we-listen-to-music-today.

12. Julia Alexander, "WarnerMedia Undergoes Major Reorganization as HBO Max Gets Higher Priority," *The Verge*, August 7, 2020, https://www.theverge.com/2020 /8/7/21359128/warnermedia-reorg-bob-greenblatt-kevin-reilly-hbo-max-jason-kilar -streaming.

13. Douglas Rushkoff, "Commodified vs. Commoditized," *Rushkoff: Blog*, 2005, http:// www.rushkoff.com/commodified-vs-commoditized/; Striphas, *Late Age of Print*, 9.

14. Tryon, *On-Demand Culture*, 19.

15. Tryon, 31; see also Charles R. Acland, "Curtains, Carts, and the Mobile Screen," *Screen* 50, no. 1 (2009): 150.

16. Tryon, *On-Demand Culture*, 60.

17. James G. Webster, *The Marketplace of Attention: How Audiences Take Shape in a Digital Age* (Cambridge, MA: MIT Press, 2014), 27–28.

18. Shira Ovide, "'Good Enough' Rules the World," *New York Times*, September 16, 2020, https://www.nytimes.com/2020/09/16/technology/good-enough-rules-the-world .html.

19. "We Want to Change the Way TV Shows Are Made in India: Nitesh Kripalani, Amazon Video," *Exchange4Media.com* (India), December 16, 2016, https://www.ex change4media.com/digital-news/we-want-to-change-the-way-tv-shows-are-made-in -indianitesh-kripalaniamazon-video-67031.html.

20. Lobato, *Netflix Nations*, 7–8.

21. Lobato, 7–8.

22. Amazon, "Prime Video: Branding Guidelines (v.3)," *Branding Style Guides*, August 2018, https://brandingstyleguides.com/guide/prime-video/.

23. Amazon, "Prime Video: Branding."

24. Karen Petruska, "Where Information Is Entertainment," in *From Networks to Netflix: A Guide to Changing Channels*, ed. Derek Johnson (New York: Routledge, 2018), 358–359.

25. Adam Levy, "Amazon Music Has Over 55 Million Listeners, and It's Growing Fast," *The Motley Fool*, January 24, 2020, https://www.fool.com/investing/2020/01/24/amazon-music-has-over-55-million-listeners-and-its.aspx.

26. Jason Del Ray, "The Making of Amazon Prime, the Internet's Most Successful and Devastating Membership Program," *Vox: Recode*, May 3, 2019, https://www.vox.com/recode/2019/5/3/18511544/amazon-prime-oral-history-jeff-bezos-one-day-shipping.

27. Blake Montgomery, "The Amazon Publishing Juggernaut," *Atlantic*, August 8, 2019, https://www.theatlantic.com/technology/archive/2019/08/amazons-plan-take-over-world-publishing/595630/.

28. Samuel Spencer, "How Many Subscribers Do Netflix, Disney+, and the Rest of the Streaming Services Have?," *Newsweek*, May 11, 2021, https://www.newsweek.com/netflix-amazon-hulu-disney-most-subscribers-streaming-service-1590463; Omri Wallach, "Which Streaming Service Has the Most Subscriptions?," *World Economic Forum*, March 10, 2021, https://www.weforum.org/agenda/2021/03/streaming-service-subscriptions-lockdown-demand-netflix-amazon-prime-spotify-disney-plus-apple-music-movie-tv/.

29. Max Signorelli, "Amazon Nipping at Netflix's Heels," *IHS Markit*, January 2018, https://technology.ihs.com/599383/amazon-nipping-at-netflixs-heels.

30. Morgan Stanley Research, "Amazon Disruption Symposium: Where So Far? Where to Next? Who Is Safe?" (slides from symposium held in New York City, September 18, 2017), 70.

31. Priyanka Pani, "Buoyed by Prime Memberships, Amazon Plans India-Specific Solutions," *Hindu Business Line* (Chennai, India), updated January 12, 2018, https://www.thehindubusinessline.com/info-tech/buoyed-by-prime-memberships-amazon-plans-indiaspecific-solutions/article9740423.ece.

32. Vidhi Choudhary, "India Has a Strong Preference for Local Content: Amazon Video's Tim Leslie," *MINT* (New Delhi, India), December 14, 2016, https://www.livemint.com/Consumer/l9Gvg6vifdsYMlZlQO8jOP/India-has-a-strong-preference-for-local-content-Amazon-Vide.html.

33. Raja Sen, "What You Should Watch (and What You Can't) on Amazon Prime India," *MINT* (New Delhi, India), December 15, 2016, https://www.livemint.com/Leisure/qsUSg4VYcyZIfSLRN8MpsO/What-you-should-watch-and-what-you-cant-on-Amazon-Prime-I.html.

34. Sergei Klebnikov, "Streaming Wars Continue: Here's How Much Netflix, Amazon, Disney+ and Their Rivals Are Spending on New Content," *Forbes*, May 22, 2020, https://www.forbes.com/sites/sergeiklebnikov/2020/05/22/streaming-wars-continue-heres-how-much-netflix-amazon-disney-and-their-rivals-are-spending-on-new-content/#440cfdc8623b.

35. Jeffrey Dastin, "Exclusive: Amazon's Internal Numbers on Prime Video, Revealed," *Reuters*, March 15, 2018, https://www.reuters.com/article/us-amazon-com-ratings-exclusive/exclusive-amazons-internal-numbers-on-prime-video-revealed-idUSKCN1GR0FX.

36. Dastin, "Exclusive: Amazon's Internal Numbers."

37. Eric Johnson, "Why Amazon Is Going to Be One of the Winners of the Stream-ing Video Wars," *Vox: Recode*, June 10, 2019, https://www.vox.com/recode/2019/6/10/18658964/amazon-prime-video-netflix-disney-plus-streaming-video-lotr-matthew-ball-peter-kafka-media-podcast?curator=MediaREDEF; Morgan Stanley Research, "Amazon Disruption Symposium: Alexa, What Happens Next?," 17; Netflix engages in the same practice: Rasmus Helles and Mikkel Flyverbom, "Meshes of Surveillance, Prediction, and Infrastructure: On the Cultural and Commercial Consequences of Digi-tal Platforms," *Surveillance & Society* 17, no. 1/2 (2019), https://ojs.library.queensu.ca/index.php/surveillance-and-society/article/view/13120.

38. *Frontline*, "Amazon Empire."

39. Dastin, "Exclusive: Amazon's Internal Numbers."

40. "In Celebration of Five Wins from the 67th Primetime Emmys, Amazon Offers Prime Memberships for Just $67," *Amazon Press Center*, September 22, 2015, https://press.aboutamazon.com/news-releases/news-release-details/celebration-five-wins-67th-primetime-emmys-amazon-offers-prime.

41. Del Ray, "The Making of Amazon Prime."

42. *Frontline*, "Amazon Empire."

43. "Introducing 'X-Ray for Movies,' Powered by IMDb and Available Exclusively on the All-New Kindle Fire Family," *Amazon Press Center*, September 6, 2012, https://press.aboutamazon.com/news-releases/news-release-details/introducing-x-ray-movies-powered-imdb-and-available-exclusively.

44. "Introducing the All-New Kindle Family: Four New Kindles, Four Amazing Price Points," *Amazon Press Center*, September 28, 2011, https://press.aboutamazon.com/news-releases/news-release-details/introducing-all-new-kindle-family-four-new-kindles-four-amazing.

45. Kari Paul, "'They Know Us Better Than We Know Ourselves': How Amazon Tracked My Last Two Years of Reading," *Guardian*, February 3, 2020, https://www.theguardian.com/technology/2020/feb/03/amazon-kindle-data-reading-tracking-privacy?utm_source=pocket-newtab.

46. Paul, "'They Know Us Better.'"

47. Jennifer Gillan, *Television and New Media: Must-Click TV* (New York: Routledge, 2011); Lee McGuigan, "Selling Jennifer Aniston's Sweater: The Persistence of Shop-pability in Framing Television's Future," *Media Industries* 5, no. 1 (2018), http://dx.doi.org/10.3998/mij.15031809.0005.101; Anthony Ha, "NBCUniversal Rolls Out Its ShoppableTV Ads," *TechCrunch*, October 28, 2019, https://techcrunch.com/2019/10/28/nbcuniversal-rolls-out-its-shoppabletv-ads/.

48. McGuigan, "Selling Jennifer Aniston's Sweater."

49. Cameron Faulkner, "Walmart May Bring 'Shoppable' TV shows and Movies to Vudu in 2019," April 19, 2019, *The Verge*, https://www.theverge.com/2019/4/29

/18522430/walmart-vudu-streaming-video-tv-shows-shoppable; Kate Taylor, "Costco Might Launch Its Own Streaming Service for 'Average Americans' to Compete with Netflix and Amazon," *Business Insider*, January 17, 2019, https://www.businessinsider .com/costco-talks-streaming-service-for-average-americans-report-2019-1\.

50. Sarah Perez, "Walmart Is Selling Its On-Demand Video Service Vudu to Fandango," *TechCrunch*, April 20, 2020, https://techcrunch.com/2020/04/20/walmart-is -selling-its-on-demand-video-service-vudu-to-fandango/.

51. Striphas, "Algorithmic Culture."

52. Rosy Cordero, "Heidi Klum and Tim Gunn Take Their New Amazon Fashion Series *Making the Cut* to Paris," *Entertainment*, June 26, 2019, https://ew.com/tv/2019 /06/26/heidi-klum-and-tim-gunn-take-their-new-amazon-fashion-series-making-the -cut-to-paris/.

53. Lee, "Amazon Is Primed."

54. Lee, "Amazon Is Primed."

55. T. L. Taylor, *Watch Me Play: Twitch and the Rise of Game Live Streaming* (Princeton, NJ: Princeton University Press), 6.

56. Mark Andrejevic, *Reality TV: The Work of Being Watched* (Lanham, MD: Rowman & Littlefield Publishers, 2004), 61.

57. Twitch, "About Twitch," n.d., https://www.twitch.tv/p/en/about/, accessed May 28, 2021.

58. *Influencer Marketing Hub*, "Top 10 Twitch Streamers by Subscriber Count," October 19, 2020, https://influencermarketinghub.com/twitch-sub-count/.

59. Taylor, *Watch Me Play*, 253.

60. *Twitch*, "Unlink Your Amazon and Twitch Accounts," 2001, https://www.ama zongames.com/en-us/support/prime-gaming/articles/unlink-your-amazon-and-twitch -accounts.

61. Kerry Flynn, "'We Have an Incredible Audience Advantage': Twitch Is Expanding Its Sales Team as It Seeks Bigger Deals," *Digiday*, May 14, 2015, https://digiday .com/marketing/twitch-cro-walker-jacobs/. See also *Influencer Marketing Hub*, "40 Useful Twitch Stats for Influencer Marketing Managers," October 26, 2020, https:// influencermarketinghub.com/twitch-stats/.

62. Julia Alexander, "Twitch Prime Changes Are Worrying Streamers Around the World," *Polygon*, August 24, 2018, https://www.polygon.com/2018/8/24/17774374 /twitch-prime-ad-free-changes-streamers-asia-japan-europe.

63. Cecilia d'Anastasio, "Amazon Wants to 'Win at Games,' So Why Hasn't It?," *Wired*, October 7, 2020, https://www.wired.com/story/amazon-wants-to-win-at-games -so-why-hasnt-it/.

64. Amazon, "Amazon Prime Membership—Prime Video" [Video], *YouTube*, 2015, https://www.youtube.com/watch?v=Q1AADPOdD78.

65. Amazon, "Amazon Prime TV Commercial: 'More to Prime: The Musical,'" *iSpotTV*, 2015, https://www.ispot.tv/ad/AIRO/amazon-prime-more-to-prime-the-musical#.

66. "Amazon Prime Video Redefines 'India Ka Naya Primetime,'" *Exchange4Media.com* (India), February 18, 2017, https://www.exchange4media.com/digital-news/amazon -prime-video-redefines-'india-ka-naya-primetime'-67776.html.

67. Mark Stewart, "The Myth of Televisual Ubiquity," *Television & New Media* 17, no. 8 (2016); Lobato, *Netflix Nations*, 41.

68. Lobato, 96–98.

69. Ben Moore, "Amazon Prime Video Review," *PC Mag*, February 26, 2020, https:// www.pcmag.com/reviews/amazon-prime-video; "Amazon Prime Video Uses AWS to Deliver Solid Streaming Experience to More Than 18 Million Football Fans," *AWS: Case Studies*, n.d., https://aws.amazon.com/solutions/case-studies/amazon-prime-video/, accessed May 28, 2021.

70. Jonathan Vanian, "Twitch CEO Emmett Shear Talks Live Streaming, Sarcasm, and Amazon Web Services," *Fortune*, October 27, 2018, https://fortune.com/2018/10 /27/twitch-ceo-emmett-shear-streaming-amazon/.

71. D'Anastasio, "Amazon Wants to 'Win at Games.'"

72. Shephard, "How Amazon Quietly Became."

73. "KDP Select," *Kindle Direct Publishing*, n.d., https://kdp.amazon.com/en_US/select, accessed May 28, 2021.

74. Matthew Ball, "How the Paradox of the Term 'Original Series' Explains the Video Industry," *MatthewBall.vc*, August 27, 2018, https://www.matthewball.vc/all /netflixoriginals.

75. Dylan Byers, "No, Mr. Bond, I Expect You to Subscribe: Amazon Buys MGM for $8.5 Billion," *NBC News*, May 26, 2021, https://www.nbcnews.com/media/amazon -acquires-movie-studio-mgm-85-billion-rcna1023.

76. "Amazon Prime Video TV Commercial, 'Let's Have Some Fun' Song by Kaskade & BROHUG & Mr. Tape Feat. Madge," *iSpot.tv*, 2020, https://www.ispot.tv/ad/Zy2w /amazon-prime-video-lets-have-some-fun-song-by-kaskade-and-brohug-and-mr-tape -feat-madge.

77. Amazon Prime Video India, "14 New Amazon Originals," *YouTube*, January 20, 2020, https://www.youtube.com/watch?v=Cwh9zmC7saE.

78. "Amazon Prime Video TV Commercial, 'Amazon Originals' Song by Summer Kennedy," *iSpot.tv*, 2019, https://www.ispot.tv/ad/oaZa/amazon-prime-video-amazon -originals.

79. Lobato, *Netflix Nations*, 186.

80. "Amazon Lowers Price on #1 Bestseller Kindle to $259 and Introduces New Addition to the Kindle Family of Wireless Reading Devices," *Amazon Press Center*, October 7, 2009, https://press.aboutamazon.com/news-releases/news-release-details /amazon-lowers-price-1-bestseller-kindle-259-and-introduces-new.

81. Dan Farber, "Amazon's Jeff Bezos Admits Kindles Are Sold at Cost," *CNet*, October 11, 2012, https://www.cnet.com/news/amazons-jeff-bezos-admits-kindles-are-sold -at-cost/.

82. Todd Spangler, "'Subscription Fatigue': Nearly Half of U.S. Consumers Frustrated by Streaming Explosion, Study Finds," *Variety*, March 18, 2019, https://variety.com/2019/digital/news/streaming-subscription-fatigue-us-consumers-deloitte-study-1203166046/.

CHAPTER 6

1. Tara Von Ho, "Amazon Wins '.Amazon' Domain Name, Aggravating South American Region and Undermining Digital Commons," *The Conversation*, June 21, 2019, https://theconversation.com/amazon-wins-amazon-domain-name-aggravating-south-american-region-and-undermining-digital-commons-118186.

2. The Governments of Brazil and Peru, *GAC Early Warning–Submittal: Amazon—BR—PE—58086*, ICANN, November 20, 2012, https://gac.icann.org/work-products/public/amazon-br-pe-58086-2012-11-20.pdf.

3. *Approved Board Resolutions: Special Meeting of the ICANN Board*, ICANN, May 15, 2019, https://www.icann.org/resources/board-material/resolutions-2019-05-15-en#1.c.

4. *Approved Board Resolutions*, ICANN.

5. "Net Perceptions."

6. Gillespie, "Politics of 'Platforms.'"

7. Hogan, "Data Flows and Water Woes," 7.

8. Andrejevic, "Surveillance in the Digital Enclosure"; Hogan, "Data Flows and Water Woes."

9. Mosco, *To the Cloud*, 3.

10. Christian Sandvig, "Seeing the Sort: The Aesthetic and Industrial Defense of 'The Algorithm,'" *Media-N: Journal of the New Media Caucus*, 2014, http://median.newmediacaucus.org/art-infrastructures-information/seeing-the-sort-the-aesthetic-and-industrial-defense-of-the-algorithm/.

11. "Encyclopedia: Cloud," *PC Magazine*, https://www.pcmag.com/encyclopedia/term/cloud.

12. Andrejevic, "Surveillance in the Digital Enclosure."

13. Raymond Williams, *Marxism and Literature* (New York: Oxford University Press, 1977), 128.

14. Day and Soper, "Amazon U.S. Online Market Share"; Wells et al., "Amazon.com, 2019," 24.

15. Robert McChesney, "Be Realistic, Demand the Impossible: Three Radically Democratic Internet Policies," *Critical Studies in Media Communication* 31, no. 2 (2014), 96; "Monopolization Defined," *Federal Trade Commission*, n.d., https://www.ftc.gov/tips-advice/competition-guidance/guide-antitrust-laws/single-firm-conduct/monopolization-defined, accessed May 28, 2021.

16. Stone, *Amazon Unbound*, 363–364; *Frontline*, "Amazon Empire."

17. *Frontline*, "Amazon Empire."

18. "Monopolization Defined," *Federal Trade Commission*.

19. Elizabeth Weise, "Cyber Monday: Biggest Online Shopping Day in U.S. History Pits Amazon vs. Walmart," *USA Today*, November 27, 2017, https://www.usatoday .com/story/tech/2017/11/27/cyber-mondays-still-got-it-840-million-spent-10-00-am /897831001/.

20. Lucy Koch, "Looking for a New Product? You Probably Searched Amazon," *eMarketer*, March 31, 2019, https://www.emarketer.com/content/looking-for-a-new -product-you-probably-searched-amazon; Garcia, "More Product Searches."

21. Renée DiResta, "How Amazon's Algorithms Curated a Dystopian Bookstore," *Wired*, March 5, 2019, https://www.wired.com/story/amazon-and-the-spread-of-health -misinformation/.

22. C. Edwin Baker, *Media Concentration and Democracy: Why Ownership Matters* (New York: Cambridge University Press, 2007); Robert McChesney, *Rich Media, Poor Democracy*, 2nd ed. (New York: The New Press, 2015).

23. Mosco, *Becoming Digital*, 10.

24. McChesney, "Be Realistic," 95.

25. McChesney, 95.

26. Marco Iansiti and Karim R. Lakhani, "Managing Our Hub Economy: Strategy, Ethics, and Network Competition in the Age of Digital Superpowers," *Harvard Business Review*, September–October 2017, 86, https://hbr.org/2017/09/managing-our -hub-economy.

27. "Issues: Tech Platforms," *Open Markets Institute*, n.d., https://openmarketsinstitute .org/issues/tech-platforms/, accessed February 2, 2018.

28. 21 Cong. Rec. 2457 (1890) (statement of Sen. Sherman).

29. "Hearing on the Subcommittee on Antitrust, Commercial, and Administrative Law," *House Judiciary GOP*, livestreamed on July 29, 2020, https://www.youtube.com /watch?v=W8QLcjS2aSU.

30. Spencer Soper and Ben Brody, "Amazon Probed by U.S. Antitrust Officials over Marketplace," *Bloomberg*, September 11, 2019, https://www.bloomberg.com/news /articles/2019-09-11/amazon-antitrust-probe-ftc-investigators-interview-merchants ?sref=1nAnrjIw; "FTC to Examine Past Acquisitions by Large Technology Companies," *Federal Trade Commission Press Releases*, February 11, 2020, https://www.ftc.gov /news-events/press-releases/2020/02/ftc-examine-past-acquisitions-large-technology -companies; Tony Romm, "House Lawmakers Ask Apple, Amazon, Facebook and Google to Turn over Trove of Records in Antitrust Probe," *Washington Post*, September 13, 2019, https://www.washingtonpost.com/technology/2019/09/13/house-lawmakers -ask-apple-amazon-facebook-google-turn-over-trove-records-antitrust-probe/.

31. Wu, *The Curse of Bigness*, 131.

32. "Antitrust: Commission Opens Investigation into Possible Anti-Competitive Conduct of Amazon," *European Commission Press Corner*, July 17, 2019, https://ec.europa.eu /commission/presscorner/detail/en/IP_19_4291; Nadler and Cicilline, *Investigation of Competition in Digital Markets*, 322–323.

33. Napoli and Caplan, "Why Media Companies Insist."

34. Victor Pickard, *America's Battle for Media Democracy: The Triumph of Corporate Libertarianism and the Future of Media Reform* (New York: Cambridge University Press, 2015), 199.

35. Jennifer Holt, *Empires of Entertainment: Media Industries and the Politics of Deregulation, 1980–1996* (New Brunswick, NJ: Rutgers University Press, 2011), 53–54.

36. Wu, *The Curse of Bigness*; Holt, *Empires of Entertainment*.

37. Lina M. Khan, "Amazon's Antitrust Paradox," *Yale Law Journal* 126 (2017): 717–722; Wu, *The Curse of Bigness*, 83–92.

38. Holt, *Empires of Entertainment*, 29–33.

39. Matthew Belvedere, "AT&T CEO: Our Proposed $85 Billion Time Warner Deal Is Aimed at Competing with Netflix and Amazon," *CNBC*, February 9, 2018, https://www.cnbc.com/2018/02/09/att-ceo-stephenson-we-expect-to-win-approval-for-time-warner-deal.html.

40. Alex Weprin, "Justice Department Moves to Terminate Paramount Consent Decrees," *Hollywood Reporter*, November 18, 2019, https://www.hollywoodreporter.com/thr-esq/justice-department-moves-terminate-paramount-consent-decrees-1255858.

41. Antonio García Martínez, "What Microsoft's Antitrust Case Teaches Us about Silicon Valley," *Wired*, February 11, 2018, https://www.wired.com/story/what-microsofts-antitrust-case-teaches-us-about-silicon-valley/.

42. García Martínez, "Microsoft's Antitrust Case."

43. Khan, "Amazon's Antitrust Paradox," 710.

44. Nadler and Cicilline, *Investigation of Competition in Digital Markets*, 263–264.

45. Frank Pasquale, "When Antitrust Becomes Pro-Trust: The Digital Deformation of U.S. Competition Policy," *CPI Antitrust Chronicle*, University of Maryland Legal Studies Research Paper No. 2017–24 (2017), https://papers.ssrn.com/sol3/papers.cfm?abstract_id=3020163.

46. Pasquale, "When Antitrust Becomes Pro-Trust," 2.

47. Khan, "Amazon's Antitrust Paradox," 710.

48. Pallante, Rasenberger, and Hill, *AAP Joint Letter to Representative Cicilline.*

49. Paul Krugman, "Amazon's Monopsony Is Not OK," *New York Times*, October 19, 2014, https://www.nytimes.com/2014/10/20/opinion/paul-krugman-amazons-monopsony-is-not-ok.html.

50. Sadowski, "When Data Is Capital," 1–2.

51. Khan, "Amazon's Antitrust Paradox," 803.

52. Pasquale, "When Antitrust Becomes Pro-Trust."

53. Soper and Brody, "Amazon Probed by Antitrust Officials"; Feng Zhu and Qihong Liu, "Competing with Complementors: An Empirical Look at Amazon.com," *Strategic Management Journal* 39, no. 10 (2018); *Frontline*, "Amazon Empire"; Jennifer Rankin, "Third-Party Sellers and Amazon—a Double-edged Sword in E-commerce," *Guardian*, June 23, 2015, https://www.theguardian.com/technology/2015/jun/23/amazon

-marketplace-third-party-seller-faustian-pact; Del Ray, "Is Amazon Too Big?"; Stone, *Amazon Unbound*, 201–204.

54. McChesney, "Be Realistic," 95; Khan, "Amazon's Antitrust Paradox," 803.

55. Laura Phillips Sawyer, *US Antitrust Law and Policy in Historical Perspective*, Harvard Business School Working Paper 19–110 (2019), 20, https://www.hbs.edu›faculty.

56. House Committee on the Judiciary, "Judiciary Antitrust Subcommittee Investigation Reveals Digital Economy Highly Concentrated, Impacted by Monopoly Power," October 6, 2020, https://judiciary.house.gov/news/documentsingle.aspx?DocumentID=3429.

57. "Amazon.com," *Open Secrets*, 2019, https://www.opensecrets.org/orgs/totals.php?id=D000023883&cycle=2018; Benjamin Wofford, "Inside Jeff Bezos's DC Life," *The Washingtonian*, April 22, 2018, https://www.washingtonian.com/2018/04/22/inside-jeff-bezos-dc-life/; MacGillis, *Fulfillment*, 86–88.

58. Derek Thompson, "Amazon's HQ2 Spectacle Isn't Just Shameful—It Should Be Illegal," *Atlantic*, November 12, 2018, https://www.theatlantic.com/ideas/archive/2018/11/amazons-hq2-spectacle-should-be-illegal/575539/.

59. Fresh Air, "How 5 Tech Giants."

60. Robin Lewis, "Amazon's Shipping Ambitions Are Larger than It's Letting On," *Forbes*, April 1, 2016, https://www.forbes.com/sites/robinlewis/2016/04/01/planes-trains-trucks-and-ships/#4fd0f6ba6d39.

61. Open Markets Institute, "Public Comments of the Open Markets Institute Submitted to the Antitrust Division Roundtable Examining 'Consumers Costs of Anticompetitive Regulation,'" May 30, 2018, 2, https://www.openmarketsinstitute.org/publications/public-comments-open-markets-institute-submitted-antitrust-division-roundtable-examining-consumer-costs-anticompetitive-regulations.

62. Open Markets Institute, "Public Comments," 2, 5.

63. Heather Long, "Amazon's $15 Minimum Wage Doesn't End Debate Over Whether It's Creating Good Jobs," *Washington Post*, October 5, 2018, https://www.washingtonpost.com/business/economy/amazons-15-minimum-wage-doesnt-end-debate-over-whether-its-creating-good-jobs/2018/10/05/b1da23a0-c802-11e8-9b1c-a90f1daae309_story.html.

64. Sarah Holder, "Amazon's Slow Retreat from Seattle," *Citylab*, April 16, 2019, https://www.citylab.com/equity/2019/04/amazon-seattle-headquarters-tech-jobs-bellevue-crystal-city/586549/.

65. Holder, "Amazon's Slow Retreat."

66. "Bringing the Spheres' Green Walls to Life," *Amazon*, January 5, 2018, https://blog.aboutamazon.com/sustainability/bringing-the-spheres-green-walls-to-life.

67. James McQuivey, "Why Amazon Will Own Your Customer and What to Do About It," *Forbes*, February 14, 2018, https://www.forbes.com/sites/forrester/2018/02/14/why-amazon-will-own-your-customer-and-what-to-do-about-it/#45d77b12ae99.

68. George Lakoff and Mark Johnson, *Metaphors We Live By* (Chicago: University of Chicago Press, 1980).

69. Cornelius Puschmann and Jean Burgess, "Metaphors of Big Data," *International Journal of Communication* 8 (2014): 1695, http://ijoc.org.

70. Cynthia-Lou Coleman, L. David Ritchie, and Heather Hartley, "Assessing Frames and Metaphors in News Coverage of Prescription Drug Advertising," *Journal of Health & Mass Communication* 1, no. 1–2 (2009): 120.

71. Lakoff and Johnson, *Metaphors We Live By*.

72. To examine usage of the term "ecosystem" by and about Amazon, I a) searched for it in Amazon's own press archive, and b) searched for "Amazon AND Ecosystem" in "HEADLINE/LEAD PARAGRAPH" in NewsBank's Access World News database, filtering for North American news sources and going back only as far as 1995.

73. "Introducing Fire—Setting an Entirely New Standard for a Tablet under $50," *Amazon Press Center*, September 17, 2015, https://press.aboutamazon.com/news-releases /news-release-details/introducing-fire-setting-entirely-new-standard-tablet-under-50.

74. Andy Ihnatako, "Amazon Appstore an Excellent Work in Progress . . . Now About That Tablet Rumor," *Chicago Sun-Times*, web only, March 23, 2011.

75. "Introducing 'Kindle for Windows 8,'" *Amazon Press Center*, October 25, 2012, https://press.aboutamazon.com/news-releases/news-release-details/introducing -kindle-windows-8.

76. "Amazon and BMW Bring Alexa to the Road," *Amazon Press Center*, September 27, 2017, https://press.aboutamazon.com/news-releases/news-release-details/amazon -and-bmw-bring-alexa-road.

77. "Amazon.com to Acquire Twitch," *Amazon Press Center*, August 25, 2014, https:// press.aboutamazon.com/news-releases/news-release-details/amazoncom-acquire -twitch; "Amazon Web Services Launches Korean Data Centers for Its Cloud Computer Platform," *Amazon Press Center*, January 6, 2016, https://press.aboutamazon .com/news-releases/news-release-details/amazon-web-services-launches-korean -datacenters-its-cloud.

78. Kim-Mai Cutler, "Amazon App Store Zeroes In on Strengths: Real Goods Purchasing and Recommendations," *Tech Crunch*, September 24, 2012, https://techcrunch .com/2012/09/24/amazon-appstore/.

79. Peter Svensson, "Barnes & Noble, Microsoft Joining Forces," *Telegraph Herald* (Dubuque, IA), May 1, 2012, https://www.telegraphherald.com/news/business/article _6c101c80-59c0-589b-868b-05ec833c528f.html.

80. Leo Sun, "Amazon Speakers Dominate," *Dayton Daily News*, August 15, 2017; Elizabeth Weise, "Best Buy Scores a Win with Amazon Fire TV Deal—TVs Will Be Available Exclusively at Retailer," *Evansville Courier and Press*, April 19, 2018.

81. "Amazon.com to Acquire Twitch."

82. Chris Anderson, and Michael Wolff, "The Web Is Dead. Long Live the Internet," *Wired*, August 17, 2010, https://www.wired.com/2010/08/ff-webrip/.

83. Berners-Lee, "Long Live the Web," 83.

84. Del Ray, "The Making of Amazon Prime."

85. Nadler and Cicilline, *Investigation of Competition in Digital Markets*, 298.

86. John McDuling, "Amazon in Australia: Starbucks, Redux?," *Sydney Morning Herald*, July 20, 2018, https://www.smh.com.au/business/companies/amazon-in-australia-star bucks-redux-20180720-p4zsp2.html.

87. Spector, *Amazon.com Get Big Fast*; *Frontline*, "Amazon Empire"; Shasta Darlington, "Battle for .Amazon Domain Pits Retailer Against South American Nations," *New York Times*, April 18, 2019, https://www.nytimes.com/2019/04/18/world/americas/amazon -domain-name.html; Graham, "CES 2019."

88. Thatcher, O'Sullivan, and Mahmoudi, "Data Colonialism Through Accumulation," 998.

89. Frontline, "Amazon Empire."

CHAPTER 7

1. Cave, "Australia's Amazon Book Battle."

2. "Alabbar: Amazon, Jeff Bezos 'Should Go Back to Seattle,'" *Arabian Business*, December 19, 2019, https://www.arabianbusiness.com/retail/435696-alabbar-amazon -jeff-bezos-should-go-back-to-seattle.

3. Stephen Cribar, "Letter to the Honourable James Moore," Canadian Booksellers Association, March 5, 2010, Internet Archive Wayback Machine, https://web.archive .org/web/20100311083515/http://www.cbabook.org/.

4. "Welcome to the Jungle! Amazon Couldn't Have Timed India Launch Better," *Nextbigwhat.com* (Bangalore, India), June 5, 2013, https://nextbigwhat.com/amazon -india-launch-analysis/.

5. Jin, "Construction of Platform Imperialism," 145.

6. Adrian Athique, "Digital Emporiums: Platform Capitalism in India," *Media Industries* 6, no. 2 (2019): 74, http://dx.doi.org/10.3998/mij.15031809.0006.205.

7. Lee McGuigan and Vincent Manzerolle, "'All the World's a Shopping Cart': Theorizing the Political Economy of Ubiquitous Media and Markets," *New Media & Society* 17, no. 11 (2015): 1833.

8. McGuigan and Manzerolle, "'All the World's a Shopping Cart.'"

9. Farhad Manjoo, "Why the World Is Drawing Battle Lines Against America's Tech Giants," *New York Times*, June 1, 2016, https://www.nytimes.com/2016/06/02/technol ogy/why-the-world-is-drawing-battle-lines-against-american-tech-giants.html.

10. Miriyam Aouragh and Paula Chakravartty, "Infrastructures of Empire: Towards a Critical Geopolitics of Media and Information Studies," *Media, Culture & Society* 38, no. 4 (2016); Scott Fitzgerald, "Over-the-Top Video Services in India: Media Imperialism after Globalization," *Media Industries Journal* 6, no. 1 (2019), http://dx.doi.org /10.3998/mij.15031809.0006.206; Lobato, *Netflix Nations*; Aswin Punathambekar and Sriram Mohan, "Digital Platforms, Globalization and Culture," in *Media and Society*, 6th ed., ed. James Curran and David Hesmondalgh (London: Bloomsbury Academic, 2019); Dwayne R. Winseck, "The Geopolitical Economy of the Global

Internet Infrastructure," *Journal of Information Policy* 7 (2017), https://www.jstor.org /stable/10.5325/jinfopoli.7.2017.0228.

11. "Sell Worldwide with Amazon," *Global Selling*, 2021, https://services.amazon .com/global-selling/overview.html.

12. J. Clement, "Global Retail E-commerce Market Share of Amazon from 2016 to 2019," *Statista*, January 22, 2019, https://www.statista.com/statistics/955796/global -amazon-e-commerce-market-share/.

13. Don Davis, "Amazon Posts Record Profits as North American Sales Jump 40% in Q1," *Digital Commerce 360*, April 29, 2021, https://www.digitalcommerce360.com /article/amazon-sales/.

14. Morgan Stanley Research, *Amazon vs. Alibaba: The Next Decade of Disruption*, May 2018, http://www.fullertreacymoney.com/system/data/files/PDFs/2018/June/6th /Amazon%20vs%20Alibaba%20-%20The%20Next%20Decade%20Of%20Disruption .pdf.

15. Koichi Iwabuchi, *Recentering Globalization: Popular Culture and Japanese Transnationalism* (Durham, NC: Duke University Press, 2002), 24.

16. Rachel Siegel and Joanna Slater, "International Pushback Disrupts Amazon's Momentum to Expand Its Empire Worldwide," *Washington Post*, May 10, 2019, https:// www.washingtonpost.com/business/economy/international-pushback-disrupts -amazons-momentum-to-expand-its-empire-worldwide/2019/05/10/76bd5d26-6507 -11e9-82ba-fcfeff232e8f_story.html.

17. Liam Cormican, "Amazon's Australian Launch Was 'Weirdly Underwhelming,'" *Sydney Morning Herald*, November 23, 2017, https://www.smh.com.au/business/com panies/amazons-australian-launch-was-weirdly-underwhelming-20171123-gzr8gm .html.

18. Sandeep Ganediwalla and Anuj Kumar, "Does Rebranding of Souq Change Anything? Stage Set for Next Round of Online Retail Battles in Middle East," *Gulf News* (Dubai, UAE), May 2, 2019, https://gulfnews.com/business/analysis/does-rebranding -of-souq-change-anything-stage-set-for-next-round-of-online-retail-battles-in -middle-east-1.63695208.

19. Jon Russell, "Amazon Finally Made Its E-commerce Service Usable for International Customers," *Techcrunch*, April 18, 2018, https://techcrunch.com/2018/04/17 /amazon-finally-made-its-e-commerce-service-usable-for-international-customers/.

20. Trefis Team, "Why India Is Crucial to Amazon's Massive International Expansion Plans," *Forbes*, November 28, 2017, https://www.forbes.com/sites/greatspeculations /2017/11/28/why-india-is-crucial-to-amazons-massive-international-expansion -plans/#452d34d0464d.

21. "Amazon.in Launches Hindi Bookstore with Over 23,000 Titles," *India Business Insight*, April 16, 2014, https://www.financialexpress.com/archive/amazonin-launches -hindi-book-store-with-over-23000-titles/1240748/.

22. Ishita Tiwary, "India—Amazon Prime Video," *Global Internet TV Consortium*, November 2018, https://global-internet-tv.com/india-amazon-prime-video/.

23. "What You Should Watch," *MINT.*

24. Chandni Mathur, "Amazon Prime Video Set for India Launch, Ties Up with Bollywood for Films, More," *Financial Express* (India), September 27, 2016, https://www.financialexpress.com/industry/amazon-prime-video-set-for-india-launch-ties-up-with-bollywood-for-films-more/392844/.

25. Tiwary, "India—Amazon Prime Video"; Siegel and Slater, "Unanticipated Pushback."

26. "Amazon Prime Video to Launch the Highly Anticipated New Series The Grand Tour on Friday, November 18," *Amazon Press Center*, September 16, 2016, https://press.aboutamazon.com/news-releases/news-release-details/amazon-prime-video-launch-highly-anticipated-new-series-grand; James Pheby, "Big-Budget Motor Show 'The Grand Tour' Praised on Amazon Debut," *Yahoo! News*, November 18, 2016, https://www.yahoo.com/news/big-budget-motor-show-grand-tour-praised-amazon-104421698.html.

27. "Clarkson's Grand Design," *Times* (London, UK), May 12, 2016.

28. Pheby, "Big-Budget Motor Show"; Craig Mathieson, "'Very Expensive' Renegades Prompt Amazon's Expansion," *Sunday Age* (Melbourne, Australia), December 22, 2016.

29. David Bond, "Amazon Poses a Double Threat to Australian Retailers," *The Conversation*, June 18, 2017, https://theconversation.com/amazon-poses-a-double-threat-to-australian-retailers-78534; Cave, "Australia's Amazon Book Battle."

30. Cave, "Australia's Amazon Book Battle"; McDuling, "Amazon in Australia."

31. Sarmistha Neogy, "Amazon India Takes 'Mass' Route to Connect with Online Shoppers," *Exchange4Media.com* (India), April 10, 2015, https://www.exchange4media.com/advertising-news/amazon-india-takes-'mass'-route-to-connect-with-online-shoppers-59636.html.

32. Anindita Sarkar and Anushree Chandran, "IPL 2014: Amazon India Bags Merchandising Rights for All Eight Teams," *Financial Express* (India), May 1, 2014, https://www.financialexpress.com/archive/ipl-2014-amazon-india-bags-merchandising-rights-for-all-eight-teams/1245847/.

33. Vidhi Choudhary, "Jaipur Literature Festival Ready to Roll with Amazon India, Amity as Sponsors," *MINT* (New Delhi, India), January 14, 2015, https://www.livemint.com/Consumer/NXn1YapwNUj0VGgm0cT7yO/Jaipur-Literature-Festival-ready-to-roll-with-Amazon-India.html; Rasul Bailay and Writankar Mukherjee, "E-tailers Turn Sponsors: Amazon Outbids Myntra & Snapdeal to Sponsor India Fashion Week," *Economic Times* (Mumbai, India), February 12, 2015, https://economictimes.indiatimes.com/industry/services/retail/e-tailers-turn-sponsors-amazon-outbids-myntra-snapdeal-to-sponsor-india-fashion-week/articleshow/46206980.cms?from=mdr.

34. "Amazon Great Indian Festival: 10th–15th October," *Amazon.in* ad published on YouTube, September 28, 2018, https://www.youtube.com/watch?v=fkd5z6wCZKM.

35. Nikhil Pahwa, "'We Have a Lot of Patience, and a Very, Very Long Term Outlook'—Amazon India's Amit Agarwal," *Medianama* (India), June 25, 2013, https://www.medianama.com/2013/06/223-we-have-a-lot-of-patience-and-a-very-very-long-term-outlook-amazon-indias-amit-agarwal/.

36. Vikas Bajaj, "India's Answer to Amazon: Order Online, Pay at Door—FlipKart Deals with Indians' Mistrust of Web Payments in Creative Way," *Bulletin* (Bend, OR), September 15, 2011.

37. Bajaj, "India's Answer to Amazon."

38. Stone, *Amazon Unbound*, 77; Priyanka Pani and Unnati Joshi, "Amazon's Mission Is to Transform the Way India Buys and Sells: Amit Agarwal," *Hindu Business Line* (Chennai, India), January 24, 2018, https://www.thehindubusinessline.com/info-tech/amazons -mission-is-to-transform-the-way-india-buys-and-sells-amit-agarwal/article7282903.ece.

39. "Souq Becomes Amazon.ae in the UAE," *Amazon Press Center*, May 1, 2019, https:// press.aboutamazon.com/news-releases/news-release-details/souq-becomes-amazonae -uae.

40. Lubna Hamdan, "Souq Says to Take Cautious Approach to Launching Amazon in Saudi Arabia," *Arabian Business*, May 1, 2019, https://www.arabianbusiness.com/retail /419174-pm-souq-will-take-cautious-approach-to-launching-amazon-in-saudi; Neil Halligan, "Dubai's Souq Launches under Amazon's Brand," *Arabian Business*, May 1, 2019, https://www.arabianbusiness.com/retail/419142-dubais-souq-relaunches-under -amazon-brand.

41. Marc Fisher and Jonathan O'Connell, "The Prince, the Billionaire and Amazon Project That Got Frozen in the Desert," *Washington Post*, October 27, 2019, https:// www.washingtonpost.com/politics/the-prince-the-billionaire-and-the-amazon-project -that-got-frozen-in-the-desert/2019/10/27/71410ef8-eb9c-11e9-85c0-85a098e47b37 _story.html.

42. "Rakuten vs. Amazon: The Battle for Japan's E-commerce Market," *CNBC* [video], April 30, 2019, https://www.cnbc.com/video/2019/04/29/rakuten-vs-amazon-the-bat tle-for-japans-e-commerce-market.html.

43. Cribar, "Letter to The Honourable James Moore"; Leah Eichler, "Amazon Launches in Canada amid Bookseller Protests," *Publishers Weekly*, June 28, 2002, https://www .publishersweekly.com/pw/print/20020701/32916-amazon-launches-in-canada-amid -bookseller-protests.html.

44. Cave, "Australia's Amazon Book Battle."

45. "Amazon.ca Launches Today, Providing Significant Savings and Great Conve- nience for Canadian Book, Music, Video, and DVD Buyers," *Amazon Press Center*, June 25, 2002, https://press.aboutamazon.com/news-releases/news-release-details/amazonca -launches-today-providing-significant-savings-and-0.

46. "Amazon.ca Supports Canadian Film Festivals and Literacy Programs with the Launch of Dedicated Online Boutiques and Event Sponsorships," *Amazon Press Archive*, September 5, 2002, https://press.aboutamazon.com/news-releases/news-release-details /amazonca-supports-canadian-film-festivals-and-literacy-programs.

47. "Amazon.com and Books in Canada Announce 2000 First Novel Award Winner: Eva Stachniak for Necessary Lies," *Amazon Press Center*, September 25, 2001, https:// press.aboutamazon.com/news-releases/news-release-details/amazoncom-and-books -canada-announce-2000-first-novel-award.

48. "Amazon Decision Demonstrates Shift in Government Policy," *Osler: Resources: Cross-Border Markets*, May 6, 2010, https://www.osler.com/en/resources/cross-border /2010/amazon-decision-demonstrates-shift-in-government-p.

49. "The Government of Canada Announces Results of Investment Canada Act Review of Amazon," *Market Wire*, April 12, 2010, Access World News.

50. The Canadian Press, "Amazon.com Dreams Big for Canada—Online Giant Gets Okay to Build Warehouse Here," *Toronto Star*, April 13, 2010.

51. Arjun Kashyap, "Flipkart Gets Jump on Amazon in India's E-shopping Market," *Yahoo! Life*, September 4, 2011, https://www.yahoo.com/lifestyle/flipkart-gets-jump -amazon-indias-071835337.html.

52. Mugdha Variyar, "Amazon India Reportedly Closing In on Flipkart," *Economic Times*, March 22, 2018, https://economictimes.indiatimes.com/small-biz/startups/news buzz/amazon-india-reportedly-closing-in-on-flipkart/articleshow/63407725.cms; "Top 10 E-commerce Sites in India 2019," *Ecommerce Nest*, May 9, 2019, https://dyhdyhdyh .wordpress.com/2019/05/09/top-10-e-commerce-sites-in-india-2019/.

53. "Amazon. vs. Alibaba: How the E-commerce Giants Stack Up in the Fight to Go Global," *CB Insights*, March 2, 2018, https://www.cbinsights.com/research/amazon -alibaba-international-expansion/.

54. Praveena Sharma, "Online Bookstore Amazon Preparing for Indian Debut," *Daily News & Analysis* (India), 2011.

55. Nikhil Pahwa, "Amazon Junglee.com Goes Live in India as an 'Advertising Service'; Our Take," *Medianama* (India), February 2, 2012, https://www.medianama .com/2012/02/223-amazon-india-junglee/.

56. Sameer Mitha, "Amazon Marketplace Goes Live in India: Currently Offers Books and Movies," *Digit Magazine* (New Delhi, India), June 5, 2013, https://www.digit.in /news/internet/amazon-marketplace-goes-live-in-india-currently-offers-books-and -movies-14919.html.

57. "Welcome to the Jungle!," *Nextbigwhat*.

58. Rasul Bailay, "Time Running Out for Amazon India to Conform to New FDI Norms in Ecommerce," *Economic Times* (Mumbai, India), April 6, 2016, https://economictimes .indiatimes.com/industry/services/retail/time-running-out-for-amazon-india-to -conform-to-new-fdi-norms-in-ecommerce/articleshow/51706311.cms?from=mdr.

59. Mihir Dalal, "Sales Rise But Loss Widens as Amazon India Chases Buyers," *MINT* (New Delhi, India), November 3, 2014, https://www.livemint.com/Industry /T8WaplWb2cscup1pTQRWaM/Sales-rise-but-loss-widens-as-Amazon-India-chases -buyers.html.

60. Rasul Bailay and Chaitali Chakravarty, "Jeff Bezos to Visit India in January, May Meet PM Narendra Modi," *Economic Times* (Mumbai, India), November 19, 2019, https://economictimes.indiatimes.com/news/politics-and-nation/jeff-bezos-to-visit -india-in-january-may-meet-pm-modi/articleshow/72118227.cms.

61. Bailay and Chakravarty, "Jeff Bezos to Visit India."

62. Chiranjivi Chakraborty, "It's Stupid! Liberal FDI Didn't Let Flipkart Become India's Amazon: Shankar Sharma," *Economic Times* (Mumbai, India), July 13, 2016.

63. Bloomberg, "Amazon Plans to Shut Down China Marketplace in Rare Retreat," *LA Times*, April 19, 2019, https://www.latimes.com/business/la-fi-amazon-china-ecom merce-pullout-20190419-story.html.

64. Tom Holland, "There's an Imperial Elephant in the Room: China," *South China Morning Post: This Week in Asia*, December 11, 2017, http://www.scmp.com/week -asia/opinion/article/2123454/theres-imperial-elephant-room-china.

65. M. Szmigiera, "The 100 Largest Companies in the World by Market Capitalization in 2021," *Statista*, May 31, 2021, https://www.statista.com/statistics/263264/top -companies-in-the-world-by-market-capitalization/.

66. "Alibaba Group: Our Businesses," *Alibaba Group*, 2018, https://www.alibabagroup .com/en/about/businesses.

67. Morgan Stanley Research, *Amazon vs. Alibaba*.

68. Morgan Stanley Research, *Amazon vs. Alibaba*.

69. Nikhil Pahwa, "Amazon Gets a Wallet License in India," *Medianama* (India), April 12, 2017, https://www.medianama.com/2017/04/223-amazon-wallet-license-india/.

70. "Alibaba and Amazon Look to Go Global," *The Economist*, October 28, 2017, https://www.economist.com/special-report/2017/10/28/alibaba-and-amazon-look -to-go-global.

71. "Amazon. vs. Alibaba," *CB Insights*.

72. Daphne Howland, "Amazon Rebrands Souq," *Retail Dive*, May 2, 2019, https:// www.retaildive.com/news/amazon-rebrands-souq/553927/.

73. Alison Hearn and Sarah Banet-Weiser, "The Beguiling: Glamour in/as Platformed Cultural Production," *Social Media and Society*, January–March (2020), doi: 10.1177 /2056305119898779.

74. Ashna Ambre, "India Post Release Amazon India Stamp," *Livemint*, June 3, 2016, https://www.livemint.com/Companies/ptJeSn2hpsUU0ATQLc3QiL/India-Post-releases -Amazon-India-stamp.html.

75. Cormican, "Amazon's Australian Launch"; McDuling, "Amazon in Australia"; Cara Waters, "'It Doesn't Meet the Hype': Amazon's Sub-Prime Delivery," *Sydney Morning Herald*, June 19, 2018, https://www.smh.com.au/business/small-business/it -doesn-t-meet-the-hype-amazon-s-sub-prime-delivery-20180619-p4zmda.html.

76. Waters, "'It Doesn't Meet the Hype.'"

77. Bond, "Amazon Poses a Double Threat."

78. "Welcome to the Jungle!," *NextBigWhat.com*.

79. "Day After Flipkart Triumph, Jeff Bezos Infuses $2bn in Amazon India," *Financial Express* (India), July 30, 2014, https://www.financialexpress.com/archive/day -after-flipkart-triumph-jeff-bezos-infuses-2-bn-in-amazon-india/1275055/.

80. Jayadevan PK and Pankaj Mishra, "Amazon Readies $5 Billion Chest for Bigger Play in India, to Launch Subscription-Based Ecommerce Services," *Economic Times*

(Mumbai, India), July 20, 2015, https://retail.economictimes.indiatimes.com/news /e-commerce/e-tailing/amazon-readies-5-billion-chest-for-bigger-play-in-india-to -launch-subscription-based-ecommerce-services/48139360.

81. "Amazon Lobbies for India FDI," *The Statesman* (India), February 3, 2014.

82. Sanket Upadhyay, "Government Snubs Jeff Bezos; Was Refused Appointment with PM, Say Sources," *NDTV*, January 17, 2020, https://www.ndtv.com/india-news /jeff-bezos-india-visit-government-snubs-jeff-bezos-was-refused-appointment-with -pm-say-sources-2165509.

83. Evelyn Fok, "How Ecommerce Portals Like Alibaba, Amazon Are Helping Merchants Sell Products Outside India," *Economic Times* (Mumbai, India), August 21, 2015, https://economictimes.indiatimes.com/small-biz/startups/how-ecommerce-portals -like-alibaba-amazon-are-helping-merchants-sell-products-outside-india/articleshow /48565719.cms?from=mdr.

84. "Amazon Launches Make in India Store," *The Hindu Business Line*, January 19, 2018, https://www.thehindubusinessline.com/economy/amazon-launches-make-in -india-store/article8232574.ece.

85. Solomon Israel, "Amazon Prime Video Streaming Could Launch in Canada on Thursday," *CBC*, November 30, 2016, https://www.cbc.ca/news/business/amazon-prime -video-canada-1.3874326.

86. Emma Koehn, "Australia's Amazon Tax Collects 300% More Revenue Than Expected," *Stuff*, March 27, 2019, https://www.stuff.co.nz/business/world/111573176 /australias-amazon-tax-collects-300-more-revenue-than-expected.

87. Natasha Lomas, "Amazon Reverses Tax-Triggered Block on US Shop in Australia," *Tech Crunch*, November 22, 2018, https://techcrunch.com/2018/11/22/amazon -reverses-tax-triggered-block-on-us-shop-in-australia/.

88. Lomas, "Amazon Reverses."

89. "Harnessing Change: The Future of Programming Distribution in Canada," *Canadian Radio-Television and Telecommunications Commission*, May 31, 2018, https:// crtc.gc.ca/eng/publications/s15/; Charles Acland and Ira Wagman, "Canada—Update (March 2019)—Global Internet TV Consortium," *Global Internet TV Consortium*, 2019, https://global-internet-tv.com/canada-update-march-2019/.

CONCLUSION

1. Jessica Bruder, "Meet the Immigrants Who Took on Amazon," *Wired*, November 12, 2019, https://www.wired.com/story/meet-the-immigrants-who-took-on-amazon/.

2. Karen Weise, "Somali Workers in Minnesota Force Amazon to Negotiate," *New York Times*, November 20, 2018, https://www.nytimes.com/2018/11/20/technology /amazon-somali-workers-minnesota.html?searchResultPosition=1.

3. Weise, "Somali Workers in Minnesota Force."

4. Bruder, "Meet the Immigrants."

5. Nandita Bose and Krystal Hu, "Insight—Could Coronavirus Help Amazon Workers Unionize?," *Reuters*, May 21, 2020, https://www.reuters.com/article/health-coronavirus

-amazoncom-workers/insight-could-coronavirus-help-amazon-workers-unionize
-idUSL2N2CG03H.

6. Evans, "Ruthless Quotas"; Peterson, "Missing Wages"; Hayley Peterson, "Amazon's Delivery Network Is Set to Explode as the Company Moves Toward One-Day Shipping," *Business Insider*, May 3, 2019, https://www.businessinsider.com/amazon -hires-drivers-expands-delivery-network-one-day-shipping-2019-5.

7. David Rising, "Amazon Workers in Germany, Italy Stage Black Friday Strike," *APNews*, November 24, 2017, https://apnews.com/a1c597ca86b04142bf5973bba87d 7824/Amazon-workers-in-Germany,-Italy-stage-Black-Friday-strike.

8. Liz Alderman, "Amazon Reaches Deal with French Unions in Coronavirus Safety Dispute," *New York Times*, May 16, 2020, https://www.nytimes.com/2020/05/16/busi ness/amazon-france-unions-coronavirus.html.

9. Hayasaki, "Amazon's Great Labor Awakening."

10. Shirin Ghaffary, "Here's Why the Amazon Climate Walkout Is a Big Deal," *Vox: Recode*, September 20, 2019, https://www.vox.com/recode/2019/9/20/20874497/amazon -climate-change-walkout-google-microsoft-strike-tech-activism.

11. Mihir Zaveri, "An Amazon Vice President Quit over Firings of Employees Who Protested," *New York Times*, May 4, 2020, https://www.nytimes.com/2020/05/04/business /amazon-tim-bray-resigns.html?action=click&module=RelatedLinks&pgtype=Article.

12. Shane, "Prime Mover."

13. Fareeha Ali, "Amazon Prime Reaches 200 Million Members Worldwide," *Digital Commerce 360*, April 16, 2021, https://www.digitalcommerce360.com/article/amazon -prime-membership/.

14. Khan, "Amazon's Antitrust Paradox," 798.

15. John Herrman, "Life Without Amazon (Well, Almost)," *New York Times*, December 29, 2020, https://www.nytimes.com/2020/12/29/style/amazon-abstainers.html.

16. Kashmir Hill, "I Tried to Block Amazon from My Life. It Was Impossible," *Gizmodo*, January 22, 2019, https://gizmodo.com/i-tried-to-block-amazon-from-my-life -it-was-impossible-1830565336.

17. Patrick M. Fahey, "Advocacy Group Boycotting of Network Television Advertisers and Its Effects on Programming Content," *University of Pennsylvania Law Review* 140, no. 2 (1991); Kasaundra M. Tomlin, "Assessing the Efficacy of Consumer Boycotts on U.S. Target Firms: A Shareholder Wealth Analysis," *Southern Economic Journal* 86, no. 2 (2019), https://doi.org/10.1002/soej.12389.

18. Sharma, "It Changes Space and Time," 73.

19. Neil Postman, *Amusing Ourselves to Death: Public Discourse in the Age of Show Business* (New York: Viking, 1985).

20. Stephanie Keith/Getty Images, "Protestors in New York City Hold 'Day of Action' Against Amazon HQ2," *Getty Images*, November 26, 2018, https://www.gettyimages .com.au/detail/news-photo/people-opposed-to-amazons-plan-to-locate-a-headquarters -in-news-photo/1065471666?uiloc=thumbnail_more_from_this_event_adp.

21. Laura Bliss, "Why Climate Strike Protestors Targeted Amazon Go," *CityLab*, September 20, 2019, https://www.citylab.com/environment/2019/09/climate-strike-san-francisco-amazon-go-store-signs/598516/.

22. *The State of the Amazon Seller 2020*, JungleScout, 2020, https://www.junglescout.com/wp-content/uploads/2020/02/State-of-the-Seller-Survey.pdf, 4.

23. Kate Crawford and Vladan Joler, "Anatomy of an AI System," *Ars Electronica*, 2018, https://ars.electronica.art/outofthebox/en/anatomy-of-ai/.

24. Kate Crawford and Vladan Joler, "Anatomy of an AI System: The Amazon Echo as an Anatomical Map of Human Labor, Data and Planetary Resources," *AI Now Institute and Share Lab*, September 7, 2018, https://anatomyof.ai.

SELECTED BIBLIOGRAPHY

Includes all cited academic sources, and books devoted wholly to Amazon.

Acland, Charles, R. "Curtains, Carts, and the Mobile Screen." *Screen* 50, no. 1 (2009): 148–166.

Acland, Charles, and Ira Wagman. "Canada—Update (March 2019)." *Global Internet TV Consortium.* 2019. https://global-internet-tv.com/canada-update-march-2019/.

Ahmed, Sara. "Affective Economies." *Social Text* 22, no. 2 (2004): 117–139. doi: 10.1215/01642472-22-2_79-117.

Ananny, Mike, and Kate Crawford. "Seeing Without Knowing: Limitations of the Transparency Ideal and Its Application to Algorithmic Accountability." *New Media & Society* 20, no. 3 (2018): 973–989. doi:10.1177/1461444816676645.

Anderson, Chris. *The Long Tail: Why the Future of Business Is Selling Less of More.* New York: Hyperion, 2008.

Andreessen, Marc. "The Three Kinds of Platforms You Meet on the Internet." *Pmarchive,* September 16, 2007. https://pmarchive.com/three_kinds_of_platforms_you_meet_on_the_internet.html.

Andrejevic, Mark. *Automated Media.* New York: Routledge, 2020.

Andrejevic, Mark. "Automating Surveillance." *Surveillance & Society* 17, no. 1/2 (2019). https://ojs.library.queensu.ca/index.php/surveillance-and-society/article/view/12930.

Andrejevic, Mark. "Surveillance in the Digital Enclosure." *The Communication Review* 10, no. 4 (2007): 295–317. doi: 10.1080/10714420701715365.

Andrejevic, Mark. *Reality TV: The Work of Being Watched.* Lanham, MD: Rowman & Littlefield Publishers, 2004.

Aouragh, Miriyam, and Paula Chakravartty. "Infrastructures of Empire: Towards a Critical Geopolitics of Media and Information Studies." *Media, Culture & Society* 38, no. 4 (2016): 559–575.

Arvidsson, Adam. *Brands: Meaning and Value in Media Culture.* New York: Routledge, 2006.

Arvidsson, Adam. "Brands: A Critical Perspective." *Journal of Consumer Culture* 5, no. 2 (2005): 235–258. doi: 10.1177/1469540505053093.

Athique, Adrian. "Digital Emporiums: Platform Capitalism in India." *Media Industries* 6, no. 2 (2019). http://dx.doi.org/10.3998/mij.15031809.0006.205.

Baker, C. Edwin. *Media Concentration and Democracy: Why Ownership Matters.* New York: Cambridge University Press, 2007.

Banet-Weiser, Sarah. "Brands." In *Keywords for Media Studies,* edited by Laurie Ouellette and Jonathan Gray, 24–27. New York: New York University Press, 2017.

Bergen, Hilary. "'I'd Blush If I Could': Digital Assistants, Disembodied Cyborgs and the Problem of Gender." *Word and Text: A Journal of Literary Studies and Linguistics* 6, no. 1 (2016): 95–113.

Berners-Lee, Tim. "Long Live the Web." *Scientific American* 303, no. 6 (2010): 80–85.

Berry, Leonard. L. "Cultivating Service Brand Equity." *Journal of the Academy of Marketing Science* 28, no. 1 (2000): 128–137.

Bogost, Ian, and Nick Montfort. "Platform Studies: Frequently Questioned Answers." *Proceedings of the Digital Arts and Culture Conference.* University of California, Irvine, December 12, 2009. https://escholarship.org/uc/item/01r0k9br.

Bonacich, Enid, and Jake B. Wilson. *Getting the Goods: Ports, Labor, and the Logistics Revolution.* Ithaca, NY: Cornell University Press, 2008.

Bonacich, Enid, with Khaleelah Hardie. "Wal-Mart and the Logistics Revolution." In *Wal-Mart: The Face of Twenty-First-Century Capitalism,* edited by Nelson Lichtenstein, 163–187. New York: The New Press, 2006.

Bonchek, Mark, and Vivek Bapat. "The Most Successful Brands Focus on Users—Not Buyers." *Harvard Business Review,* February 7, 2018. https://hbr.org/2018/02/the-most-successful-brands-focus-on-users-not-buyers.

Bond, David. "Amazon Poses a Double Threat to Australian Retailers." *The Conversation,* June 18, 2017. https://theconversation.com/amazon-poses-a-double-threat-to-australian-retailers-78534.

Brandt, Richard L. *One Click: Jeff Bezos and the Rise of Amazon.com.* New York: Portfolio/Penguin, 2011.

Braun, Joshua A. *This Program Is Brought to You By . . . : Distribution Television News Online.* New Haven, CT: Yale University Press, 2015.

Carey, James. *Communication as Culture: Essays on Media and Society*. New York: Routledge, 1988/2009.

Carillo, Kevin, Eusebio Scornavacca, and Stefano Za. "The Role of Media Dependency in Predicting Continuance Intention to Use Ubiquitous Media Systems." *Information & Management* 54, no. 3 (2017): 337–335. http://dx.doi.org/10.1016/j.im.2016.09.002.

Chambers, Jason P. "Equal in Every Way: African Americans, Consumption, and Materialism from Reconstruction to the Civil Rights Movement." *Advertising & Society Review* 7, no. 1 (2006). doi: 10.1353/asr.2006.0017.

Clough, Patricia Ticineto, and Jean Halley, eds. *The Affective Turn: Theorizing the Social*. Durham, NC: Duke University Press, 2007.

Cohen, Lizabeth. *A Consumer's Republic: The Politics of Mass Consumption in Postwar America*. New York: Knopf, 2003.

Coleman, Cynthia-Lou, L. David Ritchie, and Heather Hartley. "Assessing Frames and Metaphors in News Coverage of Prescription Drug Advertising." *Journal of Health & Mass Communication* 1, no. 1/2 (2009): 109–128.

Couldry, Nick, and Andreas Hepp. *The Mediated Construction of Reality*. Malden, MA: Polity Press, 2017.

Couldry, Nick, and Ulises A. Mejias. *The Costs of Connection: How Data Is Colonizing Human Life and Appropriating It for Capitalism*. Stanford, CA: Stanford University Press, 2019.

Crawford, Kate, and Vladan Joler. "Anatomy of an AI System: The Amazon Echo as an Anatomical Map of Human Labor, Data and Planetary Resources." *AI Now Institute and Share Lab*, September 7, 2018. https://anatomyof.ai.

Curtin, Michael, Jennifer Holt, and Kevin Sanson, eds. *Distribution Revolution: Conversations about the Digital Future of Film and Television*. Oakland: University of California Press, 2014.

Davis, Mark. "E-books in the Global Information Economy." *European Journal of Cultural Studies* 18, no. 4–5 (2015): 514–529.

Dean, Jodi. *Publicity's Secret: How Technoculture Capitalizes on Democracy*. Ithaca, NY: Cornell University Press, 2002.

Delap, Lucy. "Housework, Housewives, and Domestic Workers: Twentieth-Century Dilemmas of Domesticity." *Home Cultures* 8, no. 2 (2011): 189–209. https://doi.org/10.2752/175174211X12961586699801.

Dencik, Lina, and Jonathan Cable. "The Advent of Surveillance Realism: Public Opinion and Activist Responses to the Snowden Leaks." *International Journal of Communication* 11 (2017): 763–781.

DiNucci, Darcy. "Fragmented Future." *Print* 53, no. 4 (1999): 32, 221–222.

Draper, Nora, and Joseph Turow. "The Corporate Cultivation of Digital Resignation." *New Media & Society* 21, no. 8 (2019): 1824–1839. doi: 10.1177/1461444819833331.

Dyer, Richard. *White: Essays on Race and Culture*. London: Psychology Press, 1997.

Edwards, Paul N. "Infrastructure and Modernity: Force, Time, and Social Organization in the History of Sociotechnical Systems." In *Modernity and Technology*, edited by Thomas J. Misa, Andrew Feenberg, and Philip Brey, 185–226. Cambridge, MA: MIT Press, 2003.

Fahey, Patrick M. "Advocacy Group Boycotting of Network Television Advertisers and Its Effects on Programming Content." *University of Pennsylvania Law Review* 140, no. 2 (1991): 647–709.

Farquhar, Peter H. "Managing Brand Equity." *Marketing Research* 1, no. 3 (1989): 24–33.

Featherstone, Mike. "Ubiquitous Media: An Introduction." *Theory, Culture & Society* 26, no. 2–3 (2009): 1–22.

Fitzgerald, Scott. "Over-the-Top Video Services in India: Media Imperialism after Globalization." *Media Industries Journal* 6, no. 2 (2019). http://dx.doi.org/10.3998/mij.15031809.0006.206.

Foster, John Bellamy, and Robert W. McChesney. "Surveillance Capitalism: Monopoly-Finance Capital, the Military-Industrial Complex, and the Digital Age." *Monthly Review* 66, no. 3 (2014): 1–31.

Gallagher, Winifred. *How the Post Office Created America: A History*. New York: Penguin Press, 2016.

Gillan, Jennifer. *Television and New Media: Must-Click TV*. New York: Routledge, 2011.

Gillespie, Tarleton. "The Politics of 'Platforms.'" *New Media & Society* 12, no. 3 (2010): 347–364. doi: 10.1177/1461444809342738.

Gillespie, Tarleton, Pablo J. Boczkowski, and Kirsten A. Foot, eds. *Media Technologies: Essays on Communication, Materiality and Society*. Cambridge, MA: MIT Press, 2014.

Glenn, Evelyn Nakano. "From Servitude to Service Work: Historical Continuities in the Racial Division of Paid Reproductive Labor." *Signs* 18, no. 1 (1992): 1–43.

Goodman, Douglas J., and Mirelle Cohen. *Consumer Culture: A Reference Handbook*. Santa Barbara, CA: ABC-CLIO, 2004.

Gray, Mary L., and Siddharth Suri. *Ghost Work: How to Stop Silicon Valley from Building a New Global Underclass*. Boston: Houghton Mifflin Harcourt, 2019.

Greenfield, Adam. *Everyware: The Dawning Age of Ubiquitous Computing*. Berkeley, CA: New Riders, 2006.

Guzman, Andrea L. "Making AI Safe for Humans: A Conversation with Siri." In *Socialbots and Their Friends: Digital Media and the Automation of Sociality*, edited by Robert W. Gehl and Maria Bakardjieva, 69–85. New York: Routledge, 2017.

Hardt, Michael. "Affective Labor." *Boundary 2* 26, no. 2 (1999): 89–100.

Harvey, David. *The Condition of Postmodernity*. Malden, MA: Blackwell, 1990.

Havens, Timothy. "Netflix: Streaming Channel Brands as Global Meaning Systems." In *From Networks to Netflix: A Guide to Changing Channels*, edited by Derek Johnson, 321–332. New York: Routledge, 2018.

Hearn, Alison. "Verified: Self-presentation, Identity Management, and Selfhood in the Age of Big Data." *Popular Communication* 15, no. 2 (2017): 62–77. http://dx.doi .org/10.1080/15405702.2016.1269909.

Hearn, Alison, and Sarah Banet-Weiser. "The Beguiling: Glamour in/as Platformed Cultural Production." *Social Media and Society* 6, no. 1 (2020): 1–11. doi: 10.1177 /2056305119898779.

Helles, Ramus, and Mikkel Flyverbom. "Meshes of Surveillance, Prediction, and Infrastructure: On the Cultural and Commercial Consequences of Digital Platforms." *Surveillance & Society* 17, no. 1/2 (2019): 34–39.

Herbert, Daniel. *Videoland: Movie Culture at the American Video Store*. Berkeley: University of California Press, 2014.

Herbert, Daniel, and Derek Thompson, eds. *Point of Sale: Analyzing Media Retail*. New Brunswick, NJ: Rutgers University Press, 2019.

Hill, David W. "The Injuries of Platform Logistics." *Media, Culture, & Society* 42, no. 4 (2019): 521–536. doi: 10.1177/0163443719861840.

Hillis, Ken, Michael Petit, and Kylie Jarrett. *Google and the Culture of Search*. New York: Routledge, 2013.

Hogan, Mél. "Data Flows and Water Woes: The Utah Data Center." *Big Data & Society* 2, no. 2 (2015): 1–12. doi: 10.1177/2053951715592429.

Holt, Jennifer. *Empires of Entertainment: Media Industries and the Politics of Deregulation, 1980–1996*. New Brunswick, NJ: Rutgers University Press, 2011.

Iansiti, Marco, and Karim R. Lakhani. "Managing Our Hub Economy: Strategy, Ethics, and Network Competition in the Age of Digital Superpowers." *Harvard Business Review* September–October (2017): 84–92. https://hbr.org/2017/09/managing -our-hub-economy.

Irani, Lilly C., and M. Six Silberman. "Turkopticon: Interrupting Worker Invisibility in Amazon Mechanical Turk." *Proceedings of the SIGCHI Conference on Human Factors in Computing Systems* (2013): 611–620.

Iwabuchi, Koichi. *Recentering Globalization: Popular Culture and Japanese Transnationalism*. Durham, NC: Duke University Press, 2002.

Jaller, Miguel. "Online Shopping Is Terrible for the Environment: It Doesn't Have to Be." *Vox*, November 21, 2018. https://www.vox.com/the-big-idea/2017/12/21

/16805324/black-friday-2018-amazon-online-shopping-cyber-monday-environmental -impact.

Jin, Dal Yong. "The Construction of Platform Imperialism in the Globalization Era." *tripleC: Communication, Capitalism, and Critique* 11, no. 1 (2013): 145–172.

John, Richard R. *Spreading the News: The American Postal System from Franklin to Morse.* Cambridge, MA: Harvard University Press, 1998.

Johnson, Derek, ed. *From Networks to Netflix: A Guide to Changing Channels.* New York: Routledge, 2018.

Khan, Lina M. "Amazon's Antitrust Paradox." *Yale Law Journal* 126 (2017): 710–805.

Kielbowicz, Richard B. "Rural Ambivalence Toward Mass Society: Evidence from the U.S. Parcel Post Debates, 1900–1913." *Rural History* 5, no. 1 (1994): 81–102.

Lakoff, George, and Mark Johnson. *Metaphors We Live By.* Chicago: University of Chicago Press, 1980.

Lara, Ali, Wen Liu, Colin Patrick Ashley, Akemi Nishida, Rachel Jane Liebert, and Michelle Billies. "Affect and Subjectivity." *Subjectivity* 10, no. 1 (2017): 30–43.

Lau, Josephine, Benjamin Zimmerman, and Florian Schaub. "Alexa, Are You Listening? Privacy Perceptions, Concerns and Privacy-Seeking Behaviors with Smart Speakers." *Proceedings of the ACM on Human-Computer Interaction* 2, no. CSCW (2018): article 102, 1–31. https://doi.org/10.1145/3274371.

Lauer, Josh. "The Good Consumer: Credit Reporting and the Invention of Financial Identity in the United States." *Enterprise & Society* 11, no. 4 (2010): 688–696.

Lichtenstein, Nelson. "The Return of Merchant Capitalism." *International Labor and Working-Class History* 81 (2012): 8–27.

Lichtenstein, Nelson. "Wal-mart: Template for 21st Century Capitalism?" *New Labor Forum* 14, no. 1 (2005): 21–30.

Lobato, Ramon. *Netflix Nations: The Geography of Digital Distribution.* New York: New York University Press, 2019.

Long, Elizabeth. "The Cultural Meaning of Concentration in Publishing." *Book Research Quarterly* 1, no. 4 (1985): 3–27.

Lotz, Amanda D. *Portals: A Treatise on Internet-Distributed Television.* Ann Arbor: University of Michigan Press, 2017. https://quod.lib.umich.edu/m/maize/mpub9699689/.

MacGillis, Alec. *Fulfillment: Winning and Losing in One-Click America.* New York: Farrar, Straus and Giroux, 2021.

Manzerolle, Vincent, and Atle Mikkola Kjøsen. "Digital Media and Capital's Logic of Acceleration." In *Marx in the Age of Digital Capitalism*, edited by Christian Fuchs and Vincent Mosco, 151–179. Boston: Brill, 2016.

Marcus, James. *Amazonia*. New York: The New Press, 2004.

Marx, Karl. *Capital: A Critique of Political Economy, Volume 1*. Translated by Ben Fowkes. London: Penguin Books, 1976.

Marx, Karl. *Capital: A Critique of Political Economy, Volume II*. Translated by Ben Fowkes. New York: Penguin Classics, 1998/1978.

Maxwell, Richard, and Toby Miller. *Greening the Media*. New York: Oxford University Press, 2012.

McChesney, Robert. *Rich Media, Poor Democracy*. 2nd ed. New York: The New Press, 2015.

McChesney, Robert. "Be Realistic, Demand the Impossible: Three Radically Democratic Internet Policies." *Critical Studies in Media Communication* 31, no. 2 (2014): 92–99.

McGuigan, Lee. "Selling Jennifer Aniston's Sweater: The Persistence of Shoppability in Framing Television's Future." *Media Industries* 5, no. 1 (2018). http://dx.doi.org/10.3998/mij.15031809.0005.101.

McGuigan, Lee, and Vincent Manzerolle. "'All the World's a Shopping Cart': Theorizing the Political Economy of Ubiquitous Media and Markets." *New Media & Society* 17, no. 11 (2015): 1830–1848.

McGuigan, Lee, and Graham Murdock. "The Medium Is the Marketplace: Digital Systems and the Intensification of Consumption." *Canadian Journal of Communication* 40, no. 4 (2015): 717–726. https://doi.org/10.22230/cjc.2015v40n4a2948.

McStay, Andrew. *Creativity and Advertising: Affect, Events, and Process*. New York: Routledge, 2013.

Miller, Daniel. *A Theory of Shopping*. Ithaca, NY: Cornell University Press, 1998.

Miller, Laura J. *Reluctant Capitalists: Bookselling and the Culture of Consumption*. Chicago: University of Chicago Press, 2006.

Mitchell, Wade J., Chin-Chang Ho, Himalaya Patel, and Karl F. MacDorman. "Does Social Desirability Bias Favor Humans? Explicit–Implicit Evaluations of Synthesized Speech Support a New HCI Model of Impression Management." *Computers in Human Behavior* 27, no. 1 (2011): 402–412.

Montfort, Nick, and Ian Bogost. *Racing the Beam: The Atari Video Computer System*. Cambridge, MA: MIT Press, 2009.

Mosco, Vincent. *Becoming Digital: Toward a Post-Internet Society*. Bingley, UK: Emerald Publishing, 2017.

Mosco, Vincent. *To the Cloud: Big Data in a Turbulent World*. Boulder, CO: Paradigm Publishers, 2014.

Murdock, Andy. "The Environmental Cost of Free 2-Day Shipping." *Vox*, November 17, 2017. https://www.vox.com/2017/11/17/16670080/environmental-cost-free-two-day-shipping.

Nakamura, Lisa. "'Words with Friends': Socially Networked Reading on Goodreads." *Publications of the Modern Language Association* 128, no. 1 (2013): 238–243.

Napoli, Philip, and Robyn Caplan. "Why Media Companies Insist They're Not Media Companies, Why They're Wrong, and Why It Matters." *First Monday* 22, no. 5 (2017). https://doi.org/10.5210/fm.v22i5.7051.

Negroponte, Nicholas. *Being Digital*. New York: Vintage Books, 1996.

Nieborg, David B. and Thomas Poell. "The Platformization of Cultural Production: Theorizing the Contingent Cultural Commodity." *New Media & Society* 20, no. 11 (2018): 4275–4292. doi: 10.1177/1461444818769694.

Niemann, Greg. *Big Brown: The Untold Story of UPS*. San Francisco: John Wiley & Sons, 2007.

Pachirat, Timothy. *Every Twelve Seconds: Industrialized Slaughter and the Politics of Sight*. New Haven, CT: Yale University Press, 2011.

O'Reilly, Tim. "What Is Web 2.0." *O'Reilly*, September 30, 2005. https://www.oreilly.com/pub/a/web2/archive/what-is-web-20.html.

Packer, Jeremy, and Stephen B. Crofts Wiley, eds. *Communication Matters: Materialist Approaches to Media, Mobility, and Networks*. New York: Routledge, 2012.

Pasquale, Frank. "When Antitrust Becomes Pro-Trust: The Digital Deformation of U.S. Competition Policy." *CPI Antitrust Chronicle*. University of Maryland Legal Studies Research Paper No. 2017–24 (2017). https://papers.ssrn.com/sol3/papers.cfm?abstract_id=3020163.

Peak, Anna. "Servants and the Victorian Sensation Novel." *SEL Studies in English Literature 1500–1900* 54, no. 4 (2014): 835–851. https://doi.org/10.1353/sel.2014.0042.

Perzanowski, Aaron, and Jason Schultz. *The End of Ownership: Personal Property in the Digital Economy*. Cambridge, MA: MIT Press, 2016.

Peters, John Durham. "Calendar, Clock, Tower." In *Deus in Machina: Religion, Technology, and the Things in Between*, edited by Jeremy Stolow, 25–42. New York: Fordham University Press, 2013.

Petruska, Karen. "Where Information Is Entertainment." In *From Networks to Netflix: A Guide to Changing Channels*, edited by Derek Johnson, 355–364. New York: Routledge, 2018.

Phan, Thao. "Amazon Echo and the Aesthetics of Whiteness." *Catalyst: Feminism, Theory, and Technoscience* 5, no. 1 (2019): 1–38.

Phan, Thao. "The Materiality of the Digital and the Gendered Voice of Siri." *Transformations* 29 (2017): 23–33.

Pickard, Victor. *America's Battle for Media Democracy: The Triumph of Corporate Libertarianism and the Future of Media Reform.* New York: Cambridge University Press, 2015.

Plantin, Jean-Christophe, Carl Lagoze, Paul N. Edwards, and Christian Sandvig. "Infrastructure Studies Meet Platform Studies in the Age of Google and Facebook." *New Media & Society* 20, no. 1 (2018): 293–310. doi: 10.1177/1461444816661553.

Plantin, Jean-Christophe, and Aswin Punathambekar. "Digital Media Infrastructures: Pipes, Platforms, and Politics." *Media, Culture, & Society* 41, no. 2 (2019): 163–174. doi: 10.1177/0163443718818376.

Popp, Richard K. "The Anywhere, Anytime Market: The 800-Number, Direct Marketing, and the New Networks of Consumption." *Enterprise & Society* 19, no. 3 (2018): 702–732. doi: 10.1017/eso.2017.68.

Postman, Neil. *Amusing Ourselves to Death: Public Discourse in the Age of Show Business.* New York: Viking, 1985.

Punathambekar, Aswin, and Sriram Mohan. "Digital Platforms, Globalization and Culture." In *Media and Society*, 6th ed., edited by James Curran and David Hesmondalgh, 207–224. London: Bloomsbury Academic, 2019.

Puschmann, Cornelius, and Jean Burgess. "Metaphors of Big Data." *International Journal of Communication* 8 (2014): 1690–1709.

Radway, Janice A. *A Feeling for Books: The Book-of-the-Month Club, Literary Taste, and Middle-Class Desire.* Chapel Hill: The University of North Carolina Press, 1997.

Raji, Inioluwa Deborah, and Joy Buolamwini. "Actionable Auditing: Investigating the Impact of Publicly Naming Biased Performance Results of Commercial AI Products." *Proceedings of the AAAI/ACM Conference on AI, Ethics, & Society*, January 2019: 429–435. https://doi.org/10.1145/3306618.3314244.

Rose, Nikolas. *Governing the Soul: The Shaping of the Private Self.* New York: Routledge, 1989.

Rossman, John. *The Amazon Way on IoT: 10 Principles for Every Leader from the World's Leading Internet of Things Strategies.* Seattle, WA: Clyde Hill Publishing, 2016.

Rossman, John. *The Amazon Way: 14 Leadership Principles Behind the World's Most Disruptive Company.* North Charleston, SC: CreateSpace Independent Publishing Platform, 2014.

Sadowski, Jathan. "The Internet of Landlords: Digital Platforms and New Mechanisms of Rentier Capitalism." *Antipode* 52, no. 2 (2020): 562–580.

Sadowski, Jathan. "When Data Is Capital: Datafication, Accumulation, and Extraction." *Big Data & Society* 6, no. 1 (2019): 1–12.

Sandvig, Christian. "Seeing the Sort: The Aesthetic and Industrial Defense of 'The Algorithm.'" *Media-N: Journal of the New Media Caucus.* ISSN: 1942–017X, 2014. http://median.newmediacaucus.org/art-infrastructures-information/seeing-the-sort -the-aesthetic-and-industrial-defense-of-the-algorithm/.

Sawyer, Laura Phillips. *US Antitrust Law and Policy in Historical Perspective.* Harvard Business School Working Paper 19–110 (2019). https://www.hbs.edu/ris/Publication%20 Files/19-110_e21447ad-d98a-451f-8ef0-ba42209018e6.pdf.

Schiller, Amy, and John McMahon. "Alexa, Alert Me When the Revolution Comes: Gender, Affect, and Labor in the Age of Home-Based Artificial Intelligence." *New Political Science* 41, no. 2 (2019): 173–191. doi: 10.1080/07393148.2019.1595288.

Schiller, Daniel. *Digital Capitalism: Networking the Global Market System.* Cambridge, MA: MIT Press, 1999.

Sharma, Sarah. "It Changes Space and Time: Introducing Power-Chronography." In *Communication Matters: Materialist Approaches to Media, Mobility, and Networks,* edited by Jeremy Packer and Stephen B. Crofts Wiley, 66–77. New York: Routledge, 2012.

Slater, Don. *Consumer Culture and Modernity.* Cambridge, MA: Blackwell, 1997.

Solnit, Rebecca. "The Annihilation of Time and Space." *New England Review* 24, no. 1 (2003): 5–19.

Spector, Robert. *Amazon.com Get Big Fast: The Astounding Rise and Uncertain Future of the E-commerce Giant.* New York: HarperCollins Business, 2000.

Srnicek, Nick. *Platform Capitalism.* Malden, MA: Polity Press, 2017.

Star, Susan Leigh, and Geoffrey C. Bowker. "How to Infrastructure." In *Handbook of New Media: Social Shaping and Social Consequences of ICTS,* edited by Leah A. Lievrouw and Sonia Livingstone, 230–245. Thousand Oaks, CA: Sage, 2006.

Steiner, Ann. "Private Criticism in the Public Space: Personal Writing on Literature in Readers' Reviews on Amazon." *Participations* 5, no. 2 (2008). https://www .participations.org/Volume%205/Issue%202/5_02_steiner.ht.

Stewart, Mark. "The Myth of Televisual Ubiquity." *Television & New Media* 17, no. 8 (2016): 691–705.

Stone, Brad. *Amazon Unbound: Jeff Bezos and the Invention of a Global Empire.* New York: Simon & Schuster, 2021.

Stone, Brad. *The Everything Store: Jeff Bezos and the Age of Amazon.* New York: Little, Brown, and Co., 2013.

Strengers, Yolande, and Jenny Kennedy. *The Smart Wife: Why Siri, Alexa, and Other Smart Home Devices Need a Feminist Reboot.* Cambridge, MA: MIT Press, 2020.

Striphas, Ted. "Algorithmic Culture." *European Journal of Cultural Studies* 18, no. 4–5 (2015): 395–412.

Striphas, Ted. *The Late Age of Print: Everyday Book Culture from Consumerism to Control*. New York: Columbia University Press, 2009.

Swenson, Kristin. "Capitalizing on Affect: Viagra (In)Action." *Communication, Culture & Critique* 1, no. 3 (2008): 311–328. doi: 10.1111/j.1753-9137.2008.00025.x.

Taylor, T. L. *Watch Me Play: Twitch and the Rise of Game Live Streaming*. Princeton, NJ: Princeton University Press, 2018.

Terranova, Tiziana. "Free Labor: Producing Culture for the Digital Economy." *Social Text* 18, no. 2 (2000): 33–58.

Thatcher, Jim, David O'Sullivan, and Dillon Mahmoudi. "Data Colonialism Through Accumulation by Dispossession: New Metaphors for Daily Data." *Environment and Planning D: Society and Space* 34, no. 6 (2016): 990–1006.

Thompson, John B. *Merchants of Culture: The Publishing Business in the Twenty-First Century*. Malden, MA: Polity Press, 2010.

Tiwary, Ishita. "India—Amazon Prime Video." *Global Internet TV Consortium*, November 2018. https://global-internet-tv.com/india-amazon-prime-video/.

Tomlin, Kasaundra M. "Assessing the Efficacy of Consumer Boycotts on U.S. Target Firms: A Shareholder Wealth Analysis." *Southern Economic Journal* 86, no. 2 (2019): 503–529. https://doi.org/10.1002/soej.12389.

Tryon, Chuck. *On-Demand Culture: Digital Delivery and the Future of Movies*. New Brunswick, NJ: Rutgers University Press, 2013.

Turow, Joseph. *The Aisles Have Eyes: How Retailers Track Your Shopping, Strip Your Privacy, and Define Your Power*. New Haven, CT: Yale University Press, 2017.

Turow, Joseph. *The Daily You: How the New Advertising Industry Is Defining You and Your Worth*. New Haven, CT: Yale University Press, 2011.

Turow, Joseph, Michael Hennessy, and Nora Draper. "The Tradeoff Fallacy: How Marketers Are Misrepresenting American Consumers and Opening Them Up to Exploitation." *SSRN*. June 26, 2015. https://papers.ssrn.com/sol3/papers.cfm?abstract_id=2820060.

Turow, Joseph, Lee McGuigan, and Elena R. Maris. "Making Data Mining a Natural Part of Life: Physical Retailing, Customer Surveillance and the 21st Century Social Imaginary." *European Journal of Communication* 18, no. 4–5 (2015): 464–478.

Vaidhyanathan, Siva. *Antisocial Media: How Facebook Disconnects Us and Undermines Democracy*. New York: Oxford University Press, 2018.

Vaidhyanathan, Siva. *The Googlization of Everything (And Why We Should Worry)*. Berkeley: University of California Press, 2011.

Varian, Hal. "Beyond Big Data." *Business Economics* 49, no. 1 (2014): 27–31.

Von Ho, Tara. "Amazon Wins '.Amazon' Domain Name, Aggravating South American Region and Undermining Digital Commons." *The Conversation*, June 21, 2019.

https://theconversation.com/amazon-wins-amazon-domain-name-aggravating-south
-american-region-and-undermining-digital-commons-118186.

Weber, Christopher L., Chris T. Hendrickson, H. Scott Matthews, Amy Nagengast,
Rachel Nealer, and Paulina Jaramillo. "Life Cycle Comparison of Traditional Retail
and E-commerce Logistics for Electronic Products: A Case Study of Buy.com." *2009
IEEE International Symposium on Sustainable Systems and Technology*, 2009: 1–6. doi:
10.1109/ISSST.2009.5156681.

Webster, James G. *The Marketplace of Attention: How Audiences Take Shape in a Digital
Age*. Cambridge, MA: MIT Press, 2014.

Weil, Gordon L. *Sears, Roebuck, U.S.A.: The Great American Catalog Store and How It
Grew*. New York: Stein and Day, 1977.

Wells, John R., Benjamin Weinstock, Galen Danskin, and Gabriel Ellsworth.
"Amazon.com, 2019." Harvard Business Publishing, Case 9-716-402 (2019): 1–40.

West, Emily. "Affect Theory and Advertising: A New Look at IMC, Spreadability,
and Engagement." In *Explorations in Critical Studies of Advertising*, edited by James F.
Hamilton, Robert Bodle, and Ezequiel Korn, 248–260. New York: Routledge, 2016.

Westin, Alan F. "Social and Political Dimensions of Privacy." *Journal of Social Issues*
59, no. 2 (2003): 431–453.

White, Michele. *Buy It Now: Lessons from eBay*. Durham, NC: Duke University Press,
2012.

Williams, Raymond. *Marxism and Literature*. New York: Oxford University Press,
1977.

Williams, Raymond. *Television: Technology and Cultural Form*. New York: Schocken
Books, 1975.

Winseck, Dwayne R. "The Geopolitical Economy of the Global Internet Infrastructure." *Journal of Information Policy* 7 (2017): 228–267. https://www.jstor.org/stable/10
.5325/jinfopoli.7.2017.0228.

Wood, David Murakami, and Kirstie Ball. "Brandscapes of Control? Surveillance,
Marketing, and the Co-construction of Subjectivity and Space in Neo-liberal Capitalism." *Marketing Theory* 13, no. 1 (2013): 47–67. doi: 10.1177/1470593112467264.

Wood, David Murakami, and Torin Monahan. "Editorial: Platform Surveillance."
Surveillance & Society 17, no. 1/2 (2019): 1–6.

Woods, Heather Suzanne. "Asking More of Siri and Alexa: Feminine Persona in Service of Surveillance Capitalism." *Critical Studies in Media Communication* 35, no. 4
(2018): 334–349. doi: 10.1080/15295036.2018.1488082.

Wu, Tim. *The Curse of Bigness: Antitrust in the New Gilded Age*. New York: Columbia
Global Reports, 2018.

Wu, Tim. *The Attention Merchants: The Epic Scramble to Get Inside Our Heads.* New York: Knopf, 2016.

Wygonik, Erica, and Anne Goodchild. "Evaluating the Efficacy of Shared-Use Vehicles for Reducing Greenhouse Gas Emissions: A US Case Study of Grocery Delivery." *Journal of the Transportation Research Forum* 51, no. 2 (2012).

Zhu, Feng, and Qihong Liu. "Competing with Complementors: An Empirical Look at Amazon.com." *Strategic Management Journal* 39, no. 10 (2018): 2618–2642.

Zuboff, Shoshana. *The Age of Surveillance Capitalism.* New York: Public Affairs, 2019.

INDEX

Page numbers in italics refer to figures.